MW00773023

Gender, Violence and Criminal Justice in the Colonial Pacific

Empire's Other Histories

Series Editors: Victoria Haskins (University of Newcastle, Australia), Emily Manktelow (Royal Holloway, University of London, UK), Jonathan Saha (University of Durham, UK) and Fae Dussart (University of Sussex, UK)

Editorial Board: *Esme Cleall (University of Sheffield, UK), Swapna Banerjee (CUNY, USA), Lynette Russell (Monash, Australia), Tony Ballantyne (University of Otago, New Zealand), Samita Sen (Jadavpur University, India, and University of Cambridge, UK), Nurfadzilah Yahaya (National University of Singapore, Singapore), Onni Gust (University of Nottingham, UK), Martina Nguyen (CUNY, USA) and Meleisa Ono-George (University of Oxford, UK)*

Empire's Other Histories is an innovative series devoted to the shared and diverse experiences of the marginalised, dispossessed and disenfranchised in modern imperial and colonial histories. It responds to an ever-growing academic and popular interest in the histories of those erased, dismissed or ignored in traditional historiographies of empire. It will elaborate on and analyse new questions of perspective, identity, agency, motilities, intersectionality and power relations.

Published:

Unhomely Empire: Whiteness and Belonging, c. 1760–1830, Onni Gust, 2020.

Extreme Violence and the 'British Way': Colonial Warfare in Perak, Sierra Leone and Sudan, Michelle Gordon, 2020.

Unexpected Voices in Imperial Parliaments, edited by José María Portillo, Josep M. Fradera, Teresa Segura-Garcia, 2021.

The Making and Remaking of 'Australasia': Southern Circulations, edited by Tony Ballantyne.

Forthcoming:

Spiritual Colonialism in a Globalizing World, Christina Petterson.

Vagrant Lives in Colonial Australasia: Regulating Mobility and Movement 1840–1920, Catherine Coleborne.

Across Colonial Lines: Commodities, Networks and Empire Building, edited by Devyani Gupta and Purba Hossain.

Arctic Circles and Imperial Knowledge: The Franklin Family, Indigenous Intermediaries, and the Politics of Truth, Annaliese Jacobs Claydon.

Imperial Gallows: Murder, Violence and the Death Penalty in British Colonial Africa, c. 1915–60, Stacey Hynd.

Anti-Colonialism and the Crises of Interwar Fascism, Michael Oritz.

Gender, Violence and Criminal Justice in the Colonial Pacific, 1880–1920

Kate Stevens

BLOOMSBURY ACADEMIC
LONDON • NEW YORK • OXFORD • NEW DELHI • SYDNEY

BLOOMSBURY ACADEMIC
Bloomsbury Publishing Plc
50 Bedford Square, London, WC1B 3DP, UK
1385 Broadway, New York, NY 10018, USA
29 Earlsfort Terrace, Dublin 2, Ireland

BLOOMSBURY, BLOOMSBURY ACADEMIC and the Diana logo are trademarks of Bloomsbury Publishing Plc

First published in Great Britain 2023

Copyright © Kate Stevens, 2023

Kate Stevens has asserted her right under the Copyright, Designs and Patents Act, 1988, to be identified as Author of this work.

For legal purposes the Acknowledgements on p. x constitute an extension of this copyright page.

Series design by Tjaša Krivec
Cover image: Government House, Suva, 1880s, Dunedin, by Burton Brothers studio. Te Papa (O.036857)

All rights reserved. No part of this publication may be reproduced or transmitted in any form or by any means, electronic or mechanical, including photocopying, recording, or any information storage or retrieval system, without prior permission in writing from the publishers.

Bloomsbury Publishing Plc does not have any control over, or responsibility for, any third-party websites referred to or in this book. All internet addresses given in this book were correct at the time of going to press. The author and publisher regret any inconvenience caused if addresses have changed or sites have ceased to exist, but can accept no responsibility for any such changes.

A catalogue record for this book is available from the British Library.

A catalog record for this book is available from the Library of Congress.

ISBN: HB: 978-1-3502-7554-6
ePDF: 978-1-3502-7553-9
eBook: 978-1-3502-7552-2

Series: Empire's Other Histories

Typeset by Newgen KnowledgeWorks Pvt. Ltd., Chennai, India

To find out more about our authors and books visit www.bloomsbury.com and sign up for our newsletters.

Contents

Figures

Maps

Acknowledgements

Having a single name alone on the cover of this book obscures the collective effort that makes such an endeavour possible. This project has accumulated many debts of gratitude to people over a range of countries, universities and archives along the journey to publication. The stories explored are difficult ones, and I hope I have treated the experiences of those featured, whether named or not, with the respect and sensitivity that they deserve.

I am particularly grateful for the intellectual, emotional and practical support of a wide range of mentors, colleagues, scholars, archivists and librarians – many of whom I am also lucky to call friends. Nicholas Thomas and Sujit Sivasundaram both guided this project from the outset, and I have benefited from the depth of their knowledge of colonial history in the Pacific and elsewhere, as well as their mentorship and feedback in analysis and writing. Alison Bashford and Damon Salesa similarly provided careful and critical advice that has re-shaped the manuscript.

Angela Wanhalla supported my development as a historian from my first archival research and has been an inspiring and supportive mentor and friend ever since. She, alongside Katie Cooper, Violeta Gilabert, Lachy Paterson and Sarah Christie, all provided insightful comments on draft chapters and crucial encouragement as I edited – thank you to the 'cool people' writing hui! Tony Ballantyne, Judy Bennett, Barbara Brookes, Jacqui Leckie, Jane McCabe, Adrian Muckle, Greg Rawlings and Christine Weir have all read sections, suggested archives and provided writing, research, and funding advice at various points along the way.

In Cambridge, I shared the academic journey and benefitted from the intellectual and social companionship of Namukale Chintu, Mark Condos, Marta Costa, Noor Iqbal, Stella Krepp, Elisabeth Leake, Orla Lynskey, Kristen Meredith, Tamara Micner, Aoife Murray, Hannah Spry, Linda Stone, Erin Townsend and Danelle Van Zyl-Hermann, as well as Sujit's writing group, Emma Hunter's reading group, the Cambridge World History Workshop, Anna Abulafia and Sue Jackson of Lucy Cavendish College and the HHLCC/BC family.

I was greatly assisted by archivists and staff who were expansive with their time and expertise at a wide range of institutions. Thank you to Senate House Library, London, and the National Archives, Kew in the United Kingdom; the

Centre des Archives Nationales d'Outre Mer in Aix-en-Provence, France; the late Salesia Ikaniwai and team of the National Archives of Fiji in Suva; colleagues at the Archives Territoriales de la Nouvelle-Calédonie in Nouméa; Stephen Innes and team at the Western Pacific Archives at the University of Auckland Library, and the Presbyterian Archives, Dunedin in New Zealand; and the Mitchell Library, Sydney, and the University of Adelaide Special Collections in Australia.

Jennifer Poole and Viliame Qerawaqa in Suva, the Clegg family and Flick Stevens, Dave McEwen and family in Sydney, the Bull family in Auckland, Shane Montague-Gallagher and Elizabeth Montague in Dunedin and Lachie Munro in France generously opened their homes to me during research trips. During these travels, my research was enhanced by the conversations with and advice from Alumita Durutalo, Nic Halter, Ismet Kurtovitch, Johanna Montlouis-Gabriel, Robert Nicole, Max Quanchi, Max Shekleton, Morgan Tuimaleali'ifano and the 2014 National History Center Decolonisation seminar cohort.

At the University of Waikato, Kirstine Moffat has mentored me to ensure I found time for writing among teaching and service. 'Team archives' Maebh Long, Alice Te Punga Somerville and William Jennings ensured rich discussions over good kai. I am thankfully to the wider PACIS community at Waikato for welcoming me, especially the thought-provoking and humorous morning teas led by organizers and regulars Jess Pasisi, Jesi Bennett, Wanda Ieremia Allan and Hineitimoana Greensill. Coffee (and kava) with Apo Aporosa, Karen Buckley, Andreea Calude, Anne Ferrier-Watson, Nicola Lemberg, Chloe Wall, History colleagues and the many tearoom regulars (you know you are) provided practical advice and much needed sustenance.

Numerous others also provided good company, made the research and writing process less lonely and more fun and provided much needed breaks from work along the way. Though they are not all named here, I remember with pleasure the many coffees, lunches, dances and post-archive drinks together. While I hope I have managed to acknowledge all those who have provided me with their wisdom, time and energy here, this section was written after little sleep and much caffeine, and I apologize for any unintentional omissions.

Research costs both time and money, and the book would not have been possible without financial support for the archival work and subsequent writing. My graduate studies were made possible by a Commonwealth Scholarship. Lucy Cavendish College, the Smuts Memorial Fund, the Faculty of History and the Prince Consort and Thirlwall Trust, the University of Cambridge Board of Graduate Studies, Andrew W. Mellon Foundation, Santander and the Royal Historical Society all provided further crucial support. I am particularly privileged to return to a continuing academic role at Waikato after time away from academia, providing valuable – and increasingly rare – stability to edit the manuscript.

I would like to thank the editors and publishing team at Bloomsbury for supporting the book's development from proposal to print, especially Empire's Other Histories series editors Victoria Haskins, Emily J. Manktelow, Fae Dussart, and Jonathan Saha, and Bloomsbury editors Maddie Holder and Abigail Lane. I also acknowledge the anonymous reviewers for their thoughtful engagement with, endorsement of, and resulting improvements to, the manuscript.

Maps were thoughtfully designed by Les O'Neill. The index was expertly compiled by Daphne Lawless.

Sections of this research have been previously presented and published elsewhere, and I wish to thank these publishers for the permission to republish, as well as the valuable contributions from conference commentators and anonymous reviewers that shaped my analysis. An earlier version of part of Chapter 5 was published as '"The Law of the New Hebrides Is the Protector of Their Lawlessness": Justice, Race and Colonial Rivalry in the Early Anglo-French Condominium', *Law and History Review* 35, no. 3 (2017), 595–620. It is reprinted with permission. Revised sections of Chapter 3 are forthcoming in *Aftermaths: Colonialism, Violence and Memory in Australia, New Zealand and the Pacific*, edited by Lyndall Ryan and Angela Wanhalla (University of Otago Press) and *Suva Stories: A History of the Capital of Fiji*, edited by Nicholas Halter (ANU Press, 2022).

The author and publisher gratefully acknowledge the permission granted to reproduce the copyright material in this book. Every effort has been made to trace copyright holders and to obtain their permission for the use of copyright material. The publisher apologizes for any errors or omissions in the above list and would be grateful if notified of any corrections that should be incorporated in future reprints or editions of this book. The third-party copyrighted material displayed in the pages of this book are done so on the basis of 'fair dealing for the purposes of criticism and review' or 'fair use for the purposes of teaching, criticism, scholarship or research' only in accordance with international copyright laws, and is not intended to infringe upon the ownership rights of the original owners.

Finally, I would like to thank my family for their unwavering support: Bev (also proofreader and formatter-extraordinaire), Doug and Anna. Cat Shushi gets an honourable mention for sleeping alongside my desk and only occasionally biting me. Love and gratitude to my partner Simon for wonderful companionship and emotional and practical support throughout – it's my turn to cook dinner!

Note on Text and Translation

Following *The Contemporary Pacific*, the capitalized Islanders is used when referring collectively to peoples of the Pacific Islands. Commonly, colonial correspondence referred Indigenous peoples as a whole: as Fijians or Indians in Fiji, *canaque* in New Caledonia or New Hebridean/*néo-hébridais* in the New Hebrides. Such categories mask the diversity of these groups and reflect colonial practice of viewing island societies as largely homogenous. Where possible, I identify Islanders by their island groups or *tribu* (though the concept of *tribu* itself is an analytical term).[1] Where this information is not available in the archive, I use the collective terms ni-Vanuatu, Kanak and Fijian for Indigenous Islanders of Vanuatu, the New Caledonia Grande Terre and Fiji respectively, while acknowledging iTaukei is now used for Indigenous Fijians, and Fijians to refer to all citizens of Fiji.

For non-European individuals, colonial records frequently include only a given name, others only an anglicized name or sobriquet. These names are retained to enable individuals to be re-traced through the archives, acknowledging however that such names are not necessarily accurate reflections of individual's own identification. I hope future researchers may better restore to these individuals their fuller identities, names and genealogies.

All translations from French (and one from Spanish) are my own unless otherwise acknowledged. In other places, I rely on the translation of colonial officials, also often unnamed, who translated Indigenous languages into French or English for the colonial state but frequently failed to preserve the original words.

Note

1 Bronwen Douglas, 'Conflict and Alliance in a Colonial Context', *Journal of Pacific History* 15, no. 1 (1980), 26.

Abbreviations

ANC	Archives de la Nouvelle-Calédonie, Nouméa
ANOM	Archives Nationales d'Outre Mer, Aix-en-Provence
CCNH	Compagnie Calédonienne des Nouvelles-Hébrides
CSO	Colonial Secretary's Office, Fiji
CSR	Colonial Sugar Refining Company, Fiji
DAP	Direction des Affaires Politiques, Ministre des Colonies, ANOM
DMO	District Medical Officer, Fiji
ESM	European Stipendiary Magistrate, Fiji
JNC	Joint Naval Commission (Commission Navale Mixte in French), New Hebrides
NAF	National Archives of Fiji, Suva
NAK	National Archives at Kew, London
NHBS	New Hebrides British Service
NSM	Native Stipendiary Magistrate, Fiji
PANZ	Presbyterian Archives of New Zealand, Dunedin
PMB	Pacific Manuscript Bureau
SAI	Services des Affaires Indigènes, New Caledonia
SFNH	Société Française des Nouvelles-Hébrides
SHL	Senate House Library, London
WPA	Western Pacific Archives, Special Collections, University of Auckland Libraries, Auckland
WPHC	Western Pacific High Commission

General Maps

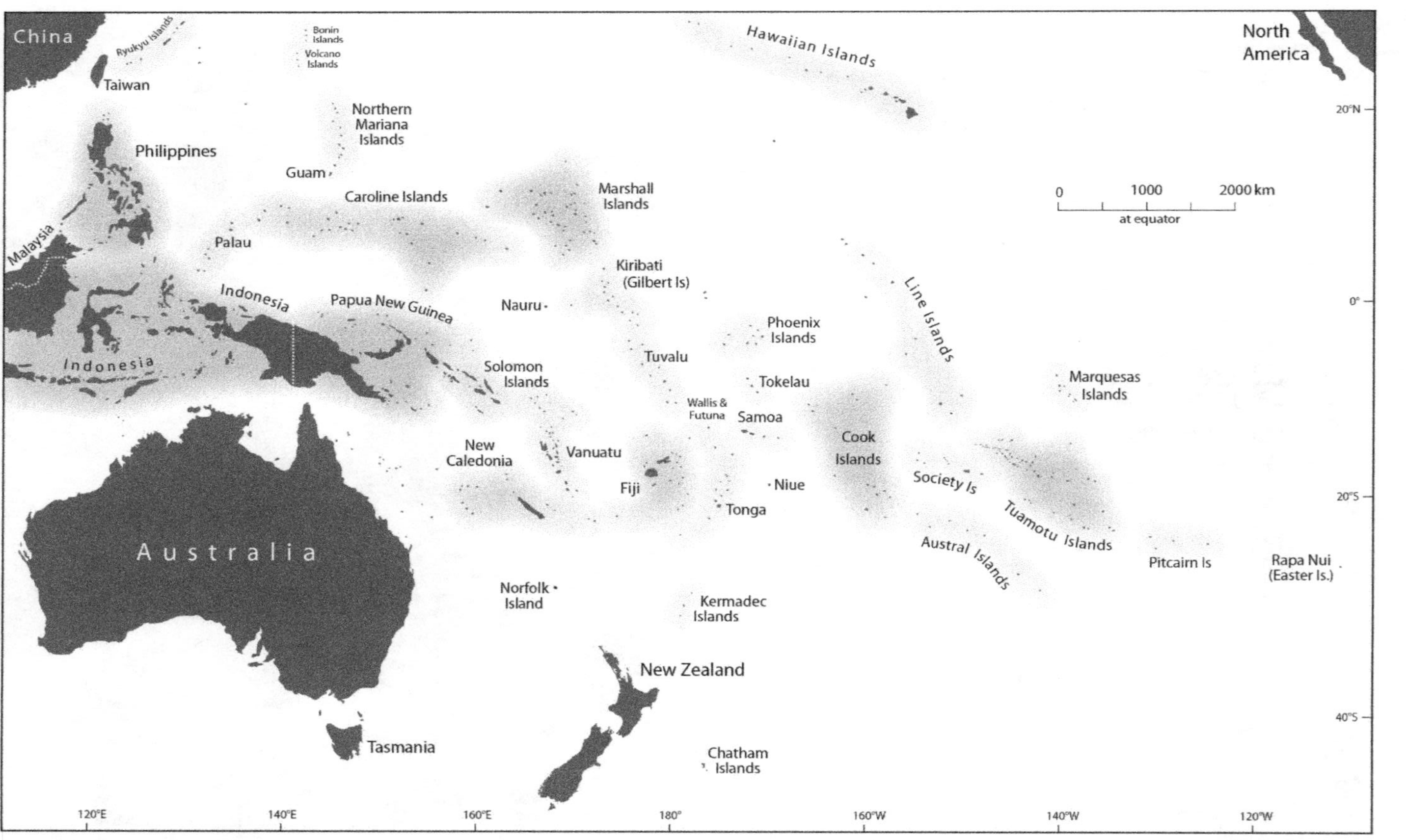

Map 1 Map of the Pacific. ©Les O'Neill.

Map 2 Map of New Caledonia, showing main locations mentioned. ©Les O'Neill.

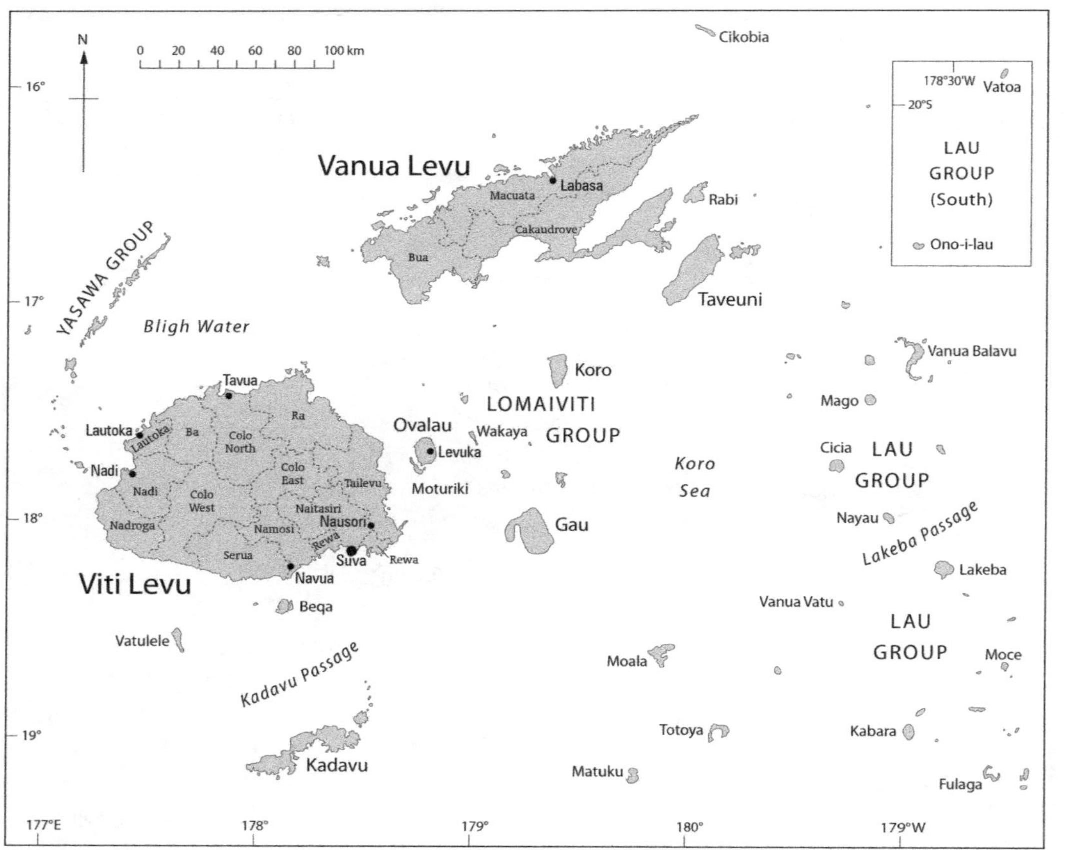

Map 3 Map of Fiji, showing main locations mentioned and the colonial district divisions. ©Les O'Neill.

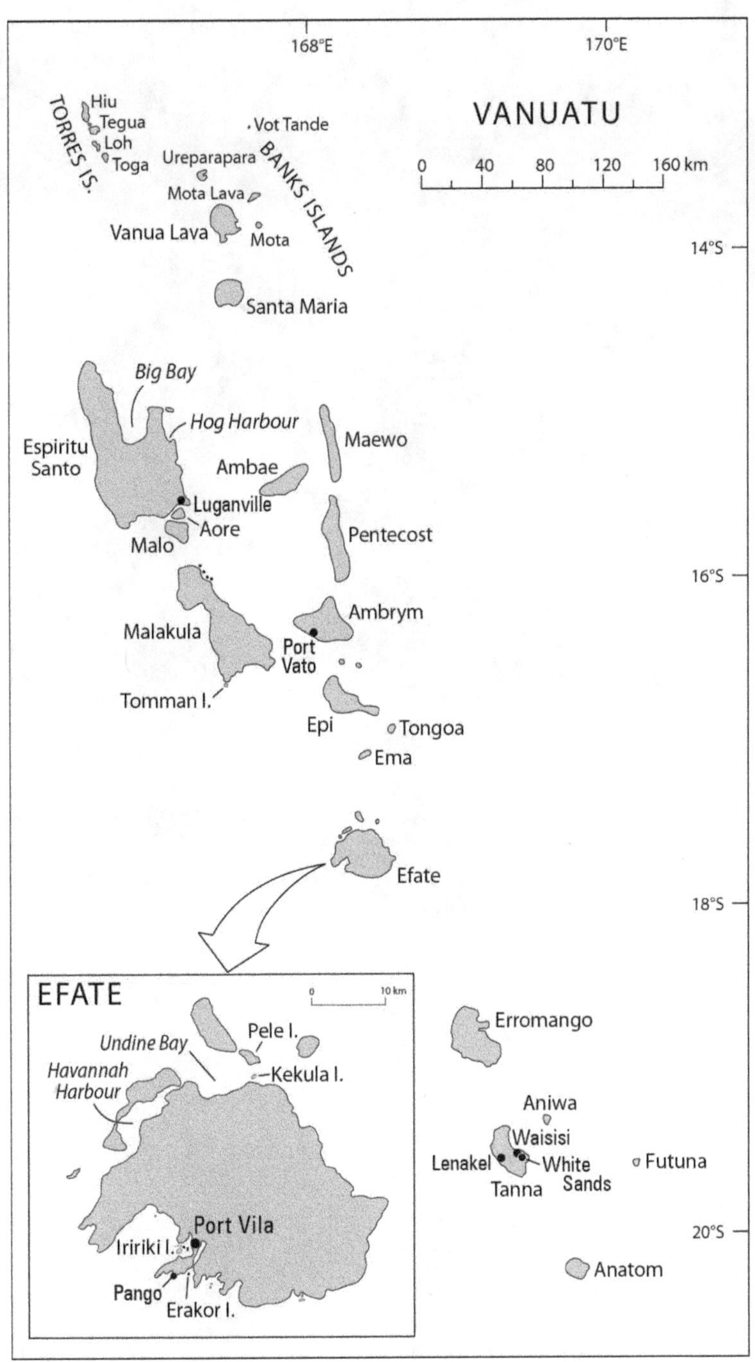

Map 4 Map of Vanuatu, showing main locations mentioned. ©Les O'Neill.

Introduction

In 1910 in a rape case heard by the Fiji Supreme Court, the complainant S, an Indian indentured labourer, stated, 'I am not a woman of loose character. I am not in the habit of alluring any men to have connection with them.'[1] She disputed both the accounts of the two accused and wider narratives of non-European women's licentiousness. In another earlier trial, the Fijian defendant M rejected the charge of rape, instead explaining that 'I took the woman to be my wife.'[2] As these contrasting examples suggest, the colonial courtroom was a space of confrontation, not just between the individuals involved in the trial but between wider experiences and differing understandings of sex, gender, violence and law.

This book examines the contested introduction of European criminal justice, its complexities and malleability, from roughly 1880 to 1920 in three Pacific colonies: French New Caledonia, British Fiji and the jointly ruled New Hebrides Condominium (Vanuatu). I focus predominantly on sexual crimes, where men and women navigated the intersection of intimacy and violence as well as the hierarchies of race, gender and status embedded by emerging colonial states. By the late nineteenth century, these three colonies included myriad social spaces ranging from Indigenous peoples, colonists and administrators living side by side in predominantly coastal colonial settlements to plantations with indentured labourers from Asia and Oceania, and Indigenous villages largely removed from day-to-day colonial governance. Within and between these communities were contested relationships and colonial hierarchies: between Indigenous chiefs, non-elite individuals and administrators; between traders, missionaries and officials; and, in the New Hebrides, between the British and French administrations, settlers and missions.

This is a story of legal pluralism and imperial practice, of how colonial administrations and island communities in the southwest Pacific adopted flexible and pragmatic approaches towards criminal justice. The legal institutions and spaces in which they operated were varied, ranging from the closed doors of the Privy Council in New Caledonia to the public rituals of the New Hebrides

Joint Court, and from naval ships to mission stations. Different forms of justice operated in these different spaces – magistrates' summary jurisdiction, violent reprisals by individuals and imperial navies and alternative missionary or settler codes of law – and existed alongside the trial-based criminal justice of the state. These alternative spaces of lawmaking were sometimes sanctioned by colonial administrations, sometimes condemned, and often existed beyond their reach.

The colonial court systems were nevertheless one place in which marginalized voices – including women – entered the archive to directly narrate their story or contest colonial legal processes. Where these records survive, examining criminal justice helps to foreground the experiences of Indigenous Islanders and indentured labourers. Cases of sexual violence were also the site of official and public debate, particularly when they crossed lines of race and gender. Judgements might be contested within local communities, official circles, newspapers and imperial networks. Drawing on these wider sources adds texture and depth to cases recorded in the colonial archive as well as illuminating some of the experiences not captured there. Such cases thus enable an exploration of the ways in which criminal justice functioned to uphold the colonial project and its underpinning hierarchies in the Pacific, while also being attentive to its limits and contradictions.

The diversity of legal institutions and practices reflected the diversity of the colonies themselves, and administrative attempts to manage the complex social landscape, which included Indigenous Islanders, Asian and Pacific Islander indentured labourers, officials, missionaries, planters, settlers, traders and penal transportees. In this context, I argue that imperial strategies of rule, and specifically the application of criminal law, were frequently adaptable and driven by pragmatics and the decisions of individual officials as much as overarching ideological concerns. This is therefore a book about the practice of empire in the Pacific, examining how laws and institutions responded to local conditions, or perceptions of them, and how Islanders and other groups engaged with and transformed legal practices. It builds on recent work that emphasizes the significance of everyday practices in constructing colonial law: frequently quotidian, contingent, ambiguous and incremental.[3]

While economic interests and visions of an Oceanic utopia drove eighteenth- and early-nineteenth-century European exploration in the Pacific, imperial administration followed only slowly, unevenly and sometimes reluctantly. Broadly, however, the second half of the nineteenth century saw a shift in the nature of European intervention in the region. Both British and French imperial involvement moved from maritime-based patrols, intended to police the labour trade, protect Islanders from unscrupulous newcomers and avenge traders and planters following 'outrages', to formal, land-based colonial administrations.[4] French interests were piqued by British expansion in Australia and New Zealand, while British settler colonists eyed French advances nearby warily. As the century progressed both metropoles staked greater claims over the ocean, islands and their resources. The Pacific became an arena for renewed Anglo-French rivalry.[5]

The three colonies examined came under colonial control at different periods from the mid-nineteenth to early twentieth centuries and exemplify different modes of colonial rule. The French annexed New Caledonia some twenty years before the British colonized Fiji and over fifty years before the inauguration of the New Hebrides Condominium. I nevertheless examine these colonies together chronologically, from roughly 1880 to 1920, for this was a formative period in which colonial administrations experimented and developed new forms of governance and law, such as the Indigénat regime in New Caledonia, indirect rule in Fiji and the Joint Naval Commission and unique Condominium structure in the New Hebrides.[6]

Throughout this period, officials, Islanders and a range of newcomers moved between the colonies. The High Commissioners for the New Hebrides were also the Suva- and Nouméa-based Governors of Fiji and New Caledonia, respectively. At a lower level, magistrates worked in several jurisdictions and French colonial inspectors touring the Pacific moved across colonial boundaries, bringing with them knowledge of other colonies and making comparisons and connections. The colonies were entwined with each other and wider imperial networks through trade, migrations and the continued and often controversial use of indentured labourers and the associated violence of recruitment and plantation life.[7] Finally this period was characterized by a degree of local turbulence in each colony, as Islander-newcomer conflict and resistance to colonial rule tested the authority of the colonial state.

In focusing on the practice of empire in the Pacific, I survey together British and French modes of imperialism. Although the colonies studied embodied quite different forms of colonial rule, I follow Donald Brenneis and Sally Engle Merry's scholarship on law in Fiji and Hawai'i, arguing that 'this comparison does not move us toward a metanarrative of colonialism but instead points to complexity and intersections'.[8] Imperial history has generally remained within the physical and linguistic borders of specific empires which, as Maya Jasanoff suggests, 'risks injecting exceptionalism into our histories, and limiting our perspectives on widespread features of imperial rule, such as settler colonialism and coercive labour regimes'. She, along with Simon Potter and Jonathan Saha, suggests further research to explore the connections, layerings and lineages that sustained imperial power across these divides.[9]

While not underplaying the distinct colonial trajectories of Fiji, New Caledonia and the New Hebrides, the perceived ideological differences between the British and French were often of less importance to how colonial justice operated and was experienced in the Pacific than how magistrates, judges and other officials dealt with the realities of small administrations and social complexities in each location. Despite the small size and populations of these possessions relative to many other British and French colonies, colonial administrations had difficulty in establishing and practicing criminal justice (and other aspects of law) across their island territories for decades after proclaiming their authority. The rule of law thus frequently existed in tension with ensuring sovereignty.[10]

Race and gender are central to this story. They shaped the experience of colonial rule, as well as the opportunities for, and experience of, engagement with new legal systems. These categories of difference also shaped and justified colonial policy. Focusing specifically on sexual crime enables us to connect colonial policy and law with private and domestic lives.[11] However, bureaucratic institutions consistently struggled to deal with the diverse realities of colonial social life. This was partly a problem of limited resources and officials, and partly one of limited knowledge. Colonial administrations, courts and magistrates grappled with their inability to oversee and make sense of intimate social practices of varied Indigenous and newcomer communities, and to delineate what constituted criminal behaviour and in what context. Similarly, imposed categories of race were never as straightforward or clearly demarcated as the state envisaged. Colonial law constructed 'racial-legal truths', defining groups as far more static and clear-cut than they actually were in spite of both shifting, contextual, and contradictory racial taxonomies and attempts to create 'universal' legal subjects.[12] Indigenous Islanders, as well as indentured labourers and other newcomers, nevertheless had to navigate these new legal concepts and practice. Through their engagement with the courts, or rejection of them altogether, individuals contested the use and meaning of colonial justice and colonial classifications.

In this context, serious violent crimes (such as rape, assault and murder) were particularly significant because all individuals were, theoretically at least, brought before the same court and subject to the same law, procedure and punishment. In practice, this was not always the case. Trials provide a significant window into the divergence between legal statute and practice in colonial settings. As Martin Weiner shows through murder trials across the British Empire, cases involving defendants and victims of different races required concrete resolution, through judgement and sentencing, of the tension between the hierarchies of difference underpinning empire and the stated equality of all before the law.[13] Colonial administrations found various ways to apply or circumvent criminal law in ways that were attentive, rather than blind, to racial difference and Indigenous subjects frequently found themselves without the right or opportunity for a trial in Pacific colonies.

Crimes of sexual violence – such as rape and sexual assault – provide particularly contentious and noteworthy case studies for understanding colonial criminal justice in action, as ideologies of gender, status and race intersected.[14] As Elizabeth Thornbury demonstrates, rape 'rendered political power as physical violence' and trials served as 'forums for disputes over political authority'.[15] Of course, focusing on the criminal necessarily emphasizes the violent and negative aspects of sexual relationships, which were but one end of a spectrum that ranged from the coercive to the consensual and affective.[16] The contestation of criminal charges of rape or sexual assault as well as official debates on where or whether certain offences should be tried nevertheless draws our attention to the disputed margins of licit and illicit behaviour. The shifting and contingent deployment of hierarchies of gender and race can be traced through multiple levels of judicial practice: in the dynamics of individual court cases, the official and public debates over judicial outcomes, and the justification for excluding groups from the jurisdiction of the colonial courts.

I argue that the inability of bureaucratic institutions to deal with the complex realities of colonial lives often meant that the courtroom became a theatrical space where authority was performed, obscuring the more complex and violent practice of colonialization and colonial lawmaking. While colonial bureaucracies engaged with and affected private lives through the court system, the difficulties of managing private lives, sex and violence also reveal the limits of colonialism's reach into Pacific communities. In this context, the courts emerge as ritual and pragmatic institutions. The trial often served as a formalized process to visibly assert European control and prestige over colonial spaces and peoples, when the court's authority was in reality hampered. This was particularly evident in the Joint Court of the New Hebrides, where both contemporaries and subsequent historians have ridiculed the rituals of judicial power as farce given the court's limited jurisdiction. However, legal procedures and performances served as potent reminders of colonial hierarchies and the increased marginalization of Islanders: male, European and medical accounts were prioritized while non-European, and especially female, testimony was devalued.

The emphasis on courtroom performance also obscured the ongoing legal violence of the state that continued in and beyond the courtroom, as well as the diverse means through which other actors sought to manage violence and pursue justice. Often considered a feature of nineteenth century imperialism, naval warships remained a regular presence in the twentieth century, particularly around Vanuatu.[17] Kanak were excluded from New Caledonia's Conseil Privé (Privy Council), which acted as a court that permitted neither witness nor defence, and were increasingly separated from the judiciary by the Indigénat regime. In Fiji, Indigenous Fijians and indentured labourers also experienced differing forms of justice in the village and plantation than in the courtrooms of Suva and Levuka. In the gaps of the criminal justice system, other options also emerged, including missionary and settler courts that challenged the authority of Indigenous leaders and colonial officials.

Tracey Banivanua Mar argues that lawless, frontier space nevertheless served an important function for emerging colonial states:

> Violence and its sanction was normalized and the frontiers, by their illegitimacy, were as deliberately central to colonial projects of settlement or resource extraction, as the administrative annexations of Indigenous lands, bodies and resources.[18]

This book picks up her argument to explore the ways in which the perceived weaknesses and limits of the judiciary remained useful in keeping space for colonial violence as a strategy of governance into the twentieth century, beyond the so-called frontier period in the Pacific.

Official reports and correspondence, legal records and court archives provide insight into the operation of colonial justice and into the uncertainties and concerns over its application. Together these sources emphasize the adaptable nature of colonial justice in the Pacific and help to break down the semblance of coherence given by the statute book or implied by terms such as indirect and direct rule. Rather, they reveal the opportunities for punitive action, individual agency and alternative forms of justices by both the colonial state as well as other groups.

In exploring legal practice on the ground, the actions and perspectives of the magistrates and officials charged with transforming written law into colonial practice are significant. Lower-level colonial agents shaped how colonial rule was enacted and experienced across the islands.[19] Their decisions, reports and memoirs contribute nuance, demonstrating how different officials approached questions of race, gender and intimate life in legal decision-making and providing a filtered view of colonial lives. As the Chief Police Magistrate in Fiji and later British Judge in the New Hebrides, Gilchrist Alexander stated, 'The Magistrate finds himself the repository of the domestic secrets not only of the native, but also of the white element of the population.'[20] Though problematic, Alexander's statement highlights how officials positioned themselves as knowledge holders over the intimate lives of colonized peoples, and how this claimed knowledge shaped colonial rule.

Where they survive, court records proved an avenue through which Indigenous voices enter the colonial record.[21] Men and women narrated their own stories of violence through trial depositions, as explored through Fiji Supreme Court cases. Their accounts offer a window into the violence of the colonial world and justice as experienced at a personal and quotidian level, particularly by women. However, their narratives were also constrained within the structures of the trial processes. From the late nineteenth century, the court became a space for supposedly rational and increasingly scientific forms of narration and victimhood that were shaped by widely held hierarchies and prejudices. The court was thus always a gendered and racialized experience. Considering intermarriage, Damon Salesa demonstrates that 'fundamentally gendered nature of colonial law regulated access to property and courts, and altered one's relationship with the state and its institutions'.[22] I show that this argument extends to criminal trials. In the arena of the court, non-European 'spheres of action were more limited than that of whites, their voices usually less audible'.[23]

Moreover, court records only exist when individuals chose to report crime and their reports were taken seriously. Rape and sexual violence have historically been both under-reported and under-prosecuted.[24] Court archives likely only represent a small sample of the incidences occurring. In the silences, we can infer the weighing up of strategic choices in responding to violence: what Arunima Datta terms the situational agencies of subaltern women, which were frequently short-term, covert and fleeting.[25] Many cases only reached the judiciary where other options for redress failed, and in many circumstances, individuals prioritized survival over revenge.[26] The colonial legal archive is unsurprisingly a partial, fragmentary one. Many Indigenous women and men appear and speak briefly before disappearing from official view: a nine-year-old Fijian girl articulating the trauma of assault before a magistrate in Chapter 3, or Jack and Toby protesting their arrest and violent treatment by the British doctor in the New Hebrides in Chapter 5 for example.

The limited audibility of Indigenous and women's voices reflects the hegemonic construction of the colonial archive and its silences. As Lisa Lowe demonstrates, the archive 'subsumes colonial violence within narratives of modern reason and progress'.[27] Danna Agmon categorizes the resultant gaps that shape historical knowledge: physical (records never created or kept, or disappeared and destroyed), historiographical (material neglected by historians due to gaps and marginalized topics in the scholarship) and epistemological (unknowability and invisibility in the records due to limits of worldview).[28] These gaps all impact the potential for recovery of Indigenous lives through colonial sources alone, and highlight significance of further research through archives and oral histories of the engagement, experience and impact of the court systems by Indigenous scholars. Indeed, historians can reinscribe the epistemic violence 'in and of the archive' if approaching sources uncritically, particularly for non-Indigenous scholars such as myself.[29] Acknowledging the power dynamics, gaps and silences that constitute the archive, I focus on unpacking how the judiciary operated to create colonial power, how the limits of its role and efficacy as a colonial institution deliberately left space for other forms of violence, and the diverse ways in which Islanders, indentured labourers, settlers and officials – men and women – worked within and around the judicial system. To do so, I attempt to read along and against the archival grain, and also highlight the 'bias grain' that structures what is absent, even between the lines, from these records.[30]

The uneven archive of the three colonies posed a further challenge to working across locations and empires.[31] The importance of the court as a site of colonial authority was distinct in each colony, and this is reflected in the nature of the legal archives.[32] Aside from the differences in court records, many archives of the Service des Affaires Indigènes in New Caledonia have been missing since their transfer in the 1950s from the colony to the Archives Nationales d'Outre Mer in France, a frustrating absence for historians interested in local interactions between the administration and Kanak, and Kanak experience of colonial rule at a quotidian level.[33] Other official sources, such as the detailed periodic reports produced by the French Colonial Inspectorate, and non-official archives therefore become crucial in addressing such topics. To allow for the varied nature of the colonial archives, different chapters foreground places and examples that are most relevant or emblematic of particular judicial and administrative practices.

The book is divided into two sections of three chapters each and structured thematically to allow connections and comparisons to be made, while also allowing for disjunctions and differences to emerge. The first section deals with the colonial court system, established as a legitimizing force for imperial rule over island communities. Chapter 1 examines the introduction and evolution of colonial law alongside European political and economic expansion in New Caledonia, Fiji and Vanuatu from the 1870s onwards, providing the wider context for the book's focus on gender, violence and justice. It details the extent to which Indigenous and indentured groups were incorporated or removed from the formal criminal justice system and the courts on the basis of race and geography, as well as the practical limitations to colonial governance. This overview reveals how ongoing tensions between complex and multi-layered colonial judiciaries and the difficulties in maintaining their practical authority created opportunities for both debate and alternative forms of justice. In this context, colonial legal systems were plural systems, significantly reshaped by local communities and specific ideas of gender, race and status across different colonial spaces.

Building from Chapter 1's argument, Chapter 2 examines the way in which officials used the courtroom as a theatrical space in the absence of substantive power in Pacific colonies. In particular, it discusses the Joint Court of the New Hebrides to highlight the way in which colonial justice was often as much about the rituals and performance of authority as the adjudication of law. The disjunction between these two elements of the court's role reflected the Joint Court's constrained jurisdiction and contributed to a legacy of farcical depictions of Anglo-French rule in the colony. Finally, this chapter explores how various individuals and communities used satire and theatre to critique colonial law and its limits in both Vanuatu and Fiji, and especially the problematic role of translation and transcription of evidence in multilingual trials.

Chapter 3 moves to analyse the testimony from specific court cases, where women and men narrated stories of intimacy and violence within the constraints of the legal system. Beyond the critiques of courtroom farce, it explores how colonial power operated in trials and how participants navigated the nuanced hierarchies in play. Using court depositions, it questions the place of race, gender and status in shaping the perception of testimony in the courtroom. The court was one of few arenas where female victims had an opportunity to articulate their experiences, and non-European defendants contested colonial ideas of guilt, violation and intimacy in relation to marriage and sex. However, the chapter argues that gendered and racial hierarchies of truth shaped the perceived credibility of evidence heard in rape and sexual assault cases, focussing on the Fiji Supreme Court where the most detailed archives remain. In contrast to the scepticism about the reliability of Indigenous and female witnesses, medical evidence was given greater weight in the trial process from the late nineteenth century, reflecting trends in Britain and elsewhere in empire.

The second section moves beyond the courtroom to consider the ways in which ideas of justice were contested more widely, including the range of intimacies and intimate violence that never made it to trial, the public debates over race, gender and colonial law, and the alternatives to the colonial courts such as missionary courts, punitive retribution and naval justice. Chapter 4 discusses varied patterns of intimacy – partnerships, marriages, mixed descent children, violent and coercive sexual encounters – and the attempts to govern these that emerged in different geographic spaces and communities. This chapter emphasizes the ways in which intimate lives and relationships, including violent ones, continued beyond the reach, or even the vision, of colonial administrations. It demonstrates how other communities, including Indigenous elites, missionaries and colonists, all had distinct interests in managing intimate and sexual relationships, as evidenced by the emergence of missionary courts, local governments and violent conflict as strategies to police and patrol intimate behaviour and interactions.

Chapter 5 explores the ways in which certain incidents of sexual violence also took on a life and significance beyond the courtroom as vehicles for broader discussions over the nature of colonial rule in the Pacific. The chapter centres on two contrasting case studies around 1915 from Vanuatu and Fiji that caused particular controversy. Indigenous men and women, colonial officials and local settlers debated 'black' and 'white peril', where anxiety over threats to, and control of, female bodies and intimate lives reflected the differing views on the role of colonial law in the Pacific. Though engaged with wider imperial debates, these cases took on greater significance in the Pacific in the context of colonial paternalism and protectionism.

Building from Chapters 4 and 5, the final chapter examines the many ways in which the colonial state addressed cases of sexual and other violence without going to trial. New Caledonia and New Hebrides administrations pursued a range of strategies to remove Islanders from the jurisdiction of courts, drawing on racial and gendered justifications to maintain practices of 'trial without witnesses'. This chapter argues that consequently government violence remained a basic response to non-European crime, both sexual and otherwise. Despite the introduction of colonial courts and the rhetoric of law's civilizing power, naval expeditions and bombardment remain the means of enforcing rule well into the twentieth century, not only justified on the grounds of Islander 'savagery' but also tied to imperial politics and rivalries of the period.

This book connects two different strands in recent imperial and Pacific history: gender, sexuality and their centrality to European imperialism; and law and legal pluralism. Gender was entwined with European perceptions of Pacific societies and practices of empire from the outset.[34] A vibrant scholarship appraises the importance of gender and sexual relations to European assessments of race, morality and civilization of societies across the Pacific Islands, and of missionary interventions into gender roles and domestic life.[35] However, the place of gender in concomitant colonial legal projects has received limited analysis in the Pacific.[36] Building upon the insights of new imperial history and especially the work of Ann Laura Stoler, historians have nevertheless demonstrated how 'private' lives and sexual relationships were not only central to the experience of imperialism, but also to the processes of empire-building and maintaining the 'intimate frontiers' of imperial rule and its boundaries.[37]

Imperial and legal histories of the Pacific more often focus on either 'civilizing' law as a justification for colonization or the critical issues of Indigenous land rights, ownership and dispossession.[38] The more quotidian operation of law in the region has not yet received adequate consideration. The imposition of criminal justice was, however, an important way in which Islanders and other colonial subjects encountered the formal structures of rule. This was, in Sally Engle Merry's phrase, 'law at its bottom fringes, where it intersects the social life of ordinary people rather than where legal doctrines are created'.[39] Criminal justice was a crucial means through which colonial authority over individuals and groups was regularly, visibly and often violently enacted and contested. As Lisa Ford argues of murder trials in settler colonies, 'much more was at stake in these trials than murder; they redefined sovereignty and its relationship to territory and jurisdiction'.[40] The colonial court and judiciary was an important space in which Islanders came into direct contact and conflict with the colonial state during the early period of colonial rule. These 'micro-judicial encounters' were critical to the gradual process of bring Indigenous peoples under European jurisdiction, as Shaunnagh Dorsett demonstrates in her nuanced scholarship on Māori engagement with magistrates' courts in mid-nineteenth century New Zealand.[41]

This book highlights the ways in which gendered rhetoric intersected with both justifications and contestations over the practice of colonial justice in the Pacific. Tropes of the degradation and mistreatment of non-European women were deployed in explanations for racially differentiated forms of justice in New Caledonia and the New Hebrides, while protests over the legal limits to patriarchal protection of white women in the New Hebrides and of Indian women in Fiji also mobilized gendered anxieties of sexual perils and critiqued colonial practice.[42] Indeed, similar discourses of sexual anxiety circulating among local settlers in 1920s Papua resulted in one of the most repressive rape laws in the British Empire.[43] While no parallel laws were passed in New Caledonia, Fiji or the New Hebrides, gender and sexuality are similarly important to understanding local imperial politics. I also add a Pacific perspective to the gendered operation of colonial courtrooms, particularly in the assessment of women's testimony and medical evidence in trials of sexual violence in Fiji.[44] The prioritization of certain types of evidence – male, European and increasingly scientific – demonstrates who was considered suitable to contribute to the production of colonial and legal knowledge and the locally specific processes by which non-European voices were devalued.

However, the production of colonial knowledge and authority in the courtroom was not complete or all-encompassing: as studies of law and empire elsewhere demonstrate, colonies often remained legally plural environments.[45] Lauren Benton and Lisa Ford emphasize the dynamic nature of law in colonial settings, where European law was but one of many legal regimes that continued to operate simultaneously, but which became hegemonic as 'everyday local practice was gradually and haltingly subordinated to jurisdiction'.[46] In thinking about these processes as they applied to colonial criminal justice in the Pacific, I aim to contribute to Nandini Chatterjee and Lakshmi Subramanian's examination of imperial rule as

> an aggregation of plural legal realities and imaginations, without losing sight of the fact that this was a plurality shaped by unequal power, and indeed characterised by zones of unbridled violence as much as the possibility of subaltern agency.[47]

Scholarship on legal pluralism that includes the Pacific has been limited, and limited Pacific history engages with this concept directly.[48] The specific dynamics of sexual violence – as crimes at the nexus of violence, gender and race – also lack an adequate history in the Pacific region, despite the fact that gender-based violence remains a pressing social issue.[49] Here I show how narratives about gender and racial difference enabled the colonial state, as well as individuals and communities, to maintain a plurality of strategies to police, punish or ignore sexual violence.

Examined together, the French administration in New Caledonia, British administration in Fiji and the Anglo-French Condominium of the New Hebrides highlight the contingent and diverse nature of colonial rule in the southwest Pacific. A tight geographical and thematic comparison adds to recent scholarship on the connections and disconnections between colonies, and between empires.[50] The places examined were also enmeshed by connected imperial practices, including the movement of officials, goods and ideas and longstanding patterns of Indigenous mobility. Pacific history has surpassed 'monograph myopia', as evidenced in a wealth of recent publications on the Pacific Islands and Pacific Rim that highlight its cosmopolitan nature (Thomas' *Islanders*), translocality (Matsuda's *Pacific Worlds*) and the multiple genealogies of the discipline (Armitage and Bashford's edited collection).[51] Focusing on three localities enables a detailed examination of the enactment of colonial rule as it was experienced by local communities, both Islander and newcomer. Here, the differing genealogies of French and British imperialism in the Pacific are considered but the operation of colonialism through its legal institutions and officials are foregrounded.

Drawing together colonies and empires requires the scope of this book to be tightly focused, with resulting limitations. The emphasis on behaviour that was considered criminal largely excludes discussion of marriage, as there were no legal provisions against interracial marriages. Secondly, heterosexual intimacy and sexual violence predominate in the book, given that few cases of homosexual crime appeared in the legal archive. Finally, the colonial archives for each place are variable in their structure and holdings, and the nature of the evidence found means that specific colonies in come into closer focus across different chapters. Practical limits to archival work, especially in the context of the Covid-19 pandemic, also restricted the scope of the research. The New Hebrides receives particular attention as it offers a window into the connections and tensions between French and British colonial practices, while joint governance resulted in an empire of paper, given the inter-imperial correspondence and duplicated systems of colonial reporting and archiving. Despite these limits, the colonial court and surrounding structures were critical institutions at the intersection between the colonial state and intimate lives in New Caledonia, Fiji and the New Hebrides. They merit detailed study.

The divergence between colonial rhetoric of 'civilized' and colour-blind criminal justice and the intersecting realities of judicial practices in the Pacific are most clearly revealed by cases of sexual violence and the diverse ways in which colonial officials and subjects navigated trials, alternative forms of justice and hierarchies of gender and race during such incidents. The theatre of the courtroom and related debates underpin the limits of colonial states' abilities to govern intimate lives, as Islanders, indentured labourers, officials and other groups navigated intimacy, violence and colonialism by pragmatic means.

Notes

1 Case 30/1910 *Rex v R and N*, Criminal Sittings, Fiji Supreme Court (FSC), NAF.

2 Case 53/1886 *Regina v M*, Criminal Sittings, FSC, NAF.

3 Lauren Benton and Lisa Ford, *Rage for Order: The British Empire and the Origins of International Law, 1800–1850* (Cambridge, MA: Harvard University Press, 2016), 3; Jonathan Saha, 'A Mockery of Justice? Colonial Law, the Everyday State and Village Politics in the Burma Delta, c.1890–1910', *Past & Present* 217 (2012), 190–1. On the significance of the quotidian implementation of law, see: Shaunnagh Dorsett, *Juridical Encounters: Maori and the Colonial Courts, 1840–1852* (Auckland: Auckland University Press, 2018); Sally Engle Merry, *Colonizing Hawai'i: The Cultural Power of Law* (Princeton, NJ: Princeton University Press, 2000); Jonathan Saha, *Law, Disorder and the Colonial State: Corruption in Burma c.1900* (Basingstoke: Palgrave Macmillan, 2013). On law and empire in the Pacific more generally, see: Tracey Banivanua Mar, 'Frontier Space and the Reification of the Rule of Law: Colonial Negotiations in the Western Pacific, 1870–74', *Australian Feminist Law Journal* 30, no. 1 (2009), 23–39; Stuart Banner, *Possessing the Pacific: Land, Settlers and Indigenous Peoples from Australia to Alaska* (Cambridge, MA: Harvard University Press, 2007); Donald Brenneis and Sally Engle Merry (eds), *Law and Empire in the Pacific: Fiji and Hawai'i* (Santa Fe: School of American Research, 2004); Lisa Ford, 'Law', in David Armitage and Alison Bashford (eds), *Pacific Histories: Land, Ocean, People* (Basingstoke: Palgrave Macmillan, 2014).

4 Deryck Scarr, *Fragments of Empire: A History of the Western Pacific High Commission 1877–1914* (Canberra: Australian National University Press, 1967); Isabelle Merle, *Expériences Coloniales: La Nouvelle-Calédonie 1853–1920* (Paris: Belin, 1995), 32–5; Robert Aldrich, *The French Presence in the South Pacific, 1842–1940* (Basingstoke: Macmillan, 1990); Tracey Banivanua Mar, *Decolonisation and the Pacific: Indigenous Globalisation and the Ends of Empire* (Cambridge: Cambridge University Press, 2016), chapter 1.

5 Nicholas Thomas, *Islanders: The Pacific in the Age of Empire* (New Haven: Yale University Press, 2010), 129–30, 162–3.

6 Isabelle Merle and Adrian Muckle, *L'Indigénat. Genèses dans l'empire français. Pratiques en Nouvelle-Calédonie* (Paris: CNRS Éditions, 2019); Scarr, *Fragments of Empire;* Peter France, *The Charter of the Land: Custom and Colonisation in Fiji* (Melbourne: Oxford University Press, 1969).

7 For example: Tracey Banivanua Mar, *Violence and Colonial Dialogue: The Australia-Pacific Labor Trade* (Honolulu: University of Hawai'i Press, 2007); Bril V. Lal, *Chalo Jahaji: On a Journey through Indenture in Fiji* (Canberra and Suva: Australian National University and Fiji Museum, 2000); Brij V. Lal, Doug Munro and Edward D. Beechert (eds), *Plantation Workers: Resistance and Accommodation*

(Honolulu: University of Hawai'i Press, 1993); Clive Moore, 'Revising the Revisionists: The Historiography of Immigrant Melanesians in Australia', *Pacific Studies* 15, no. 2 (1992), 61–86; Doug Munro 'The Labor Trade in Melanesians to Queensland: An Historiographic Essay', *Journal of Social History* 28, no. 3 (1995), 609–27; Dorothy Shineberg, *The People Trade: Island Labourers and New Caledonia, 1865–1930* (Honolulu: University of Hawai'i Press, 1999).

8 Donald Brenneis and Sally Engle Merry (eds), Introduction to *Law and Empire in the Pacific*, 6. See also: Ann Laura Stoler, *Carnal Knowledge and Imperial Power: Race and the Intimate in Colonial Rule, with a New Preface* (Berkeley: University of California Press, 2010), x–xv.

9 Maya Jasanoff, 'How Can We Write the History of Empire?' in Suzannah Lipscomb and Helen Carr (eds), *What Is History, Now?* (London: Weidenfeld & Nicolson, 2021), 97–9; see also: Simon J. Potter and Jonathan Saha, 'Global History, Imperial History and Connected Histories of Empire', *Journal of Colonialism and Colonial History* 16, no. 1 (2015). Examples of scholarship across imperial borders include: Jennifer Pitts, *A Turn to Empire: The Rise of Imperial Liberalism in Britain and France* (Princeton, NJ: Princeton University Press, 2005); Julia Martínez, Claire Lowrie, Frances Steel and Victoria Haskins, *Colonialism and Male Domestic Service across the Asia Pacific* (London: Bloomsbury, 2018); David Todd, 'A French Imperial Meridian 1814–1870', *Past and Present* 210 (2011), 155–85; Martin Thomas, *Violence and Colonial Order: Police, Workers and Protest in the European Colonial Empires, 1918–1940* (Cambridge: Cambridge University Press, 2012); Josep M. Fradera, *The Imperial Nation: Citizens and Subjects in the British, French, Spanish, and American Empires*, translated by Ruth MacKay (Princeton, NJ: Princeton University Press, 2018).

10 Nasser Hussain, *The Jurisprudence of Emergency: Colonialism and the Rule of Law* (Ann Arbor: University of Michigan Press, 2003).

11 Durba Ghosh, *Sex and the Family in Colonial India: The Making of Empire* (Cambridge: Cambridge University Press, 2006), 10; Ann Laura Stoler, 'Rethinking Colonial Categories: European Communities and the Boundaries of Rule', *Comparative Studies in Society and History* 13, no. 1 (1989), 134–61.

12 Renisa Mawani, *Colonial Proximities: Crossracial Encounters and Juridical Truths in British Columbia, 1871–1921* (Vancouver: UBC Press, 2009), 22–5; Sally Engle Merry, 'Law and Colonialism', *Law & Society Review* 25, no. 4 (1991), 895; Elizabeth Kolsky, *Colonial Justice in British India: White Violence and the Rule of Law* (Cambridge: Cambridge University Press, 2010), 10; John L. Comaroff, 'Colonialism, Culture and the Law: A Forward', *Law and Social Inquiry* 26, no. 2 (2001), 309. Jennifer Anne Boittin, Christina Firpo and Emily Musil Church, 'Hierarchies of Race and Gender in the French Colonial Empire, 1914–1946', *Historical Reflections/Réflexions Historiques* 37, no. 1 (2011), 60–90; Sue Peabody

and Tyler Stovall, 'Introduction: Race, France, Histories', in Sue Peabody and Tyler Stovall (eds), *The Color of Liberty: Histories of Race in France* (Durham: Duke University Press, 2003), 1–8; Sylvie Laurent and Thierry Leclère (eds), *De quelle couleur sont les Blancs? Des «petits Blancs» des colonies au «racisme anti-Blancs»* (Paris: La Découverte, 2013). On the construction of race in the Pacific, see for example: Nicholas Thomas, *In Oceania: Visions, Artifacts, Histories* (Durham: Duke University Press, 1997), chapter 5; Bronwen Douglas and Chris Ballard (eds), *Foreign Bodies: Oceania and the Science of Race 1770–1940* (Canberra: ANU E-Press, 2008); Margaret Jolly, Serge Tcherkézoff and Darrell Tyron (eds), *Oceanic Encounters: Exchange, Desire, Violence* (Canberra: Australian National University Press, 2009); Maile Arvin, *Possessing Polynesians: The Science of Settler Colonial Whiteness in Hawai'i and Oceania* (Durham: Duke University Press, 2019).

13 Martin Wiener, *An Empire on Trial: Race, Murder, and Justice under British Rule, 1870–1935* (Cambridge: Cambridge University Press, 2009), 5–6.

14 Pamela Scully, 'Rape, Race and Colonial Culture: The Sexual Politics of Identity in the Nineteenth-Century Cape Colony, South Africa', *American Historical Review* 100, no. 2 (1995), 335–59; Jonathan Saha, 'The Male State: Colonialism, Corruption and Rape Investigations in the Irrawaddy Delta c.1900', *Indian Economic and Social History Review* 47, no. 3 (2010), 343–76. More generally, see: Joanna Bourke, *Rape: A History from 1860 to the Present* (London: Virago, 2007); Anna Clark, *Women's Silence, Men's Violence: Sexual Assault in England, 1770–1845* (London: Pandora Press, 1987); Shani D'Cruze, 'Sexual Violence in History: A Contemporary Heritage?' in Jennifer Brown and Sandra Walklate (eds), *Handbook on Sexual Violence* (London: Routledge, 2011), 23–51; Louise A. Jackson, *Child Sexual Abuse in Victorian England* (London: Routledge, 1999); Emily J. Manktelow, *Gender, Power and Sexual Abuse in the Pacific Rev. Simpson's 'Improper Liberties'* (London: Bloomsbury, 2018), 35–51; and Georges Vigarello, *A History of Rape: Sexual Violence in France from the 16th to 20th Century* (Cambridge: Polity Press, 2000).

15 Elizabeth Thornbury, *Colonizing Consent: Rape and Governance in South Africa's Eastern Cape* (Cambridge: Cambridge University Press, 2018), 10.

16 Matt K. Matsuda, *Empire of Love: Histories of France in the Pacific* (New York: Oxford University Press, 2005), 4.

17 Jane Samson, *Imperial Benevolence: Making British Authority in the Pacific Islands* (Honolulu: University of Hawai'i Press, 1998).

18 Banivanua Mar, 'Frontier Space', 28.

19 Dorsett, *Juridical Encounters;* David Lambert and Alan Lester (eds), *Colonial Lives across the British Empire: Imperial Careering in the Long Nineteenth Century* (Cambridge: Cambridge University Press, 2006); John McLaren, *Dewigged, Bothered and Bewildered: British Colonial Judges on Trial, 1800–1900* (Toronto: University of Toronto Press, 2011); Zoe Laidlaw, *Colonial Connections, 1815–45: Patronage,*

the *Information Revolution and Colonial Government* (Manchester: Manchester University Press, 2006).

20 Gilchrist Alexander, *From the Middle Temple to the South Seas* (London: John Murray, 1927), 82, 84–5.

21 John Kelly, '"Coolie" as Labour Commodity: Race, Sex, and European Dignity in Colonial Fiji', *Journal of Peasant Studies* 19, nos. 3–4 (1992), 262; John Kelly, 'Gaze and Grasp: Plantations, Desires, Indentured Indians, and Colonial Law in Fiji', in Lenore Manderson and Margaret Jolly (eds), *Sites of Desire, Economies of Pleasure: Sexualities in Asia and the Pacific* (Chicago: University of Chicago Press, 1997), 73–98.

22 Damon Salesa, *Racial Crossings: Race, Intermarriage, and the Victorian British Empire* (Oxford: Oxford University Press, 2011), 184.

23 Renisa Mawani, 'Law's Archive', *Annual Review of Law and Social Science* 8 (2012), 337–65.

24 Bourke, *Rape*, 390–4.

25 Arunima Datta, *Fleeting Agencies: A Social History of Indian Coolie Women in British Malaya* (Cambridge: Cambridge University Press, 2021), 17–18; see also: Clare Anderson, *Subaltern Lives: Biographies of Colonialism in the Indian Ocean World, 1790–1920* (Cambridge: Cambridge University Press, 2012).

26 Nicole, *Disturbing History*, 164.

27 Lisa Lowe, *The Intimacy of Four Continents* (Durham: Duke University Press, 2015), 2.

28 Danna Agmon, 'Historical Gaps and Non-Existent Sources: The Case of the Chaudrie Court in French India', *Comparative Studies in Society and History* 63, no. 4 (2021), 985–7.

29 Marisa J. Fuentes, *Dispossessed Lives: Enslaved Women, Violence, and the Archive* (Philadelphia: University of Pennsylvania Press, 2016), 5–6. Emily J. Manktelow further highlights that 'giving voice' both 'troubles the authority of the past and the archive, but relies upon and idealizes the authority of the historian – which itself is troubling'; Manktelow, *Gender, Power and Sexual Abuse*, 5.

30 Ann Laura Stoler, *Along the Archival Grain: Epistemic Anxieties and Colonial Common Sense* (Princeton, NJ: Princeton University Press, 2010); Fuentes, *Dispossessed Lives*, chapter 3.

31 Dorsett and McLaren suggest the depth of archives for certain jurisdictions (and not others) has resulted in scholarship focused on a single site and helps explain why 'colonial legal historians … have responded more slowly to the challenges of the new imperial history'. Shaunnagh Dorsett and John McLaren, 'Laws, Engagements and Legacies: The Legal Histories of the British Empire: An Introduction', in Shaunnagh Dorsett and John McLaren (eds), *Legal Histories of the British Empire: Laws, Engagements and Legacies* (Abingdon: Routledge, 2014), 2.

32 Mawani, 'Law's Archive'.
33 Isabelle Merle, 'De la «législation» de la violence en context colonial: Le régime de la Indigènat en question', *Politix* 17, no. 66 (2004), 155–6; though see: Adrian Muckle and Benoît Trépied, 'Note on French Gendarmerie Archives Relating to New Caledonia', *Pambu News* 26 (July 2009) for details on surviving records available from 1913 onwards.
34 Patty O'Brien, *The Pacific Muse: Exotic Femininity and the Colonial Pacific* (Seattle: University of Washington Press, 2006); Lee Wallace, *Sexual Encounters: Pacific Texts, Modern Sexualities* (New York: Cornell University Press, 2003); Matsuda, *Empire of Love.*
35 For example: Margaret Jolly, '"To Save the Girls for Brighter and Better Lives": Presbyterian Missions and Women in the South of Vanuatu: 1848–1870', *Journal of Pacific History* 26, no. 1 (1991), 27–48; Patricia Grimshaw, *Paths of Duty: American Missionary Wives in Nineteenth Century Hawai'i* (Honolulu: University of Hawai'i Press, 1989); Margaret Jolly and Martha Macintyre (eds), *Family and Gender in the Pacific: Domestic Contradictions and the Colonial Impact* (Cambridge: Cambridge University Press, 1989); Manktelow, *Gender, Power and Sexual Abuse*; Kalpana Ram and Margaret Jolly (eds), *Maternities and Modernities: Colonial and Postcolonial Experiences in Asia and the Pacific* (Cambridge: Cambridge University Press, 1998). Beyond the Pacific, see: Antoinette Burton, *Burdens of History: British Feminists, Indian Women, and Imperial Culture, 1865–1915* (Chapel Hill: University of North Carolina Press, 1994).
36 But see: Kelly, 'Gaze and Grasp'; Sally Engle Merry, 'Narrating Domestic Violence: Producing the "Truth" of Violence in 19th- and 20th-Century Hawaiian Courts', *Law and Social Inquiry* 19 (1994), 967–93; Sally Engle Merry, 'Comparative Criminalization: Cultural Meanings of Adultery and Gender Violence in Hawai'i in 1850 and 1990', *Pacific Studies* 25, no. 1 (2002), 203–20; Angela Wanhalla, 'Intimate Connections: Governing Cross-Cultural Intimacy on New Zealand's Colonial Frontier', *law&history* 4, no. 2 (2017), 45–71.
37 Ann Laura Stoler, *Carnal Knowledge and Imperial Power: Race and the Intimate in Colonial Rule* (Berkeley: University of California Press, 2003). See also: Anne McLintock, *Imperial Leather: Race, Gender, and Sexuality in the Colonial Context* (New York: Routledge, 1995); Philippa Levine (ed.), *Gender and Empire* (Oxford: Oxford University Press, 2007); Julia Clancy-Smith and Frances Gouda (eds), *Domesticating the Empire: Race, Gender, and Family Life in French and Dutch Colonialism* (Charlottesville: University Press of Virginia, 1998); Emmanuelle Saada, *Empire's Children: Race, Filiation, and Citizenship in the French Colonies*, translated by Arthur Goldhammer (Chicago: University of Chicago Press, 2012); Tony Ballantyne and Antoinette Burton (eds), *Bodies in Contact: Rethinking Colonial Encounters in World History* (Durham: Duke University Press, 2005);

Tony Ballantyne and Antoinette Burton (eds), *Moving Subjects: Gender, Mobility and Intimacy in an Age of Global Empire* (Urbana: University of Illinois Press, 2009); Gilles Boetsch, Nicolas Bancel and Pascal Blanchard (eds), *Sexualités, identités & corps colonisés. XVe siècle-XXIe siècle* (Paris: CNRS Editions, 2019); Judith Surkis, *Sex, Law, and Sovereignty in French Algeria, 1830–1930* (Ithaca, NY: Cornell University Press, 2019). For recent overviews see: Dagmar Herzog and Chelsea Schields (eds), *The Routledge Companion to Sexuality and Colonialism* (Abingdon: Routledge, 2021) and Louise Edwards, Nigel Penn and Jay Winter (eds), *The Cambridge World History of Violence*, vol. 4, 1800 to present (Cambridge: Cambridge University Press, 2020), especially Part II – Gendered and Intimate Violence.

38 Banner, *Possessing the Pacific*; Bain Attwood, *Empire and the Making of Native Title: Sovereignty, Property and Indigenous People* (Cambridge: Cambridge University Press, 2020); Howard Van Trease, *The Politics of Land in Vanuatu: From Colony to Independence* (Suva: Fiji Times, 1991 [1987]); Joël Dauphiné, *Les spoliations foncières en Nouvelle-Calédonie (1853–1913)* (Paris: Éditions L'Harmattan, 1989); Alain Saussol, *L'héritage: essai sur le problème foncier mélanésien en Nouvelle-Calédonie* (Paris: Société des Océanistes, Musée de l'homme, 1979); Alan Ward, *Land and Politics in New Caledonia* (Canberra: Australian National University Press, 1982).

39 Merry, *Colonizing Hawai'i*, 8.

40 Lisa Ford, *Settler Sovereignty: Jurisdiction and Indigenous Peoples in America and Australia, 1788–1836* (Cambridge, MA: Harvard University Press, 2010), 2.

41 Dorsett, *Juridical Encounters*.

42 Claudia Knapman, *White Women in Fiji, 1835–1930: The Ruin of Empire?* (London: Allen & Unwin, 1986); Carina E. Ray, 'Decrying White Peril: Interracial Sex and the Rise of Anticolonial Nationalism in the Gold Coast', *American Historical Review* 119, no. 1 (2014), 78–110.

43 Amirah Inglis, *'Not a White Woman Safe': Sexual Anxiety and Politics in Papua, 1920–1934* (Canberra: Australian National University Press, 1974).

44 Jonathan Saha, 'Whiteness, Masculinity and the Ambivalent Embodiment of "British Justice" in Colonial Burma', *Cultural and Social History* 14, no. 4 (2017), 527–42.

45 Lauren Benton, *Law and Colonial Cultures: Legal Regimes in World History, 1400–1900* (Cambridge: Cambridge University Press, 2002); Benton and Ross (eds), *Legal Pluralism and Empires 1500–1850*; Dorsett and McLaren, *Legal Histories of the British Empire;* Renisa Mawani, 'Law and Colonialism: Legacies and Lineages', in Austin Sarat and Patricia Ewick (eds), *Law and Society Handbook* (Malden: John Wiley and Sons, 2015), 417–32; Barry Godfrey and Graeme Dunstall (eds), *Crime and Empire 1840–1940* (Uffculme: Willan Publishing, 2005).

46 Ford, *Settler Sovereignty*, 11; Benton, *Law and Colonial Cultures.*

47 Nandini Chatterjee and Lakshmi Subramanian, 'Law and the Spaces of Empire: Introduction to the Special Issue', *Journal of Colonialism and Colonial History* 15, no. 1 (2014).

48 But see: Brenneis and Merry, *Law and Empire;* Etherington, 'The Gendering of Indirect Rule'; Merry, *Colonizing Hawai'i*; Adrian Muckle, 'Troublesome Chiefs and Disorderly Subjects: The Internment of Kanak under the Indigénat – New Caledonia, 1887–1946', *Journal of French Colonial History* 11 (2010), 131–60.

49 United Nations Entity for Gender Equality and the Empowerment of Women Pacific Sub-Regional Office, *Ending Violence Against Women and Girls: Evidence, Data, and Knowledge in Pacific Island Countries – Literature Review and Annotated Bibliography*, 2nd edn (Suva: UN Women Pacific Sub-Regional Office, 2011); Aletta Biersack, Margaret Jolly and Martha Macintyre (eds), *Gender Violence & Human Rights: Seeking Justice in Fiji, Papua New Guinea and Vanuatu* (Canberra: Australian National University Press, 2016).

50 John McLaren, 'Chasing the Chimera: The Rule of Law in the British Empire and the Comparative Turn in Legal History', *Law in Context* 33, no. 1 (2015), 21–36.

51 Kerry R. Howe, 'Pacific Islands History in the 1980s: New Directions or Monograph Myopia?' *Pacific Studies* 3, no. 1 (1979), 81–90; Thomas, *Islanders*; Matt K. Matsuda, *Pacific Worlds: A History of Seas, Peoples, and Cultures* (Cambridge: Cambridge University Press, 2012); David Armitage and Alison Bashford (eds), *Pacific Histories: Land, Ocean, People* (Basingstoke: Palgrave Macmillan, 2014).

Part 1

'A stranger in our midst': Criminal justice in the colonial courts

Figure 1 Postcard from the 1913 voyage of the *Kersaint*, showing the shipboard arrest of ni-Vanuatu men. Credit: Campagne du 'Kersaint', G. de Béchade, No. 26. NOUVELLES-HÉBRIDES. Arrestation d'une tribu. Private collection.

Figure 2 Postcard from the 1913 voyage of the *Kersaint*, showing the arrival of arrested 'murderers' in Port Vila. Credit: Campagne du 'Kersaint', G. de Béchade, No. 27. NOUVELLES-HÉBRIDES. Débarquement d'assassins à Port-Vila. Private collection.

1

Creating European law in the Pacific

At the first meeting of the Bose Vakaturaga (Council of Chiefs) in 1875 shortly after British annexation, the Fijian elite expounded the difference between European and Fijian law. One magistrate Mafi asserted, 'In England, the law is the great Chief; there it governs all and has done so for ages. We have had English law in Fiji for some time, but it is still a stranger in our midst.'[1]

By contrast, on his appointment as chief police magistrate of Fiji in 1907, Gilchrist Alexander recalled that he 'left the Colonial Office still uncertain whether I should be required to live in a native hut and hold a Court under the shade of a palm tree'.[2] On his arrival, Alexander found the native hut of his imagination was in fact a courthouse in the colonial township of Suva, still rather different from the august architecture of the London inns. The numerous doors of the court, kept open onto the surrounding verandahs to let in the breeze during tropical days, let in many unexpected intruders: wandering dogs disrupted proceedings and sand proved a constant menace to the desired cleanliness and order of the courthouse.[3] The refractory island environment was but one of many novel elements which European judges, lawyers and officials who ventured to the Pacific encountered and attempted to control.

As the contrasting words of the Fijian and Europeans magistrates demonstrate, lawmaking in the Pacific was a contested process. Far from the colonial view that the expansion of 'civilized' law and justice was the 'supreme gift' of imperial expansion over 'uncivilized' peoples, European forms of law were not simply transplanted from imperial metropoles onto colonial spaces.[4] Nor were newly acquired colonies a tabula rasa upon which new ideologies of justice could be imposed: Indigenous societies of the Pacific (like all societies) contained their own proscriptions, codes of behaviour and sanctions that maintained stability and order and structured conflict.

The extension of 'civilised', and therefore European, law and justice throughout the imperial world was both a motivation – at least to the extent that the actions of European settlers needed to be policed – and a justification for colonial domination of Indigenous people and their territories.[5] Colonial law was a vital instrument and expression of imperial rule.[6] However, its effect was by no means inevitable or straightforward: different legal traditions, changing public opinion, the influence of individual governors and officials, the specificities of local conditions and especially Indigenous society and politics all converged to shape the practice of justice in unique ways. These contradictions were evident in Fiji Governor Arthur Gordon's speech to settlers upon his departure in 1880, when he thanked the chief justice 'for the improvement of different branches of the law which have given to our Statute Book a value and a character distinctively its own'.[7]

This chapter examines the introduction and evolution of colonial law alongside European political and economic expansion in New Caledonia, Fiji and Vanuatu from the 1870s onwards, providing the wider context for the book's focus on gender, criminal justice and violence. It focuses on the extent to which Indigenous and indentured groups were incorporated or removed from the formal criminal justice system and the courts on the basis of race and geography, as well as the practical limitations to colonial governance. Traced through the late nineteenth and early twentieth centuries, we see recurrent tensions between complex and multilayered colonial judiciaries and the difficulties in maintaining their practical authority, creating space for both debate and alternative forms of justice. In this context, colonial legal systems were plural systems, significantly reshaped by local communities and specific ideas of gender, race and status across different colonial spaces.

The chapter begins with an overview of emerging justice systems in each colony in relation to broader patterns of colonization and the attempts (or lack of) to interpret and incorporate Indigenous customs and traditions into colonial governance. I then examine the practical limits to the operation of these legal systems. Island geographies, Indigenous resistance and the small size and resourcing of each bureaucracy shaped the implementation the rule of colonial law. I conclude with an examination of the broad connections and differences between judicial structures in these three Pacific colonies.

Local circumstances, British and French experience of colonial rule in other parts of empire, and broader imperial politics resulted in convergence and divergence in judicial institutions. Each colony developed a multifaceted legal system. The evolution of a plurality of courts divided criminal cases, deliberately or otherwise, along the boundaries of race as well as geography, frequently separating Indigenous and European subjects (and indentured labourers in Fiji) within the judicial system. In Fiji this was achieved through the institution of chiefly authority, Native Regulations and village courts, while in New Caledonia and the New Hebrides, Islanders were largely excluded from the jurisdiction of the courts.

The specific judicial structures created in each colony were locally contingent. Divergent motivations, modes of imperialism – from penal colonization, attempted settler colonialism to direct and indirect rule – and perceptions of each locale and its inhabitants were important factors governing this process. While not underplaying the haphazard nature by which the legal architecture developed, I argue that, in creating its judiciary, each colony addressed similar practical and ideological challenges, which ranged from very local to much broader debates about the nature and role of imperial justice and rule. These included imperial rivalries, public pressures, quotidian frustrations and attempts to overcome the contradiction between the liberal ideals of judicial equality and citizenship of late-nineteenth-century Europe, the rhetoric regarding the protection and trusteeship of 'native' peoples, and the authoritarian nature of colonial rule.[8]

New Caledonia

France claimed possession of New Caledonia in 1853, motivated by imperial rivalries, the desire for a naval stronghold in the region and to find a solution to metropolitan penal problems.[9] Following the appointment of the first local Governor Charles Guillain in 1862, the colony developed its own administration and infrastructure.[10] Its identity began, first and foremost, as a *bagne* or penal colony: over 22,000 criminals and political prisoners arrived on New Caledonian shores from 1864 until transportation terminated in 1897.[11] The penitentiary played an important role in the development of the economy and infrastructure of the early colony with prison labour contributing to construction projects and mining. It also added social complexity, firstly because of the diversity of the transportees themselves and secondly because many remained permanently, significantly influencing the demographics of the colony.[12]

The size of the Grande Terre, along with a belief in the fertility of the climate and soil that emerged in the mid-nineteenth century, fed into hopes amongst French officials that New Caledonia would become an agrarian settler colony, or 'la France australe'.[13] Penal transportation evolved into penal colonization as *bagnards* with records of good behaviour were offered plots of land upon their release. In 1884, 110,000 hectares were allocated for this purpose, primarily around Bourail, La Foa, Diahot, Pouembout and Prony.[14] Working to end deportation in the 1890s, reformist Governor Paul Feillet encouraged 'colonisation libre' (free, non-penal settlement).[15] Under Feillet's scheme, new settlers and some freed convicts were given land grants and encouraged to grow coffee and other crops, with the aim of transforming the colony agriculturally.[16] By 1896, around 9,300 settlers along with over 3,000 colonial officials and soldiers had arrived and remained on New Caledonian soil, along side a population of 8,200 convicts or paroled individuals.[17] By comparison, the Kanak population had apparently declined to under 30,000 in the problematic 1901 census count.[18] Over the first five decades of French rule, almost 300,000 hectares of land were appropriated, leased or sold.[19] Despite the limited success of Feillet's immigration drive, French visions for the colony quickly impinged upon Indigenous land use and ownership, becoming a source of conflict as well as a driving factor behind laws and policies to exclude Kanak from European jurisdiction and rights.[20]

As elsewhere in the French empire, imperial governance in New Caledonia rested upon distinctions between subjects and citizens, distinctions overlaid on categories of race, and concepts of civilization and justice. These were embodied in the notion 'to each race, its law, and to each law, its race'.[21] Racial understandings, however nebulous, fed into strategies for rule and hardened throughout the second half of the nineteenth century. From the outset, the colonial administration was predicated on a range of divisions that filtered into the legal system. Alongside the distinction between Kanak and colonists, New Caledonia's European society was fractured by the division of *libéré* and *colon*, and metropolitan and locally born.[22] As Adrian Muckle, Bronwen Douglas and Chris Ballard argue, concepts of race in Pacific colonial discourse were shaped as much by legal, administrative and political necessity and utility as by scientific understanding.[23] Moreover, the category of the *indigène* had blurry borders which could be negotiated, appropriated and redefined, and was further complicated by continuing intermarriages and indentured labour migrations from French Indochina, Japan and the Pacific.[24] The limits of colonial legal binaries were particularly evident at the intersections between the categories of *indigène* and *métis*; between Kanaks of the Grande Terre and the Loyalty Islands; and *indigènes* of New Caledonia and other Pacific Islanders in the colony, including ni-Vanuatu and Tahitians.

New Caledonian courts nevertheless largely mirrored the judicial organization of metropolitan France, envisaged as it was to become a 'colonie de peuplement' or settler colony. When the first Governor arrived in 1862, the judicial structure was skeletal. The 1843 ordinance, which established French legal norms in the Marquesas, was applied to New Caledonia in 1855 as an initial framework. Subsequent laws in 1859 laid out the practical organization of the courts and promulgated the Code Napoleon, applying French law in New Caledonia.[25] By 1866, the judiciary comprised a Procureur de la République (a prosecuting attorney or public prosecutor) and deputy; a Tribunal de Première Instance composed of a single judge and a *lieutenant de juge* (performing the role of examining magistrate and deputy judge), a Tribunal d'Appel with a sole judge, a Tribunal de Commerce comprising five notable businessmen; along with a Tribunal Supérieur, again with a single judge, to hear appeals.[26] The Tribunal de Première Instance dealt primarily with criminal affairs when it sat in its capacity as the Tribunal de Simple Police or Tribunal de Police Correctionnelle.

Given the colony's foundation of deportation and penal labour, the issues of law and lawlessness were ever present in the minds of officials. In 1888, Governor Mouët expressed his concern over the large and ever rising number of cases before the Tribunal Correctionnel and Tribunal Criminel, which he attributed to the preponderance of *libérés* and *indigènes* in the colonial population.[27] Concerns regarding the moral standing of the settler community also emerged, as 'they are most often poor people who have a fortune to make or remake, and whose moral sense is not always as elevated'.[28] Officials were troubled by the potentially negative influence of these unprincipled European newcomers upon an 'uncivilised' and 'undeveloped' Indigenous population, a concern also expressed across British Pacific colonies. Such contact was considered detrimental to the social fabric of the colony and a contributing factor to severe population decline observed in the Kanak population.[29]

From the mid-1860s calls for increased powers over the management of the Kanak population began to circulate in the metropole. The Minister of the Navy and Colonies argued that

> in the face of a population still unfamiliar with the ideas of civilisation, the French authorities should be vested with the necessary powers to assure the security of our possession; it therefore seems to me that there shall be occasion to employ the means of repression which experience has already shown to be effective in Algeria.[30]

The Arrêté (decree) du 24 Decembre 1867 recognized the concept of the *tribu* (tribe) as the organizational base of Kanak society, legally enshrining both collective ownership of property and collective responsibility for crimes and disorder.[31] The following year, another decree further defined Kanak land rights and initiated the process of *cantonnement* (containment) of the Indigenous population in reserves, thus freeing up land for European use.[32] The only French colony to use *cantonenment* so extensively, it did not prevent conflict as Kanak sought to protect their lands and rights.

Indigenous resistance and Kanak-French conflict was recurrent following colonization as Kanak sought to protect their lands and lives, including in the south around Nouméa from 1856 to 1859; the northern Grande Terre from 1856 to 1862; and continuing in the centre-north to 1869.[33] New Caledonia was particularly shaken by the eruption of conflict around La Foa in June 1878, which marked the start of war between the *tribus* around Ouraïl and Bouloupari-Thio lead by chiefs Ataï and Naïna, and the French military and their Kanak allies.[34] The 1878–9 war marked a watershed as the last major conflict of the nineteenth century. By January 1879, aided by Kanak allies, the French suppression of Indigenous resistance seemed complete, heralding an era of aggressive European expansion that obscured continued Kanak resilience and resistance. Nevertheless, for New Caledonia the so-called revolt of 1878–9 was reminiscence of the impact of the 1857 Indian rebellion.[35] In both cases, neither settlers nor officials anticipated the violent uprising of their subjects, though the consequences for the attitudes and style of imperial rule were long-lasting. The conflict awakened local European anxieties concerning Kanak: the 'fantôme' of further violence left a legacy within the colonial imagination.[36]

Nine years later, a new strategy for managing a troubling Indigenous population was implemented: the Code de l'Indigénat, or simply the Indigénat. The New Caledonia legislation was modelled on French practices of rule elsewhere, notably Algeria and Indochina.[37] Alongside labour corvées and taxation, the Décret du 18 juillet 1887 outlined specific infractions that, committed by *indigènes non-citoyens français*, would be policed and disciplined by the head of Service des Affaires Indigènes (SAI) and Kanak chiefs appointed by the administration.[38] Initially restrictions included prohibitions on disobeying orders, being found outside one's district without permission, carrying of 'armes canaques' in areas inhabited by Europeans, the practice (or accusation of) sorcery, entering inns or drinking places, nudity on the roads or European towns, entering European houses without authorization and disturbing order or work in settlements, workshops, factories or stores. Kanak women were subject to particular surveillance under these regulations, given the moral anxieties around prostitution, interracial relationships and disorder.[39]

Additional decrees in 1888 and 1892 extended the list to include an 8 pm curfew in Nouméa as well as proscriptions against disrupting the peace in the streets of the colonial townships. As the Indigénat legislation was renewed in 1907, 1915 and 1928, further infractions were added. While the 1887 law provided the basis for its implementation, the Indigénat in its broader sense comprised a range of legislation and strategies that defined Indigenous experience of imperial rule for over sixty years, until Kanaks gained citizenship at the end of the Second World War and the laws underpinning it were dismantled.[40] The Indigénat is thus better conceptualized as a regime than a code.

The result of the 1867 legislation and the 1887 Indigénat was segregation on racial and spatial lines, a characteristic of French rule in New Caledonia until the end of the Second World War. The idea of containment and management of Kanak in reserves and control of Indigenous mobility was initially closely linked to the predicted decline, pacification and absorption of the Indigenous population. The Indigénat hinged upon the removal of one basic pillar of democratic governance: the separation of judicial and administrative powers. It granted administrators summary powers to discipline Kanak, without reference to the judicial system, with sentences of up to fifteen days imprisonment or fines of up to 100 francs.[41] For more serious threats or offences, the Governor, supported by the Conseil Privé (Privy Counsel), could intern individual *indigènes* on the Îlot Amadée, Île des Pins, Loyalty Islands or occasionally Tahiti: another form of enforcing physical and geographical separation, which reflected increased judicial segregation.[42]

During Feillet's *fin-de-siècle* governorship, the differing status of Kanaks was deemed necessary on civilizing grounds: a means of very gradual development towards European civilization.[43] The Indigénat initially was presented as a temporary and exceptional measure, in place until *indigènes* either passed away or could be integrated into French civil society. By the early twentieth century, however, colonial officials became disillusioned with the optimistic belief in the so-called progress towards civilization among the Kanak and sceptical of expectations of racial decline. Subsequent colonial inspections criticized assumptions about Indigenous annihilation or absorption, as Kanak communities survived and thus remained an administrative problem.[44]

While each decree had a limited lifespan, their continual renewal and expansion prompted criticism. In 1907, Colonial Inspector Fillon reported scathingly of the 'arbitrary extension of punishments … and serious illegalities' that continued under the regime:

> The Indigénat is in most colonies a quick and simple system of repression, often useful for the prestige of the local administration and the success of their

> indigenous policy. But it is an exceptional regime that infringes upon individual liberty: the powers of administration and judge are conferred upon the same people, who are not bounded by the conclusive proof required in ordinary criminal matters. [45]

Despite the critical voice of the Colonial Inspectorate, the codification of local custom 'remain[ed] largely ignored by our administration' and 'arbitrary' administration through the Indigénat continued.[46]

While there was little attempt to record and codify Kanak custom in New Caledonia (as occurred in Fiji), the Indigénat had some features of indirect rule more commonly associated with British imperialism. Appointed Kanak chiefs invested with not only the right but also the responsibility to oversee their *tribu*, and the enactment of regulations specific to the Indigenous population, overseeing labour required for works and the collection of head taxes for the colonial state. In light of the limited resources of the SAI, during the late nineteenth and early twentieth centuries the administration was frequently reliant on the compliance of chiefs in establishing order and authority outside limited areas of European settlement.[47] The result was 'an intense localisation of the local, for Kanaks in particular, accompanied by multiple forms of segregation, through the differentiation of rights and spaces'.[48] The Indigénat was a defining aspect of the colonial experience for Kanak but also defined the colonial order, creating legal and physical demarcations on the basis of race.

Fiji

The development of the Indigénat occurred at a similar time to British colonization of Fiji, where early officials experimented with indirect rule. In the 1850s and 1860s the British Colonial Office was wary of acquiring further territories with little perceived prospect of economic reward. By the eve of British colonization of the Fijian archipelago in 1874, disputes over land sales and political authority between Bauan chief Cakobau's government, other Indigenous leaders and newcomers had become sufficiently detrimental to British interests and reputation to overcome official reluctance for formal intervention.[49] Law and justice was thus a key tenet of imperial rule in Fiji and its legitimation. Sir Arthur Gordon, Governor of Fiji from 1875 to 1880, emphasized in a speech to Indigenous chiefs in 1875 that 'laws are necessary; a country without laws would be in a pitiable condition'.[50]

Nevertheless, the Colonial Office had little desire to closely manage a distant colony and even less to fund one, and charged Gordon with making Fiji a financially self-sufficient possession. Gordon's policies regarding native administration, and his implementation of indentured immigration as the basis of the sugar plantation economy, formed the foundation for the key racial, economic and political divisions in colonial and post-colonial Fiji. His coterie of administrators and successors would maintain much of this system into the twentieth century.[51]

Gordon's patronage and education underpinned the confidence and ambition that he carried though a career of governorships spanning the British empire over nearly thirty years from 1861 to 1890.[52] Gordon 'was no amateur': he brought with him experience in plantation colonies and well-formed plans for ensuring the economic viability of the island colony.[53] His economic policy of government-administered indentured labour migration was intimately entwined with aims for a protectionist and highly paternalistic approach to Indigenous governance. He saw poor administration and unfettered interaction between 'natives' and unscrupulous settlers as the cause of Fijian population decline.

While this view was based on observations made around the imperial world, Gordon's arrival in Fiji in June 1875 coincided with the height of a severe measles epidemic that killed around 20 per cent of the Fijian population. The epidemic strengthened his pre-existing belief in racial decline and his desire for a 'better' form of imperial rule.[54] The depopulation narrative was a long-standing element of colonial thought in Fiji. However, as Nicholas Thomas notes, the causes of depopulation were increasingly perceived as internal to Fijian society, thereby justifying colonial intervention in intimate and village life on the grounds of improving sanitation and hygiene.[55]

Protection of Indigenous Fijians from the perceived pernicious effects of cultural contact and colonial market forces was achieved through indirect rule, which instituted and solidified chiefly authority and preserved 'traditional' village culture and land tenure. In fact, 'traditional' authority and cultural practices were largely European constructs.[56] What Gordon and his administration understood as 'native' tradition derived predominantly from the regions and chieftainships with which they had most interaction (such as Bau on the east of Viti Levu). Formalizing these traditions erased, in the statute books at least, the diversity and fluidity that existed on the ground. Cultural differences within Fijian society were framed through a hierarchical view. Cakobau's 'heathen Kai Colo' opponents of Viti Levu's interior were deemed less civilized and more volatile than the inhabitants of the coastal polities, views compounded by the 1876 war.

Indirect rule supported an interpretation of Fijian society weighted towards elite and Bauan views, while 'ordinary Fijians ... sometimes had to be told by white men what their customs were'.[57]

The reification of chiefly authority was subject to some contemporary criticism, such as missionary Lortimer Fison's grave predictions of a feudal society emerging due to restrictions on labour mobility imposed on non-elite Fijians.[58] Moreover, Gordon's protectionist policy inevitably frustrated the settler population, who chafed at having access to land and a convenient labour source cut off by an interfering colonial administrator.[59] Aware of the unpopularity of such policies, Gordon saw indentured labour from India (and elsewhere) as his trump card: it offered a cheap and seemingly abundant workforce, simultaneously solving the issues of labour shortages, and preserving his 'benign' native administration.[60]

Over the nearly four decades from 1879 to 1916, over 60,000 *girmitiyas* or Indian indentured labourers arrived to work the plantations on five-year contracts. Labourers who re-indentured for a further five years earned their return passage to India. Most remained in Fiji, set up communities on the outskirts of the plantations or migrated to towns and established agricultural and trading businesses after the *narak* (hell) of indenture. As a rich body of scholarship on the indenture experience recalls, the work was harsh, conditions of life dispiriting, and contracts were frequently contravened or ignored by plantation managers and overseers. The associated dislocation and social breakdown were reflected in high levels of violent crime, murder and suicide amongst migrants.[61]

From a judicial perspective, as well as economically and socially, the colonial structure was predicated on racial divisions. On his voyage to Fiji, Gordon read J. W. B. Money on Java, who emphasized that 'each race has its allotted sphere'. His plans for the new colony developed along these lines even before his arrival.[62] He consequently resisted land issues and related disputes being heard in the courts, believing that a European-dominated institution would not uphold justice for Fijians, and thus removed Fijian land cases from the courts as far as possible. Given Gordon's hands-on, even authoritarian approach, he preferred to have the arbitration of land claims under the authority of the Executive Council, not the judiciary. This policy developed before Gordon and others in the administration understood how Indigenous land tenure functioned, instead emerging from ideas outside the Fijian context.[63] This aspect of 'native' governance was achieved through separate courts and Native Regulations that removing the majority of Indigenous legal cases from the colonial courts of Suva and Levuka.[64]

The pattern of courts across the colony broadly reflected the compartmentalization of racial groups in different geographic and economic spaces. Fijians were encouraged to maintain a 'traditional' lifestyle and non-monetary economy in villages. Native Regulation No. 5 (1878) restricted Fijians' movements, requiring chiefly permission to leave the village or to take up paid labour.[65] Though restrictions on entering paid labour were relaxed somewhat in 1912, the importance of village life and obedience to chiefs was maintained though regulations and courts. Indentured labourers were also subject to restrictions. They were housed in plantation 'lines' (cramped and unsanitary blocks of housing) and labour laws curtailed their freedom to travel. Though Europeans managing plantations lived in relative isolation, traders, officials and settlers mostly congregated in the urban centres. Norman Etherington outlines how different court systems existed in these different spaces broadly contiguous with these socio-economic fault lines. He found

> a system articulated into four separate legal worlds operating side by side. What mattered most was not the race or national origins of persons charged, but the arena in which those persons operated. Town justice was different from plantation justice, and both were in their turn different from justice meted out in the Provincial Courts.[66]

I argue however that race did play a large part in determining legal outcomes, as the different arenas of the plantation and the village were demarcated along racial, as well as economic, lines.

These racial, social and economic demarcations were manufactured and sustained through ordinances, regulations and their implementation. Early officials solidified the administrative division of the islands into twelve districts headed by Roko Tui (government-appointed district chiefs), and subdivided them into smaller areas presided over by Buli (local or minor chiefs). The Native Affairs Ordinance of 1876 established the Native Regulation Board and courts that operated under the authority of the Roko and colonial officials.[67] Native Stipendiary Magistrates (NSMs) assisted in enforcing chiefly jurisdiction and the associated Native Regulations over the villages. A Chief Native Commissioner oversaw this hierarchy. The colonial chiefly elite, which was based largely on aristocratic lineage, exercised considerable influence through the Bose Vakaturaga or Council of Chiefs, an annual forum which drew together the Roko, Buli and native magistrates from across the islands to debate and advise on Indigenous affairs.[68] In the opening decade of colonial rule, the views of this group were crucial in shaping Native Regulations, justice and punishments, particularly regarding obedience towards chiefs, labour recruitment, marriage, divorce and adultery, communal services and taxation.

Chiefs strove to ensure that their authority was maintained or enhanced in the colonial era. The Roko Tui Ba (district chief of Ba) declared that 'most of us know that the law will take hold of evil doers, but the great body of the people know of no law nor understand any other authority than the will and word of their Chief'.[69] The Bose Vakaturaga strongly advocated that 'the law shall take hold of the people through us'.[70] Their concerns over safeguarding traditional authority in the face of the *vakapiritania* ('the British way') mirrored the British administration's wish to keep Fijians sequestered from the developing colonial economy. The intersection of these stances was crucial for the establishment and support of the Provincial Courts.

District and Provincial Courts were charged with disciplining infractions of the Native Regulations and hearing cases arising amongst Indigenous Fijians generally. The local Roko or Buli and NSM presided over the court, assisted by a European Stipendiary Magistrate (ESM) acting as assessor.[71] Punishments ranged from fines to imprisonment for men, while women were more often sentenced to labour within the village for a set period of time or a set number of tasks, such as mat-making.[72] Though designed to preserve the aspects of traditional society deemed acceptable to missionaries and officials, Fijian chiefs and ESMs also utilized the law in unexpected ways. For example, the magistrate at Bua, Henry Anson, reported in 1880 that the Buli at Kubalau had been 'administering laws of his own', which 'are greatly at variance with the ordinance of the colony'. He had run into debt with local Europeans and appeared to be using the court to raise fines and therefore his credit.[73]

European magistrates were also criticized for overstepping their mandate and setting their authority above that of the Fijian chiefs and magistrates. In 1883, the Roko Tui Ba exclaimed that

> the European Magistrate's eyes are as the eyes of needles; he sees this, and he sees that, and instantly reports; but he knows not the seriousness of it to us, or even understands our customs. Strangers come to us, and they partake of food with us. Who plants the food? They (the Magistrates) report to Suva, and are believed. The European Magistrates have given rise to this, for they oppress us and write to the Governor. He does not, I think, wish this.[74]

Overall, particularly in cases around sexual conduct, there was confusion over who had the power to prosecute and punish, and frustration that cases only came to light if offenders 'fail to find favour in the eyes of their chiefs'.[75]

By contrast, on the plantations power clearly lay with managers, labour inspectors and European magistrates. Most cases on the court circuits related to infractions of labour contracts. Labour infractions ranged from desertion and unlawful absence, neglect or refusal to complete allotted tasks, disorderly conduct, time spent in hospital and stealing rations.[76] The prosecutions for labour violations enabled frequent extension of the indenture contract. Many indentured Indians were forced to work longer than their five-year term to cover fines imposed or working days lost to court cases and imprisonment.[77] Cases of violent crime between indentured migrants were also frequent. While workers could bring their employers to court for overtasking, withholding wages or assault, cases against managers or *sirdars* were rare and conviction rates were low. Indeed, the number of convictions of Indian indentured labourers drew critical comment from the Indian government.[78] Yet the cases before the plantation courts tell only half the story: violence, intimidation and complicity between plantations overseers and colonial magistrates meant many incidents were never brought to court, forcing indentured workers to find alternative ways to seek retribution and justice for plantation exploitation.

Police courts, which operated in Suva and Levuka, dealt with crimes stemming from the problems of urban settlement (theft, drunkenness and offences to public order and morals) and operated like their equivalents in Britain or British settler colonies. The Supreme Court adjudicated on serious crime, including murder, assault, rape and sexual assault. These cases were forwarded from magistrates or the lower courts to the criminal sittings held quarterly in Suva or Levuka. Trials could be conducted by jury but only if all parties involved were European, or by assessors, who advised the Chief Justice but did not have a decisive vote in the outcome of the case. The Criminal Procedure Ordinance of 1875 ensured that any cases involved Fijians were tried by assessors, as the impartiality of a European jury in judging crimes involving non-Europeans was deemed dubious at best. Trial by assessor was extending to Indian, Chinese and Pacific Islanders in 1883.[79] This was justified on the basis of similar procedures in India, but nevertheless irked settlers who regarded trial by jury as a British birthright.[80]

The lives of colonial subjects were frequently entangled in undesired or unexpected ways that demonstrate the constructed nature of these legal spheres. Still, as Gordon optimistically articulated in 1880, the Fijian statute book developed its own unique character, predicated on distinctions based on race and socio-economic status. It was marked by the differing interest in, and protection given to, Indigenous Fijians and indentured Indians and by indirect rule that sought to impose a unified system of chiefly custom upon a diverse

Fijian society. Yet these judicial divisions were also contested and subverted by different groups and individuals, including magistrates themselves, who were often less confident of law's positive impact in Fiji.

The New Hebrides Condominium

While colonial administration in Fiji sought to reify aspect of Indigenous custom as law, officials of the New Hebrides Condominium sought to integrate two imperial legal systems in 'an unprecedented juristic experiment'.[81] This effort took up the energy of both British and French officials, who initially paid scant attention to the legal position of ni-Vanuatu in the Condominium. Upon the opening of the New Hebrides Joint Court in 1910, the British judge stated:

> The Court's historic task is to adjust, parallel to each other, two differing national legal systems. This is an unprecedented juristic experiment, but is likely to prove that the essential ideals of justice differ much less than its outward forms.[82]

His opinion proved overly optimistic in a system of colonial governance marred by practical constraints and fraught with tension over the inability to reconcile differing motivations behind European involvement in the New Hebrides. These tensions were present well before the formal annexation of the group. British and French rivalry culminated in an attempt at imperial co-operation with the joint colonization of the islands under the Anglo-French Condominium of 1906. The unique Condominium arrangement was the consequence of failed policies of non-intervention and half-baked attempts to maintain order, as trading, land sales, land grabs and 'blackbirding' (unscrupulous recruiting of Islanders as indentured labour) saw disorder escalate through the late nineteenth century.

Britain and France acknowledged the other's stake in the archipelago: unilateral colonization would provoke diplomatic discord. In 1878, an agreement in which both London and Paris recognized the independence of the New Hebrides solidified this position.[83] In fact, the British Colonial Office had little appetite for annexation, but local Presbyterian and Anglian missions and public opinion in the Australasian colonies prevented Britain relinquishing its interest.[84] By contrast, French commercial and political interest in the archipelago surged in the closing decades of the century. From the 1880s, John Higginson and his Compagnie Calédonienne des Nouvelles-Hébrides (CCNH) purchased the plantations of bankrupt British planters and claimed extensive land holdings 'bought' from ni-Vanuatu on Malekula, Epi and Santo. In 1885, the French

Naval Minister had instructed that his officers should 'combat English influence by all legal means, to eliminate as much as possible British interests from the archipelago and substitute French interests'.[85] Most significantly, the French government bailed out the struggling CCNH in 1894, which was renamed the Société Française des Nouvelles-Hébrides (SFNH). Thereafter France had a vested interest in stimulating local economic activity, ensuring the success of French plantations and confirming their land claims.

By 1886, pressure from their respective nationals with interests in the New Hebrides – be they spiritual or material – influenced Britain and France to begin negotiations over the status of the islands.[86] Discussions focused on protecting their citizens' interests and finding a solution to land disputes. The resulting convention, signed on 16 November 1887, established the Joint Naval Commission (JNC). It was 'charged with the duty of maintaining order, and of protecting the lives and property of British and French subjects in the New Hebrides'. The JNC, comprising British and French naval officers, empowered warships to patrol the waters. Unilateral action by either was discouraged except in urgent circumstances. Given infrequent patrols through the islands and the difficulty of assembling warships from both nations, this requirement severely hindered the effectiveness of the commission. However, more problematic was the final point in the agreement: 'The Commission … shall not interfere in disputes concerning the title to land, or dispossess of their lands any persons, natives or foreigners.'[87] Navy officers were not deemed equipped to mediate on land issues. The crux of the New Hebrides problem was thus left unaddressed by the 1887 Convention, effectively undermining the Commission before it even began.

France and Britain re-entered negotiations for a 'sphere of joint influence' in 1904.[88] Almost intractable differences remained between British and French intentions and involvement in the New Hebrides. Britain focused on limiting French power, to mitigate missionary fears and Australian anxieties; France on a swift and favourable resolution of land issues to enable increased economic development of the islands. After protracted negotiations, the final wording limited the shared governance powers, with many functions left to the two national administrations.[89] The resulting Convention, signed on 20 October 1906 and ratified on 9 January 1907, established the Anglo-French Condominium.[90]

The Condominium was governed by a joint administration, with a British and a French administration each headed by a resident commissioner, accountable to the Governor of the Western Pacific High Commission in Suva and the Governor of New Caledonia in Nouméa, respectively. However, the Condominium functioned more as two parallel administrations than one, with essentially separate police forces, mail services and courts. The Bislama term for the Condominium, *tufala gavman*, encapsulates the divided nature of New Hebrides colonialism: 'the government of two fellows'.[91] The Condominium quickly became unwieldy and unsatisfactory and prompted calls for a single imperial administration or partition of the islands. In response, the 1906 Convention was revised in London in 1914. The ratification of the resultant Protocol was delayed by the outbreak of the First World War and not implemented until 1922. The 1914 Protocol made few substantial changes to the original agreement and remained largely in place until independence in 1980.[92]

The attempt to meld two legal traditions and judicial cultures in the Joint Court proved difficult. Alexander, a former British judge to the Joint Court, described it as 'a small international body … in a setting and with a machinery unique and cumbrous … it was calculated to drive one to distraction'.[93] With neither power ready to concede jurisdiction over its own subjects, the 1906 agreement resulted in separate British and French national courts where individuals were tried according to their own law and procedure. Further complicating the matter, the settlers and traders residing or visiting the islands were a diverse group of German, American, Prussian, Danish, Swiss and Hungarian nationals – who could choose their jurisdiction – in addition to the British subjects and French citizens.[94]

The National Courts were limited to civil and criminal cases between their own subjects. Disputes between British and French or European and ni-Vanuatu – at least with regards to land – were heard before the Joint Court. While established primarily to resolve and confirm disputed land titles, the Joint Court also oversaw cases on labour recruitment and the sale of alcohol or arms to ni-Vanuatu and presided over criminal and civil cases that crossed lines of nationality or race. In structure, like much of the Condominium, the bench of the Joint Court was unwieldy: it comprised a British judge, a French judge, a president appointed by the king of Spain, a registrar and public prosecutor, along with a Native Advocate to represent ni-Vanuatu rights. This 'cour franco-brittanique-espagnole-hollandaise' looked far more impressive in appearance than in practice.[95] The court did not open until 1910, after court buildings and official housing had been constructed in manner fitting the prestige of each power.[96] Plagued by problems of language and translation, procedure, delays and frequent closures, it also held no executive power, leaving individual national administrations to enforce the verdicts and punishments meted out, much to the ire of the Joint Court judges.[97] The sentences imposed were limited to imprisonment of up to one month or fines of £20, and even these were often not enforced.[98]

While both Fiji and New Caledonia established some form of 'native administration', this was conspicuously absent in the early Condominium. The 1906 agreement stated:

> The High Commissioners and their Delegates shall have authority over the native Chiefs. They shall have power to make administrative and police regulations binding on the tribes, and to provide for their enforcement.[99]

However, aside from continued visits under the umbrella of the JNC, few specific provisions were enacted to this end.[100] In late 1911, the High Commissioners made the first step towards extending Condominium rule outside Efate with the appointment of two British and two French District Agents to supervise recruiting and labour based on Tanna, Santo, Raga and Malekula.[101] The number of posts was expanded under the 1914 Protocol, which provided for a British and a French agent in each district. However, with each District Agent only having responsibility over their own nationals, the efficacy of this skeletal arrangement once again wilted in the face of imperial divisions.[102]

Missionaries sometimes sought to fill the void by providing local courts and administrative structures (see Chapter 4). In response, there was a gradual move to establish criminal jurisdiction over ni-Vanuatu though the Joint Court and local Native Courts in the late 1910s and 1920s. This was a slow and contested process, owing to different economic imperatives, differing views of ni-Vanuatu readiness for such laws and of what offences should be codified.[103] In 1917, a Joint Regulation enabled the Joint Court to try serious offences, including murder, rape, assault and arson.[104] A decade later, Native Courts were formally established.[105] For two decades after the Condominium's arrival therefore, 'life, and sometimes violent death, went on as before':[106] ni-Vanuatu experience of colonial rule was predominantly through warship visits or informal agents of imperialism, missionaries, traders and recruiters.

The result was three distinct courts in which the few hundred Europeans based in the islands could be tried or could bring civil cases, while the approximately 50,000 ni-Vanuatu were effectively stateless. It seemed there were 'three justices in the New Hebrides: one for the French, one for the British and one for the natives'.[107] The 1914 Protocol explicitly denied ni-Vanuatu nationality or citizenship of either imperial power, thus limiting their options for representation, legal recourse and economic opportunities throughout the Condominium period.[108] During the opening decade of the twentieth century, there were no courts in which ni-Vanuatu could bring cases to deal with internal conflicts, no due process nor ability to appeal Joint Court judgements. Though effectively disenfranchised and subject to repressive justice, the limits of Condominium governance left some ni-Vanuatu largely free from official interference, and on occasion Islanders proved adept at using the divisions between the colonial powers to their advantage.[109]

Disconnections between paper and practice: The limits to colonial law

In 1912, a group of Pentecost men refused to come to Port Vila when summoned as, when they had visited earlier regarding the return of a kidnapped woman, 'no one saw them or spoke to them of the subject of their affair'. After unsuccessful weeks in Vila, the men returned home and 'nor will they leave it again since they maintain that it is but a waste of time for them to come here, where, as they say, the white men "gammons" (deludes) them "too much"'.[110] Their disillusionment draws attention to the very real limitations of the law's application in the Pacific.

Law's extension seemingly heralded the successful arrival of the colonial order, but the ongoing challenges to its enforcement served as a constant reminder of the fragility of European authority in the islands. In New Caledonia and the New Hebrides especially, practical and financial limitations constrained the ability of colonial institutions to enforce the rule of law. As geographically and geopolitically remote colonies (from a metropolitan perspective), budgetary constraints were a significant consideration in determining colonial policy. As this section discusses, officials in all three colonies were often frustrated by such hinderances, which effectively curtailed their jurisdiction.

Serious crimes, such as rape, sexual assault, assault and murder, had to be reported and forwarded to the higher courts, which sat only periodically in the colonial capitals. The accused and witnesses had to be transported to Nouméa, Suva, Levuka or Port Vila, housed and maintained while awaiting trial, which might be weeks or months away. This process burdened limited budgets and resources. Firstly, the outer islands or remote provinces had insufficient administrators to transport prisoners back to the local metropole without leaving their posts unattended, and such journeys could be lengthy or subject to long delays given the scarcity of official transportation. In cases involving labourers in Fiji or the New Hebrides, employers could be reluctant to go to court, as they risked losing their workforce for a sustained period.[111] Secondly, the expenses of feeding and housing defendants and witnesses stretched resources, particularly in Port Vila where there was nowhere to house Indigenous witnesses and the prisons were notoriously under-provisioned and unfit for purpose.[112]

Colonial administrators were often forced to wear many hats. This limited the attention they could devote to their functions as police or magistrates and raised questions over their neutrality in investigating and assessing crimes. A blurring of legal and administrative roles resulted: individuals filled multiple positions in both official and unofficial capacities, particularly in New Caledonia, where the *gendarmerie* were assigned a range of auxiliary roles.

Financial constraints resulted in frequent complaints regarding the limitations of the judiciary and requests for increased funding and personnel.[113] In 1859 the New Caledonian Governor was particularly concerned that officials also acted as judges on civil cases while a Conseil de Guerre presided over criminal cases in the absence of suitable magistrates, resulting in conflicting roles and a lack of judicial separation from other administrative functions.[114] Moreover, the lack of accountability to a higher official diminished the sense of responsibility of presiding magistrates, and was especially problematic given the limited scope for appeals in a small colony.[115] Consequently the first Governor reported there were 'frequent indecisions' amongst judges and confusion over the application of the law in New Caledonia and the legality of their judgements.[116] One official noted:

> At a pinch, you could consider this primitive organisation sufficient in the era when New Caledonia had neither commerce nor industry. [But] today the activity of the colony is attested to by the number of trials.[117]

The wealth of correspondence to the Minister in Paris demanding further judges and magistrates, as well as strategic attempts to improve the funding and support received from the metropolitan government, reflected these concerns.

From 1898, with a dearth of suitable alternatives, *gendarmes* could also be *syndics* of Indigenous affairs, with one *syndic* in each of the thirty-four brigades.[118] In 1916, the core of the SAI consisted of just the head Alfred Fourcade, his clerks, and two agents based in the Loyalty Islands. The outbreak of the First World War resulted in further depletion of the already limited number of *gendarmes* working as SAI syndics.[119] By 1918, a report from the Colonial Inspectorate noted that *gendarmes* in New Caledonia were variously acting as police officers, prosecutors, bailiffs, officers of the Etat Civil, members of the Sanitary Commission, *syndics* of Indigenous affairs, agents of public works and *syndics* of immigration.[120] Such overlaps had budgetary benefits but as Inspector

Bougourd argued, it resulted in officials 'both ill-prepared and ill-placed to perform the delicate functions they must fulfill'.[121]

This problem was dramatically exposed by the outbreak of war around Koné, Hienghène and Tipindjé in 1917, where *gendarmes* failed to read and investigate warnings and rumours of Kanak discontent. Knowledge of local conditions was an important but frequently lacking aspect of SAI work in monitoring and controlling the Kanak population.[122] While this situation had existed since the turn of the century, it took the largest conflict since the 1878–9 war to draw metropolitan and official attention. These events and subsequent investigations point to tensions within the colonial administration between balancing the books and maintaining the appearance of an effective system for Indigenous governance. Inspector Bougourd stated that most *gendarmes* knew neither the local languages nor culture and had little opportunity to acquire such knowledge given the time spent in long and difficult journeys over the territory of a *tribu*.[123]

While *gendarmes* were burdened with multiple official duties, many also maintained personal business interests in the colony. The potential conflict of interest raised questions over the neutrality of colonial agents and their commitment to official duties. Inspector Bougourd reported they were sometimes 'inclined to regrettably confuse their own interests and those for which they are responsible'.[124] The entanglement between judicial and other official capacities, and blurred boundaries between official and personal interests, appeared inevitable in the early colonial period, partly owing to the small size of the imperial administrations and settler communities.

Similar issues over the efficacy and ability of magistrates arose in Fiji and especially in the New Hebrides.[125] In the latter, Edward Jacomb, Gilchirst Alexander, and Joint Court clerk H. Pieremont pointed to the perceived isolation and irrelevance of these colonies and the poor rates of pay as deterrents to attracting competent qualified candidates to local bureaucratic posts.[126] The French suffered from a particularly high turnover of officials.[127] Moreover, New Hebrides officials expended much energy wrangling over their pay, leave, housing and benefits, and debating joint Condominium expenses, amassing files of archival correspondence in the process.[128] Notably, president of the Joint Court, Count Buena Esperanza, spent much of his appointment on leave.[129]

As in New Caledonia, agents of the New Hebrides Condominium were occasionally permitted to take other work alongside their official roles. For example, the public prosecutor for the Joint Court took private cases to supplement his salary, but at the expense of his formal duties.[130] At times court officials had insufficient work.[131] A constant tension in the New Hebrides existed between judicial officials lacking work, given the frequent closures of the Joint Court and the delays in addressing land claim cases, and the lack of suitable officials to undertake the work that did exist. Overall, there was a concentration of high officials (with the duplication of roles under the dual administration – two resident commissioners, three judges) but a paucity of lower-level administrators. Thus, Felix Speiser wrote:

> In spite of the great number of officials, the Government does not make itself much felt outside the larger settlements … There are not yet magistrates on each island, so that the Government heard only so much about the crimes committed on the islands as the planters care to tell, and naturally they do not tell too much.[132]

In all three territories, criticism of the judicial system was often directed towards Indigenous employees and appointed chiefs upon whom the administrations depended, revealing frustrations over reliance on Islanders for the operation of colonial law. In the New Hebrides, British Commandant of the Constabulary Edwin Harrowell impressed upon his superiors the need for a European commanding officer in Port Vila during his absence. He highlighted the need for constant supervision and the problems of respect and insubordination that arose when a 'native' was in charge of cases involved interactions with European settlers.[133] In Fiji, magistrate Mark Spence complained that, despite his best attempts to 'impress a sense of duty' upon the NSMs of Bua and Cakaudrove, breaches of regulations were common.[134] The frequent internment of administration-appointed chiefs in New Caledonia suggests the administration often felt their Kanak appointees failed to effectively support French rule over the Grande Terre.[135] Recurrent colonial frustrations suggest divergent Indigenous priorities.

Islanders were not oblivious to these views, and had their own concerns about European officials, as the Pentecost men who opened this section articulated. In New Caledonia, Kanak also viewed the actions and motivation of the *gendarmes* and *syndics* with suspicion. In 1898, Commandant Laporte described the *gendarmerie* as having 'lack of tact' in their relations with the Kanak inhabitants of the Grande Terre.[136] As Bougourd reiterated some twenty years later:

> The native sees in him [the gendarme] a dispenser of justice much more than a protector and the attitude that prevails among the soldiers of the detachment … is such as to justify certain apprehensions regarding the integrity of their conduct vis-à-vis the natives.[137]

Such concerns undoubtedly limited Kanak engagement with colonial administrators. Within the *tribu*, there was considerable latitude to resolve disputes internally as social structures remained largely intact well after formal colonization.

The nature of the island geography further posed a challenge for the small land-based administrations of the Pacific. In the New Hebrides, Fiji and to a lesser extent New Caledonia, the multitude of islands that made up each colony and the dispersed population made surveillance and policing virtually impossible, with communications and inadequate transportation key limiting factors.[138] It was not only the maritime landscape that tested these colonial administrations. *La brousse* (bush) in New Caledonia, the Viti Levu interior dominated by the 'hill-tribes' of Fiji, and the domains of 'man-bush' (as opposed to 'man-saltwater') in the New Hebrides were also conceptualized as spaces removed from law and order, possible 'hearts of darkness' from whence disorder and rebellion might stem. Missionaries contributed to these views, drawing sharp distinctions between the civilization and behaviour of converted Islanders, who frequently resided around the coast, and their 'heathen' counterparts. Such views derived their power from the administrations' inability to know and police such regions, to extend their hegemony beyond the bounds of small urban administrative centres.

In an era of continued mobility across the region, the disappearance of suspected criminals (both European and Islander) into the bush or across the ocean reinforced perceptions of a troublesome geography that circumscribed colonial power. For European accused, the most frequent way to evade summons and arrest was to ship out of the colony altogether, safe in the knowledge that the island administrators generally lacked the will or resources to track them. One example from Fiji involved the disappearance of William Peckham, accused of indecent assault of a 'half-caste' girl aged fourteen in 1880. In September, Taveuni magistrate A. Taylor reported that Peckham had not responded to the summons and 'there now seems little doubt that he has left the Colony in schooner "Nudge"'.[139] In the New Hebrides, Alexander noted that Europeans could escape the colony and avoid their sentences, such as recruiter Leclerc did in 1912.[140] From New Caledonia, penal colony escapees aroused Australian anxieties.[141]

For Islanders, retreat into the bush, often aided by their family or community, was the easiest means of evading European officials, though departing under indenture also remained an option for ni-Vanuatu. Colonial administrators in Fiji, New Caledonia and the New Hebrides all agonized over the disappearance of island suspects into the bush and the refusal of communities to hand over the accused.[142] The early prisons in Fiji and the New Hebrides were inadequate to keep prisoners who wanted to escape in.[143] For example, concerned with the insecure and unsanitary prison, the British resident commissioner in the New Hebrides argued the need for improved facilities in 1912 because 'in a country like this … escapes can only rarely be followed by rearrest if the accused desires to evade it'.[144] The difficulties in capturing and containing suspects and prisoners in all three colonies fostered the perception of the islands as remote and uncivilized. For colonial magistrates and police, the isolation, the bush and the ocean were all hindrances to the effective fulfilment of their duties and the extension of European law across the colonial territory.

The belief that officials were on the back foot in governing the island landscape was compounded by the fact that individual officers in the field had limited contact with their superiors in the colonial capitals. The 1918 inspection of New Caledonia revealed ongoing resourcing issues that prevented the *gendamerie* from patrolling in a systematic and disciplined manner, and in turn prevented regular oversight of these brigades. Reports to Paris emphasized the impossibility of regular inspections of outlying administrative posts.[145] In 1919, Pegourier noted some posts had not been visited since 1914 or 1916, which meant that

> the gendarmes enjoy a wide freedom. The situation of the colony, from the perspective of communication, is such that most posts, outside of the only road (Nouméa-Bourail) or the immediate neighbourhood of the capital, can only be reached by sea after days of travel. The visit of the commander of the detachment cannot in the slightest degree, in these circumstances, offer the unexpected character that would be necessary to make the surveillance effective.[146]

Reports highlight the level of individual authority and discretion afforded to *gendarmes* outside the Nouméa-Bourail region as a result of the economic and environmental circumstances under which the SAI operated.

The loss of manpower during the First World War magnified personnel constraints, but the situation described by the 1918 Colonial Inspection reflected the conditions under which the administration had operated for decades. For example, in 1913 the New Caledonian Governor wrote to the Minister of Colonies highlighting a lack of coordination between the colonial administration and the Navy. Lack of transport made rapid and regular tours of the colony all but impossible. In support of his request for greater funding and assistance from Paris, he noted his colleague in Fiji had four vessels at his disposal.[147] In these conditions, the colonial administration had little insight into or ability to intervene in local affairs without the aid of the administrative Kanak chiefs, or local missionary or settler informants. Thus, court cases and Conseil Privé debates over Indigenous crime and its punishment relied upon community support to apprehend troublesome individuals.

The limits of communication and transportation facing magistrates were even greater in the New Hebrides. The Condominium lacked sufficient maritime transport to patrol the waters of the archipelago, transport judges and magistrates from Port Vila to other islands, and accused and prisoners from outer islands to Port Vila.[148] There was initially no official vessel for judicial work and the frustrated president of the Joint Court wrote that he lacked the authority and the transportation to investigate land claims or criminal cases 'on the spot'.[149] For the most part, the administrations relied on their imperial navies to assist in law enforcement by sending men-of-war to the islands as a presence to deter crime against Europeans and to transport accused. At times, imperial politics further hindered judicial work. For example, in 1912, French officials denied the Native Advocate's request for transport to speak with ni-Vanuatu communities he represented, to delay land claims against French nationals.[150]

The realities of governance in a remote island colony with a dispersed population shaped how European law spread across Fiji, New Caledonia and the New Hebrides. The budgetary bottom line imposed by London and Paris resulted in insufficient personnel and resources to govern across the island and maritime spaces. Individual magistrates were frequently expected to cover large tracts of territory, often without access to regular transportation, though they simultaneously wielded their authority with limited oversight from superior officers.

Despite the best efforts of the colonial state, lone officials or small brigades circuiting a province in the New Hebrides, New Caledonia or Fiji were often ineffective in policing and punishing Islanders, especially if individuals put themselves beyond the bounds of *gendarme* posts, colonial townships or Indigenous villages. Such difficulties contributed to an official view of the islands as potentially hostile spaces, especially in the interiors, and opened the way for alternative and violent forms of justice. In these circumstances, bringing Islanders and others before the colonial courts required a degree of consent and support from the community, which might engage with the colonial judiciary when it suited to remove a problematic individual. Indigenous social structures in many communities or *tribus* frequently remained outside the influence of the colonial administration, and individuals could and did choose to resolve violence and disputes without reference to the courts.

Conclusion: Drawing connections across oceans and empires

All three colonies were connected by the flows of indentured labour, capital, goods and European missionaries, traders and settlers. The perceived need to control these flows of people and goods helped precipitate imperial expansion in the region. But colonialism in the southwest Pacific proved remarkably adaptable, with each colony and its legal architecture taking a unique form specific to local, regional and imperial political and economic exigencies. There was however a convergent evolution towards the judicial and physical separation of Islanders, Europeans and – in Fiji – indentured Indian labourers in response to intersecting perceptions of race and island space. Islanders were thus increasing removed from the European systems of courts, though whether this was deliberate policy or unplanned development differs from colony to colony. The results were complex systems of courts and legal administration, often disproportionate to the colonies' size and relative importance to their metropolitan governments. This was particularly true in the New Hebrides, owing to the duplication of roles through the dual national administrations. The bureaucratic exchange of paperwork was similarly swollen in consequence of the need for each decision and expenditure to be negotiated between French and British officials.

In New Caledonia, the introduction of the Indigénat in the wake of the 1878 revolt and on the heels of similar regimes across the French empire differentiated and compartmentalized Kanak from the settler and penal population. It underpinned the physical and legal *cantonnement* (containment) of Kanak from 1887, with local officials given summary jurisdiction and the Conseil Privé the ability to try Kanak without judicial process. The logic of containment drew inspiration from the longer history of penal transportation to New Caledonia and the importation of strategies from Algeria and French Indochina, as well as the need to open lands for European settlement. This regime relied on enshrining in law the collective responsibility of the *tribu* and the appointment and assistance of administration-appointed chiefs to ensure that Kanak conformed to colonial law. In this we see a structure resembling the indirect rule more common to British colonies.

While the policy of indirect versus direct rule is one of the key differences often identified between British and French imperialism, in fact there are parallels between the New Caledonian system and Fijian indirect rule. Certain chiefs were recognized and invested with limited authority by the colonial state and held accountable for maintaining order and overseeing labour and taxes among their tribes and communities. However, unlike Fiji, New Caledonian chiefs had little input into defining the laws and regulations that applied to the Kanak population, placing administration-appointed chiefs in the difficult position of being legally accountable for restrictive laws over which they had no control.

In Fiji, quite different motivations drove attempts to maintain 'traditional' Fijian life in villages removed from European settlements or plantations. Gordon's reign over 'a Crown Colony of a severe type' enabled his administration to push through the protectionist programme of indirect rule deemed necessary to shelter Fijians from the ravages of colonial contact. His paternalism was funded by the use and abuse of Indian indentured labour. Both Indigenous Fijians and indentured Indians came within the orbit of the colonial courts, but the laws they were expected to follow, the infractions and crimes for which they were tried and the punishments received in the legal spheres of the village and the plantations respectively were far removed from the courts operating in Suva and Levuka.

Compared to the New Caledonian Indigénat, the Fijian system involved chiefs in the process of codifying and enforcing 'native' custom to a much greater degree. New Caledonian policies were more focused on maintaining the boundaries of European communities with, for example, restrictions on Kanak movement and clothing in Nouméa. These differences can be explained partially by different perceptions of race. In Fiji, the interest and recognition accorded to Fijian chiefly culture by Gordon and others meant ceremonial and social engagement with the Fijian elite, including the negotiation of cession in 1874, was common from the outset. Such patterns of interaction never occurred at an official level in New Caledonia, where Kanaks of the Grande Terre were perceived as less amenable to 'civilisation', in part owing to a contact history of conflict. In explaining these differences, we must also consider political and economic motivations. In Fiji, the British stance was that European settlement was not to occur at the expense of Fijian society, though the underside of this seeming benevolence was the installation of the indentured plantation system with exploitation and violence it entailed for Indian immigrants. In New Caledonia, the attempts to build an agriculturally driven settler colony created different priorities. Kanak did not fit easily into this vision, except as labour extracted through the Indigénat. Thus, while in both colonies the legal status and rights of Islanders were defined against those of Europeans and a certain form of chieftainship reified, the basis for such policies was quite different.

By contrast, the requirements of joint action constrained the development of a 'native policy' in the New Hebrides Condominium. If Islanders were largely excluded from Condominium jurisdiction, this omission was due to oversight rather than deliberate strategy. Almost an afterthought in an imperial expansion embroiled in European rivalries, ni-Vanuatu had little legal recourse or protection from either the French or British administration yet found themselves under the surveillance of navy patrols from both nations. The limited power given to the Condominium and the constant need for negotiation of decisions between the two Residencies meant political attention and policy continued to focus more on the Anglo-French relationship than that between Europeans and Islanders. In consequence, for many ni-Vanuatu, colonial magistrates and courts were notable only in their absence in the opening decades of Condominium rule. When legislation covering ni-Vanuatu did emerge, it was often the result of advocacy on the part of missionaries, traders or settlers or perceived threats from these groups to Anglo-French authority.

Despite the differences between the colonies, elements of convergence are visible as imperial governments and colonial administrations grappled with the tensions between the economic and ideological imperatives of empire and the practicalities of governance in the racially diverse terrain of these islands. In contrast to the expansion of settler sovereignty – defined by Lisa Ford as territorial jurisdiction demonstrated through trial and incarceration of Indigenous people – in Australasia or America, the place of colonial law in the Pacific was a more fragile and less all-encompassing venture, yet of far-reaching consequence for many colonial subjects.[151]

The plurality of judicial structures in New Caledonia, Fiji and Vanuatu was defined by spatial as well as racial separation and by geographical divisions that mirrored ideological ones. Strategies of rule were nuanced by differing ideological and legal traditions, local specificities and economic motivations, though there was also overlap between them. Stemming in part from the rivalry between the two metropoles that played out in Oceania, especially the New Hebrides, local administrations and metropolitan governments peered across the oceans – particularly the Channel and Pacific, but also the Atlantic and Indian oceans – to discern the strategies and strategic interests of the other, to evaluate their own policies in light of the other's practices. The solutions dovetailed in certain elements, but the impact on individual engagement with and experiences of the judicial process was distinct, as subsequent chapters explore.

Notes

1 Mafi (magistrate), [16th?] September 1875, 'Proceedings of the Native Council or Council of Chiefs', Draiba, Ovalau, NAF.

2 Alexander, *From the Middle Temple*, 28.

3 Ibid.; No. 32/81 SM for Lau, Swayne, to Colonial Secretary, 5 May 1881, Lau Provincial Office – Official Correspondence 1876–83, NAF.

4 Karuna Mantena, *Alibis of Empire: Henry Maine and the Ends of Liberal Imperialism* (Princeton, NJ: Princeton University Press, 2010), 90–1.

5 Lisa Ford, 'Law', in David Armitage and Alison Bashford (eds), *Pacific Histories: Land, Ocean, People* (Basingstoke: Palgrave Macmillan, 2014), 220–6; Scarr, *Fragments of Empire*, 7–8.

6 See Benton *Law and Colonial Cultures* and Merry, *Colonizing Hawai'i.*

7 Governor's Speech on Leaving the Colony, Papers Relating to Her Majesty's Colonial Possessions. Fiji 1880, Reports for 1880, 1881 and 1882, NAF.

8 Wiener, *An Empire on Trial.*

9 Martyn Lyons, *The Totem and the Tricolour: A Short History of New Caledonia since 1774* (Kensington: New South Wales University Press, 1986), 41–2; Aldrich, *The French Presence*, 18; Merle, *Expériences Coloniales*, chapter 4.

10 Throughout the 1850s, New Caledonia was governed by the Establissements de l'Océanie based in Tahiti, some 4600 kilometres away.

11 Merle, *Expériences Coloniales*, 115; Robert Aldrich and John Connell, *France's Overseas Frontier: Départements et territoires d'outre mer* (Cambridge: Cambridge University Press, 2006), 46; Stephen A. Toth, *Beyond Papillon: The French Overseas Penal Colonies, 1854–1952* (Lincoln: University of Nebraska Press, 2006).

12 On the varied origins of prisoners: Alice Bullard, *Exile to Paradise: Savagery and Civilization in Paris and the South Pacific, 1790–1900* (Stanford: Stanford University Press, 2000); Merle, *Expériences Coloniales*, 116–25; Karin Speedy, 'Who Were the Reunion "Coolies" of 19th-Century New Caledonia?' *Journal of Pacific History* 44, no. 2 (2009), 123–40; J.-C. Roux, 'Les Indiens de la Nouvelle-Calédonie (Une ethnie disparue par assimilation)', *Bulletin de la Société de l'études historiques de la Nouvelle-Calédonie* 58 (1984), 311.

13 Patrick Pillon and François Sodter, 'The Impact of Colonial Administrative Policies on Indigenous Social Customs in Tahiti and New Caledonia', *Journal of Pacific History* 26, no. 2 (1991), 152.

14 Angleviel, 'A History of New Caledonia', 56.

15 Stephen A. Toth, 'Colonisation or Incarceration? The Changing Role of the French Penal Colony in *Fin-de-siècle* New Caledonia', in Annick Foucrier (ed.), *The French and the Pacific World, 17th–19th Centuries: Explorations, Migrations and Cultural Exchanges* (Aldershot: Ashgate, 2005), 117–32.

16 Alain Saussol, 'The Colonial Chimera, 1853–1976', in Michael Spencer, Alan Ward and John Connell (eds), *New Caledonia: Essays in Nationalism and Dependancy* (Brisbane: University of Queensland Press, 1988), 38–9. However, Merle notes that in fact only a small proportion of the penal population became and remained *concessionaires*. Merle, *Expériences Coloniales*, 142–7.

17 Alain Saussol, 'Nouvelle-Calédonie: le choc d'une colonisation singulière', in Alban Bensa et al. (eds), *Comprendre l'identité kanak* (Paris: Centre Thomas Moore, 1990), 42.

18 Dorothy Shineberg, 'Un nouveau regard sur la démographie historique de la Nouvelle-Calédonie', *Journal de la Société des océanistes* 76 (1983), 41, but note the problems with the accuracy of these figures discussed.

19 Alain Saussol, *L'héritage. Essai sur le problème foncier mélanésien en Nouvelle-Calédonie* (Paris: Société des Océanistes, 1979), 42.

20 Merle, *Expériences Coloniales*, 85–8.

21 Emmanuelle Saada, 'Citoyens et sujets de l'Empire français. Le usages de droit en situation coloniale', *Genèses* 53 (2003/4), 20.

22 Frédéric Bobin, 'Caldoches, Metropolitans and the Mother Country', *Journal of Pacific History* 26, no. 2 (1991), 303–12.

23 Adrian Muckle, 'The Presumption of Indigeneity: Colonial Administration, the "Community of Race" and the Category of Indigène in New Caledonia, 1887–1946', *Journal of Pacific History* 47, no. 3 (2012), 309–28; Bronwen Douglas and Chris Ballard, 'Race, Place and Civilisation: Colonial Encounters and Governance in Greater Oceania', *Journal of Pacific History* 47, no. 3 (2012), 245–62.

24 Infractions under the Indigénat were frequently also extended to indentured labourers; Merle and Muckle, *L'Indigénat*, 282–4.

25 Extrait d'un rapport, 2 juin 1862, rémis à Gouveurneur Guillain par M. Durand, ancien Commandant de la Nouvelle Calédonie, SG-NC Carton 234, ANOM.

26 Décret du 28 novembre 1866, SG-NC Carton 160; Note on 'L'organisation judiciaire de la Nouvelle Calédonie', n.d., SG-NC Carton 234, ANOM.

27 M. Mouët, Gouverneur de la Nouvelle Calédonie à Ministre de la Marine et des Colonies, 5 mai 1888, SG-NC Carton 235, ANOM. See also Adrian Muckle, '"Natives", "Immigrants" and "Libérés": The Colonial Regulation of Mobility in New Caledonia', *Law Text Culture* 15, no. 1 (2011), 135–61.

28 F. Laisesse [?], President du Tribunal Supérieur, à Monsieur Le Gouverneur, Nouméa, 15 février 1875, SG-NC Carton 234, ANOM.

29 Commissariat de Police, 'Rapport Annuel sur la marche du Service de la Police pendant l'année 1910', encl. in Rapport d'Ensemble 1910, DAP Carton 1AFFPOL/271, ANOM.

30 Rapport à l'Empereur; from Ministre Secrétaire d'Etat de la Marine et des Colonies, Paris, octobre 1866, SG-NC Carton 234, ANOM.

31 Arrêté du 24 décembre 1867. *Bulletin Officiel de la Nouvelle Calédonie*; see 'No. 104 Affaires Indigènes', Inspecteur L. Bourgourd à Ministre des Colonies, 23 mai 1919, ADC Carton 826; and Secrétaire d'Etat á M. Moncelou, delégue de la Nouvelle-Calédonie au Conseil Superieur des Colonies, 11 août 1884, SG-NC Carton 234, ANOM.

32 Christiane Terrier, 'Le «Grand Cantonnement» des indigènes (1897–1903)', in Eddy Wadrawane and Frédéric Angleviel (eds), *La Nouvelle-Calédonie: Les Kanaks et l'histoire* (Paris: Les Indes Savantes, 2008), 255–81; Merle, *Expériences Coloniales*, 87, 97–106; Isabelle Merle, 'La construction d'un droit foncier colonial: De la propriété collective à la constitution des réserves en Nouvelle-Calédonie', *Enquête: Anthropologie, Histoire, Sociologie* 7 (1999), 97–126.

33 Bronwen Douglas, 'Conflict and Alliance in a Colonial Context', *Journal of Pacific History* 15, no. 1 (1980), 21–51.

34 Douglas, *Across the Great Divide*, 197–203. Note that Kanak involvement on both sides was entwined with inter-tribal politics as much or more than anti-French sentiments.

35 Merle, *Expériences Coloniales*, 112, 153–4; Douglas, *Across the Great Divide*, 215.

36 Adrian Muckle, 'Killing the "Fantôme Canaque": Evoking and Invoking the Possibility of Revolt in New Caledonia (1853–1915)', *Journal of Pacific History* 37, no. 1 (2002), 25–44.

37 See the excellent Merle and Muckle, *L'indigénat* on the imperial genealogy of the regime and its implementation.

38 Décret du 18 Juillet 1887, *Bulletin officiel de la Nouvelle Calédonie*, 664–5. Indigénat regulations were sometimes applied to other Pacific Islanders and immigrant labourers, especially if they lived in Kanak community, though these groups were never formally included in the regime's orbit. See Merle and Muckle, *L'Indigénat*, 455–73 for summary of infractions.

39 Merle and Muckle, *L'Indigénat*, 285–90.

40 Merle, 'De la «législation»' 154–5; Ismet Kurtovitch and Jean Guiart, 'Sortir de l'indigénat: cinquantième anniversaire de l'abolition de l'indigénat en Nouvelle-Calédonie', *Journal de la Société des Océanistes* 105, no. 2 (1997), 117–39.

41 Décret du 18 Juillet 1887, *Bulletin officiel de la Nouvelle Calédonie*, 664–5.

42 'Affaires Indigenes', Inspecteur Maurice Méray à Ministre des Colonies, 24 mai 1902, ADC Carton 821, ANOM; Adrian Muckle, 'Troublesome chiefs and disorderly subjects'.

43 Discours prononcé par M. Paul FEILLET, Gouverneur de la Nouvelle-Calédonie et Dépendances, à l'Ouverture de la Session Ordinaire du Conseil Général, 3 juin 1901 (Nouméa: Impremerie Calédonienne, 1901), 8 and 10–11, in DAP Carton 1AFFPOL/266, ANOM.

44 See 'No. 104 Affaires Indigènes', Inspecteur L Bougourd à Ministre des Colonies, 23 mai 1919, ADC Carton 826, ANOM.

45 'No 22 Régime de l'Indigénat', Inspecteur Fillon à Ministre des Colonies, 15 mai 1907, ADC Carton 822, ANOM.

46 'No. 104 Affaires Indigènes', Inspecteur L. Bougourd à Ministre des Colonies, 23 mai 1919, ADC Carton 826, ANOM. Adrian Muckle, 'Calling Colonialism to Account? France's Colonial Inspectorate in Oceania', Pacific History Association Conference, 6–8 December 2012, University of Victoria Wellington.

47 Adrian Muckle, *Specters of Violence in a Colonial Context: New Caledonia, 1917* (Honolulu: University of Hawai'i Press, 2012), 12–13; Michel Naepels, *War and Other Means: Violence and Power in Houaïlou (New Caledonia)* (Acton: ANU Press, 2017), chapter 3.

48 Naepals, *War and Other Means,* 132.

49 J. D. Legge, *Britain in Fiji, 1858–1880* (London: Macmillan, 1958), 15–35; France, *The Charter of the Land*, chapters 5 and 6; Scarr, *Fragments of Empire*, 7–8.

50 Quoted in John D. Kelly, 'Gordon Was No Amateur: Imperial Legal Strategies in the Colonisation of Fiji', in Sally Engle Merry and Donald Brenneis (eds), *Law and Empire in the Pacific: Fiji and Hawaii* (Santa Fe: School of American Research Press, 2003), 67–8.

51 On successors: Bridget Brereton, *Law, Justice and Empire: The Colonial Career of John Gorrie, 1829–1892* (Barbados: University of the West Indies Press, 1997), xvi, 98–9, 104, 111, 116; Legge, *Britain in Fiji*, 207–8; Deryck Scarr, *The Majesty of Colour: A Life of Sir John Bates Thurston* (Canberra: ANU Press, 1973–80); R. B. Joyce, 'Sir William MacGregor – a Colonial Governor', *Historical Studies: Australia and New Zealand* 11, no. 41 (1963), 18–31.

52 On Gordon see: Colin Newbury, *Patronage and Politics in the Victorian Empire: The Personal Governance of Sir Arthur Hamilton Gordon* (Amherst, NY: Cambria Books, 2010); and J. K. Chapman, *The Career of A. H. Gordon* (Toronto: University of Toronto Press, 1964); Lord Stanmore, *Fiji: Records of Private and Public Life 1875–1880*, four volumes (Edinburgh: R. and R. Clark, 1897–1912).

53 Kelly, 'Gordon Was No Amateur'; Laurence Brown, 'Inter-Colonial Migration and the Refashioning of Indentured Labour: Arthur Gordon in Trinidad, Mauritius and Fiji', in Lambert and Lester (eds), *Colonial Lives*, 204–27.

54 Brereton, *Law, Justice and Empire,* 108; David M. Morens, 'Measles in Fiji, 1875: Thoughts on the History of Emerging Infectious Diseases', *Pacific Health Dialog* 5, no. 1 (1998), 119–28; Sara H. Somner, 'Idealism and Pragmatism in Colonial Fiji', *Hawaiian Journal of History* 18 (1984), 140–55; Jane Samson, *Imperial Benevolence.*

55 Thomas, *Colonialism's Culture*, 112–15.

56 Stanmore, *Fiji,* vol. 1, 195–9; Thomas, *Colonialism's Culture*, 108, 118; Nicholas Thomas, 'The Inversion of Tradition', *American Ethnologist* 19, no. 2 (1992), 213–32; Eric Hobsbawn and Terence Ranger (eds), *The Invention of Tradition* (Cambridge: Cambridge University Press, 1992 [1983]).

57 Thomas, *Colonialism's Culture*, 108; Deryck Scarr, 'A Roko Tui for Lomaiviti: The Question of Legitimacy in the Fijian Administration 1874–1900', *Journal of Pacific History* 5 (1970), 3–31.

58 Lortimer Fison, 'Land Tenure in Fiji', *Journal of the Anthropological Institute of Great Britain and Ireland* 10 (1881), 332–52; France, *The Charter of the Land*, 117–20.

59 Stanmore, *Fiji*, vol. 1, 194–5; William Des Voeux, *My Colonial Service in British Guiana, St. Lucia, Trinidad, Fiji, Australia, New-Foundland, and Hong Kong with interludes*, vol. 1 (London: John Murray, 1903), 348.

60 K. L. Gillion *Fiji's Indian Migrants: A History to the End of Indenture in 1920* (Melbourne: Oxford University Press, 1962), 1–15; Ralph Shlomowitz, 'The Fiji Labor Trade in Comparative Perspective, 1864–1914', *Pacific Studies* 9, no. 3 (1986), 108–52; 'Atu Bain, 'A Protective Labour Policy? An Alternative Interpretation of Early Colonial Labour Policy in Fiji', *Journal of Pacific History* 23, no. 2 (1988), 119–36.

61 See Lal, *Chalo Jahaji*; Gillion, *Fiji's Indian Migrants* especially chapter 6; Vijay Naidu, *The Violence of Indenture in Fiji* (Lautoka: Fiji Insitute of Applied Studies, 2004); Ahmed Ali, *Girmit: The Indenture Experience in Fiji* (Suva: Fiji Museum, 2004 [1979]).

62 J. W. B. Money, *Java; or, How to Manage a Colony*, quoted in Kelly, 'Gordon Was No Amateur', 88; Stanmore, '*Fiji*', vol. 1, 196–7.

63 Kelly, 'Gordon Was No Amateur', 65–6; France, *The Charter of the Land*, chapter 7.

64 Native Affairs Ordinance (No. 35 of 1876), Fiji Certified Copies of Acts 1875–80, CO 84/1, NAK, and Native Regulation No. 2 of 1877 (Respecting Courts), *Regulations of the Native Regulation Board 1877–1882* (London: Harrison and Sons, 1883), 8–15.

65 Regulation No. 5 1878, *Regulations of the Native Regulation Board: 1877–1882* (London: Harrison and Sons, 1883), 38–9.

66 Norman Etherington, 'The Gendering of Indirect Rule: Criminal Law and Colonial Fiji, 1875–1900', *Journal of Pacific History* 31, no. 1 (1996), 45–6.

67 Native Affairs Ordinance (No. 35 of 1876), Fiji Certified Copies of Acts 1875–80, CO 84/1, NAK, and Native Regulations No. 1 of 1877 (For the Better Administration of Provincial Affairs) and No. 2 of 1877 (Respecting Courts), *Regulations of the Native Regulation Board 1877–1882*, 3–15; Section IV – Native Affairs, Fiji Colonial Report No. 848 (Report for 1914), Fiji Colonial Reports 1905–20, NAF, provides an overview of the administrative and judicial organization created by this ordinance.

68 Colin Newbury, 'Bose Vakauraga: Fiji's Great Council of Chiefs, 1875–2000', *Pacific Studies* 29, nos. 1/2 (2006), 82–127.

69 Roko Tai Ba, 18 September 1875, 'Proceedings of the Native Council', Draiba, NAF.

70 Roko Tui Bua, 17 September 1875, 'Proceedings of the Native Council', Draiba, NAF.

71 Legge, *Britain in Fiji*, 209–10; Native Affairs Ordinance (No. 35 of 1876), Fiji Certified Copies of Acts 1875–80, CO 84/1, NAK; and Native Regulation No. 2 of 1877 (Respecting Courts), *Regulations of the Native Regulation Board 1877–1882*, 8–15.

72 Etherington, 'The Gendering of Indirect Rule'; P. S. Friend, SM Lower Rewa, to Colonial Secretary, 19/1/1877, CSO MP 77/104; and G. R. Le Hunte, SM Loma Loma, to Colonial Secretary, 12/3/1877, CSO MP 77/330, NAF.

73 Henry Anson, Stipendiary Magistrate Bua, to Colonial Secretary, 6 December 1880, CSO MP 80/2102, NAF; see also R. Swanston to Colonial Secretary, 2/5/1876, CSO MP 76/742, NAF.

74 Roko Tui Ba, 23 May 1883, 'Proceedings of the Native Council', Naduri, May 1883, NAF.

75 Henry Anson, Stipendiary Magistrate Na Wi, to Colonial Secretary, 1 January 1881, CSO MP 80/69, NAF. See also Provincial Inspector Mark Spence to Native Commissioner, 7/3/1899, CAO 1252/1899; Case 11/1901 Rex v A, Criminal Sittings, FSC, CSO MP 80/423; CSO MP 80/561; CSO MP 77/330, and No. 4/82 SM for Lau Swayne to Colonial Secretary, [Jan 1882], Lau Provincial Office – Official Correspondence 1876–83, NAF.

76 See Annual Reports on Indian Immigration in the *Journal of the Legislative Council* (held at NAF) for full details and numbers of violent offences. Naidu also compiles offences between labourers for 1885–1920 in *The Violence of Indenture*, 72–8.

77 Lal, *Chalo Jahaji*, 188; Naidu, *The Violence of Indenture*.

78 Governor-General of India in Council to Secretary of State for India, Department of Commerce and Industry, Simla, 15 October 1915, Council Paper No. 36 of 1916 – Indian Immigration. Correspondence with Secretary of State relating to – In continuation of C. P. No. 12 of 1916, *Journal of the Legislative Council* 1916, NAF.

79 Peter Duff, 'The Evolution of Trial by Judge and Assessors in Fiji', *Journal of Pacific Studies* 21 (1997), 189–213.

80 Wiener, *An Empire on Trial*, 83.

81 Speech of the British judge reported in 'Britain and France in the New Hebrides. Opening of the Joint Court', *The Times*, 30 November 1910.

82 Ibid.

83 'Exchange of Notes Arrangement between Great Britain and France, Respecting the Independence of the New Hebrides Group [1878] PITSE 1 (18 January 1878)', Pacific Islands Treaty Series, Pacific Islands Legal Information Institute, accessed 19 January 2022, http://www.paclii.org/pits/en/treaty_database/1878/1.html.

84 Howard Van Trease, *The Politics of Land in Vanuatu: From Colony to Independence* (Suva: Fiji Times, 1991 [1987]), 35; Scarr, *Fragments of Empire*, 176; Howard Van Trease, 'The Colonial Origins of Melanesian Politics', in Howard Van Trease (ed.), *Melanesian Politics: Stael Blong Vanuatu* (Christchurch, New Zealand: Macmillan

Brown Center for Pacific Studies, University of Canterbury; Suva, Fiji: IPS, USP, 1995), 7; Roger C. Thompson, *Australian Imperialism in the Pacific: The Expansionist Era 1820–1920* (Melbourne: Melbourne University Press, 1980).

85 Quoted in Van Trease, *The Politics of Land,* 40.

86 'Declaration between Great Britain and France, for the Constitution of a Joint Naval Commission for the Protection of Life and Property in the New Hebrides [1888] PITSE 1 (26 January 1888)', Pacific Islands Treaty Series, Pacific Islands Legal Information Institute, accessed 19 January 2022, http://www.paclii.org/pits/en/treaty_database/1888/1.html

87 'Declaration (26 January 1888)'; 'Convention between Great Britain and France, Respecting Abrogation of the Declaration of the 19th June 1847, Relative to the Islands to the Leeward of Tahiti and for the Protection of Life and Property in the New Hebrides [1887] PITSE 1 (16 November 1887)', Pacific Islands Treaty Series, Pacific Islands Legal Information Institute, accessed 19 January 2022, http://www.paclii.org/pits/en/treaty_database/1887/1.html.

88 D. P. O'Connell, 'The Condominium of the New Hebrides', *British Year Book of International Law* 49 (1968–9), 76.

89 Scarr, *Fragments of Empire*, 230. See Van Trease, *The Politics of Land,* 44–7, for an excellent discussion of these negotiations.

90 'Convention between the United Kingdom and France Concerning the New Hebrides. Signed at London, October 20, 1906. (Ratifications Exchanged at London, January 9, 1907)', *American Journal of International Law* 1, no. 2, Supplement: Official Documents (1907), 179–200.

91 William F. S. Miles, *Bridging Mental Boundaries in a Postcolonial Microcosm: Identity and Development in Vanuatu* (Honolulu: University of Hawai'i Press, 1998), 41.

92 'Protocol between Great Britain and France Respecting the New Hebrides [1906] PITSE 2 (27 February 1906)', Pacific Islands Treaty Series, Pacific Islands Legal Information Institute, accessed 19 January 2022, http://www.paclii.org/pits/en/treaty_database/1906/2.html.

93 Alexander, *From the Middle Temple*, 187.

94 Subjects of neither British nor French nationality had six months from arrival to choose whether to place themselves under the French or British legal system. If they did not elect a jurisdiction in this time, the choice was made by the Resident Commissioners. Notice from Resident Commissioner, 8/5/1908, in Folder 4/1908, NHBS 1/I Vol. 1, WPA.

95 Paul Ad. Serre, Consul de France à Auckland, quoted in 'Note pour le Cabinet du Ministre', Directeur de Institut National d'Agrinomie Colonie, 2 mai 1927, SG-NH Carton 9, ANOM.

96 Margaret Rodman, 'Portentous Splendour: Building the Anglo-French Condominium', *History and Anthropology* 11, no. 4 (1999), 479–514.

97 For example, the Joint Court initially delayed hearing land cases to enable time for surveys, but was closed through much of the First World War as communications from Marseille were cut off and various officials left to join the war effort in Europe. The court did not reopen to hear land claims until 1927 with the return of the President, the Count de Buena Esperanza. Keith Woodward, 'Historical Note', in Brian J. Bresnihan and Keith Woodward (eds), *Tufala Gavman: Reminiscences from the Anglo-French Condominium of the New Hebrides* (Institute of Pacific Studies, USP, 2002), 36; and Count of Buena Esperanza to Secretary of State for Colonies, 26/2/1926, Folder 51/1926, NHBS 1/I Vol. 2, WPA.

98 Folder 14/1923 (Executions of Judgements of Joint Court under Protocol of 1914), NHBS 1/I Vol. 2, WPA.

99 Article VIII 3, 'Convention between the United Kingdom and France Concerning the New Hebrides 1906'.

100 'New Hebrides. Joint Court', *Sydney Morning Herald*, 28 December 1911.

101 Scarr, *Fragments of Empire*, 243.

102 Woodward, 'Historical Note', 36.

103 See discussion on 'Tribunaux Indigènes' in Inspecteur Revel à Ministre des Colonies, 5 juin 1922, SG-NH Carton 31, ANOM; Ministre des Affaires Etrangères à Ministre des Colonies, 18 décembre 1915, DAP Carton 1AFFPOL/1916; and Rapport Trimestriel Octobre–Décembre 1917, SG-NH Carton 12, ANOM.

104 Scarr, *Fragments of Empire*, 240.

105 Joint Regulation No. 2 of 1928 – Insitution of Native Courts, Pacific Islands Legal Information Institute, http://www.paclii.org/vu/legis/joint_reg/ioncr1928445/.

106 Woodward, 'Historical Note', 27.

107 M. Paul Ad. Serre, quoting views of missionary Frederick Paton, in 'Note pour le Cabinet du Ministre', 2 mai 1927, SG-NH Carton 9, ANOM.

108 Greg Rawlings, 'Statelessness, Human Rights and Decolonisation', *Journal of Pacific History* 47, no. 1 (2012), 45–68; and Miles, *Bridging Mental Boundaries*, 36–7.

109 Miles, *Bridging Mental Boundaries*, 41.

110 Resident Commissioner to High Commissioner, 14 November 1912, Folder 57/1912, NHBS 1/I Vol. 1, WPA.

111 'Main d'oeuvre tonkinoise et javanaise. Service d'Immigration', Inspecteur Coste à Ministre des Colonies, 8 septembre 1929, Carton 31 SG-NH, ANOM.

112 Margaret Rodman, '"My Only Weapon Being a Pencil": Inscribing the Prison in the New Hebrides', *Journal of Pacific History* 33, no. 1 (1998), 29–49; Rapport d'Ensemble, au Janvier 1910, du Commissaire-Résident de France p.i. [M. Colonna] aux Nouvelles-Hébrides à Haut Commissaire, in Gouverneur à Ministre des Colonies, 10 février 1910, Carton 11bis, SG-NH ANOM; No. 79/5 SM Swayne to Colonial Secretary, 27/1/1879 and No. 79/21, SM Swayne to Colonial Secretary, 18/4/1879, S. M. Lau – Copies of Outward Letters 1876–82, and No. 153/83

Swayne to Colonial Secretary, 13 June 1883, S. M. Lau – Outward Letter Book 1882–3, Lau Provincial Council Records, NAF.

113 See for example Le Secrétaire d'Etat à Gouverneur de la Nouvelle Calédonie, 28 juin 1884, SG-NC Carton 234, ANOM.

114 Extrait d'un Rapport du Gouverneur de la Nouvelle Calédonie, 15 mars 1859, SG-NC Carton 234, ANOM.

115 Note on 'L'organisation judiciaire de la Nouvelle Calédonie', n.d., SG-NC Carton 234, ANOM.

116 Gouverneur Guillain à Ministère des Colonies, 29 novembre 1869, SG-NC Carton 234, ANOM.

117 Note on 'L'organisation judiciaire de la Nouvelle Calédonie', n.d., SG-NC Carton 234, ANOM.

118 Merle and Muckle, *L'Indigènat*, 198; Arrêté du 9 Août 1898 (Organisation of SAI), *Bulletin Officiel de la Nouvelle-Calédonie* 1898, 366–76.

119 Muckle, *Specters*, 12.

120 Service de la Gendarmerie. Rapport fait par M. PEGOURIER, 12 septembre 1918, ADC Carton 827, ANOM.

121 No. 104 Affaires Indigènes, Inspecteur L. Bougourd à Ministre des Colonies, 23 mai 1919, ADC Carton 826, ANOM.

122 Muckle, *Specters*, 113.

123 No. 104 Affaires Indigènes, Inspecteur L. Bougourd à Ministre des Colonies, 23 mai 1919, ADC Carton 826, ANOM.

124 No. 36 Gendameries, Inspecteur L. Bougourd à Ministre des Colonies, Nouméa, 7 janvier 1919, ADC Carton 826, ANOM.

125 Service de la Curatelle, Inspecteur M. Revel à Ministre des Colonies, Nouméa, 20 mai 1920, SG-NH Carton 31; Dossier Fonctionement de Tribunal Mixte, DAP Carton 1AFFPOL/1676, ANOM. On the poor state of the police force see Rapport d'Ensemble sur la situation des Nouvelles-Hébrides en 1910, Carton 11bis, SG-NH ANOM.

126 Letter to A. W. Jose, 24/4/1914, MS 894/24 Edward Jacomb diary 1914; Letter from H. Pieremont, 5/11/1920 and Letter to Charlies, private, 18/1/1920, MS 894/30 Edward Jacomb Diary 1920–21, SHL; Alexander, *From the Middle Temple*, 40–1; See for example Personnel locaux 1910–28 – Tribunal Mixte, DAP Carton 1AFFPOL/1915, ANOM; Gouverneur et Haut-Commissaire Repiquet, à Ministre des Colonies, 23 mars 1923, DAP Carton 1AFFPOL/1915, ANOM.

127 Revel à Ministre of Colonies, 3 juin 1912, SG-NH Carton 31, ANOM; Letter from H. Pieremont to Jacomb, 5/11/1920, MS 894/30 Edward Jacomb Diary 1920–21, SHL.

128 For example, see Folder 115/1909 (Native Advocate (4 parts) 1909–24), NHBS 1/I Vol. 1, WPA on debates over the appointment, salary and housing of the Joint

Court's Native Advocate; Folder 80/1910 (Joint Court – Requirements in re staff, equipment, etc.), Folder 39/1912 (Particulars of costs in various court cases. 1911–12.), Folder 119/1912 (Delay in hearing of cases before the Joint Court.), Folder 5/1913 (General Affairs of the Joint Court. (2 parts, five folders) 1913–14.), Folder 85/1913 (Police. Correspondence relating to stores, appointments, regulations, reports and arrests (3 parts in six folders) 1913–24.), Folder 18/1914 (Joint Court (10 parts in 17 folders) 1913–24.), NHBS 1/I Vol. 1, WPA; Folder 74/1924 (Return of and Expenses of, Count of Buena Esperanza. 1924), NHBS 1/I Vol. 2, WPA.

129 President du Conseil, Ministre des Affaires Etrangères à Ministre des Colonies, 17 juin 1921, SG-NH Carton 12; Rapport Trimestriel sur la Situation des Nouvelles-Hébrides, Octubre – Décembre 1914, SG-NH Carton 12; and Service de l'Administration Générale – Rapport fait par M. Bougourd, novembre 1918, SG-NH Carton 31, ANOM. See also Dossier Proposition de fermer provisionnement le Tribunal Mixte, DAP Carton 1AFFPOL/1676; and Rapport sur le fonctionnement du Tribunal Mixte pendant 1923, DAP Carton 1AFFPOL/1916, ANOM.

130 Edward Jacomb, *France and England in the New Hebrides* (Melbourne: G. Robertson and Company, 1914).

131 Alexander, *From the Middle Temple*, 187; President du Conseil, Ministre des Affaires Etrangères à Ministre des Colonies, 1 avril 1914, SG-NH Carton 5, ANOM.

132 Speiser, *Two Years*, 16–17.

133 Folder 8/1908 (Suggests that the commandant of Police should have the assistance of a White N. C. O), NHBS 1/I Vol. 1, WPA.

134 Provincial Inspector Cakaudrove and Bua (Mark Spence) to Native Commissioner, 7/3/1899, CSO 1252/1899, NAF.

135 Muckle, 'Troublesome Chiefs', 137. Fijians chiefs were also deported on occasion: see Nicole, *Disturbing History*, chapter 2 and 133; and Roko Tui Rewa and Buli Burebasaga, Toga and Vutia to Governor, 8 April 1889, CSO 89/990, NAF.

136 Gouverneur Feillet à Ministre des Colonies, 24 mai 1898, SG-NC Carton 5, ANOM.

137 No. 104 Affaires Indigènes, Inspecteur L. Bougourd à Ministre des Colonies, 23 mai 1919, ADC Carton 826, ANOM.

138 Des Voeux, *My Colonial Service*, vol. 1, 356; see also correspondance in Dossier Fonctionnement de Tribunal Mixte, DAP Carton 1AFFPOL/1676, ANOM.

139 A. Taylor, Stipendiary Magistrate Taviuni, to Colonial Secretary, 8 September 1880, CSO MP 1594/1880, NAF.

140 Alexander, *From the Middle Temple*, 195–6. On Leclerc, see Resident Commissioner to High Commissioner, 14 November 1912, Folder 57/1912, NHBS 1/I Vol. 1, WPA.

141 Russell Brennan and Jonathan Richards, '"The Scum of French Criminals and Convicts": Australia and New Caledonia escapees', *History Compass* 12, no. 7 (2014), 559–66.

142 G. Aubrey-Lecomte à Commissaire General de la Republique Française dans le Pacifique, 6 novembre 1901, SG-NH Carton 4, ANOM; Alexander, *From the Middle Temple*, 219–20; Henry Anson, Stipendiary Magistrate Na Wi, to Colonial Secretary, 1 January 1881, CSO MP 80/69, NAF.

143 Acting Colonial Secretary to Office, 1/12/1899, CSO 5317/1899, NAF; Rodman, 'My Only Weapon Being a Pencil'; Margaret Rodman, *House Far from Home: British Colonial Space in the New Hebrides* (Honolulu: University of Hawai'i Press, 2001), 84–101; and Rapport sur le fonctionnement du Tribunal Mixte pendant 1923, DAP Carton 1AFFPOL/1916, ANOM.

144 Resident Commissioner to Jacomb, 20/9/1912, in Folder 35/1912, NHBS 1/I Vol. 1, WPA.

145 No. 36 Gendarmerie, Inspecteur L. Bougourd à Ministre des Colonies, janvier 1919, ADC Carton 826, ANOM.

146 Service de la Gendarmerie. Rapport fait par M. Pegourier, 12 septembre 1918, ADC Carton 827, ANOM.

147 Gouverneur à Ministre des Colonies, 24 octubre 1908, and Gouverneur à Ministre des Colonies, Nouméa, 30 septembre 1908, SG-NC Carton 231, ANOM.

148 Le President p.i. du Tribunal Mixte Borgesius à Ministre des Colonies, 22 décembre 1916, DAP Carton 1AFFPOL/1676, ANOM.

149 'Note of Interview with President of the Joint Court', in Folder 283/1908, NHBS 1/I Vol. 1, WPA. See also discussions in Dossier Fonctionnement de Tribunal Mixte, DAP Carton 1AFFPOL/1676, ANOM.

150 Scarr, *Fragments of Empire*, 239; Commissaire Resident à Procureur Général, 23 décembre 1910, DAP Carton 1AFFPOL/1676, ANOM.

151 Ford, *Settler Sovereignty*, 6.

2

Courtroom theatre and colonial prestige

In memoirs recounting his time as chief police magistrate in Fiji from 1907, Gilchrist Alexander evoked the typical scene at his arrival at court:

> Under the shade of the mango tree outside the Court House would be gathered a little group recalling the Biblical pictures of one's boyhood … it would comprise one or two white-bearded patriarchs who had come in the immigrant ships from India in the eighties and nineties. With them would be their wives and married sons or daughters and their grandchildren – a whole village community. A chapter in some age-long quarrel in the little settlement of Muanivatu would no doubt be staged for the day, and few of the residents of the little hamlet would miss the entertainment. My arrival stirs them all to interest. In the chops and changes of official life they are never sure whether the Chief Police Magistrate himself or a deputy will try the case, and, like all theatre-goers, they clamour for the principal actor himself and not for the understudy.[1]

Exemplifying paternalistic colonial humour, Alexander explicitly framed the court as theatre. Implying that, for the audience, the performative aspect was a critical part of the court's role, he suggests that a court case was a welcome distraction from their everyday lives. Private lives and 'age-old quarrels' were publicly played out for the diversion of those attending. The court thus represented an arena in which domestic incidents and local disagreements could take on dramatic proportions through their retelling. However, Alexander's account also trivializes the lives and experiences of local Indian residents and instead centres the European official as the 'principal'. This tension, between the court's performative qualities and the minimization of its impact on the lives of Islanders or indentured labourers, is a theme that runs through this chapter.

The concerns of European Stipendiary Magistrate Le Hunte in Fiji serve as a counterpoint to Alexander's vignette. In reference to a case of fornication that involved eight schoolboys and two very young girls, Le Hunte lamented to his superiors:

> I take far too great a personal interest in these people not to feel that the spectacle of ten children, dressed up as for a fête, appearing in open court before a large number of spectators for an offence, at times discreditable, but in such [illegible word] young persons absolutely disgusting, was not one that should be seen in Fiji.[2]

Le Hunte demonstrated an awareness of how the court as a space of 'spectacle' compromised the dignity of the young defendants and victims. He implied that only certain subjects were suitable for public consumption in the theatre of court, drawing the line at children. This example highlights the difficulty in reconciling the intimate nature of sexual cases with the public grandeur and drama inherent in the colonial court as a public space of confrontation. The protectionism central to the Fijian administration's native policy contributed to the discomfort with this juxtaposition. Nevertheless, officials generally played the starring roles in the courtroom, with the voices of Islanders, indentured labourers and others heard largely through translators, if at all.

This chapter examines how officials used the courtroom as a theatrical space in the absence of substantive power in Pacific colonies. In particular, the Joint Court of the New Hebrides' operation highlights that colonial justice was often as much about the rituals and performance of authority as the adjudication of law. The disjunction between these two elements reflected the Joint Court's constrained jurisdiction and contributed to a legacy of farcical depictions of Anglo-French rule in the colony. Finally, this chapter explores how various individuals and communities used satire and theatre to critique colonial law and its limits in both Vanuatu and Fiji, and especially the problematic role of translation and transcription of evidence in multilingual trials.

Observers called into question the authority and ability of presiding magistrates and their courts through humour. In the New Hebrides especially, the Joint Court was a popular target for parody. There is a wealth of commentary on its functioning and memoirs from legal officials and observers.[3] Administrators themselves joked that it was a 'mésentente cordiale'.[4] This view is reflected in subsequent historiography of the Condominium, which scholars have described as a 'comic opera pomp', or 'a system of joint neglect'. Others have labelled it 'asinine', a 'bastard', as well as the oft-quoted 'Pandemonium'.[5]

Assessments of officials adopted a similar tone. For example, D. L. Oliver suggested that the Spanish president of the Joint Court 'was truly neutral, having understood little French, less English, and no Melanesian; but this was no additional handicap, because he was also deaf'.[6] This historiography contrasts with that of Fiji and New Caledonia, which has focused on the traumatic consequences of colonial rule, especially regarding indenture. I argue that satiric portrayals of colonial rule in the New Hebrides frequently originated as colonial critiques and then question the impact that the predominance of such depictions has had on our understanding of colonialism's impact. As Oliver notes, 'along with such comedy, the condominium also had its tragic side'.[7]

While revealing the limited efficacy of the colonial systems, courtroom performances did serve significant purposes for the administration. The theatre of the courtroom attempted to impose authority over subjects – both Indigenous and European – and endowed prestige upon the presiding officials as representatives of the colonial state. The primacy given to enacting authority, often ahead of passing judgment and sentence, in the colonial court was entwined with other strategies of enforcing the law. The theatre functioned to divert attention from the violence of colonial justice pursued outside the constraints of the court (see Chapter 6).

Magistrates did not always interpret or apply the law in expected or desired ways. Colonial administrations were sometimes wary of handing power over judicial decisions to magistrates (and on occasion to juries) and thus lose control over a key moment in which authority was exercised, as colonial laws and statutes were enforced through judgments and sentences. In consequence, the courts and the trial process were commonly sites where the rhetoric of equality and justice was invoked and performed, where justice could be seen to be done while less liberal aspects of imperial rule continued outside the judicial process.[8] This is particularly evident in the deployment of the Indigénat regime in New Caledonia and in the pursuit and punishment of Indigenous violence by 'man-of-war' expeditions in the New Hebrides. Many cases involving Kanak defendants never went to trial in New Caledonia. Rather, the Governor's Conseil Privé adjudicated on serious crimes including murders and cases of persistent sexual assaults or violence. Lesser offences were dealt with summarily by local colonial administrators, without referral to the judiciary or to Nouméa. Removed from public view in the colony, these cases do not offer the same sense of drama evident in the other colonies.[9]

In Fiji, by contrast, the court was ubiquitous: four levels of courts operated across the islands.[10] The humanitarian bent of Gordon and his successors and distrust of settlers' ability to judge fairly in cases involving racial difference meant that officials resisted calls for trial by jury and instead attempted to retain tighter control of the court process.[11] However on the Fijian plantations, Indian indentured labourers were subjected to a wide variety of coercive tactics, including in the court itself. Humanitarian idealism had little place in the plantation courts. While courtroom dramas provided fodder for a magistrate's memoirs, their version of colonial justice failed to recount indentured Indians' (and other subjects) experience of colonial law. However, unlike Alexander, other commentators recognized the problems with colonial justice, deploying drama and humour to critique the courts.

As in Fiji, the rule of law was a prominent justification for European imperialism in the New Hebrides. The Joint Court sat at the apex of colonial rule, not least because the court building itself was an imposing marker on the landscape of Efate. Yet this view of the Condominium obscured authoritarian forms of justice that bore striking parallels to New Caledonia. While highly visible, the court was also commonly denounced for being ineffectual, a combination that lent the Joint Court an air of play-acting and opened it to ridicule as in Edward Jacomb's satirical play *The Joy Court* and Thomson Reid Cowell's Gilbert and Sullivan-inspired 'Pandemonia, or a Franco-British Fantasy'.[12] Such accounts trivialize and obscure the serious and traumatic impact of Condominium rule. As in New Caledonia, executive, and often retributive, authority was the more common method for dealing with Indigenous crime across the archipelago. Margaret Rodman has said of the pre-Condominium period that 'government presence was largely punitive and always transitory', and I argue that to a significant degree this remained the case after 1906, despite the grandeur of the Joint Court and other performances of colonial rule (such as flag raising) in Port Vila.[13] The courtroom stage represented each legal regime and colonial authority in potent ways, while also obscuring the realities of colonial violence that are explored in Part 2.

Performing authority and prestige

As Deutsch observes, in colonial Tanzania 'the colonial public sphere emerged out of the repetitive symbolic display of power by the colonial government'.[14] The everyday spectacle of authority was crucial to attempts by small imperial administrations to awe and impress their power and prestige on the much larger Indigenous populations they governed, and on settler communities who were often at odds with officials. The colonial court was one of the most powerful arenas for such displays.[15] In this section on the New Hebrides Joint Court, I examine how imperial power was manifested. Attempts to instil a sense of the Condominium's authority in both Indigenous and European subjects ranged from the grand architecture of the courthouse to the mundane performance of bureaucratic rituals. The example is particularly potent given the wide disparity between the rhetoric and ambitions of joint Anglo-French rule and the unfulfilled reality. While these performances were an important part of colonial authority in the New Hebrides, they also served to highlight the limits of Condominium power.

The Joint Court building, along with the residences of the president and judges, were by far the largest and grandest in the emerging Port Vila, illustrating the centrality of the judicial system to the Condominium. Indeed, over a third to a half the Condominium budget went into running the Joint Court.[16] These buildings visibly imposed colonial authority upon the landscape, looming large over the ramshackle assemblage of trade stores and houses around the harbour.[17] While the buildings served as grand symbols of the arrival of European rule, the reality of imperial expansion was less certain to those residents in Vila and around the archipelago. Influenced by colonial bungalow architecture, the façades of the new court buildings were impressive, but the less polished interiors provide a metaphor for the fragility of colonial power in the New Hebrides.[18] The judges' seat was an impressive 'elevated and ornamentally carved horse-shoe Bench'.[19] However, as Jacomb recorded, only the 'Judges' Stadium … is backed with oak', the remaining walls being made of cheaper plaster. Jacomb likened the building to 'the inside of an enormous square bandbox', with small inoperable windows, awkwardly sticky benches and floors and the acoustics of 'a large swimming bath'.[20] And while the windows would not open, the doors would not lock.[21]

The minutiae of archival minutes complaining of such issues are emblematic of the state of the judicial system more generally, where reality failed to meet the grander vision underpinning the Joint Convention for an integrated, effective and benevolent legal system. As Alexander opined, 'the magnitude of our work, I fear, did not correspond with the magnificence of our *milieu*'.[22]

As much as it riled individual officials on both sides of the *entente cordiale*, the fact that the law functioned as a site of performance rather than a genuine and effective code of practice served a political end in the New Hebrides. As President Manuel Bosch Barrett experienced as late as the 1930s, the court existed 'only in name', perhaps unsurprising given 'passivity is the most effective weapon in the colonies'.[23] The French preferred to maintain the powers of their national administration at the expense of the joint jurisdiction of the Condominium. Neither party was satisfied by the joint arrangement (and nor were their respective settlers, missionaries or colonists in New Caledonia and Australia), meaning there was little incentive to improve the functioning of the Condominium or the Joint Court. The failures of the system lent weight to petitions for an end to Condominium rule.[24] With the respective Residents pinching pennies and ready to debate and oppose any contribution to the joint Condominium expenses, the delays, suspensions in hearing land claims and closures of the Joint Court (during the First World War and from 1919 to 1928) were powerful indictments of the Anglo-French imperial regime.[25] After all, the Joint Court's role in resolving the land disputes was a key *raison d'être* for the Condominium itself. The ills plaguing the administration added fuel to the voices of those campaigning for single colonial rule or partition into two separate colonies, which included Presbyterian missionaries and their Australian supporters on the British side, and the planters and traders on the French.

While the photographs of the court exterior and judges' houses sitting high on the natural terraced hillside of Vila Harbour provide a striking example of colonialism's mark on the landscape, few images exist to add a visual dimension to the descriptions of the theatrical performances taking place inside the court. A postcard of ni-Vanuatu men charged with the murder of the Clapcott family on Santo in 1923 nevertheless suggests an interest in the visual consumption of the trial.[26] It is a glimpse into the court and the trial as a troubling site of entertainment and fascination for Europeans settlers and observers. The case was described as 'the longest and most exciting trial in the history of the New Hebrides'.[27] The image shows Indigenous murderers of a European family brought to justice as an event worthy of commemoration – 'an exceptional occurrence' – as a symbol of the advance of European law and civilization, but also highlighting the continued threat of 'savage' violence.[28] Other postcards showing arrests of ni-Vanuatu men circulated through imperial networks to hail the advance of European authority, as depicted in the opening of Part 1 (Figures 1 and 2).[29]

Just as postcards and the physical surroundings of the court attempted to demonstrate authority, so too did dress act as a signifier of both power and difference. Both Alexander and Jacomb chronicled the importance of appearance for the personnel of the Joint Court. Alexander described the companionable costuming of the judges before entering the stage of the court.[30] Jacomb provided further details and pointed barbs regarding the appearance of other officials and Condominium employees:

> Various native policemen lounge at the big folding doors, or promenade the verandah outside. The British police are arrayed in shabby dungaree with gilt buttons, and green woollen caps with tufts at the top. The French police boast khaki uniforms, scarlet puttees and scarlet fezes. The costumes of the judges are

> equally picturesque. The President wears a black gown with plush collar, white lace cuffs and a black sexagonal hat with a nob on the top. The French Judge also has a sexagonal hat and a black gown with a tail of rabbit skin thrown over his shoulders. The British Judge wears a wig and gown, the Public Prosecutor (a foreigner) the gown of a Bachelor of Arts of the University of Oxford (which he has borrowed), and the Registrar nothing (except of course his ordinary clothes).[31]

Such visible markers of identity and difference highlighted the dual nature of the judicial system, signalling that the two powers of the Condominium remained divided rather than integrated in the exercise of imperial authority. The attention given to dress suggests that the tenuous veneer of British and French authority had to be continually re-enacted and re-enforced. Though costuming was equally a quotidian part of judicial practice in London or Paris, Swanepoel argues that dress took on even greater importance in the colonies as a signifier of imperial identity.[32] The combination of judicial robes in the New Hebrides was nevertheless unique, with magistrates using dress to define themselves not only against Islanders but also against the imperial other.

The court structure lent itself to performance, with a raised horseshoe bench for the presiding officials, which was approached from the public gallery by four steps. The shape of the courtroom echoed the architecture that emerged in metropolitan courtrooms during Second Empire France.[33] Katherine Fischer Taylor argues that, in the context of increasingly public trials and the greater weight given to oral procedure (relative to pre-trial investigation), 'the architectural effect … is to convert the courtroom to a stage, in which space, sightlines and acoustics are critical'.[34] In this respect, the difference between the accusatorial model of Anglo-American legal tradition and the inquisitorial model of the French has sometimes been overstated. Certainly, in the Anglo-French Joint Court, the performative aspect of trial was a common element.

Before each court sitting and after every break, the entry of the high officials was a delicate and public display. According to Jacomb's play, the president, two judges and public prosecutor

> reach their allotted seats, stand for an instant, and then sit down simultaneously with military precision. There are questions of precedence at stake, but all is well if they sit down at the same moment. There is a slightly pause to enable the Public to resume its seats, and to impress it with the dignity of the Court. Both objects are successfully and visibly achieved.[35]

The balance of the imperial arrangement hinged on small performances – sitting down simultaneously or raising flags at the same moment and to precisely the same height – which detracted from the delicate larger questions over the effective functioning of the joint arrangement. The emphasis on performance, prestige and precedence helped obscure, at least temporarily, the fact that the Joint Court lacked the effective jurisdiction to confront and resolve more significant issues facing the court, such as land claims and the continued recruitment of Islanders against the terms of the 1906 Convention.

The result is a peculiar situation in which what survives is more nuanced detail pertaining to the dress and appearance of the judiciary, debates over the division of Joint Court expenses, and more material satirizing Anglo-French interactions than specifics of their judicial function and work.[36] However, as there was little connection between the sentences the Joint or National Courts imposed and the actions of the national administrations (at least in the case of the French) to ensure their fulfilment, it is perhaps unsurprising that a large degree of the court's time and attention ended up devoted to activities predominately for show.[37] Fines imposed were never collected, and others provided reprieves. For example, in 1911 Leclerc was referred to the French National Court to be tried for murder after the unscrupulous recruitment of seventeen Santo men and shooting one who jumped overboard to escape. Leclerc and his compatriots, though found guilty, were immediately released under the *lois de sursis* (conditional sentencing) and departed the colony, while the British mate served out his sentence after being tried in the British National Court. Many officials expressed these very frustrations: that the Joint Court was a shadow, a play at justice, given the lack of substantial authority to give weight to the court's decisions.[38]

For all that magistrates and settlers complained regarding inaction of the Joint Court, Britain and France maintained divergent interests and made little headway towards improving the situation. The curtailed powers suited French economic interests, while the British felt that the Condominium was 'the best we can do with France just at present … that *must* be made the best of'.[39] As Rodman writes, 'one suspects that only diplomats with a well-developed sense of humour could devise this travesty of civil authority'.[40] Critics of the Condominium took to humour both as a means to indict the system and simply to express and channel their frustration and despair at the Gilbert and Sullivan-esque Joint Court. Yet humour obscured the substantive impact of colonial rule in the New Hebrides. As the French desired, a large proportion of law enforcement and justice was left in the hands of national administrations. In the gaps between performance and practice, patrolling navies, individual subjects and communities also formed independent ideas of justice. These alternative forms of justice are the focus of Part 2.

Satire and farce in the court

> Of happiness the very pith,
> In Pandemonia you may see:
> A monarchy that's temper with,
> Republican equality.
> This form of Government we find
> The *ne plus ultra* of its kind –
> Except for natives, never mind –
> We've absolute fraternity.[41]

Thomson Reid Cowell, assistant resident commissioner in the New Hebrides in the 1950s deployed musical comedy – 'with humblest apologies to Gilbert and Sullivan' – to highlight the absurdities of the Condominium system, including this chorus from a scene set in a courtroom of 'Vanilla, Pandomonia'.[42] The limitations of the colonial judiciary in the New Hebrides made the Joint Court and its officials an easy subject to satirize, even by individuals connected and invested in the administration itself. Indeed, the local *Bulletin du Commerce* described the Joint Court as 'a tower of Babel' and an 'opéra-bouffe', while *Le Néo-Hébridais* published a dialogue in which a *colon* interrogates the French judge on the lack of clerks (all on leave) needed for the court to function.[43] Such ridicule played to the mutual desires of many British and French settlers, missionaries and officials to dissolve the Condominium and claim the islands for the sole benefit and authority of their respective nations. Nevertheless elements of court procedure and particularly the difficulties of linguistic diversity and translation in the court clearly lent themselves to such satiric portrayals.

The farcical nature of the Joint Court received its most thoroughly treatment in Edward Jacomb's 1929 satire *The Joy Court: Comédie Rosse*.[44] The play's title itself reflects a derisive local name for the Joint Court. These fictional accounts provide valuable insight into the functioning of the court, for they were produced by individuals with intimate knowledge of the judiciary and magistrates. As a British colonial employee turned Condominium critic, Jacomb became a vocal campaigner against Anglo-French governance of the New Hebrides. After a brief period in Fiji, Jacomb established himself as the assistant to the British resident commissioner in the New Hebrides, Merton King, in 1907.[45] His career with the civil service was short-lived and dominated by tense relationships with his colleagues and superiors. The fact that Jacomb did not shy away from condemning the shortcomings of the Condominium system and its officials (particularly the inability of many to speak both French and English) no doubt contributed to these tensions. He resigned in 1911 in order to establish his own legal practice representing ni-Vanuatu, a move that was to make him highly unpopular with the French administration, settlers and many local Britons and Australians.[46] Indeed, planter Tom Wright described him as 'an arch-blackmailer and a hypocrite whose sensibilities were only aroused by the dink of native gold'.[47] More generally the French accused Jacomb of extortion of money from ni-Vanuatu.[48] During Jacomb's private practice, British Resident Merton King barred the lawyer from attending British Residency functions for fear of causing offence to the French. Such were the fault lines in the European community within early colonial New Hebrides.

In *The Joy Court*, the fictional defendant Hughes, a lawyer, was modelled on Jacomb himself and his experiences when tried before the Joint Court. In January 1913, over seventy 'Mélé boys' from the Stuart and Wright plantation came to him with complaints about their treatment including being forced to work on Sundays, fines and floggings, payment in trade and tokens (instead of cash) and insufficient food and medical attention.[49] Jacomb feed the men who had come to Vila, while seeking new work for them and redress for their ill treatment. Yet soon after Jacomb had forwarded a formal complaint to the public prosecutor against Stuart and Wright, he found himself in court for illegal detention of their labour.[50]

On 1 July 1913, he was found guilty and fined £1 plus costs, though he and many British felt the case was unjust and '*au fond* … a struggle between the two residencies'.[51] Certainly the French administration appreciated it would be beneficial to them if Jacomb was convicted and disqualified from his practice representing ni-Vanuatu.[52] Stuart and Wright came before the court twice themselves between May and July on charges related to illegal recruitment and non-repatriation of labour, and in the first case were found guilty but fined just 5 francs.[53] These cases highlight the political divides of Port Vila, which spread into social life as French boycotted the monthly Club dinner, while most British members resigned in protest after the French entertained mixed-descent Robert Petersen Stuart at the Club.[54]

Even more scandalous was the incident that followed the murder of planter Emile Guitel on Epi in August 1913. In the absence of legal protection to prevent

European encroachment on ni-Vanuatu land and with land registration cases still months or years away, Jacomb had advised ni-Vanuatu to resist, with force if necessary, any attempts to dispossess them.[55] The French warship *Kersaint* arrested Sam Miley and others for the murder. French settlers in Vila were quick to connect Guitel's murder to Jacomb, and a confession made under duress by Jimmy Tamares seemed to confirm their fears.[56] The French requested the British sanction Jacomb, though Acting Resident Mahaffy, supported by Sir Edward Grey in London, refused.[57] However, the ni-Vanuatu were found guilty of murder, and Jimmy Tarames died in the French prison in Vila the morning of their trial. Though the men claimed they were subject to physical abuse and lack of food while in custody, no enquiry was held 'for the native complainants were not heard'.[58] The injustice of their treatment and the other events of 1913 provided impetus for Jacomb's first book, which was highly critical of Condominium rule.[59] Though Jacomb was disparaging of French colonialism, the French High Commissioner recognized that his book provided a true representation of the antagonistic situation in the New Hebrides.[60]

Around this period, Jacomb was the frequent subject of vitriol in the French press, particularly in the *Le Néo-Hébridais*.[61] The Société Française des Nouvelles-Hébrides also produced a report of over 100 pages detailing their complaints against Jacomb.[62] Jacomb's diaries and publications detail the 'petty insults' and feuds in the court over the use of English and French law, highlighting a lack of co-operation between both officials and participants, as well as what he saw as the 'French (or Latin)' bias of the court, the 'spite' and politics underpinning decisions.[63] He felt that 'all the Joint Court work could easily be done by a single magistrate', and that the high costs, closures and delays were unnecessary.[64] Many of his critiques related to the treatment of ni-Vanuatu, the subject of his books and correspondence with the Aborigines Protection Society.[65] Though he was hardly an objective or dispassionate observer, the situations he depicts resonate with the accounts of Thomson Reid Cowell, Robert Fletcher, Gilchirst Alexander and French Colonial Inspector Bougourd.[66]

The Joy Court was a part of a series of publications in which Jacomb aired his critiques of the Condominium.[67] Perhaps as his previous publications had failed to initiate the change he desired, Jacomb turned to drama and satire to unmask the flaws he saw in the system in a more arresting fashion. In the foreword, Jacomb articulated his aim to

> preserve for the delectation of posterity, in an approximation to photographic form, some few of the almost incredible inanities that happened before this

> Tower-of-Babel tribunal, which played at law in pretentious and portentous splendour on the sun-lapped coral shores of a distant Melanesian island. The author apologises for the vulgarity of his little play – but the Joint Court WAS vulgar.[68]

Set around 1913, the action revolves around a trial in which English lawyer Henry Hughes is brought before the Joint Court by M. Libéré, the French counsel representing two French proprietors from the Banks Islands, Messrs. Dupont and Dubois. Dupont and Dubois attempt to convict Hughes for a 'terrible smell' emanating from his house, the breathing of which resulted in a severe 'malady of the throat' and necessitated a lengthy and expensive trip to the Vila hospital. Accordingly, the two men claim costs of travelling from Banks to Vila, sixty-two days of hotel expenses, hospital expenses and damages for 'the material prejudice that they have suffered which also directly results from their … obligatory absence from their plantation for two long periods during which time fifty of their boys who have been working on their plantations for the past eighteen years ran away', particularly given the difficulties in obtaining labour in the colony.[69] From the outset, the amount claimed seems ridiculous to the reader in light of the evidently spurious accusation.

The audience in the fictional courtroom thinks otherwise: as Jacomb highlights, the overwhelmingly French audience of 'braves colons' have 'the eager air of hounds scenting blood'.[70] This description echoes a contemporary account from occasional court translator Robert Fletcher:

> The place is a seething pit of racial hatred, and every man, English and French alike, has his own pet grievance against some other fool.[71]

The fictional audience is convinced of Hughes' guilt before the proceedings begin and intractable attitudes of mutual distrust and dislike between French and British settlers are emphasized throughout.

The poor acoustics of the courtroom mean that the audience 'can only hear snatches of the proceedings, and know nothing of the merits of the case, they know, or know of, the accused, and so have no doubt as to his guilt'.[72] Here in another manner, we see how the content of the trial before the court was secondary to the performance and the imperial rivalries that dominated European colonial society in the New Hebrides. Indeed as one report on the colony confirmed, the enactments of the court 'represented, at one time, the great distraction of Port Vila'.[73]

The trial itself begins with the grandiose ritual of the judges' entrance but quickly descends into confusion as uncertainty over the appropriate procedure and functioning of English legal process emerges. In line with the defendant's nationality, English procedure should be followed. However, it quickly becomes evident that the French judge, the public prosecutor and M. Libéré are completely unversed in English law. The whole case then proceeds at a comically slow pace, hindered by the frequent need for translation, the public prosecutor's confusion over his role and debates over the admissibility of evidence in English law. At the earliest opportunity, the French judge cries for the panel to deliberate ('Délibérons!') and the judges retire, marking the end of scene.

Each scene ends in such fashion, indicating the lethargic approach to the dispensation of justice as well as the imprecision of the Condominium laws and of the judges' knowledge of them. The recurring fictional motif reflects contemporary frustrations with the Joint Court, as former British Judge Alexander recalled:

> On one occasion, I succeeded in getting the Court to sit every day for a week, but there was much shrugging of shoulders and upturning of eyes and heartfelt murmurs of '*beaucoup de travail*.'[74]

Indeed during 1913, for example, the court sat for just 24 hours a month, as well as being closed for periods of two months.[75] Overall, the play is characterized by inaction, with inordinately long periods of time spent on debating and recapitulating basic points of procedure. In this way the play echoes Alexander's complaint that the court was plagued by 'executive supineness or obstruction … needless over-elaboration of forms and procedure'.[76] While the accusations and evidence border on absurdity, it is the inept functioning of the court officials that contribute most to the farcical elements of the play.

The prickly exchanges between French and English judges modelled on their real counterparts add further drama, and caricature the challenging reality of the *entente cordiale*. In particular, the French judge is quick to take offence at the attempted interrogations of Hughes:

> *French Judge*. [*Rising.*] 'That is to say that you accuse the Commander of the French Police of falsification of documents. In these circumstances, you understand that I will not stay here and listen to a French official insulted in this manner! Deliberate!'[77]

In another instance, the frustrated French judge orders Hughes not to smile.[78] Scene IV ends in uproar and the French judge 'flounces' out of the court in protest, in the belief that Hughes has accused the French Commandant of lying and of casting religious insults.[79] By contrast, the British judge's accommodation in the play of all French demands reflects real frustrations local British settlers felt at the frequent acquiescence of long-standing British Resident Merton King to his French counterpart.[80]

Throughout the play, the prestige of the court and its officials is of utmost importance. On multiple occasions, the president orders Hughes that 'The Administration must be respected', effectively barring attempts to question or indirectly accuse Condominium employees, such as the police, of inappropriate or illegal behaviour.[81] In his defence, Hughes draws attention to the fact that the *milice française* had themselves defied the regulations of the Joint Convention in entering his house in his absence. However, his complaints are quickly quashed:

French Judge. 'It's a crime! I will not stay here to hear the French administration insulted in such a fashion!' [*Rises.*]
President. 'Chut! Chut! … M. 'Ug, you may defend yourself, but not by attacking the French administration.'
Hughes. 'M. le Président, we are in English procedure …'
President. 'Yes, but we are also in the Condominium!'[82]

The importance of respect for the Condominium, the dual administrations and their representatives thus looms above that of adjudicating the case at hand, following procedure and ensuring individual rights. The ready dismissal of individual subjects' rights is a bone of contention for the author, who proclaims in his introduction:

> Had some of those statesmen who had so light-heartedly created it without reference to such vital considerations, been compelled by circumstances to appear before it, either as plaintiffs or defendants, their experiences might have caused them (and their successors) to refrain afterwards from inaugurating similar grotesque tribunals in other parts of the world.[83]

Here Jacomb speaks from personal experience, not so much as a former Condominium employee but as a former defendant in the court.

The play ends questioning the validity of the proceedings and highlighting their absurdities. Defendant Hughes is convicted and fined. In response, Hughes requests summons against all parties involved in adjudicating and bringing the case, asserting he will find them all guilty of the very same offence for which he was just convicted. The curtains come down as the case adjourns, leaving a final impression of the judges' alarmed faces. The play did not receive the same level of attention as Jacomb's previous work but was nevertheless used as a means to discuss the limits and absurdity of the combined judiciary in newspapers from Sydney to Madagascar.[84]

The Joy Court centres on the administrators and judiciary, with little room for voices of ni-Vanuatu. Through a critique of the justice system and the limits of communication in the multilingual colonial courtroom, it also reinforced officials and Europeans' power to speak back against specific colonial structures but left colonialism itself unscathed.

Language and courtroom narration

As *The Joy Court* highlighted, language and translation were not only open to complaint and satire but also critical to courtroom performance across the New Hebrides, New Caledonia and Fiji. While French and English were the official languages of the courts, the diverse ethnic and linguistic divisions across the islands meant that translation was often necessary. Under-resourced imperial administrations were not well equipped with officials skilled in Indigenous languages, or those of Indian indentured migrants and other sojourners. The confidence of most officials in the superiority of European language, culture and law further compounded the issue, with proficiency in the lingua franca not required. Adapted from missionary descriptions of the New Hebrides archipelago with some hundred Indigenous languages, the characterization of the Joint Court as a 'tower of Babel' was particularly apt.[85] While the misunderstandings and incomprehension caused by difficulties in language, translation and cultural differences were easy to ridicule, the implications for those appearing before the courts were very real. As Taylor writes, 'the defendant, like the other evidence in the trial, was forced to be eloquent'.[86] Proficiency in speaking the language of the courtroom, including responding to the appropriate social, cultural and legal cues and expectations, was an important part of a successful performance as a trustworthy victim, defendant or witness, as further explored in the following chapter.

Lack of fluency either in Bislama or in English by French officials (and vice versa) was a bugbear for Jacomb; complaints appeared in both his published works and private correspondence. The issue creates one of the most amusing scenes in *The Joy Court*, when the French Police Commandant claims to have questioned his ni-Vanuatu *miliciens* (Indigenous constables in the French Police Force) despite not speaking a common language. When Hughes exposes the

French Commandant's inability to understand Bislama, instead of dismissing the French Commandant's statement, the French judge rebukes Hughes for mocking the court – 'M. 'Ug doesn't have the right to speak bêche-la-mer. We are not Canaques!' – and the president orders him to stick to the official languages, French or English.[87] For the French judge and the president, the trial was not about communication but about respect. Actors within the court above all had to demonstrate deference to the administration. As such, courtroom presentation became a theatrical act signifying hierarchy and authority, not simply communicating the facts, evidence or argument of the case.

While Jacomb's dialogue is imagined, the reality was not far from the mark. In his 1914 account of the political situation in the New Hebrides, he notes that forty-one out of fifty-four Condominium officials were 'for all intents and purposes' unable to communicate in the other official language of the colony, and close to none in Bislama, impacting on the efficiency and quality of the court's work.[88] As Miles argues, language was a key boundary-marker in both colonial and post-colonial Vanuatu, and this was epitomized in the Joint Court.[89]

The inability or refusal of the Joint Court to deal in the lingua franca Bislama illustrated another level in which the judiciary was ill-placed to adjudicate across the boundaries of race and nationality, and further hindered ni-Vanuatu access to the court system. The figures of the 'some hundreds of native witnesses in every variety of clothing and some without clothing at all' underline that ni-Vanuatu attempted to engage with the judicial process. Their presence was nevertheless described as 'picturesque' in the *Sydney Morning Herald*'s account of the Joint Court's circuit around some of outer islands in 1911. Roseby recounted to the newspaper that

> considerable patience, and resource was necessary in certain instances in arriving at the interpretation of their evidence. In some cases this could only be done by securing a native interpreter, who translated the evidence into 'pidgin English,' this being put into intelligible form by one of the clerks of the Court, who was an expert in that jargon, and finally interpreted into French by a third official for the benefit of the President of the Court and the French Judge. A great difficulty that the Court had to contend with was the looseness and inaccuracy of this 'pidgin English,' and on account of its exceedingly limited vocabulary one word was often capable of a dozen different interpretations.[90]

With three levels of translation, the process was clearly prone to misunderstandings and miscommunication. Amusing as the vignette was supposed to appear to readers, it reflected an assumed superiority of European language and perceived imprecision of non-European speech, rather than any serious effort to engage with the challenges of working across linguistic boundaries.

Parallel problems arose in Fiji as the first Indian lawyer in colony, D. M. Manilal, advised the Colonial Secretary in 1915:

> Time and again I have attended the Sessions of the Supreme Court of Fiji and I have often been impressed with the necessity of more correct interpretation of the Hindi language than we actually are accustomed to.[91]

Manilal cited the example of the verb *katal karna*, which he noted was often translated by interpreter Mr Kinderdine as 'to murder' when a more accurate and neutral translation would have been 'to cut up' or 'slaughter'. Even more seriously, he suggested that Kinderdine inappropriately jumped to the conclusion of a 'guilty' plea as soon as he heard the word 'yes' from the defendant, not allowing the accused to make their case or plead innocent.[92] Despite the gravity of the complaint, the minutes from the Colonial Secretary's office quickly dismissed Manilal's concerns. The official minute (signed CSP) replied:

> I have no reason whatever for supposing that [Mr Kinderline's] interpretation is not satisfactory. My knowledge of Hindi does not enable me to check the correctness of his work, but I am satisfied, from long experience, that if his rendering of Hindi into English and vice versa were seriously faulty my attention would have been drawn to the fact, and, even without a knowledge of Hindi, I can form a pretty good opinion as to whether witness and interpreter understand each other or at cross purposes. Misunderstandings must at times occur, but these are certainly not more frequent in the case of Mr Kinderline than with other interpreters. As regards what Mr Manilal says about pleas of 'guilty' there is no danger, with a judge who knows his business, of a plea of 'guilty' being attempted unless it is clear that the accused understands the meaning of the plea.[93]

Linguistic fluency was rendered irrelevant to this magistrate's ability to adjudicate. Appearances and interactions thus became critical to the magistrate's assessment of the situation and of the translation. The ability of either the interpreter (or the judge himself) was of little import, British identity signifying reliability. Again, the words themselves become secondary to the performance of accuracy and credibility on the part of the interpreter.

The courts were in constant need of interpreters and translators. Indeed, Gilchrist Alexander described Suva as 'a congerie of island nationalities' and the local Magistrate's Court thus offered, he argued

> a unique opportunity … of studying human nature in the raw. Before one passed a procession as varied in nationality and in colour as it was possible to imagine. I remember a case in which a China-man charged a Fijian with assault. An Indian witness gave evidence. We had three interpreters employed in that case. The Hindustani interpreter rendered the evidence into English. Then the Chinese interpreter took up the running, followed by the Fijian interpreter. On the same day in another case an Italian interpreter was employed. I can recall evidence been given on various occasions in French, German, Spanish, Italian, Japanese, Chinese, Hindustani, Tamil, Madrasi, various dialects of Fijian, and even in pidgin-English for a Solomon Island case.[94]

While the ethnological possibilities fascinated Alexander, the challenge of finding suitably qualified translators weighed upon the minds of the administration. In the New Hebrides, frequent delays were caused by a lack of individuals fluent in both French and English, let alone local languages. For example, in 1912 the dismissal of one inept translator left the Joint Court scrambling for a new interpreter so it could continue sitting.[95]

With all these shortcomings, colonial interpreters played a crucial role in mediating the way in which statements and pleas were translated and recorded in the legal archive. For example, the surviving depositions in the Fijian Supreme Court archives are all recorded in English. For the historian, the voices of Indigenous witnesses in the colonial legal archive are almost always mediated through often-unidentified interpreters and transcribers. Though the colonial courtrooms of the Pacific might have been theatres, not all the actors had equal footing as the judiciary favoured certain types of performances, narration and evidence. The focus on colonial authority and prestige minimized the importance and voices of Islanders and indentured labourers, while the inadequacy of translation frequently silenced the possibilities for real and effective communication in colonial trials.

The art of not listening in Fiji's plantation courts

As in the New Hebrides, the Fijian judicial system received critique from local residents and visiting observers in the early twentieth century. In missionary and observer reports, the treatment of Indian indentured labourers by the courts, the extremely high conviction levels and the perceived complicity between magistrates and plantations managers were all a concern and the subject of reproach.[96] A series of satirical vignettes of the Fijian courtroom published in 1921 by G. L. Barrow, a European trader resident in Colo West, illustrated the same criticism in a memorable fashion. Barrow's account also underlines that historical actors had a clear understanding of the weaknesses and biases of the judicial system.

The issue of communication cut to the heart of these scenes. Just as translation plagued the cosmopolitan colonial courts in the urban centres of Suva and Levuka, magistrates and officials proved adept at not listening and not hearing certain voices and certain versions of events. The first recounted various episodes involving the same Stipendiary Magistrate (SM). The scene begins at the magistrate's house at dawn. The official is still in his pyjamas when plantation manager Mr Sweetener arrives, and requests the arrest of a 'coolie fellow' for 'impudence'. The SM hands Sweetener his handcuffs, a symbol that magistrates were in the pocket of commercial interests, before Sweetener invites him for dinner. In the second case, the SM attempts to arrest, on a trumped-up charge, a free Indian labourer brought to him as a witness for the police: 'I don't care if he is a jury. Planting season is almost over, and I want another man very badly.' In the final case, the SM sentences labourers on the basis of evidence provided over the phone by their manager, though the charge is unclear: 'They are guilty of something; take them away.'[97]

Barrow concludes that 'It sounds ridiculous, but that was justice as she was extended to the coolie by one SM. The cases we instance are by no means exaggerated.'[98] In essence, it did not matter what the 'coolie' had said or had to say: that he spoke at all was sufficient to cast him as insolent. In these anecdotes, the collusion between officials and labour employers is evident, and European judicial and economic interests overlap. Though presented in dramatic manner, Barrow's account parallels other archival sources. For example, close social relationships between magistrates, labour inspectors and European planers raised questions over the objectivity of colonial justice in the minds of Indian immigrants: 'how could these coolie inspectors see our difficulties when they sat at our master's table and consumed brandy?'[99]

In another vignette, Barrow highlights the lack of impartiality on the part of presiding magistrates and the loose application of the rules of evidence:

Coolie on trial.	'All evidence has been heard.'
Magistrate to Prosecutor:	'Mr. –, I don't think there is enough evidence to convict, do you?'
Prosecutor:	'Oh, yes, there is.'
S.M.:	'You think so? Oh, very good. Six months each.'[100]

In the context of courtroom drama, this episode clearly highlights the reliance upon and weight given to certain voices in the trial at the expense of others. Like the earlier anecdote where the magistrate accepts without question the claims brought by manager Mr Phatdyner, the European actors in the colonial trial loomed large while the counter-narratives of Indian defendants, victims and witnesses were marginalized. Barrow's final dramatic sketch reinforces this point:

Coolie, battered and bleeding, to S.M.:	'I want to take out a summons against Mr. Woods for assaulting me with a horsewhip.'
S.M.:	'Mr Woods! Why, I know Mr. Woods. Just you tell him, *baboo*, that if he dares to take out a summons against Mr. Woods and he swears in Court that Mr. Woods assaulted him in that brutal manner, I will give him six months' imprisonment for contempt of Court.' (Exit coolie nursing a grievance.)[101]

Barrow concludes by situating the mistreatment and ignoring of Indian complaints as a potential threat to European security in the islands, with reform needed for this reason as much as to ensure equality and justice. His anecdotes nevertheless suggest that settlers were aware of the problematic and racist nature of the courts. However, as a trader in Colo West, Barrow has his own economic interests in critiquing the administration, and was desirous of less restriction upon Fijians' economic involvement and labour.[102]

Nevertheless, his accounts are borne out by court statistics. From 1885 to 1916, the conviction rate of Indian immigrants for labour offences ranged from 75 per cent to just over 95 per cent, with a large percentage (up to 40 per cent) of the adult indentured population convicted of an offence in any one year.[103] By 1915, reports reached India in the context of anti-indenture movement, prompting the Governor-General of India to express concern:

> The extraordinary high proportion of convictions to prosecutions is significant even in such simple cases as labour offences. It is alleged by the opponents of the system that justice is not done; that the coolie is largely in the hands of the interpreter who is apt to take the side of the employers; that magistrates are in many cases themselves employers, or necessarily favour the employers; and that the witnesses are servants of the prosecutor. Some of these facts are obviously true; but of the truth of others no authoritative evidence is forthcoming … But the possibilities of injustice which obviously

exist, coupled with the very high percentage of convictions, give rise to uncomfortable suspicions.[104]

In Barrow's account, the theatre of the court itself is less important than the use of bleak humour to critique the indenture system and the ongoing judicial prejudices after its end. He demonstrated who was given prerogative to speak and to be heard and believed in Fiji's plantation courts. In this account, the appearance of the actors was of utmost significance to the outcome of the incidents: the appearance of a 'coolie' – indistinguishable and interchangeable in the eyes of the SM – was enough to imply guilt, while the shared racial heritage and social standing of the magistrate and plantation managers underpinned an implicit bond of trust.

Conclusion: Humour as critique of colonial law?

The court was often a source and subject of drama in colonial Pacific life. In the New Hebrides Condominium, the theatre of colonial rivalries and prestige often sustained the court when it had limited casework and even less substantive authority. The function of the Joint Court was often to impress (or at least attempt to impress) colonial subjects with the power of imperial Britain and France despite its lack of effective jurisdiction. For critics of the Condominium, the pomp and ceremony of courtroom architecture and procedure was juxtaposed against the backdrop of the rough and ready township of Port Vila and limited reach of the state beyond Efate. The incongruity between the court and its milieu made it an easy target of ridicule. Both officials and observers drew attention to the farcical elements of the performance of the Joint Court, often with the aim of transforming the structure of the imperial administration. Humour was a strategy designed to discredit. However, satirizing had little effect, and perhaps there was little to do but laugh in despair at the inadequacies and inanities of the system. Instead, while the Joint Court delivered a semblance of law and order, other authoritarian forms of justice predominated outside the confines of the courtroom, explored in Chapter 6.

The connection between the court and theatre is not unique to the New Hebrides. But the frequency with which satirical, theatrical or humorous descriptions of the Joint Court and the Condominium appear in contemporary accounts and in the historiography leaves us with the question of how such depictions impact upon our understanding and analysis of imperial rule in the New Hebrides. Does the image of the Condominium as nothing more than a bumbling, ineffectual, and by implication harmless, Janus figure prevent us from fully appreciating the real negative effects and authoritarian nature of imperial rule in the New Hebrides? Such humorous accounts do not take seriously the impact of colonial law on Islanders. Indeed though intended to critique the Condominium courts, at some point the ability to find humour in proceedings only becomes sustainable if you ignore Indigenous suffering under the colonial system. As Nagriamal leader Jimmy Stephens described in 1991, 'The British and the French were like two wild dogs, fighting for a bone between them – and we were the bone … Each pulled the other in a different direction.'[105] For all its limits, the court, and the law it imposed or equally failed to impose, had a real impact on those brought to trial, or in the case of many Islanders, those denied the opportunity to bring their grievances to court.

Moreover, the performances were powerful in demonstrating a commitment to the rule of law in the islands, while acting as a smokescreen for other repressive aspects of colonial rule such as trials of ni-Vanuatu without witnesses or defence and violent naval expeditions. The image of the Joint Court as comical or farcical has also been perpetuated in the historiography, and often dominates accounts on law in the New Hebrides. This view needs to be problematized. We must also consider what a seemingly 'inept' judiciary enabled, and who this system benefited. There was efficacy in the inefficacy of the courts. Satire hid the more authoritarian aspects of colonial rule and the extent to which the Condominium employed illiberal and punitive measures throughout the islands, in spite of, or perhaps because of, the existence of the Joint Court.

Like Jacomb and Cowell in the New Hebrides, Barrow employed humour to highlight the persistent inequalities of the legal system in Fiji with a particular focus on the plantation courts. His dramatic anecdotes underline that the theatre of the trial itself was deadly serious for those involved, as the ability to subscribe to the norms of courtroom appearance and narration had real consequences for victims and defendants. This was particularly evident with regards to language in both Fiji and New Hebrides, as Jacomb, Manilal and Barrow all demonstrated how non-European defendants and witnesses were disadvantaged or even silenced on the basis of their race and their inability to speak the colonial languages of English or French.

Drawing upon observations made by a recent jurist, Katherine Fischer Taylor argues that 'a trial is two dramas, that of the case nested within that of the courtroom proceedings'.[106] The theatre presented in this chapter has been twofold: the performative nature of the judiciary itself and deployment of theatrical humour and satire to critique the judiciary. This chapter has nevertheless been primarily concerned with the drama of the proceedings and the procedure, while the following chapter considers the dynamics unfolding within specific cases of sexual crimes. Judicial theatre in the colonial courts served to reinforce European imperial authority, while the patriarchal theatre within specific cases of rape and sexual assault reflected and normalized masculine authority in both the court and domestic space. It is to these more intimate dramas and narratives we now turn.

Notes

1 Alexander, *From the Middle Temple*, 75. On Alexander: Cyril Glasser, 'In Foreign Parts: Reflections on British Lawyers Abroad', in Gavin Drewry and Charles Blake (eds), *Law and the Spirit of Enquiry: Essays in Honour of Sir Louis Blom-Cooper, QC* (London: Kluwer Law International, 1999), 187; Paul Swanepoel, 'Transient Justice: Colonial Judges on Circuit in Interwar Tanganyika', *Stichproben: Wiener Zeitschrift für kritische Afrikastudien* 13, no. 24 (2013), 69–70.

2 G. R. Le Hunte, Stipendary Magistrate, Loma Loma, to Colonial Secretary, 12 March 1877, CSO MP 77/330, NAF.

3 Joel Bonnemaison, *The Tree and the Canoe: History and Ethnogeography of Tanna* (Honolulu: University of Hawai'i Press, 1994), 94.

4 Miles, *Bridging Mental Boundaries*, 30.

5 R. A. S. Forster, 'Vanuatu: The End of an Episode of Schizophrenic Colonialism', *The Round Table: The Commonwealth Journal of International Affairs* 70, no. 280 (1980), 370; Jeremy MacClancy, *To Kill a Bird with Two Stones: A Short History of Vanuatu* (Port Vila: Vanuatu Cultural Centre, 1980); Andrew Stuart, *Of Cargoes, Colonies and Kings: Diplomatic and Administrative Service from Africa to the Pacific* (Oxford: Radcliffe Press, 2001), 133; Miles, *Bridging Mental Boundaries*, 29–30, summarizes these other terms.

6 D. L. Oliver, *The Pacific Islands* (Cambridge, MA: Harvard University Press, 1951), 178. See also 'Asterisk', *Isles of Illusion*, 76–8.

7 Oliver, *The Pacific Islands*, 178.

8 Sidney Abrahams, 'The Colonial Legal Service and the Administration of Justice in Colonial Dependencies', *Journal of Comparative Legislation and International Law* 30, nos. 3/4 (1948), 10.

9 The missing archives of the Services des Affaires Indigènes (SAI) limit what can be said in this study about the operation and impact of New Caledonia law on Kanak outside serious offences dealt with in Nouméa.

10 Etherington, 'The Gendering of Indirect Rule'.

11 Duff, 'The Evolution of Trial'.

12 Edward Jacomb, *The Joy Court: Comédie Rosse* (London: Braybrook and Dobson, 1929); Thomson Reid Cowell, 'Pandemonia, or a Franco-British Fantasy', MSS 0077, University of Adelaide Special Collections.

13 Rodman, *Houses Far from Home*, 31.

14 Jan-Georg Deutsch, 'Celebrating Power in Everyday Life: The Administration of Law and the Public Sphere in Colonial Tanzania, 1890–1914', *Journal of African Cultural Studies* 15, no. 1 (2002), 95.

15 On the importance of court performances in legally plural contexts, see Merry, 'Courts as Performances'. On performing legality in colonial land title and purchases, see Siobhan McDonnell, 'Exploring the Cultural Power of Land Law in Vanuatu: Law as a Performance That Creates Meaning and Identities', *Intersections: Gender and Sexuality in Asia and the Pacific* 33 (2013).

16 Thirty-eight per cent of Condominium budget spent on Joint Court in 1918, according to L. Bougourd à Ministre des Colonies, 9 décembre 1918, SG-NH Carton 31, ANOM; Bresnihan and Woodward (eds), *Tufala Gavman*, 41.

17 Rodman, 'Portentous Splendour', 479–514; and Rodman *Houses Far from Home*.

18 Margaret Purser, 'The View from the Verandah: Levuka Bungalows and the Transformation of Settler Identities in Later Colonialism', *International Journal of Historical Archaeology* 7, no. 4 (2003), 293–314.

19 Alexander, *From the Middle Temple*, 198.

20 Jacomb, *The Joy Court*, 7.

21 Count de Buena Esperanza, President of the Joint Court to BRC, 6/12/1910, Folder 80/1910, NHBS 1/I Vol. 1, WPA.

22 Alexander, *From the Middle Temple*, 189.

23 Quotes from Count of Buena Esperanza to Secretary of State for Colonies, 26/2/1926, Folder 51/1926, NHBS 1/I Vol. 2, WPA; and Manuel Bosch Barrett, *Tres Años en las Nuevas Hébridas 1936–1939* (Barcelona: Alqueria, 2009 [1943]), 126.

24 Edward Jacomb, *France and England in the New Hebrides: The Anglo-French Condominium* (Melbourne: George Robertson and Company, 1914), 195.

25 Van Trease, *The Politics of Land*, 63, 66; Margaret Jolly, 'Custom and the Way of the Land: Past and President in Vanuatu and Fiji', in Robert Borofsky (ed.), *Remembrance of Pacific Pasts: An Invitation to Remake History* (Honolulu: University of Hawai'i Press, 2000), 345.

26 Frédéric Angleviel and Max Shekleton, '"Olfala Pija blong Niuhebridis blong Bifo": Old Pictures of the Early New Hebrides (Vanuatu)', *Pacific Studies* 20, no. 4 (1997), 172, 174–5; Kate Stevens, 'Visualizing Violence and Performing Law: Postcards of the Kersaint in the New Hebrides', *New Zealand Journal of History* 52, no. 1 (2018), 69–89.

27 'Hebrides Murder', *Northern Advocate*, 17 November 1923.
28 Angleviel and Shekleton, 'Olfala Pija', 171.
29 Stevens, 'Visualizing Violence'.
30 Alexander, *From the Middle Temple*, 198.
31 Jacomb, *The Joy Court*, 7.
32 Swanepoel, 'Transient Justice', 72.
33 Katherine Fischer Taylor, *In the Theater of Criminal Justice: The Palais de Justice in Second Empire Paris* (Princeton, NJ: Princeton University Press, 1993); Elwin Hofman, 'Spatial Interrogations: Space and Power in French Criminal Justice, 1750–1850', *law&history* 7, no. 2 (2020), 155–81.
34 Taylor, *In the Theater*, 10. See also Yann Robert, *Dramatic Justice: Trial by Theater in the Age of the French Revolution* (Philadelphia: University of Pennsylvania Press, 2019).
35 Jacomb, *The Joy Court*, 9.
36 For example: Folder 115/1909 (Native Advocate (4 parts) 1909–24), NHBS 1/I Vol. 1, WPA on debates over the appointment, salary and housing of the Joint Court's Native Advocate; Folder 80/1910 (Joint Court – Requirements in re staff, equipment, etc.), Folder 39/1912 (Particulars of costs in various court cases. 1911–12.), Folder 119/1912 (Delay in hearing of cases before the Joint Court.), Folder 5/1913 (General Affairs of the Joint Court. (2 parts, five folders) 1913–14.), Folder 85/1913 (Police. Correspondence relating to stores, appointments, regulations, reports and arrests (3 parts in six folders) 1913–24.), Folder 18/1914 (Joint Court (10 parts in 17 folders) 1913–24.), NHBS 1/I Vol. 1, WPA; Folder 74/1924 (Return of and Expenses of, Count of Buena Esperanza. 1924), NHBS 1/I Vol. 2, WPA.
37 Scarr, *Fragments of Empire*, 233–4. On the non-collection of fines and reluctance to prosecute, see Folder 200/1908 (Regulations concerning the sale and consumption of alcoholic liquor. Joint Court cases re infringements (2 parts) 1909–12), Folder 77/1913 (Views held by the French Resident Commissioner with regard to prosecutions of French Nationals before Joint Court for Breaches of Convention concerning Recruiting of Native Labour), NHBS 1/I Vol. 1, WPA; Folder 14/1923 (Executions of Judgements of Joint Court under Protocol of 1914), NHBS 1/I Vol. 2, WPA; and on continued recruitment issues from 1908 alone, see Folders 102/1908 (Illegal Recruitment), 142/1908 (Marriage difficulty of certain natives. 1908–9), Folder 210/1908 (Complaint against Master of the French recruiting vessel *Tamarino*. 1908–9), Folder 211/1908 (Alleged illegal recruitment of two Tangoan girls. 1908–9), Folder 212/1908 (Proceedings of Salvan's Recruiting vessel in Malekula), Folder 242/1908 (Complaints as to illegal recruiting by Rev. Stenley Howard and F. J. Purdy. 1908–11), Folder 263/1908 (Case of illegal recruitment of two Santo women by Mr. F. Whitford in 1901. 1908–9), Folder 264 (Engagement of women and children. 1908–24. Regulation concerning employment of labour.),

and Folder 283/1908 (Joint Court – Appointments, Accommodation, Orders etc. (3 parts) 1908–14), NHBS 1/I Vol. 1, WPA.

38 Miles, *Bridging Mental Boundaries*, 29–30; William Stober, 'Isles of Illusion: Letters from Asterisk to Mowbray', *Journal of Pacific History* 39, no. 3 (2004), 361, 365; Service de l'Administration Générale – Rapport fait par M. Bougourd, 1918, SG-NH Carton 31, ANOM; Marcel Ludeau à Ministre des Colonies, Port-Vila, 29 octobre 1914, SG-NH Carton 8, ANOM; British Judge R. S. de Vere to President of the Joint Court, 27/11/1923, Folder 14/1923, NHBS 1/I Vol. 2, WPA.

39 Letter from Arthur W. Jose to Jacomb, 23 June 1913, MS 894/23 Edward Jacomb Diary 1913, SHL.

40 Rodman, *Houses Far from Home*, footnote 8, 213.

41 Cowell, 'Pandemonia', 26. According to the archival listing, 'Pandemonia' was performed at the fifty-year anniversary of Condominium rule in 1956 but I have found no further information about this performance to date.

42 Cowell, 'Pandemonia'.

43 Quoted in Service de l'Administration Générale – Rapport fait par M. Bougourd, 1918, SG-NH Carton 31, ANOM; 'Encore un arrêté commun. (Oh! combien!)' *Le Néo-Hébridais*, 25 octubre 1914.

44 Jacomb, *The Joy Court.*

45 For more detail on his career, see MS894 Edward Jacomb diaries and papers, 1907–55, SHL.

46 Note to letter from Mother to Charlie, 29/10/1908, MS 894/18 Edward Jacomb Diary 1907–8; Letter to Mother, 17/10/1919, MS 894/29 Edward Jacomb Diary 1919, SHL.

47 Entry for 31/1/1913, MS 894/23, Edward Jacomb Diary 1913, SHL.

48 'Rapport d'Ensemble sur la situation des Nouvelles-Hébrides en 1910', 20 avril 1911, and the various Rapports Trimestriels for 1913 and 1914, SG-NH Carton 11bis; Comissaire-Résident de France à Haut Commissaire, 12 octubre 1911, SG-NH Carton 7, ANOM.

49 Entry for 8/1/1913 and 31/1/1913, MS 894/23, Edward Jacomb Diary 1913, SHL.

50 Letter to Charlie, 24/02/1913, MS 894/23, Edward Jacomb – Diary 1913, SHL.

51 Criminal Action – No. 186 Public Prosecutor v Jacomb, 1 July 1914, Vanuatu Unreported Judgements Joint Court of the New Hebrides, Volume 2 (1913–15), http://www.paclii.org/vu/indices/cases/VanUnR_Cases2.html; Entries for 10/5/1913 and 27/7/1913; Resumé of Case Public Prosecutor and Stuart and Wright v Jacomb, MS 894/23, Edward Jacomb Diary 1913, SHL.

52 Extrait du rapport du Capitaine de Frégate commandant le 'Kersaint', SG-NH Carton 7, ANOM.

53 Ministère Public et Mtre Jacomb c MM. Stuart et Wright [1913] VUTM 39; [1913] No 183 (30 May 1913), Décision du Tribunal Mixte des Nouvelles-Hébrides, http://www.paclii.org/vu/cases/VUTM/1913/39.html.

54 From Jacomb's account it is unclear how much this protest was linked to the case or to the question of race. Entry for 4/4/1913, MS 894/23, Edward Jacomb Diary 1913, SHL.

55 Edward Jacomb to Monsieur Kaspar [Gaspard], Vila, 9 février 1913; Gouverneur à President du Tribunal Mixte, 5 août 1913; and Gouverneur et Haut Commissaire à Ministre des Colonies, 7 août 1913, SG-NH Carton 7, ANOM; Van Trease, *The Politics of Land*, 59.

56 Commissaire-Résident à Haut Commissaire, 8 août 1913; Bruenet à Ministres des Colonies, 19 juillet 1913 and Ministre des Colonies à Ministre des Affaires Etrangères, 12 août 1913, SG-NH Carton 7, ANOM; Newspaper clipping and 'Report of the Proceedings. Meeting of French Subjects held at the Doutreleau Hall at Vila, Efate, on 2nd December 1913', MS 894/23, Edward Jacomb Diary 1913, SHL; Jacomb, *France and England*, 121–4.

57 Sir E Grey to Paul Cambon (French Ambassador in London), 16 March 1914 and Ministre des Affaires Etrangeres à Ministre des Colonies, Paris, 22 octubre 1913, SG-NH Carton 7, ANOM; Van Trease, *The Politics of Land*, 59.

58 Jacomb, *France and England*, 123–6.

59 Ibid.

60 Gouverneur et Haut Commissaire à Ministre des Colonies, 23 novembre 1913, DAP Carton 1AFFPOL/1915, ANOM; see also R. J. Fletcher to Jacomb, [not dated, *c.* July 1918]. MS 894/28 Edward Jacomb Diary 1918–19, SHL.

61 For example, 'Nouvel Assassinat commis par des indigènes contre un blanc. Jacomb coupable d'excitation au meutre', *Le Néo-Hébridais*, 16 aôut 1913; 'Jacomb … Toujours Jacomb …' *Le Néo-Hébridais*, 13 septembre 1913; 'Notre Enquête sur l'affaire Guitel', *Le Néo-Hébridais*, 6 décembre 1913. See also 'Report of the Proceedings. Meeting of French Subjects held at the Doutreleau Hall at Vila, Efate, on 2nd December 1913', MS 894/23, Edward Jacomb Diary 1913, SHL.

62 Rapports addresses par Monsieur Vigoureux, Directeur de la S. F. N. H. à Haut-Commissaire (1915), SG-NH Carton 7, ANOM.

63 Entries for 12/7/1913 and 27/7/1913, MS 894/23, Edward Jacomb Diary 1913, and Edward Jacomb to Arthur W. Jose, 31/3/1914, MS 894/24 Edward Jacomb Diary SHL; Jacomb, *France and England*, 106–10.

64 Letter to A. W. Jose, 25/10/1915, MS 894/24 Edward Jacomb Diary 1915 SHL. See also 28/10/1907, MS 894/18 Edward Jacomb Diary 1907–8, SHL.

65 Entry for 26/8/1913, MS 894/23 Edward Jacomb Diary 1913; Entry for 2/4/1914 MS 894/24 Edward Jacomb Diary 1914, and Appendices to MS 894/26 Edward Jacomb Diary 1916, SHL; 'The New Hebrides Problem' and 'The Annual Meeting', *The Anti-Slavery Reporter and Aborigines' Friend* 4, no. 2 (July 1914); Folder 122/1913, NHBS 1/I Vol. 1, WPA.

66 See Alexander quoted this chapter; and President du Conseil, Ministre des Affaires Etrangères à Ministre des Colonies, 1 avril 1914, SG-NH Carton 5, ANOM; Service

de l'Administration Générale – Rapport fait par M. Bougourd, 1918, SG-NH Carton 31, ANOM; Letter from R. J. Fletcher, 10 February 1918, MS 894/28 Edward Jacomb Diary 1918–19, SHL.

67 Jacomb, *France and England*; Edward Jacomb, *The Future of the Kanaka* (London: P. S. King and Son, 1919).

68 Jacomb, *The Joy Court*, foreward.

69 Ibid., 20.

70 Ibid., 8.

71 'Asterisk' (Robert James Fletcher), *Isles of Illusion: letters from the South Seas*, edited by Bohun Lynch (London: Constable, 1928 [1923]), 67.

72 Jacomb, *The Joy Court*, 8.

73 Service de l'Administration Générale – Rapport fait par M. Bougourd, 1918, SG-NH Carton 31, ANOM.

74 Alexander, *From the Middle Temple*, 190.

75 RC to President of the Joint Court 17/2/1913, in Folder 5/1913, NHBS 1/I Vol. 1, WPA.

76 Alexander, *From the Middle Temple*, 187. See President du Conseil, Ministre des Affaires Etrangères à Ministre des Colonies, 1 avril 1914, SG-NH Carton 5, ANOM, for a French critique.

77 Jacomb, *The Joy Court*, 31.

78 Ibid., 40.

79 Ibid., 43.

80 Scarr, *Fragments of Empire*, 229.

81 Jacomb, *The Joy Court*, 42, 44.

82 Ibid., 42.

83 Ibid., foreward.

84 'The Court of Babel', *Sydney Morning Herald*, 6 July 1929; 'Georges Courteline aux Nouvelles Hébrides', *La Tamatave*, 5 août 1929 and *L'Echo de Tananarive*, 7 août 1929.

85 'Asterisk', *Isles of Illusion*, 67, 76–8.

86 Taylor, *In the Theater*, 47.

87 Jacomb, *The Joy Court*, 45–7.

88 Jacomb, *France and England*, 82–4. See also *Bulletin du Commerce*, 12 Octubre 1918, in Service de l'Administration Générale – Rapport fait par M. Bougourd, 1918, SG-NH Carton 31, ANOM.

89 Miles, *Bridging Mental Boundaries*, 5.

90 'New Hebrides. Joint Court. The Picturesque Side. Land Titles', *Sydney Morning Herald*, 28 December 1911.

91 D. M. Manilal, Rewa, to Colonial Secretary, 13/5/1915, CSO MP 4241/15, NAF. See Lal, *Broken Waves*, 46–8; and Hugh Tinker, 'Odd Man Out: The Loneliness of the Indian Colonial Politician – the Career of Manilal Doctor', *Journal of Imperial and Commonwealth History* 2, no. 2 (1974), 226–43, for brief biography of Manilal Doctor in Fiji.

92 D. M. Manilal, Rewa, to Colonial Secretary, 13/5/1915, CSO MP 4241/15, NAF.

93 Minute from CSP to His Excellency, 19/8/1915, MP 4241/15, NAF.

94 Alexander, *From the Middle Temple*, 59–60.

95 'Asterisk', *Isles of Illusion*, 66–7 and 76–8.

96 C. F. Andrews and W. W. Pearson, *Indian Indentured Labour in Fiji: An Independent Enquiry* (Calcutta: Star Printing Works, 1916), 29–30.

97 G. L. Barrow, *Fiji for the Fijians: A Protest and a Plea* (Korolavu, 1921?), 4–5.

98 Ibid.

99 Sanadhya quoted in Naidu, *The Violence of Indenture*, 59; Gill, *Turn Northeast*, 38, 43–5.

100 Barrow, *Fiji for the Fijians*, 5.

101 Ibid.

102 Lal, *Broken Waves*, 52; James Heartfield, '"You Are Not a White Woman!" Apolosi Nawai, the Fiji Produce Agency and the Trial of Stella Spencer in Fiji, 1915', *Journal of Pacific History* 38, no. 1 (2003), 74.

103 Naidu, *The Violence of Indenture*, 56–7.

104 Governor-General of India in Council to Secretary of State for India, Department of Commerce and Industry, Simla, 15 October 1915, Council Paper No. 36 1916. Indian Immigration. Correspondence with Secretary of State relating to – In continuation of C. P. No. 12 of 1916, NAF.

105 Interview quoted in Miles, *Bridging Mental Boundaries*, 29. From 1967, Stephens lead the Santo-based secessionist movement that was particularly concerned with preventing the appropriation of ni-Vanuatu lands and was based around a rejection of European practices and their replacement with 'kastom'.

106 Taylor, *In the Theater*, 4.

3

Bodily and narrative performances in the court

Witness:	'He's a dirty, mean little wretch, your honour; a low –'
Magistrate (sternly):	'Silence!'
Witness:	'Well, your honor, it's the truth.'
Magistrate:	'It doesn't matter. We want none of it here.'[1]

This page filler, printed in the *New Hebrides British Association Gazette* in 1912, suggests the colonial settler population in the New Hebrides Condominium were aware of the tenuous relationship between justice and truth. Clearly much was else at stake and at play in the colonial courts aside from establishing the truth of an accusation. As Kali Israel argues, 'the entire court system depended on the telling of stories, and the divorce court relied especially on the elicitation of sexual stories'.[2] Her statement equally applies to cases of sexual violence heard in the colonial courtrooms of the Pacific.

This chapter examines the relationship between truth, justice and narration in trials of sexual crimes from 1875 to 1920. Moving beyond the critiques of courtroom farce, it explores how colonial power operated in trials and how participants navigated the nuanced hierarchies in play. Just as judicial rituals were critical to the authority of the court, specific cases required performances from victims, defendants and witnesses. The court was one of few arenas where female victims had an opportunity to articulate their experiences, and non-European defendants contested colonial ideas of guilt, violation and intimacy in relation to marriage and sex. However, I argue intersecting hierarchies of gender and race and concepts of morality shaped the accounts of individuals under investigation or on trial, their perceived credibility and the judicial outcomes. In contrast to the scepticism about the reliability of Indigenous and female witnesses, medical evidence was given greater weight in the trial process from the late nineteenth century, reflecting trends in Britain and elsewhere in empire.

The key archive for this chapter comes from the Supreme Court of Fiji, where surviving files for specific cases include the transcribed depositions from complainants, defendants and witnesses. These files provide a unique body of historical evidence: they are often more detailed than comparative newspaper reports of the criminal court sittings. Moreover, no parallel records have currently been found for New Caledonia or the New Hebrides Condominium. The Supreme Court files examined include depositions for rape, attempted rape, carnal knowledge, attempted carnal knowledge and indecent assault, as well as other serious violent crimes, though this paper trail was often fragmented. Verdicts and sentences were not always recorded in individual files (particularly after 1889), complicating efforts to assess longer-term patterns and trends in rape and sexual assault cases and the relationship between evidence, testimony and the outcome. Alongside the issue of non-reporting, magistrates chose not pursued many cases beyond the lower courts. For example, magistrate Valla requested instruction on this matter from the Colonial Secretary, noting that

> many cases occur from time to time, some of them are actually rape, but I find that so far, the cases sent to the Att Gen. have not sufficient evidence in his option to ensure a *conviction* for rape and in consequence the accused is dismissed with absolutely no punishment – even for assault.[3]

The cases that did progress to the highest court nevertheless offer insight into how official and local ideas about sexuality, morality, race and gender intersected and diverged through the types of proof and testimony required from complainants and defendants. Cases of rape centred on questions of vaginal penetration and consent. Indecent assault covered cases of sexual assault short of penetrative rape, with charges similarly requiring proof of a lack of consent, though the physical evidence required for conviction was less clearly defined. Carnal knowledge – the charge for rape or indecent assault of (female) children – specified that if the victim was under sixteen years or, more commonly, under twelve or thirteen years, the question of consent was irrelevant.[4] Only physical proof of the assault was required, though this could be problematic to establish in the courtroom setting.

The adversarial nature of the trial resulted in the narration of differing versions of the same violent incident. The expected detachment and objectivity of judges in assessing traumatic stories was part of the 'construction of imperial white masculinity', as Jonathan Saha demonstrates in colonial Burma.[5] The job of the judge or investigating magistrate (as well as assessors or jury) was thus to disentangle the facts and establish the truth in order to make judgement. As Nancy Erber and George Robb discuss with regards to British and French *fin de siècle* court cases, 'although narrative competition waxed intense, there remained a strong, and typically Victorian, desire for a single truth or meaning'.[6] Thus, in contrast to Chapter 2, the court and presiding magistrates were positioned as 'anti-theatrical' in individual cases, while defendants, witness and lawyers were compared 'to actors, predisposed to subterfuge … the court's role [was] to distinguish play-acting from truth'.[7]

Establishing truth was particularly fraught in cases of a sexual nature, due to the perceived difficulty of establishing consent and ambiguous interpretations of physical evidence. Cases of sexual crime thus involved both physical evidence and moral judgement, shaped by gendered, racialized hierarchies of knowledge, respectability, behaviour and reliability. Underpinning these trials was the pervasive influence of Hale's warning that 'rape is … an accusation easily to be made and hard to prove, and harder to be defended by the party accused, tho never so innocent'.[8] Hale drew attention to his (unsubstantiated) fears of false and pernicious rape accusations, arguing the importance of a fresh complaint and corroborating evidence. As many contemporary commentators and historians on rape acknowledge, such implicit distrust of women's testimony disadvantaged female victims in British and French courtrooms and frequently focused attention on the victim's actions, morality and credibility.[9] The female body had to be proved innocent in cases of sexual crime.

In the colonial court, racialized assumptions about the reliability of non-Europeans were overlaid upon the broader mistrust of female testimony. Non-European women were 'doubly suspect suspects'.[10] The 'native' witness was variously portrayed as either deceitful and untrustworthy, or naïve, confused and therefore unreliable. Non-European and Indigenous actors were perceived as unable to contribute to, and excluded from, an increasingly masculine and 'scientific' legal project on the basis of empire-wide concepts of racial difference. These perceived differences were themselves the products of an increasingly rigid and scientific discourse of race, further contributing to a damaging cycle that reinforced colonial hierarchies within the courts.[11]

The court's ability to produce justice free from such hierarchies was considered laughable by indentured Indian labourers. As Jadnandan Singh reportedly told a missionary, 'The Court! The Court! There is not justice there – not for the man who speaks the truth.'[12] Despite claims to objectivity and equality, the trial centred on gender and racial identities as well as their performance. As Singh implied, speaking the truth was not enough to achieve justice if one was not European. The perceived reliability of different individuals, and individuals' ability to conform to the gendered and racialized behaviour expected of victims and defendants, shaped the unfolding trial to create a nuanced hierarchy of truth amongst those testifying before the court.

Defining credible witnesses

Colonial legislation defined who had the power to speak in Fiji's court at all, as well as who would adjudicate depending on the crime and participants. Both racism and official perception of racial bias among colonists shaped these laws. The early colonial administration felt that Europeans in the colony were unlikely to adjudicate fairly on trials involving Fijians and Europeans. The Criminal Procedure Ordinance of 1875 legislated for trial by the Chief Justice with the aid of assessors (whose advice was non-binding) instead of juries in cases involving a Fijian defendant or victim, though juries were allowed in 'all-European' cases.[13] The provision for trial by assessor was extended in 1883 to include cases involving Indians, Chinese and other Pacific Islanders.[14] This legislation vexed settlers, who believed trial by jury was their unequivocal right as British citizens.[15]

Nevertheless, both juries and assessors were solely comprised of colonists. Juries of seven were selected from English-speaking men over twenty-one years with annual income over £50 and no serious convictions, while assessors were chosen from an annually published list of men who were 'qualified by their education and character' in the judgement of senior officials.[16] In practice, the panel of two to five assessors operated like a jury, though 'the whole purpose of dispensing with the jury was to allow the judge, if necessary, to counter any racial bias by overruling the opinions of the assessors'.[17] Whereas in nineteenth-century India, trial by jury was intertwined with liberalism, in Fiji trial by judge and assessors was enshrined as a key tenet of humanitarian imperial rule.[18]

Testimony was to be taken from any witnesses considered relevant to the case, with practice following the British High Court. Depositions could be used in cases where a witness was unable to be present. All proceedings were to be in English, with any other testimony interpreted.[19] Subsequent regulation enabled the court to hear 'native' testimony without taking an oath (which it was felt not all Fijians understood) from 1883 and to 'protect' young witnesses before the court. For example, 'native' women and children under fourteen could not give evidence before the Supreme Court unless 'accompanied by such persons as necessary for her or its protection.'[20] Under an 1889 amendment, the evidence of girls or children of 'tender years' could be accepted without an oath if magistrates deemed them 'possessed of sufficient intelligence … to understand the duty of speaking the truth.'[21]

Despite these limited, paternalist attempts to mitigate colonial bias, both Indigenous Fijians and indentured Indians were the subject of discourse that equated whiteness with credibility and rationality; non-whiteness with unreliability. This discourse enabled colonial law to 'enunciate equality while fabricating a racial taxonomy through which to operate unequally'.[22] Racially specific but shifting understandings are evident in official reports, public commentary and implicit in the cases themselves. Writing in 1910, missionary John Burton described Fijians as among 'the most law abiding subjects of empire'. In his opinion, Fijians were 'not naturally truthful' but this was a cultural characteristic: 'A man must be cautioned not to speak *vakaviti* – after the manner of Fiji – else he may not even attempt to put accuracy into his statements.' However, this was attributed to the 'natural disposition to oblige', rather than a deceitful character.[23] Other official reports characterized Fijians as honest to a fault in court. Indeed, one 1884 report commended 'the excellent moral régime enjoyed in this Colony by its native race'.[24]

However, according to Governor des Voeux, the influence of cultural contact and 'vakapiritania' ('the British way') had quickly had a troubling impact upon Fijian interactions with the justice system. As early as 1881, he reported that 'native criminals are now, though slowly, learning to defend themselves by lying, and in time native prisoners will doubtless endeavour to regain their liberty by breaking gaol'.[25] Given the colonial aim to protect and preserve Fijian society from such changes, the pernicious infiltration of outside influence was the subject of official anxiety. Des Voeux's account reflected and was bolstered by similar concerns aired in the Bose Vakaturaga. By contrast, Burton argued that Fijian character and morality had improved under mission tutelage. Nevertheless, he asserted that Islanders' tendency towards lying and licentiousness remained just below the surface.[26] Both officials and missionaries saw the honesty and morality of the Fijian as under threat, either from the detrimental influence of Indian immigrants or the breakdown of traditional authority.

Others, including some magistrates and European settlers, were much more critical of Indigenous witnesses. A prominent example of the disjunction between the colonial executive and local magistrates occurred in *Aromasi et al. v G. B. Evans and J. Rannie*, the first civil case taken by Fijians to the Supreme Court in 1877 for fraudulent recruitment. The Kadavu magistrate originally dismissed the case, but in the Supreme Court the plaintiffs' claim for the cancellation of their labour contracts and damages succeeded. Chief Justice John Gorrie wrote:

> I have no sympathy with what seems to have been the ground of the decision in the case before the Magistrate ... that we are not to believe the evidence simply because it comes from native witnesses. I have heard that often argued in regard to negroes, and Indians, as well as now in regard to Fijians, and if a Judge were to allow himself to be led away by such arguments, it would simply mean that the native races were to be left as the prey of white men.[27]

This case suggests that the protectionist stance held by Governor Gordon and Chief Justice Gorrie did not necessarily extend to colonial officials serving under them. Doubtless not all magistrates were so dismissive of Fijian complainants, but individual views on race varied in ways that had a critical impact in the courtroom. The outcome of the Aromasi case outraged the settler public, whose ire was stirred by the local press.[28]

Appeals to European public opinion were a common strategy for colonists who found themselves convicted for crimes against Indigenous Islanders in early colonial Fiji. For example, in 1882, Henry Lee published a pamphlet attacking the colonial justice system and demanding that his conviction for assaulting a Fijian be investigated. He complained of his undignified treatment imprisoned alongside Fijians and overseen by a Fijian gaoler. The disgruntled European defendant protested that 'a greater degree of reliance' was placed upon Fijian testimony than on his own. This, Lee argued, was problematic because Fijians had a less rigid view of the truth and were more susceptible to undue influence:

> The education and instincts of the Fijian have not up to the present time impressed upon his mind the sanctity of an oath, and it is a recognised fact that pressure of circumstances, more particularly the influence of a chief, will induce him to depose to any statement however ridiculous.[29]

Lee's frustrations and his scathing perception of Fijian witnesses, fellow prisoners and gaolers highlight the limits of protectionist ideals outside official circles. His assessments of the 'native' character were common among fellow settlers and fed into local frustration with the colonial administration for seeming to favour the Indigenous population.

Given settler racism, jury trials could lead to what officials called a 'miscarriage of justice', such when an all-white jury acquitted Patrick Scanlon of the murder of his 'Polynesian' labourer in 1877. Solomon Island labourer Masiomo died after a flogging by Scanlon. Finding the legislation unclear, the Chief Justice had bowed to pressure to allow a jury trial, which acquitted Scanlon on the ground he acted in self-defence.[30] In 1875 a jury acquitted two Europeans for the death of twenty-four 'Polynesian' labourers in their care, having failed to provide adequate food or shelter.[31] These cases likely fed into the expansion of trial by assessor for a wider range of non-European subjects in 1883. Lawyer Edward Jacomb reiterated the problem with jury trials in Pacific colonies, following the acquittal of Arthur Ashton in Suva for assault at his Havannah Harbour plantation in the New Hebrides. He argued that lawyer Scott got Ashton off 'but I believe that he would have got off undefended – for records of similar cases here show that it is almost impossible to secure a conviction of a white man for the killing of a native'.[32] To demonstrate jury bias, Jacomb collected statistics on convictions and acquittals (Table 1).

Table 1 Criminal trials in the colony of Fiji from 1887, tabulated by Jacomb in 1907[a]

Trials before …	Total number of cases	Convictions	Acquittals
Jury	17	3	14
Assessors	10	5	5

[a] Note from 14/10/1907, MS 894/18 Edward Jacomb Diary 1907–8, SHL. Jacomb created this table in 1907 for a letter to the Western Pacific Herald about the merits of trial by assessor in certain contexts.

Colonial officials faced another challenge: how to appropriate adjudicate upon Indigenous cultural and social practices criminalized under the new legal system. One prominent example of this arose over the Native Regulation criminalizing abortion and attempts to procure abortion.[33] This legislation arose out of concerns over the decreasing Indigenous population, problematically linked to maternal behaviour.[34] Officials expressed concern that this law would be impossible to fairly enforce, because such cases were

> full of intricate native technicalities and the interpretation is often extremely difficult more especially when native midwives are permitted to fully express what they know.[35]

Intimate practices were considered to some extent unknowable to European officials, despite their judicial power over such cases. Local magistrates, supporting by Native Stipendiary Magistrates (NSMs) and chiefs, were often considered better able to navigate the complexities of local custom than judges in Suva or Levuka, though the relationship between European and Fijian magistrates could be a fraught one.[36]

The other objection to the abortion legislation related to the perceived problem of obtaining clear testimony from Fijians more generally. According to Allardyce:

> Native witnesses under the most favourable conditions have a diffiulty [*sic*] in publicly stating facts as they saw them; many are extremely nervous after being on oath more especially when there is a sprinkling of Europeans in the Court, and least of all can they stand being badgered by a lawyer or lawyers. Under cross examination by a lawyer it frequently happens that they become so bamboozled that they really do not know what they are saying and straightway contradict and deny what they have already said.[37]

He concluded that 'the cross-examination of Fijians by lawyers goes far to defeat the ends of justice'. The practices of the European court were considered frequently at odds, if not fundamentally incompatible, with the behaviour and legal understanding of Fijians.

European Stipendiary Magistrates (ESMs) and NSMs were mutually critical of the other's neutrality and judgement, causing tension over who had the right to administer justice. Both acted beyond their official mandate at times: the NSMs and chiefs used their discretion in bringing charges for sexual and other offences based on local relationships and rivalries, much to the chagrin of European officials for whom this contravened principles of impartiality. Similarly, ESMs occasionally dispensed summary justice for criminal assault or carnal knowledge in the Provincial Courts when their authority to do so was questionable, while their interpretations of Fijian custom triggered complaints from chiefs and NSMs. At core lay questions about the purpose of colonial law: whether it should impose European practices and ideals of justice and morality, maintain order in local communities, or shore up Indigenous custom and chiefly power. The answer differed depending on the magistrate. Indirect rule enabled colonial agents, Fijian and European alike, to administer justice with limited effective oversight from central authorities, and the resulting practices did not always align with the statute books or expectations from the colonial capital or London.[38] Incidents of abortion, adultery and sexual assault and the debates they provoked illustrate the limits of British law over intimate Fijian lives and, 'reading against the grain', are suggestive of the many sexual and moral crimes that occurred beyond the purview of the courtroom.

Colonial perceptions of indentured Indians witnesses framed them as a foil to the 'naïve' Indigenous population. John Burton wrote:

> The mendacity of the race makes it difficult to make any impression upon their life and character. The class of people in Fiji, especially, are steeped in falsehood. Often, it is true, they lie so artistically as almost to provoke admiration. Tears of innocence trickle down injured cheeks whenever any fault is complained of. Indian evidence in court is practically valueless if there is nay other opposed to it. Often when the litigant has a really good case he spoils it by trying to strengthen it with lies.[39]

Before the rise of anti-indenture movements forced some reappraisal in the 1910s, a wealth of unfavourable traits were routinely associated with the indentured Indian community, providing catch-all explanations for the ills of plantation life. In the courtroom 'the majority of overseers and stipendiary magistrates thought in terms of stereo types [*sic*], stressing the necessity to maintain strict discipline and not to show weaknesses before the Indians'.[40]

More generally, Burton stressed the perceived incompatibility of Indian temperament with rational English procedure: 'The oriental has somewhat primitive and summary ideas of justice, and cannot understand our calmer and slower methods.'[41] The very high level of Indian convictions and extremely low rate of success in cases where Indian labourers brought charges against their employers indicate how such bias played out in the courts.[42] Employers brought more cases against labourers and had much higher rates of successful convictions than vice versa: close to 10,000 versus 311 cases brought from 1890 to 1897, with 82 per cent versus 35 per cent convictions.[43]

Indian labourers were quite aware of this bias. They were observant of the personal relationships between European officials, plantation owners and managers, and how these muddied the waters when it came to judicial neutrality. As Totaram Sanadhya noted, distrust and suspicion of officials, including those supposedly employed to oversee labour and living conditions for indentured Indians, prevented some individuals making complaints against their employers:

> In every district a coolie-inspector was appointed by the Immigration Department, to look after our welfare, but how could these coolie inspectors see our difficulties when they sat at our master's table and consumed brandy?[44]

The problem was also recognized by some colonial administrators in 1885, who argued against the practice of holding courts at planters' houses.[45] However, some thirty years later overt friendships between plantation overseers and the Immigration Inspectors and magistrates were still observed by Colonial Sugar Refining Company employee Walter Gill, who noted the problematic reliance of colonial agents upon the hospitality of the very managers and overseers against whom labourers' complaints were directed.[46] Unsurprisingly, the neutrality of magistrates and labour inspectors was brought into question by the close social interactions with employers. Coupled with the high success rate of charges against labourers, this enhanced Indian immigrants' belief in their inequality in colonial law and deterred them from bringing claims before the courts.

The issue was compounded by the unequal opportunity and ability of indentured Indians to present their case against European employers comparatively well-versed in law and fluent in the English language and norms.[47] For example, in 1900, Immigration Inspector James Harper reported from Labasa on a case in which overseer R. A. Harricks was accused of assault upon a 'poor defenseless woman'. Though Harricks had a record of violence, he presented himself as 'mild and inoffensive' before the magistrate. In fact, he had successfully defended himself against all previous charges. One Indian woman complainant even found herself convicted of conspiracy and jailed instead after bringing a complaint against an overseer. Expressing his distaste for violence, Harper asserted, 'I did not intend to stand on one side and see Immigrants loose [*sic*] their cases and expenses owing to their inability to conduct them properly in court.'[48] In the absence of any lawyers to represent Indians in the colony before 1912, Immigration Inspectors such as Harper provided a rare settler voice highlighting the disadvantages that Indians faced before the colonial judiciary.

While court cases in colonial Fiji mainly involved Indians or Fijians, European settlers and other Pacific Islanders occasionally featured as complainants, defendants or witnesses. Like Fijians, 'Polynesian' immigrants (in fact predominantly from the New Hebrides or Solomon Islands) were deemed of good character. Low levels of crime were appreciated in Blue Book reports on 'Polynesian Immigration':

> Away not only from his own island, but often separated from his former associates and protectors, he feels no reliance in his own ability to look after his private interests, and, as a matter of fact, rarely goes to the slightest trouble to secure them. If, as in the great majority of cases, the immigrant be free from innate vice and the employer an upright man, the relations between them may be compared to those of a confiding passenger towards the skilful commander of a vessel at sea. This influence is probably conducive to the paucity of crimes found in the registers of the Courts recorded against Polynesian immigrants.[49]

The seemingly childlike 'Polynesians' were characterized as exemplary subjects of empire when under the tutelage of 'benign' Europeans. Furthermore, the

'Polynesian' was reputedly a model prisoner, in contrast to non-cooperative Indian prisoners.[50]

Some Europeans came under scrutiny from the colonial administration for interfering with the justice system. In particular, conscientious Immigration Inspectors (for they were not all so) as well as visiting anti-indenture campaigners frequently expressed disquiet about managers of Indian and Pacific Island plantation labourers. Overseers were variously accused of preventing witnesses coming to court, and bribing sirdars or other employees to provide false testimony.[51] The same overseers were vocal in their criticism when they felt that their judicial rights were impinged. Other officials supported their grievances. Chief Medical Officer William Macgregor complained:

> The ruling idea is that the employer of a black or brown man is a cheat and a conspirator. Anson cannot see that men are under a contract, and that there are reciprocal obligations. Men are persecuted, worried by inquiries irritated by interference and that too often over such trifles. A genuine case of bad treatment is far from common here.[52]

Despite potential tensions, bonds of race, language and education tied administrators and planters together into a social network in the small colony. Consequently, some magistrates were reluctant to rock the boat, while the economic influence exerted by the Colonial Sugar Refining Company provided the company with much political influence. These factors meant that while critiques of European behaviour in the court were articulated in official correspondence, little was done to address the imbalance of power.

Comparative trial records for the New Hebrides Condominium and New Caledonia are limited for this period. However, official correspondence suggests similar discourses regarding the reliability of Islanders' testimony shaped courtroom experiences. As early as 1899, a naval captain reported that ni-Vanuatu 'lie in the most systematic manner' and would shift responsibility for a crime depending on local tribal alliances and enmity.[53] In contrast, in 1919 Jacomb wrote:

> Every one … who has had any experience of courts of law where native and white interests come into conflict knows quite well it is as hard in a case of alleged murder to secure the acquittal of a native as it is to secure the conviction of a white man … Facts are usually capable of being interpreted in different ways, and it is always easy to mistrust the word of a native, and hard to doubt that of a white man.[54]

He argued patronizingly that the 'Kanaka' was 'too simpleminded' to fabricate and lie when charged with a crime. As in Fiji, there were a variety of attitudes to ni-Vanuatu and their reliability and honesty.

Gendered prejudices were also clearly at play. A 1929 memo noted that an 'excessive' amount of the New Hebrides Native Courts' time was occupied with adultery charges, and that even unmarried men and women were convicted. Alongside legal reform of the definition of adultery, the writer focused on the question of evidence. Magistrates were advised:

> In cases of adultery it is desirable that the evidence of the accused in relation to his or her partner in guilt should be in some way corroborated, otherwise great injustice may be done. To convict on the uncorroborated evidence of a woman puts any man at the mercy of a woman who chooses to say that she has committed adultery with him – by doing so, she can, at a cost to herself of 15/s (the fine for a first offence) ensure that any man who has before been convicted of adultery, shall be sentenced to 90 days imprisonment without the option of a fine. This is a dangerous weapon to put into the hands of a native woman.[55]

This statement suggests a strongly gendered suspicion of ni-Vanuatu motivations and honesty in bringing adultery cases, and the need for corroboration focuses on women. Paralleling Hale's warning against false rape accusations, ni-Vanuatu women were characterized as vindictive.

Unlike Fiji, the use of medical evidence in rape cases was considered 'impracticable or even impolitic' in the New Hebrides. Determining the accuracy of the charges again rested upon an assessment of character:

> The burden of proof of 'Seduction' by the male, and of virginity in the female should be borne in every case by the complaining parties … 'virginity' may be 'proved' by the testimony as to good previous moral character of the girl given by a number of respectable persons who know her well, and also may frequently be corroborated by the tactful cross-questioning of the girl herself, though this alone will not suffice.[56]

In contrast to the professionalization and increasing turn to the expert elsewhere, ni-Vanuatu complainants and defendants were to be assessed on morality and respectability. As in Fiji, intimate knowledge over Islanders' lives was considered key but problematic in criminal cases, and race entangled with gender in these narratives.[57] These examples highlight the limits to, and the prejudices underpinning, colonial and legal knowledge of Pacific societies. But the Condominium judiciary did not often give ni-Vanuatu the opportunity to speak, so for the remainder of this chapter we return to the Fiji Supreme Court.

Indigenous voices in the colonial court

Entrenched stereotypes of non-European character and behaviour coloured the reception of Fijian, Indian and Pacific Islander complainants, witnesses and defendants in the courtroom. In this context, only certain stories of violence progressed through the judicial process to trial in the Supreme Court of Fiji. Many victims chose to avoid the courts altogether, while magistrates were selective in the cases they forwarded. When they chose to engage with the colonial legal system, each complainant's case was filtered through various levels of the judicial process, from reporting to depositions heard by the local court before being dismissed or forwarded to the Supreme Court. Consequently, the narratives of violence in the legal archives were heavily structured by the court process. As Jonathan Saha eloquently describes:

> The historian is confronted with the details of terrible crimes and traumatic events that are rendered in the detached language of an imperial judge. Where the testimonies of survivors have been preserved, these passages are often framed, picked apart and occasionally undermined by this surrounding legalistic prose.[58]

Despite their traumatic nature, many incidents of sexual violence described by the victims were almost formulaic. Women likely 'calibrated' their accounts to meet courtroom expectations, as Thornbury describes in South Africa.[59] Common elements included the isolated location (in remote gardens, paths or sugar cane fields), the use of force, and attempts (often stifled) by the victim to cry out or resist the assailant. For example, indentured labourer A described her rape by a fellow labourer at Vucimaca Estate in 1910:

> On Wednesday last … the accused came up to me about 1pm. He asked me to have connection with him. I told the accused to shut up and not to talk like that. He then took hold of my hand, knocked me down pulled up my cloths and had connection with me. He put a cloth on my mouth to prevent me calling out. I tried to call out … Lachmi came. Then the accused got off me and ran away. I reported the matter to the sardar.[60]

Given the reluctance, difficulties and suspicion often associated with such complaints, these common elements were critical in shaping which cases successfully proceeding from initial complaint, through the lower courts to trial in Suva or Levuka. This trend resonates with findings of rape and sexual assault trials from colonial India, New Zealand and the Cape Colony as well as nineteenth- and twentieth-century England. Moreover, in the courtroom arena the leading actors in a trial were often the offender and the officials.[61] Performing authority took precedence. Rather than giving voice to the variety of victims' emotional experiences, trials represented those incidents that most closely embodied the strict legal definition and prevailing cultural perceptions of rape.

Nevertheless, when faced with insinuations or direct slurs against their morality in court, both Indian and Fijian women stood up for their virtue. In the trial of R and N for rape, victim S, an indentured labourer of the Vancouver Sugar Company, testified that 'I am not a woman of loose character. I am not in the habit of alluring any men to have connection with them. I swear that with the exception of my man and the accused no one has had connection with me since my introduction to Fiji.'[62] In some cases, this was not necessarily sufficient to allay the court's suspicions, as in *Rex v OK*. Because the attack occurred at a *meke* (dance), concerns were raised about the character of victim, as did the accused's statement that he and accuser V had consensual intercourse previously. OK was acquitted.[63]

Occasionally, victims provided a brief glimpse of the physical or emotional impact that the violence and the subsequent reporting process had upon them. Many victims and witnesses mentioned they felt afraid to report the crime, especially if the offender was a chief or an overseer. For example, Fijian woman S told the court she had been sent by the accused ER to bring the fifteen-year-old victim Em to him. She said she did this because she 'was afraid as [ER] is a big chief'.[64] Others focused on the physicality of the attack. For example, in 1917 K highlighted the physical violence of rape, describing how the accused 'lifted her bodily', 'fisted' her thighs and shoulders so she was 'rendered weak and he overcame me'.[65] By contrast, M emphasized her fear of S, stating, 'When near I saw the expression of his eyes were not good. I was afraid and ran away.'[66] R, an indentured labour viciously assaulted and raped by a group of men on the plantation one night in 1907, described feeling she was 'silly' and lost her senses after the attack.[67]

Women articulated the sense of shame and resultant suffering caused by sexual assaults and drew attention the court's attention to the emotional as well as the physical violence of the attack. After describing her physical wounds, rape victim TB said simply, 'My mind also is in pain.'[68] In an 1881 rape case, witness S reported that Solomon Islands labourer L told her the accused, 'M has forced me and made a fool of me.'[69] Tokelauan woman K said, 'A Fijian has insulted me as if I were a pig.'[70] These accounts go beyond a description of the assault itself to hint at the devastating physical and psychological effect of sexual crime. Other accounts focus on the physical act alone, though it is unclear whether this reflected an inability or unwillingness to articulate emotional suffering before a magistrate or in the public courtroom, or that the process of translation and transcription of their testimony obscured the victim's tone and emotion.

Despite the constraints in their retellings, all these women 'chose to voice … the wrongs done against them, while being fully aware that by exhibiting such agency of efforts to negate others' agency, they could invite further violence.'[71] Some women who did speak out in court found themselves on trial again – literally – for perjury. In 1886, on the recommendation of the assessors, N was sentenced to eighteen months hard labour for making a false charge of rape against *sirdars* D and L on Nakoroqaqa plantation in Rewa.[72] Disentangling the conflicting accounts between N, D and L was difficult and, on cross-examination by the magistrate, N claims she lied on the promise of money from G. While N's conviction may have indeed been a rare case of false rape accusation that Hale warned of, it most likely spoke to colonial stereotypes of the mendacity and mercurial nature of Indian women.

Contested concepts of guilt in the courtroom

Defendants contested both the details of the accusation and its legal interpretation, providing insight into the tensions between legal and social meanings of consensual and non-consensual sexual intercourse. While many accused made no statement or reserved their defence for the Supreme Court trial, those who made statements used the opportunity to debate the interpretation of legal concepts. In a number of cases, Fijian, Islander and Indian defendants pleaded not guilty yet implicated or admitted to their role in the crime. Such cases demonstrate an ongoing divergence between understandings of what constituted criminal or unacceptable behaviour, as well as the limits to the knowledge, spread and acceptance of colonial concepts of legality, guilt and responsibility.

Compared to other crimes, defendants in rape and sexual assault cases appear to have been particularly willing to challenge colonial law. For example, in the Supreme Court criminal sitting of Tuesday 2 May 1876, fifteen Fijians appeared before the court for seven different charges including rape, obtaining money under false pretences, manslaughter, larceny and breaking gaol. The seven men charged with two instances of rape were the only ones to plead not guilty.[73] Similarly, missionary Burton cites a case of an Indian indentured labourer who was careful to specify that, though he killed his adulterous wife, he did not murder her. Her infidelity seemingly justified his actions.[74] In another example, Fijian man B pleaded not guilty to the murder of V's husband R in 1883, on the grounds he was acting on V's request and that the deceased 'troubled' and threatened his wife. The court did not accept B's defence: he was found guilty and sentenced to death.[75]

An 1886 case suggests a conception of guilt that separated intention from action.[76] Two Polynesian labourers Mk and Mt appeared before the Supreme Court, charged respectively with raping and aiding and abetting the rape of Santo woman V of the Maqo Island Company's Tabuca plantation.[77] On 5 September, V was heading towards Vaqa to collect bananas when the two accused grabbed her, carried her into the trees and pulled her down. She explained to the magistrate for Lau, Swayne, that Mt held her arms as Mk raped her. V cried out, successfully calling the attention of her companions R and T, who served as witnesses for the prosecution. In his defence, Mk expressed his confusion regarding the charges her faced:

> I do not understand this. Yesterday I took this woman's legs. J___ took her hands. We laid her on the ground I tried to have connection with her but I failed. I did not have connection with her.[78]

His co-accused Mt reiterated Mk's assertion: the failure to achieve penetration made the charge inappropriate while also seeking to minimizing the impact on V. Their accounts prioritized the action of completed intercourse in defining rape as a crime, ahead of the motivation, intention or attempt at intercourse that were all important from a British legal perspective. The men were both found guilty, with Mk sentenced to nine months hard labour and Mt to six months hard labour. The relatively short sentences indicate the defence may have some bearing on the judges' decision in spite of witnesses supporting of V's account.

Other cases demonstrated unexpected interpretations of the role of British law and courts. Indian labourer G felt that the government must protect him when he found himself before the court charged with carnal knowledge in 1917: 'I have nothing to say except the Government have brought me from India and is my father and mother and may protect me.'[79] The possibility of conviction also loomed large in the mind of one Fijian defending himself on a charge of rape in 1881. Defendant K showed both fear for the potential power of the law and a simultaneous disregard for it when accused of raping his cousin WR on the road on 22 January 1881. WR reported the attack immediately to her husband, who was an officer in the village. Witness S reported that defendant K told him:

> I took hold of the woman and she began to cry and I let go her hand again. Then he said in my own mind now I have take hold of this woman and let her go again perhaps she will go and make a charge against me and I shall get punished for nothing I may as well have her fully.[80]

The outcome was not reported in the Supreme Court file, but the evidence reveals K's understanding of colonial justice: if he might be accused, he may as well have actually committed the crime. His actions may also have reflected his concern with village dynamics, as he was surely aware of the official role and relative power of WR's husband. K's statement shows a conscious evaluation of the possible legal consequences of grabbing and raping WR.

Such evaluation was also evident when Sm refused to help his friend Sa in catching his wife in the act of adultery with E. Sa was accused of clubbing and wounding E after seeing his wife enter the victim's house. Sm refused to get involved, stating, 'this is the time of law. It is the duty of the ovisa and the husband'.[81] These cases underline the way in which concepts of colonial law and its reach were present in the minds of Fijian men by the early 1880s, though they intersected with rather than displaced other factors that shaped sexual and domestic crimes and their reporting, such as village hierarchies.

Magistrates found it particularly challenging to determine the boundary between acceptable and coercive sexual relationships in cases where the accused claimed some form of engagement or marriage with the victim in local custom. For example, when Mk of Viria in Rewa was arrested for rape in 1915 he was surprised, for he claimed that fourteen-year-old Ma was his wife. However, Ma denied this and asserted she would not have gone with him to work in the bush if she had known what he intended to do.[82] In *Rex v N and VS* in 1916, the Buli Matailokau reported a rape to Wesleyan minister Taito Raukuni. Raukuni implied such cases occurred as older customs had not been fully replaced: 'It was a former practice in Fiji if a woman refused to cohabit with a man to shut them both up together until he had had his will of her.'[83]

Fijian rape-accused Ma's view of marriage was at odds with European ideals when tried in the October 1886 Supreme Court sitting. MVC was fishing for prawns with Me when they encountered the defendant on the path carrying taro. Ma appeared again when the two women had cast their nets into the stream, at which point Me ran away – presumably fearful of the man's intentions. Ma took MVC by the hands and said, 'we will go together'. MVC told the magistrate that she tried to talk him out of it, but Ma took her off into the bush, threw her down and raped her at knifepoint. In his account Ma revealed a view of marriage in which sexual intercourse could make a woman one's wife:

> I remembered M___ was a widow. I thought I would go and take her for my wife and go to the law when enquiry could be made ... She did not refuse me ... I took the woman to be my wife.[84]

His view of the incident reflected customary practice of elopement by young Fijian couples where parents disapproved of the union. MVC countered Ma's claims, stating that, as the accused was her father-in-law, sexual connection was prohibited by custom. She further noted Ma was worried by how his actions would be perceived by 'the law'. Addressing him directly, she noted, 'You were not afraid to force me while in the bush. I ask you to go into the town but you forced me here.'[85]

Despite MVC's prompt reporting and Me's corroboration of events leading up to the rape – factors that would often support a conviction – Ma was found not guilty. No medical evidence was presented, but aside from this it is difficult to assess the grounds on which this case was dismissed. The Chief Justice may have found it problematic to adjudicate since claims to Indigenous customary practice and taboos featured prominently in both sides. The trial demonstrated a collision of values in marriage and sexual relationships, not only between Fijian and European but also between defendant and victim. Brereton discusses incidents that posed similar challenges for the first Chief Justice John Gorrie, such as imposing a death sentence for uxoricide on a 'Polynesian' labourer when such an act may not have been a crime on his home island, and a 1878 rape case where the accused was the cousin of the victim and may have therefore had sexual rights over her as a potential wife.[86] In such cases, magistrates had to decide the limits of protectionism when local custom was unclear and potentially contradicted British law and values.

Trials involving Indian indentured labourers also involved thorny assessments of morality. As John Kelly analyses in a 1907 rape case, the defendants suggested that the Indian victim was a prostitute. This narrative aligned with pre-existing stereotypes, and introduced sufficient doubt that the men accused were acquitted.[87] Other prominent trials featured young Indian girls married to or cohabiting with older men on the plantation. One such case, an accusation of carnal knowledge, came to official attention in 1891 when J, an Indian labourer, tried to register his marriage to ten-year-old A.[88] These cases were often taken to court by the girl's family, reflecting divisions within the Indian community on the appropriate age of marriage and consent. An 1892 example saw labourer C charged with carnal knowledge on M, a girl of less than thirteen years.[89] M and C had cohabited for around eight months when M's mother A brought a charge against the defendant. A stated that while she was present at their marriage two years prior, she did not consent to C living with M, as her daughter was still too young.

Age of consent was also the key issue in the 1881 trial of *Rex v J* for indecent assault.[90] Eleven-year-old D was married to the accused a year prior and had cohabited with him on Mr Tucker's plantation for six weeks. D's mother explained that the girl had been sent to cook for J and nothing more, but D told magistrate Alex Eastgate that she lived and slept with her husband, though full penetration had not occurred. J's earlier accusation to policeman John Forster against Mr Tucker for raping D complicated the case. This charge was discharged when Forster arrested J, presumably on the basis of his wife's young age. In magistrate's court, J pleaded guilty to indecent assault and was committed to trial in Levuka. However, in the Supreme Court eleven days later he changed his plea and was found not guilty. On the available evidence it is difficult to assess the truth of J's accusation against Tucker, why J changed his plea or the reasons behind the court's acquittal. However, the case highlights that the police officer was quick to dismiss the charges made against the plantation manager and equally quick to arrest J despite no complaint having been made against him. Forster sought to protect D from sexual relations as a minor but also reinforced with commonly held prejudices about Indian mendacity.

Relatively few cases of interracial rape or assault appeared the Supreme Court. The most common were between indentured Islanders and Fijians in Suva, given its more cosmopolitan population. By contrast European men rarely faced trial. Until 1920, there were just seven cases brought against European men for the abduction, rape or carnal knowledge of Fijian and Indian women or children, and no cases for the years between 1876 and 1897.[91] In the first case of a European man on trial, JB was found not guilty of the abduction of a Fijian girl N. At the heart of the case was the question of whether her family had the authority to prevent her departure and whether JB had taken her to work in good faith.[92] In 1898, TF was found not guilty of carnal knowledge of twelve-year-old K, despite the fact the girl had given birth to a visibly mixed descent ('half-caste') infant.[93] Though there were witnesses supporting the prosecution, overseer JMJ was found not guilty of rape at Batinika, Navua, as another overseer's alibi placed them together at the picture house.[94] Such acquittals, and the comparatively light sentences imposed in the few cases successfully prosecuted, suggest a leniency towards European men.

A number of cases had European or mixed-descent children, and occasionally women, as victims. In one case, R of Cavanadi village was charged with the rape of JS, a mixed-descent woman who spoke some Fijian and resided in Muanicula with William Henry Chapman. JS reported encountering R and refusing his advances on the road when returning home from her uncle's house. Chapman and JS's sister, Anna, provided evidence based on a physical examination of JS's genitals. R pleaded guilty and was sentenced to three years hard labour.[95] This pattern was largely typically of rape and assault cases in Britain or other colonies, as customary practice or marriage could not be used in mitigation of the accused's actions. The protection of white women generally overrode notions about their perceived propensity for false accusations when the accused was a man of colour.[96]

European children, some very young, were the victims of sexual assaults more frequently than adult women. In 1904, G, indentured at Labasa, was found guilty of carnal knowledge. The victim was the three-year-old daughter of mill manager William Gosling. There were no eyewitnesses, but Dr Farrington reported finding seminal fluid on the child's labia and on the accused. The age and race of the victim saw a long sentence (seven years' penal servitude) imposed.[97] Indeed, in the rape or assault of particularly young victims, longer sentences were generally imposed regardless of race.[98] In these cases, the home was a space of vulnerability: a site of intimate interaction but also of policing and anxiety. Domestic servants, household visitors and family members were frequently cited as defendants in charges of carnal knowledge.[99] Indeed, cases of interracial sexual crime almost exclusively involved European children and non-European domestic servants. The disquiet of the European parents of young victims echoes Stoler's work on anxieties over domestic space in the Dutch East Indies.[100] Overall, the large number of sexual cases involving child victims is striking. This likely reflects their vulnerability, official perceptions of innocence linked to age that were somewhat independent of race, and the role family played in bringing complaints.[101]

Medicalization and moralization of gender violence

Faced with conflicting testimony, 'unreliable witnesses' and the challenges of navigating between British law and local cultural norms, medical evidence presented in rape and sexual assault cases seemingly provided magistrates with a clearer path to establishing the facts. Donald Denoon writes, in the context of colonial depopulation theories, that

> by invoking Western science, doctors reinforced the colonialist dichotomy between rational administrator who enjoyed access to western science and technology, and irrational native who had to make do with superstition.[102]

The late nineteenth century similarly saw the emergence of 'scientific' methods of criminology in Britain and France, with growing emphasis placed on expert testimony such as that of medical professionals.[103] These trends are echoed in the colonial context. While the focus here is Fiji, medical examinations were also considered increasingly important in determining rape cases in New Caledonia.[104] 'Scientific' evidence was a prominent element of many, though not all, trials for rape and sexual assaults.

Colonial medical officers (District Medical Officers or DMOs) provided expert testimony for numerous cases of rape, and especially carnal knowledge, in the Fiji Supreme Court. On occasion, Fijian or Indian women, Fijian midwives or Native Medical Practitioners also presented the results of a physical examination but were increasingly displaced by European medical officers after the turn of the century. Between 1875 and 1882, there were between four and ten medical officers across the colony. In 1891 there were eight DMOs, increasing to eighteen by 1921.[105] Some simultaneously acted as magistrates in the colony, indicative of their overlapping roles and influence.[106]

On the basis of physical examinations of the victim and, more rarely, of the accused, DMOs provided their opinion firstly on whether penetration had occurred and to what extent, on the basis of the size of the victim's genitals, any swelling or bleeding and the presence or absence of a hymen. They also commented upon any other marks of violence or assault on the body that might indicate a struggle, and frequently drew attention to the absence of bruises or scratches to imply that intercourse was consensual. On occasion, the presence or absence of venereal disease was used to infer the likelihood of sexual contact between individuals.

The centrality of medical testimony is evident in Supreme Court case *Rex v RB*.[107] Complainant OK was the nine-year-old daughter of P and a European man named FM. Around 6.00 pm on Wednesday 3 August 1910, she was in the empty labourers' house at Korovatu playing with her younger two siblings while her mother cooked in the kitchen some fifty yards away. Soon after, RB, a local Fijian man indentured at Korovatu, entered. OK told the Labasa Police

Court that she picked up her infant sibling and made to leave, when the man took the child from her and carried OK to the bed. Pulling her pinafore up, her *sulu* down and stuffing his own white *sulu* in her mouth to prevent her cries, RB 'then had connection with me gently. He did not penetrate far and his semen was spent on my two thighs'. Her mother P arrived as RB wiped OK's thighs clean with another *sulu* and, hearing her approach, he scrambled to cover himself with a mat.

P questioned her daughter. After hearing OK's account, she approached RB about the incident. According to P's statement, RB was reluctant to answer but after repeated questioning stated, 'Yes, it is true. I got on to her but I did not have connection: it is true I have committed an offence.' When questioned again while working the plantation the following day, RB asserted the incident 'was O___'s fault; she comes into our house and plays with Leweni [another labourer] and I indecently'. The degree to which OK participated and encouraged such sexual interactions would be a key focus in the court proceedings. RB disappeared when P went to Mr Mess at the store in Naqiqi to write a letter to Police Inspector Stanlake, but was found and arrested the following day in Labasa, and brought before the Labasa Police Court on 10 August 1910.

The testimony centred on the accounts of the victim OK and her mother P, as well as the expert testimony provided by Labasa DMO, Gilbert Emerson Arnold. These depositions were forwarded to the Supreme Court under the charge of carnal knowledge, where Acting Chief Justice Ehrhardt heard the case on 21 September. The accused's plea and statement are missing from the Supreme Court file, but RB was found guilty and sentenced to eighteen months hard labour and twenty lashes. The facts of the case were not in question. RB admitted what had occurred to P but tried instead to place guilt and responsibility on OK by insinuating she frequently sought to play 'indecently' with the Fijian labourers. OK firmly denied this on RB's cross-examination, stating, 'I am not in the habit of going in there every day and pulling down my sulu and lying on the bed and playing with you.' The differing narratives presented by the prosecution and defence hinged around OK's purported history of sexual interaction with the accused. *Rex v RB* is thus a clear example of the way in which sexual cases frequently centred on the actions, comportment and character of the victim, even when of a very tender age.

The expert testimony of DMO Arnold is striking for his assessment of OK's morality and sexual behaviour extrapolated from his physical examination of the child. On 5 August, two days after the assault, Arnold first questioned OK and, with her permission, performed a genital examination in the presence of Constable Orisi. Presenting his findings, Arnold emphasized his belief that OK demonstrated bodily knowledge and behaviour beyond her years. Surprised by OK's straightforward and open responses to his medical questions, the DMO reported he was

> struck by her extreme precocity. She showed an intimate knowledge of all sexual matters about which she spoke in a matter-of-fact and deliberate way like a woman of the world; in a perfectly serious, and not ribald, way.

OK's lack of reserve and her articulate understanding of sexual matters was problematic to the European DMO, who clearly felt that a child of nine could not and should not have such intimate knowledge except if gained through sexual experience. Louise A. Jackson calls this 'the paradox of innocence': 'A girl who really was innocent and virtuous should be ignorant of the language and meaning of sexual acts and would, therefore, be unable to articulate what had happened to her.'[108] In speaking out about her experience, OK contradicted gendered expectations about modesty and ignorance of sexual matters: the very act of speaking out against the perpetrator implicated her own character.

Arnold also reported on his physical examination of the girl's genitals. He noted that OK's hymen was intact and genitals too small for full penetration, but found the vulva 'deep and dilated', a state consistent with OK's description of the molestation. Arnold further noted 'considerable redness and signs of irritation of the whole of the genital organs', yet these facts did not add weight to his view of the likelihood of assault. Instead they lead Arnold to conclude that, despite OK's denial, 'the child is sexually precocious and has probably been addicted to the habit of masturbation and possibly incomplete intercourse with boys and men'. Although Arnold notes it is only an opinion, the physical examination was used to support the DMO's initial hypothesis of sexual precocity. Far from its purported objectivity, the medical evidence was marshalled to support a moral judgement.

Arnold concluded to the court that 'I found her condition to be consistent with both their [OK's and RB's] stories.' Yet the overwhelming tenor of his statement, and the frequent references to the girl's precocity, favoured RB's insinuations that OK was a Lolita of sorts: sexually mature and encouraging of inappropriate intimacies with the older labourers. Ultimately RB was found guilty: OK's tender age meant that the question of consent was irrelevant to the charge. However, the narrative of sexual precocity likely contributed to the relatively short sentence. Although the charge related to RB's carnal knowledge of OK, both the expert testimony and the accused's statements instead focused the court's attention on

OK's own sexual knowledge, suggesting her responsibility in participating or even encouraging sexual interaction. Although RB was convicted, the outcome came down to the fact that OK was a minor and thus the question of consent was not salient.

Rex v RB provides a particularly clear example of the way in which the body often needed to, in Elizabeth Kolsky's words, 'evidence the crime'.[109] Her analysis of rape trials in India shows that physical evidence (semen, broken hymen and bruises or scratches as signs of a struggle) was needed to support the victim's statements and obtain a conviction in court cases that pitted a female Indian victim against a male European (or on occasion Indian) accused. In Fiji, a lack of supporting physical evidence could similarly be detrimental to a victim's case. In some cases, medical evidence contributed to a reduction or dismissal of the criminal charge.[110] In the trial of Indian man R for carnal knowledge and indecent assault, George Augustus Lynch, the medical officer in Suva, found that, despite her pain in walking, 'there were not any marks of violence about the private parts' of eleven-year-old victim P.[111] R was consequently found guilty only of the lesser charge of indecent assault, and sentenced to six months hard labour. DMO Charles Hirsh encapsulated this view in *Regina v P et al.*, where he argued that 'if one or more tried to ravish a vigorous woman against her will that even if they should succeed in spite of her strong opposition … there would be some marks of violence'.[112]

Some medical officers stuck closely to the physical evidence furnished by their examination of the victim, which could support the victim's case in a more straightforward manner. In *Rex v B*, resident officer at the Colonial Hospital Lynch confirmed 'external marks of violence' around the body and vagina of eleven-year-old victim R, helping secure a conviction. B was sentenced to nine months' hard labour with twenty lashes.[113] S was sentenced to five years penal servitude and twenty-four lashes for carnal knowledge of L, seven-year-old daughter of HW in 1907, after the medical officer at Kadavu Hospital recorded evidence of bloodstains, semen, a broken hymen and pain and inflammation around her privates.[114] In another 1910 case, the strong physical build of the two men led DMO William Ramsey to conclude rape was possible, supporting their conviction.[115] In other cases, the inconclusive nature of medical evidence was irrelevant, given the strength of other evidence. In a particularly horrific gang rape at the Vatamai Estate, six of the ten accused received sentences of ten to twelve years penal servitude despite the fact the lack of a microscope meant that Superintendent of Lautoka Hospital William Baddeley was unable to complete an accurate physical exam.[116]

While it was often influential, the impact of medical evidence and the outcomes of rape cases in Fiji was not always clear cut or consistent. RB's trial nevertheless highlights the prioritization of medical interpretation over the voices of Indigenous subjects and the ways in which race and gender prejudices inflected the trial. It also demonstrates the way questions of the child's morality were deployed even when not relevant to the charge. Though consent was immaterial to carnal knowledge cases, it was nevertheless often discussed at length.

Conclusion

In the courts of Fiji, as in other colonies, perceptions of gender differences intersected with, and were overlaid by, concepts of racial difference to create hierarchies of truth and credibility in the courtroom. The increasing use of, and the high esteem according to, medical expert testimony in rape and sexual assault cases rendered the colonial court as a rational space. The establishment of British legal practice in Fiji coincided with the growing professionalization of courts and the turn to science and forensic medicine, and more rigid categorization of race. In the theatre of the colonial court, those actors with the ability to present their evidence in terms of scientific and rational, and by implication masculine and European, knowledge therefore had louder voices in the archives, in the trial and often in determining the outcome of rape and assault cases. Yet medical evidence was imbued with ideas about morality, as accounts of physical examinations moved from anatomical description to assessments of personal character and sexuality read upon the female body.

Victims and non-European witnesses and defendants could be excluded from this 'scientific' conceptualization of the court by virtue of their irrationality and excitability, their violence or mendacity. These characterizations were flexible: to missionaries, Indigenous Fijians could be increasingly honest despite the spectre of their 'savage' past; or increasingly corrupted by cultural contact as some officials and chiefs feared. The result was a reduction of possible courtroom narratives that could successfully be told in cases of sexual violence. Fijian, Islander and Indian women's accounts of their experiences were often factual in nature and frequently betrayed little of the full impact of violence on the victim. The recurrent elements in their narratives are striking, and reflect women's strategic, situational agency to voice their suffering with an awareness, and sometimes rejection, of colonial power structures.[117]

Given the low rates of reporting and the many rape and sexual assault cases not brought to trial, the cases in the Supreme Court often conformed to similar narratives that reflected a limited idea of true victimhood: an isolated location, a struggle, silenced cries for help and sometimes eyewitnesses or supporting medical testimony. As Caroline Strange has demonstrated, a 'defendant's fate was thus closely linked to the stories he told and the stories that were made of him, his victim, and the crime'.[118] The influence of Hale's warning and perceptions of female deceitfulness reached into the Pacific, restricting the experiences of sexual assault that could be told and believed in the colonial court. Among these restrictions, complainants nevertheless took the opportunity to speak of their experience of violence, and show glimpses of their physical and mental pain and their strength.

The court was also a space where divergent views of acceptable sexual relationships were articulated. Defendants' explanations highlight various ways in which they conceptualized intimacy and sex, or sought to absolve their behaviour from criminal responsibility. In some cases, they simply made excuses for themselves or misunderstood European law, but in others their statements illuminate locally held ideas and practices regarding marriage, intercourse and concepts of guilt. Legal definition of crimes of rape, indecent assault and carnal knowledge were clearly not hegemonic outside the courtroom. Sexual relationships and related violence could be a source of conflict between individuals and families, as well as between Indigenous Islanders, indentured labourers, settlers and the state.

The most notable absence from this chapter has been the voices of ni-Vanuatu or Kanak, whose voices have not been preserved in trial records. However, the adjudication of many criminal cases involving Islanders in New Caledonia or the New Hebrides Condominium, took place outside of the courtroom, as will be explored through Part 2.

Notes

1 Extract from *New Hebrides British Association Gazette* 1, no. 3, September 1912, SG-NH Carton 8, ANOM.

2 Kali Israel, 'French Vices and British Liberties: Gender, Class and Narrative Competition in a Late Victorian Sex Scandal', *Social History* 22, no. 1 (1997), 9.

3 Memo for the Assistant Colonial Secretary, SM Valia, 13/1/93 CSO 304/1893, in CSO 2320/1985, NAF.

4 Supreme Court Ordinance 1875 (No. 14) Criminal Procedure Ordinance 1875 (No. 23), and Summary Offences Ordinance 1876 (No. 17), Fiji Certified Copies of Acts 1875–80, CO 84/1, NAK. 'Criminal Law and Procedure Amendment Ordinance 1889 (No. 4)', *The Ordinances of the Colony of Fiji: A New Edition* (Suva: Edward John March, Government Printer, 1906), 637–42.

5 Jonathan Saha, 'Whiteness, Masculinity and the Ambivalent Embodiment of "British Justice" in Colonial Burma', *Cultural and Social History* 14, no. 4 (2017), 529.

6 Nancy Erber and George Robb (eds), Introduction to *Disorder in the Court: Trials and Sexual Conflict at the Turn of the Century* (London: Macmillan Press, 1999), 8.

7 Taylor, *In the Theater*, 28–9.

8 Matthew Hale, 1778, quoted in Estrich, 'Rape', 1094–5.

9 See Estrich, 'Rape'; Bourke, *Rape*; Vigarello, *A History of Rape*.

10 Kolsky, 'The Body Evidencing the Crime', 111; Margaret Mishra, '"Your Woman Is a Very Bad Woman": Revisiting Female Deviance in Colonial Fiji', *Journal of International Women's Studies* 17, no. 4 (2016), 67–78.

11 Nancy Stepan, *The Idea of Race in Science: Great Britain 1800–1960* (London: Macmillan, 1982).

12 John W. Burton, *The Fiji of To-Day* (London: Charles H. Kelly, 1910), 291–3; see also Kelly, 'Gaze and Grasp', on limits of colonial legal and scientific positivism in the courts.

13 Criminal Procedure Ordinance 1875 (No. 23), Fiji Certified Copies of Acts, CO 84/1, NAK; Duff, 'The Evolution of Trial by Judge and Assessors in Fiji', 190–1.

14 Unsworn Testimony Ordinance 1875 (No. X) and Criminal Procedure Ordinance 1875 (No. 23), Fiji Certified Copies of Acts, CO 84/1; see also: Native Witness Protection Ordinance 1883 (No. 3), Certified Copies of Acts of the Fiji Islands 1881–7, CO 84/2, NAK.

15 Wiener, *An Empire on Trial*, 83.

16 Criminal Procedure Ordinance 1875 (No. 23), Fiji Certified Copies of Acts, CO 84/1, NAK.

17 Duff, 'The Evolution of Trial by Judge and Assessors in Fiji', 191–2, 197. Only after 1950 were non-Europeans included on jury and assessor lists.

18 Christopher Bayly, *Recovering Liberties: Indian Thought in the Age of Liberalism and Empire* (Cambridge: Cambridge University Press, 2012), 61–71.

19 Criminal Procedure Ordinance 1875 (No. 23), Fiji Certified Copies of Acts, CO 84/1, NAK. See also: The Indictable Offences Procedure Ordinances 1896 (No. 3).

20 Native Regulation No. 2 of 1877 respecting Courts, *Fiji Government Gazette*, no. 3, vol. 6, 26 May 1877, CO 86/1, NAK; 'The Native Witness Protection Ordinance 1883 (No. 1)', *The Ordinances of the Colony of Fiji: A New Edition* (Suva: Edward John March, Government Printer, 1906), 412–13; Criminal Procedure Ordinance 1883 (No. 8), Certified Copies of Acts of the Fiji Islands 1881–7, CO 84/2, NAK.

21 Criminal Law and Procedure Amendment Ordinance 1889 (No. 4), *The Ordinances of the Colony of Fiji: A New Edition* (Suva: Edward John March, Government Printer, 1906), 638–9. See also: Unsworn Testimony Ordinance 1875.
22 Damon Salesa, *Racial Crossings: Race, Intermarriage, and the Victorian British Empire* (Oxford: Oxford University Press, 2011), 42.
23 Burton, *The Fiji of To-Day*, 45.
24 'Annual Report on Polynesian Immigration 1884', *Journal of the Legislative Council*, 1886, 23.
25 Governor G. W. Des Voeux to Earl of Kimberley, 4 November 1881, Papers Relating to Her Majesty's Colonial Possessions, Reports for 1880, 1881, and 1882, NAF.
26 Burton, *The Fiji of To-Day*, 156.
27 Quoted in Brereton, *Law, Justice, Empire*, 131.
28 Ibid., 131–2.
29 George Henry Lee, In the Supreme Court, Fiji: Regina v. Lee; affidavit of G. H. Lee and his remarks thereon, 343.988/L, Mitchell Library Sydney. See also: Martin Wiener, *An Empire on Trial*, chapter 3.
30 Case 2/1877 Regina v Scanlon, Criminal Sittings, Fiji Supreme Court, NAF; Brereton, *Law, Justice, Empire*, 132.
31 Lord Stanmore, *Fiji: Records of Private and Public Life 1875–1880*, vol. 1 (Edinburgh: Printed by R. and R. Clark, 1897), 145–7.
32 Entry for 11/9/1907, 22/9/1907, 28/10/1907 and 14/10/1907, MS 894/18 Edward Jacomb Diary 1907–8, SHL.
33 Native Regulation No. 2 of 1887, Fiji Native Regulation Board, *Records of the Native Regulation Board 1887–1895* (Suva: Edward John March, Govt. Printer, 1898); Thomson, *The Decay of Custom*.
34 *Report of the Commission Appointed to Inquire into the Decrease of the Native Population* (Suva: Edward John March, Govt. Printer, 1896); see also: Vicki Luker, 'A Tale of Two Mothers: Colonial Constructions of Indian and Fijian Maternity', *Fijian Studies: A Journal of Contemporary Fiji* 3, no. 2 (2005), 357–74; Margaret Jolly, 'Other Mothers: Maternal "Insouciance" and the Depopulation Debate in Fiji and Vanuatu, 1890 to 1930', in Ram and Jolly (eds), *Maternities and Modernities*, 177–212.
35 Minute WLA to A. C. S., 3/11/1897, CSO 304/1893 in CSO 2320/1895, NAF; 'Asterisk', *Isles of Illusion* (1928 [1923]), 243.
36 Ordinance 14 of 1875 enabled the Governor to exempt districts from Supreme Court jurisdiction, an 1878 rape case was tried by local court for the same reasons. See: Brereton, *Law, Justice, Empire*, 136–7.
37 W. L. A to A. C. S., 3/11/1897, CSO 304/1893 in CSO 2320/1895, NAF.
38 For comparative discussion, see Dorsett, *Juridical Encounters*, 2–3, 12–3, 26–7, 62, 211–15.

39 Burton, *The Fiji of To-Day*, 340.
40 FRG 1901, A/R 1900, quoted in Naidu, *The Violence of Indenture*, 56.
41 Burton, *The Fiji of To-Day*, 270.
42 Lal, *Chalo Jahaji*, 182–4.
43 Doug Munro, 'Patterns of Resistance and Accommodation', in Brij V. Lal, Doug Munro and Edward D. Beechert (eds), *Plantation Workers: Resistance and Accommodation* (Honolulu: University of Hawai'i Press, 1993), 16; Lal, *Chalo Jahaji*, 182–4.
44 Totaram Sanadhya, Fiji Dweep Me Mere Ikkis Varsh (My 21 years in the Fiji Islands), quoted in Naidu, *The Violence of Indenture*, 59.
45 Minute signed JM, in W. L. Allardyce, Stipendiary Magistrate Navua, to Colonial Secretary, 18/4/85, CSO 85/1084, NAF.
46 Walter Gill, *Turn Northeast at the Tombstone* (Adelaide: Rigby, 1970), 147.
47 Naidu, *The Violence of Indenture*, 56–9.
48 Extract from Inspr. James Harper Labasa Report (No. 721 – 1900), CSO 2065/1900, NAF.
49 'Annual Report on Polynesian Immigration for 1884', *Journal of the Legislative Council*, 1886, 23.
50 Ibid., 26.
51 Lal, *Chalo Jahaji*, 184.
52 Quoted in Joyce, *Samuel Walker Griffith*, 80, in Wiener, *An Empire on Trial*, 93.
53 Captain A. M. Farquhar, quoted in Roger C. Thomson, 'Natives and Settlers on the New Hebrides Frontier, 1870–1900', *Pacific Studies* 5, no. 1 (1981), 8.
54 Jacomb, *The Future of the Kanaka*, 121–2.
55 Memo 'Native Courts (Criminal)', F. E. W., 25/2/1929, in Folder 5/1 Part One, NHBS 15/I, WPA.
56 Resident Commissioner to British District Agent Tanna, 18/3/1930, in Folder 5/1 Part One, NHBS 15/I, WPA.
57 Fletcher to Jacomb, 10 February 1918, MS 894/28 Edward Jacomb Diary 1918–19, SHL.
58 Saha, 'Whiteness, Masculinity', 527.
59 Thornbury, *Colonizing Consent*, 26–7.
60 Case 40/1910 Rex v R, Criminal Sittings, Fiji Supreme Court (hereafter FSC), NAF. Victims and defendants are referred to by their initials throughout this chapter given the young age of many and the potential for identification, following Adrian Bingham et al., 'Historical Child Sexual Abuse in England and Wales: The Role of Historians', *History of Education* 45, no. 4 (2016), 423–6.
61 Wiener, *An Empire on Trial*, 10.
62 Case 30/1910 Rex v R and N, Criminal Sittings, FSC, NAF. See also: Case 1/1881 Regina v L.

63 Case 39/1918 Rex v OK, Criminal Sittings, FSC, NAF.

64 Case 6/1910 Rex v ER; see also: Case 13/1875 Regina v S Case 27/1879 Regina v TVB, Criminal Sittings, FSC, NAF.

65 Case 89/1917 Rex v LR, Criminal Sittings, FSC, NAF.

66 Case 7/1881 Regina v S, Criminal Sittings, FSC, NAF.

67 Case 21/1907 Rex v J and others, Criminal Sittings, FSC, NAF.

68 Case 16[?]/1879 Regina v N and VS, Criminal Sittings, FSC, NAF.

69 Case 13/1881 Regina v M, Criminal Sittings, FSC, NAF.

70 Case 6/1891 Regina v P, Criminal Sittings, FSC, NAF.

71 Datta, *Fleeting agencies*, 17.

72 Case 33/1886 Regina v N, Criminal Sittings, FSC, NAF.

73 One group of men were found guilty, the other not guilty. Calendar Supreme Court Criminal Sittings, Tuesday 2 May 1876, contained within 1876 Supreme Court Criminal case files, NAF.

74 Burton, *The Fiji of To-Day*, 316–17.

75 Case 40/1883 Regina v B and B, Criminal Sittings, FSC, NAF. V was acquitted.

76 Case 44/1886 Regina v Mk and Mt, Criminal Sittings, FSC, NAF. See also Case 1/1881 Regina v L, where accused admits and regrets his actions but pleads not guilty to the charge of rape.

77 Case 44/1886 Regina v Mk and Mt, Criminal Sittings, FSC, NAF.

78 Statement of accused, Case 44/1886, Criminal Sittings, FSC, NAF. See also Case 4/1883 Regina v M, where accused pled guilty to attempted rape on grounds he found himself impotent.

79 Case 36/1917 Rex v G, Criminal Sittings, FSC, NAF.

80 Case 10/1881 Regina v K, Criminal Sittings, FSC, NAF.

81 Case 17/1890 Regina v S, Criminal Sittings, FSC, NAF. No verdict was recorded in the case file.

82 Case 40/1915 Rex v M, Criminal Sittings, FSC, NAF. See also: Case 20/1881 Regina v RB, Case 5/1905 Rex v SS and K and Case 66/1908 Rex v SV.

83 Case 16[?]/1879 Regina v N and VS (for rape, and aiding and abetting, respectively), Criminal Sittings, FSC, NAF.

84 Case 53/1886 Regina v M, Criminal Sittings, FSC, NAF.

85 Ibid.

86 Brereton, *Law, Justice, Empire*, 135–6, quoting CO 83/8 Carnarvon to Gordon 22/3/75 no. 2 and Ordinance 14 of 1875.

87 Kelly, 'Gaze and Grasp', 88–90.

88 Case 6/1891 Regina v J, Criminal Sittings, FSC, NAF. See also: Case 42/1895 Rex v M and C 14/1901 Rex v G.

89 Case 21/1892 Regina v C, Criminal Sittings, FSC, NAF.

90 Case 11/1881 Regina v J, Criminal Sittings, FSC, NAF.

91 Based on surviving records, they included Case 24/1876 Regina v B; Case 4/1897 Regina v A; Case 15/1898 Regina v H; Case 30/1898 Regina v TF; Case 25/1907 Rex v MF; Case 26/1909 Rex v JS; Case 43/1912 Rex v J (rape), K and R (accessories before the fact); and Case 28/1919 Rex v CB. See also Case 3/1898 Regina v P, in which accused was charged with procuring a girl to have connection with John Williams. All Criminal Sittings, FSC, NAF.

92 Case 24/1876 Regina v B, Criminal Sittings, FSC, NAF.

93 Case 30/1898 Regina v TF, Criminal Sittings, FSC, NAF.

94 Case 43/1912 Rex v J (rape), K and R (accessories before the fact), Criminal Sittings, FSC, NAF.

95 Case 38/1903 Rex v R, Criminal Sittings, FSC, NAF.

96 Though see James Heartfield, 'You Are Not a White Woman!' 69–83, on the discourse of white solidarity and prestige in a case in which the magistrate considered that 'Spencer had put herself outside white society by consorting with natives' (p. 79).

97 Case 12/1904 Rex v G, Criminal Sittings, FSC, NAF. See also an unnumbered case from 1901 (Rex v A), a rare case of sodomy, the accused was found guilty of intercourse with a boy of less than twelve years.

98 Case 25/1909 Rex v K, and Case 32/1904 Rex v B; Criminal Sittings, FSC, NAF.

99 Case 48/1906 Rex v G, Case 10/1882 Regina v M, Case 52/1917 Rex v S, Criminal Sittings, FSC, NAF.

100 Stoler, *Carnal Knowledge and Imperial Power.*

101 See for example: Case 13/1908 Rex v OD; and Case 42/1908 Rex v RR Criminal Sittings, FSC, NAF.

102 Donald Denoon, 'An Untimely Divorce: Western Medicine and Anthropology in Melanesia', *History and Anthropology* 11, nos. 2–3 (1999), 347; Kelly, 'Gaze and Grasp', 93–4.

103 Erber and Robb (eds), *Introduction to Disorder in the Court*, 6. Willemijn Ruberg, 'Trauma, Body, and Mind: Forensic Medicine in Nineteenth-Century Dutch Rape Cases', *Journal of the History of Sexuality* 22, no. 1 (2013), 85–104; M. Anne Crowther and Brenda White, *On Soul and Conscience: The Medical Expert and Crime* (Aberdeen: University of Aberdeen Press, 1988); Michael Clark and Catherine Crawford, *Legal Medicine in History* (Cambridge: Cambridge University Press, 1994); Jackson, *Child Sexual Abuse*, chapter 4.

104 No. 1913, Juge de paix (F. Ursleur?) Ouégoa en tournée à Hyenghène, 2 novembre 1891, 23W C11, ANC.

105 Brewster, *The Turtle and the Caduceus*, 34–5; 'Colonial Medical Service', *Lancet* 198, no. 5113 (27 August 1921), 471–2.

106 'Colonial Medical Service', *Lancet* 198, no. 5113 (27 August 1921), 472; Jacqui Leckie, *Colonizing Madness: Asylum and Community in Fiji* (Honolulu: University of Hawai'i Press, 2019), 118.

107 All material related to this trial found in Case 74/1910 Rex v RB, Criminal Sittings, FSC, NAF. Spelling also recorded as Muller.

108 Jackson, *Child Sexual Abuse*, 99.

109 Kolsky, 'The Body Evidencing the Crime', 109–30.

110 Case 42/1908 Rex v RR, Criminal Sittings, FSC, NAF; Case 87/1910 Rex v D.

111 Case 31/1901 Rex v R, Criminal Sittings, FSC, NAF.

112 Case 40/1895 Regina v P, A, M and HS, Criminal Sittings, FSC, NAF. See also: Case 82/1893 Regina v B.

113 Case 7/1905 Rex v B, Criminal Sittings, FSC, NAF. See also: Case 48/1906 Rex v G.

114 Case 20/1907 Rex v S, Criminal Sittings, FSC, NAF.

115 Case 30/1910 Rex v R and N, Criminal Sittings, FSC, NAF.

116 Case 21/1907 Rex v J and others, Criminal Sittings, FSC, NAF.

117 Datta, *Fleeting Agencies*, 17–18; Thornbury, *Colonizing Consent*, 27.

118 Strange, 'Masculinities', 313.

Part 2

'Rough justice indeed'? Creating and contesting law beyond the courts

Figure 3 A Kanak engraved bamboo depicting a sexual relationship between an Indigenous woman and a European man, acquired by the British Museum in 1913 from Louis-Joseph Bouge, a colonial administrator and collector. Oc1913,1115.369, © The Trustees of the British Museum.

4

Colonial intimacies below and beyond the law

On 23 March 1909, Jesse Hopson, a government official in the New Hebrides, reported to the Brisbane Immigration Agent from Big Bay on Espiritu Santo that

> an aboriginal woman named Jemima who came to the Islands with her husband some 15 months ago and had two children was anxious to know if she could return to Queensland. She was married in Townsville Sept. 1901 and has had one child since she has been on Santo … The husband wants to get rid of her and has knocked her about a good deal, he says if something cannot be done he will kill her for he has another woman in his eye and wishes to marry her native style … I cannot keep her here or find work for her and now more especially, for a new regulation has just been received from England which prohibits the recruiting or employment of native women.[1]

This letter appears amongst archival tables listing ni-Vanuatu, predominately men, repatriated from Queensland plantations. The men had served periods of indenture where some had formed relationships with women, primarily of Aboriginal descent. They were repatriated with the emergence of 'white Australia' policies following the Federation of the Australian states at the beginning of the twentieth century. Jemima was not the only woman who chose to follow her partner to the islands and who subsequently wished to return to Australia. Lizzie Wilson appealed to the British administration for assistance to return to Queensland, due to homesickness and abuse.[2]

These archival trails quickly grow cold: whether either woman returned home is unclear. Many similar relationships never came to official attention, either because they ended with or before the repatriation of indentured labourers or because the individuals were absorbed into the local community.[3] However, they indicate the complex and unexpected networks developed within and between the islands during the nineteenth and twentieth centuries, building on longer histories of mobility.[4] Beyond the court, colonial administrations were occasionally entangled with domestic disputes and personal relationships, as imperial expansion and informal empire facilitate new patterns of interaction.[5] The archival evidence is fragmentary but signals towards relationships from affectionate to violent, which only occasionally surfaced in official records or progressed to trial.

This chapter highlights the intersection of intimacy, conflict and control through an array of intimate relationships – partnerships, marriages, mixed descent children, violent and coercive sexual encounters – and the attempts to govern these that emerged in different geographic spaces, social groups and communities. Examining court cases alone obscures the ways in which intimate lives and relationships, including violent ones, continued beyond the reach of colonial administrations. In these Pacific colonies, the state was most often interested in policing intimacy when it challenged the administration's tenuous authority, or when Indigenous elites (such as Fijian chiefs) sought colonial support for their position.[6] However, administrations generally lacked the resources to enumerate and manage intimate frontiers, making relationships and violence difficult to quantify, while officials often struggled to look beyond racist 'civilising' narratives.

I draw on specific examples to illustrate the multiple and adaptable intimacies that existed before, beyond or below the law in each colony. These emphasize the fluid and evolving nature of island societies and individual agency over which officials had limited oversight. Paula Bryne argues that 'ordinary people … made their own law; they mapped their own boundaries of legality and illegality. They both clashed with and supported the magistrates, judges and juries who interpreted statute law'.[7] In the same vein, I demonstrate how individuals and communities ranging from Indigenous elites to missionaries and settlers all had distinct approaches to forming and managing intimate and sexual relationships. Missionary courts, local governments and violent conflict were all strategies to police and patrol intimate interactions beyond the judiciary and, read carefully, demonstrate individuals' agencies even where their voices are not recorded. Collectively, these examples highlight the gradual and uneven progress of British and French law across the Pacific, and suggest the broader range of relationships, and attempts to manage them, that existed beyond the control, or even the gaze, of the colonial judiciary.

Beyond colonial perceptions of intimacy

As we have seen, the judicial regulations imposed upon Indigenous or indentured groups were shaped by racist official perceptions of local societies. Though removed from local realities, their impact was critical in fashioning the colonial experience and the nature of imperial incursions into intimate life. Part of the early colonial project was a limited and flawed attempt to record and understand Indigenous cultural practices and incorporate Indigenous custom into European law and modes of governance, if only to govern more efficiently in remote spaces on limited colonial budgets. Official archives, missionary accounts and other European writing about the islands reveal how perceptions of intimacy and sexuality beyond the criminal shaped official understanding of racial difference in New Caledonia, Fiji and the New Hebrides.

Official narratives regarding the changes between the pre- and post-colonization eras framed the story as one of incomplete development from savagery to civilization.[8] Developmentalist narratives had a long-standing and pervasive influence in Oceania, underpinning beliefs in an 'intimate causal liaison between race and level of civilisation'.[9] While the degree of intervention varied, missionaries had, for decades longer than colonial officials, been engaged in similar endeavours to reform island cultures in the model of 'civilised' Victorian Christianity.[10] While sometimes at variance, missionaries and officials had overlapping interpretations and interests in knowing and controlling intimate practices. In 1919, French Inspector Bougourd credited missionaries in New Caledonia with aiding 'the general evolution of morals and ideas' of Kanak towards European 'civilisation', highlighting the 'use of clothing, the disappearance of polygamy, [and] the reduction of abortion practices'.[11] Similar patterns of change were observed in the converted communities in Fiji, Vanuatu and elsewhere, though missionaries were often frustrated that Islanders selectively adopted and adapted the precepts of Christianity and civilization, converting 'Christianity as much as … converted by it'.[12]

Missionary-influenced tropes emphasized lawlessness and the lack, or violent form, of justice before the advent of European imperialism. Alexander compared the genteel punishment of fines and prison or labour sentences in Fiji to 'the old days' when

> the adulterer had met with rude justice from the club of the injured husband, but with the advance of government and civilisation 'club law' had given place to Native Regulations.[13]

In Vanuatu and New Caledonia, intertribal warfare was described as incessant, and the kidnapping of women considered a frequent cause of violence between individuals and groups.[14] Such teleological narratives served to underline the beneficial influences and perceived progress towards Christian civilization under the auspices of the missions, while emphasizing the scope of work that yet remained.[15] For officials, the emphasis on an incomplete journey towards civilization justified continued subjugation of Indigenous communities. The Indigénat in New Caledonia and protectionism in Fiji were both unveiled as temporary measures until Indigenous subjects were considered ready to take up the full rights and responsibilities of European law and citizenship. Yet after decades of colonial rule, neither group was deemed to have advanced sufficiently to end them.

In all three colonies, the 'dying native' theory served as a counter-narrative to that of progress towards civilization.[16] For example, in New Caledonia some officials believed that the Indigénat system of reservations was in place only until the population became extinct. Reports from the colonial inspection of 1895–6 stated that the Kanak race would disappear within a few years, though twenty years later inspectors demonstrated this error underpinned 'the repression of Kanak in the mountains and their confinement in reserves whose settlement depended on administrative arbitrariness'.[17] Such ideas circulated between colonies and imperial powers, with relatively widespread currency in the late nineteenth century. Bougourd noted that the accuracy of depopulation theory was disproved by the late 1910s, but they continued to influence official attitudes and the structures of Indigenous governance inherited and continued by twentieth-century administrations.

Outsiders' perceptions of Indigenous gendered social norms and practices were crucial to these contrasting depictions of island societies. The improvement of the place of women within their family and community was a critical marker of the progress towards 'civilisation'.[18] In all three colonies, Indigenous women were viewed as 'beasts of burden', degraded by a life of hard labour forced upon them by their male family and chiefs.[19] Polygamy, abortion, infanticide and localized practices, such as knocking out of married women's teeth in Malekula, were further targets for critique and missionary or imperial intervention.[20] Indeed, paternalistic interventions were often predicated on attempts to avert racial extinction. Population decline was attributed to cultural factors such as abortion, lack of maternal qualities or unsanitary village conditions, situating the cause within the island societies (rather than the 'fatal impact' of contact), justifying further intrusion in domestic and intimate life.[21] Intimate lives of Islanders were thus conceptualized in relation to broader trans-imperial debates about race, civilization and decline, and projects of transformation by European and Islander missionaries often continued by the colonial state. Yet both in and beyond these reductive accounts, we glimpse a complex network of relationships and strategies to manage these at interpersonal and community levels often unknown – and unknowable – to the colonial state.

New Hebrides

Mobility of both Europeans and Islanders in the colonial New Hebrides underpinned new relationships and new strategies to manage these at interpersonal and community level. From the 1860s, missionaries were particularly concerned about 'blackbirding' in Vanuatu (and elsewhere) and the subsequent treatment of Islanders recruited for plantations locally and New Caledonia, Fiji and Queensland.[22] Indentured recruitment occasioned specifically gendered anxieties. Women being 'kidnapped' and the use of women as decoys on recruiting vessels to entice men aboard were especially emotive and considered important grounds for European intervention.[23] Questions over whether indentured recruitment was a new form of slavery, an unscrupulous and abusive practice inflicted upon Islanders, or a process in which Islanders had economic and other motivations, if not agency, sparked debate then and now.

Many Islanders chose indenture despite the contractual inequality and abuse experienced on plantations. Dorothy Shineberg, Clive Moore and others highlight the new economic opportunities, adventure, freedom from missionary oversight and the desire to escape an unhappy or violent marriage or to elope with a partner disapproved of by community and family.[24] Nevertheless ongoing criticisms and attempts to monitor the recruitment provided an influential context in which other attempts to establish social order took place. The prominence of indenture in imperial debates and its impact on local societies provides an important backdrop to three cases studies from the New Hebrides. They include the complex relationship between Robert Fletcher ('Asterisk') and his Ambaean partner Onéla Kohkonne on Lemaru plantation, Epi; local attempts at governance underpinned by desires for respectability in the emergent settlement of Franceville; and the mission or 'native' courts on Tanna where control over sexual and moral norms became central to local and imperial politics tensions in the early twentieth century.

The home was a key space of interaction between Islanders and Europeans in colonial and postcolonial Vanuatu, with some indentured women working in domestic service.[25] Margaret Rodman notes that 'masters could and did cross intimate boundaries. Occasionally, a colonial officer's affair with a house girl became general knowledge, but this was probably the tip of a rather large iceberg'.[26] A close reading of one intimate relationship established on an early-twentieth-century plantation provides insight into the personal and social dynamics and the underpinning power dynamics that shaped colonized women's experiences.

Robert James Addison Fletcher, a 'sometime medical student, bank clerk, Oxford graduate and schoolmaster', arrived in the New Hebrides in 1912 by way of New Caledonia.[27] Inspired by Robert Louis Stevenson, he hoped ultimately to find his own Pacific utopia. Despite growing disillusionment with the climate and society, economic and personal circumstances kept Fletcher in the New Hebrides. Like many contemporaries, he worked in various capacities: as a plantation manager, a surveyor and an interpreter-translator for the Joint Court, then as a planter at Lemaru, Epi. In early 1916, Fletcher took a fifteen-year-old Ambae (Aoba) woman, Onéla Kohkonne or so-called Topsy, as his 'woman'. Their son, Bilbil, was born a year later.[28] Abandoning his family, Fletcher departed in 1919.

While Fletcher died in obscurity in 1965 his correspondence ensured notoriety. *Isles of Illusion* was published in 1923, a collection of letters from Fletcher (under the anonymous name 'Asterisk') to the volume's editor, J. G. Bohun Lynch.[29] The book, offering candid insights into life during the early Condominium, was a 'best-seller' and appeared in various translated editions.[30] Fletcher was an unusual commentator: a product of the attitudes and prejudices of his period but also deeply critical of his own society and compatriots. Few escape his censure: not bumbling officials, missionaries, planters, 'natives' (especially 'mission natives'), 'half-castes', nor Fletcher himself. He encapsulates the ambivalence of the joint colonial experiment and its divided nature.[31]

Yet what of Onéla Kohkonne's own experience? Her experience is relayed through Fletcher's letters, who romanticizes the power imbalance and the young woman's vulnerability away from her home and community support. Communication difficulties surely marked the early relationship. Fletcher attempted to teach Kohkonne Bislama or to learn Aobese himself, suggesting they did not have a common language during the early years of their relationship.[32] What we can deduce of Kohkonne's perspective is thus heavily filtered through Fletcher's interpretations. She is described as 'the most faithful womanly woman and an insanely blind adorer of me'. He goes so far as to claim, 'I am her god and her heaven and her earth.'[33]

Though surely an exaggeration, Kohkonne appeared loyal to Fletcher, and keenly followed his instruction on childcare in a manner that suggested she was eager to please or appease him. Fletcher also emphasized Kohkonne's distress whenever he mentioned the possibility of his impending departure, implying that, whether for emotional or practical reasons or simply personal safety on a different island, she wanted the partnership to continue.[34] While we cannot know her emotions and motivations, Kohkonne adapted through barriers and difficulties. To whatever extent she felt them, she ably performed the emotions of admiration and adoration expected by self-proclaimed 'God' Fletcher – an important form of agency within the circumstances. As such she arguable embodied the Ambae proverb that a girl 'is like a branch of nanggalat – a stinging-nettle tree – whatever the ground you stick it in, it will grow. A girl can thrive in any place, planted in any ground'.[35]

Indenture and her relationship with Fletcher were perhaps a means for Kohkonne to escape the customary order, providing a space of freedom or opportunity. Her character in the fictionalized *Gone Native* arrived on the plantation to escape unhappy and burdensome marriage on Ambae.[36] More generally, Ambae woman frequently recruited, possibly because they had independence and high status in some parts of the island.[37] However with Fletcher also being Kohkonne's employer, it was never a relationship of equals. Aside from Fletcher's own confident white supremacy, differences of class and of age were at play. The fact that Fletcher was twenty years her senior certainly affected their interactions, increasing Fletcher's racialized perception and treatment of Kohkonne as childlike and naïve. The dynamic of their relationship was structured by inequalities.

Fletcher often expressed real affection towards Kohkonne, but always qualified by his ongoing disapproval of interracial partnerships, a continuing juxtaposition between affection and self-censure.[38] Tension between his emotional investment and disdain manifested itself with the birth of Fletcher and Kohkonne's son, Bilbil (John James Friday or 'Man Friday'), around May 1917. On discovering Kohkonne's pregnancy, Fletcher expressed curiosity in seeing his son but vowed he would not acknowledge the child: 'junior shall be brought up as a native. These islands teem with half-castes brought up as "white" and I hate them individually and collectively'.[39] From Bilbil's birth, Fletcher battled with his distaste for 'half-castes' and his contradictory love for his son. Though a 'sweet little baby', he quickly asserted 'the sooner I get rid of him the better' and he even expressed relief at the death of his second child.[40] Fletcher was nevertheless the doting and proud father, frequently singing the child's praises to Lynch. He declared, 'if I do not love Bilbil, then I am incapable of understanding that sensation'.[41]

His affection for both Onéla Kohkonne and Bilbil were contingent on the colonial island setting. Fletcher pours scorn on Australian men who upheld exclusionary politics of race at home, while engaging in relationships with Indigenous women in the islands.[42] Thus, though there were no laws against miscegenation in either Australia or the New Hebrides, the acceptance of colonial interracial intimacies was geographically dependant. Fletcher himself found this to be true when he imagined taking his own mixed family outside Epi. Regarding Kohkonne, Fletcher confided: 'Do you think I could tolerate her in civilisation? Not for a week! That is the difference that the islands make.' Moreover, Fletcher was convinced that Kohkonne would not survive in England, though with little evidence of consulting her.[43]

Fletcher did entertain the idea of bringing Bilbil back to England with him, despite the racial prejudices he believed they would encounter there. However, he worried that British social mores might override the love he felt for his son in the colony where prejudice was less. Fletcher admitted, 'I am so afraid that, if I take Bilbil away and get him among whiter things, I shall straightaway begin to hate him.'[44] The meaning and impact of racial identity and of interracial relationships thus shifted from place to place, and Fletcher's own attitudes shifted with it. Such relationships were made possible, even permissible, by colonial expansion into the New Hebrides, a geography of emotion that was mapped onto the colonial world.

After much equivocation, Fletcher decided to abandon Bilbil upon his departure in 1919. He considered sending Kohkonne and Bilbil back to Ambae, but eventually arranged for Bilbil to be adopted by German planter Adopholus Zeitler. Kohkonne's life beyond this moment is notably absent in Fletcher's arrangements for his son, which he reasoned would enable Bilbil to gain the rights and privileges of French citizenship. By contrast, British law in the New Hebrides offered no legal means to adopt a child.[45] Zeitler legally adopted Bilbil, who became Jimmy Zeitler. Though he confessed contempt for the 'French' tolerance of *métis* in the islands and missionary attempts at assimilation, Fletcher nevertheless sought to capitalize on such attitudes for Bilbil's benefit, to help overcome the 'disability' of 'half-caste' status.[46] In doing so, Fletcher was flexible, or at least opportunistic, when it came to conceptualizing racial difference and legal possibilities in the Condominium.

For Fletcher, affection for his Ambaean partner and their son co-existed with a general racism towards ni-Vanuatu, and particularly to 'half-castes' and 'mission natives'. He embodied the complexity of contemporaneous understandings of race, which were uneven, shifting and applied circumstantially. More generally

Fletcher's observations frequently contrasted English and French attitudes to racial mixing. The perceived French treatment of 'half-castes' as equals and as white he abhorred: 'No snuff and butter coloured citoyen français for me.'[47] The English boycott of the club Cercle de Port Vila after Indigenous men were allowed to drink on the verandah alongside European members indicates that Fletcher's attitude was not uncommon. However, it also reflected a stereotypical view of French imperialism, which was equally underpinned by racist attitudes even when condoning concubinage and assimilation.

Other settlers in the New Hebrides were similarly concerned by the respectability of their lifestyle and legality of their intimate relationships. Some sought self-government as the solution prior to the Condominium's inauguration. Captain Kane of HMS *Calliope* reported on the newly established government of Franceville, Efate, proclaimed on 9 August 1889:

> M. Chevillard explained that he and other whites living in that part of Vate Islands had found the necessity for some form of government therefore he said a certain number of residents associated themselves together and by common consent established what they called the Commune or Muncipality of Franceville, and elected a Council with M. Chevillard as Mayor. They have established a registry of births and deaths, and a form of civil marriage; they have made roads for the public use … They have established a sort of Court of Justice for whites and natives alike. As far as I understand, one white, nationality unknown, was accused of shooting a black. M. Chevillard nominated a Commission of three persons by whom the accused was tried and acquitted.[48]

Sending their flag to officials in Fiji and New Caledonia, Ferdinand-Albert Chevillard and his government claimed to be 'practically' an independent power under the protection of both British and France.[49] The short-lived Commune of Franceville provides an example of alternative forms of power and justice established in the islands as an attempt to manage the changing social, political and economic relationships.[50]

Franceville consisted of around 40 Europeans (predominantly French) and 500 ni-Vanuatu. Its leaders claimed authority over the settler population as well as interactions between Europeans and Islanders, though not over matters within ni-Vanuatu society.[51] The administration emerged from settler frustrations over the lack of legal authority in the islands to punish crimes or manage civil matters. In particular, the question of marriage registration loomed large in the minds of French settlers, who were forced to travel to Nouméa to regularize unions according to civil law and to register their children as legitimate citizens. Among them were a number of men living with ni-Vanuatu women, including

Chevillard.[52] Given the limited resources of many settlers, this journey was 'always troublesome and sometimes impossible'.[53] Adding insult to injury was the fact that English law recognized marriages solemnized by missionaries or clergy. While some pursued this route to marry, the problem of French recognition remained. The situation was further complicated by marriages that crossed boundaries of nationality.[54] The *Hawaiian Gazette* applauded the new government's progressiveness for adopting universal suffrage regardless of race and gender (though only white men could hold office).[55]

However, Franceville as an independent state was an unacceptable incursion upon joint imperial power exercised under the 1887 Convention, being 'outside of [the metropoles'] laws'.[56] The French representative of the Joint Naval Commission (JNC), Commandant Bigant, quickly ordered the dissolution of the municipality in 1890.[57] The settler government had hoped their initiative would receive imperial endorsement. But in the delicate balance of power between British and French interests, the nascent French settler commune was viewed with great suspicion from Australia, Britain and even France.

While its authority was technically void, local attempts to establish jurisdiction continued in the 1890s including local tribunals, marriages 'celebrated in the name of public morality', and an 1895 Arbitration Court comprising both British and French judges (also vetoed by the JNC).[58] While these attempts at locally led governance on Efate had little long-term success, they highlight settlers' desires for regular family life and community-based governance.

The Commune of Franceville exemplified the ways in which newcomers to the New Hebrides sought to establish social and political norms in the absence of the state. In contrast to an image of complete lawlessness in contemporaneous depictions of labour recruiting, Franceville residents aimed to establish themselves and their families as legitimate and respectable by European standards. The settlement was a 'combination of Western economic practices with island social and sexual mores'.[59] Yet seeking to prevent the impression of attempted unilateral annexation, the French swiftly quashed their ambitions, while the JNC guarded Anglo-French imperial claims. Franceville did however have a longer history as a site of governance in the New Hebrides, evolving into Condominium capital, Port Vila.

The settlers of Franceville were not the only ones concerned with regularizing social and political norms in the New Hebrides. Presbyterian missionaries on Tanna also attempted to codify and police social practices in line with Christian morals, holding courts to try and punish transgressors. They emulated missions in Tahiti and Hawai'i that had similarly established codes of law by which their converts and communities were expected to live.[60] After decades of slow progress, many Tannese had converted to Christianity in the 1890s and coastal mission communities were firmly established around Lenakel, Waisisi and White Sands.[61] In addition, the HMS *Prometheus* and *Cambrian* had been influential in peacemaking in 1906 by encouraging nascent 'Native Courts' for dispute resolution.[62] The first British Condominium Agent on Tanna Wilkes explained that the 'war-wearied' Tannese welcomed this alternative to violent conflict.[63] In gratitude, the Tannese gave Captain Bentinet many magic stones that had been involved in fermenting and continuing the island's disputes.[64]

These events empowered missionaries Dr Nicholson and Rev. Thomas Macmillan to take on a greater role in governing local affairs in the early twentieth century alongside ni-Vanuatu leaders. The missionaries endorsed leading converts such as Lohmai and Koukarei as 'chiefs', organized a system of police and held sway over the courts.[65] The years 1905–6 were the apogee of the 'era of Tanna Law': the political authority asserted by Christian chiefs across the island (including over non-converts) replaced the more fluid and egalitarian power dynamics that characterized the preceding period.[66] Noting the ever-widening scope of the population and offenses subsumed under the auspices of the Tannese mission courts, Wilkes wrote in 1912:

> The Worshipping people from the commencement of missionary influence were a law unto themselves. They now became a law within a law, the new regime of course embracing the whole people.[67]

The courts coalesced the interests of missionaries and certain Indigenous elites in controlling sexuality and sociability within their community. Although rape cases were rare, other sexual offences, along with attempts to prevent recruitment, were a substantial part of the courts' work. During this period, no records of the court sittings were kept so the exact number of cases is unknown. However, two decades later, sexual offences remained prominent in the cases heard by the Tanna Native Courts, which were now formally established under Condominium law. Between October 1925 and June 1927, fifty-one adultery cases, five divorces, four attempted indecent assault and one indecent assault case, two cases of interfering with women, one attempted seduction, one seduction and one attempted abortion case came before the court.[68] Similarly high levels of prosecution for adultery and seduction were heard in the Fijian District Courts, suggesting that male Indigenous elites in both Tanna and Fiji were interested in controlling the personal lives of their communities.

This reflected the intersection of long-held male Tannese concerns to prevent the 'stealing' of women with both Christian proscriptions against premarital sex and protectionist policies against 'blackbirding'. Polygamy, adultery (including consensual sex between unmarried individuals), ritual exchanges such as the *toka*, which included 'sing-sings' or dances where men and women mingled, were suppressed as immoral. Sexual initiation for young men was banned, as was kava-drinking and other 'transgressions' such as sorcery.[69] The suppression of cultural practices was led by converts, and resisted by non-converts.

Converts and non-converts alike nevertheless pursued adultery cases, suggesting marriage and sexual relationships were considered of enduring community importance.[70] Wilkes argued the courts were preferable for dealing with such offences, as

> this act was in the old days called 'stealing' a woman, considered merely as property – without any question of morality entering into the matter – and constituted such a breach of convention that if discovered might lead to the male offender being clubbed or killed at the hands of the person whose 'property' was 'stolen.'[71]

Wilkes further wrote that such a sentence was not final: a cycle of retribution often followed. The courts also wrought changes to traditional patterns of sister marriages between groups, by allowing men and women greater freedom of movement. Joel Bonnemaison, Ron Brunton and David Richardson argue such social changes contributed to the rise of the Jon Frum movement reasserting local custom in the 1940s.[72] The impact of these courts on intimate life on Tanna was therefore contradictory. Certain Tannese social practices and proscriptions such as adultery aligned with missionary attitudes, while other attempts to radically transform 'kastom' saw the mission and its converts firmly opposed by non-converts.

More broadly, the place of the Tanna courts in Condominium-era New Hebrides was the subject of debate and disagreement. Advocating for similar courts in Epi in the face of French suspicion, the British High Commissioner's stance reflected the religious divides, the differing economic interests of the French and British, and diverging imperial attitudes to indirect versus direct rule of Indigenous populations:

> Native Government is to be encouraged. Indeed it must be established in some form or other, because for many years to come the Government of the Protectorate will not be able to afford a purely European administration. Mr King has encouraged the people to settle their own petty disputes and offences

> against morality, such as adultery and seduction, in accordance with native custom. At one time the natives were in the habit of imposing fines in money for the offences their village authorities dealt with. Mr King stopped this practice and punishment is now usually inflicted by fining the delinquents in pigs. I have no doubt that the missionaries encourage these embryonic attempts at local government. On the other hand the French settlers and local officials appear to be strongly opposed to them. They are jealous of any influence over the natives but their own, and they disapprove of any but official government of natives.[73]

Despite the frequent complaints from Tanna-based French traders and the official French view that ni-Vanuatu had no existing forms of law that could be codified, French High Commissioner Jules Louis Richard was persuaded to support some form of 'native government' as was established in New Caledonia.[74] Consequently the mission-run courts were initially sanctioned by the Condominium in 1909.[75]

The origin of the courts was disputed, reflecting different views of the Tannese past and present. Supporters situated them as an extension of local custom, legitimizing their authority:

> The courts are said by some to be a survival and natural elaboration of the ancient tribal conferences which were held to determine the guilt of an individual and in which the dictum of the Chief of Chiefs was the sentence pronounced.[76]

By contrast, Koukarei argued that the inauguration of the courts and mission were in fact a break with the past, expressed in the conventional evangelical metaphor of pre-Christian darkness. His words nevertheless suggest some Islanders experienced a certain freedom and sense of security arising from the new courts that he oversaw:

> In the old dark days we lived in dread. No man could walk about alone; women were in terror, and children too. But ever since it was declared that there was to be one law for everyone in the island, we have been conscious of improvement.[77]

Wilkes, and French settlers aggrieved at the mission's perceived overreach, argued instead that the nascent 'Native Courts' had been co-opted by missionaries to serve their own ends.[78] The Commandant of the HMS *Pegasus* in 1909 was similarly unable to attribute agency to Indigenous leaders:

> Nominally the Chief holds the Court but Mr. MacKenzie controls the Chief and that men are punished whenever Mr. MacKenzie considers fit … he seems to have acted during the whole of the last few years in a quite unwarrantable

> manner, dealing out punishment to Natives whenever he thought fit and stating he was doing so by order of the Government.[79]

Arguing that MacKenzie should be tried for unlawful arrest, he noted that 'every missionary' felt they could arrest Islanders on 'the flimsiest pretext', often simply for having offended the mission, and while missionaries were important allies of the administration, their power was clearly open to abuse. The well-resourced Presbyterian mission at this time embodied the French accusation that they were 'veritable religious fiefs'.[80]

By 1912 missionaries MacMillan and Nicholson were widely viewed as overzealous and authoritarian in Port Vila, a view encouraged by Wilkes. Wilkes had a legal background and was thoroughly opposed to the 'potential arbitrary and utterly illegal local courts'.[81] The same year, a French recruiter, Mattei, arrived on the *Clotilde* and, pretending to act under Government authority, attempted to persuade the Tannese he met that the Condominium had ordered the courts be abolished.[82] In response, Koukarei wrote complaining that the Islanders were receiving contradictory messages from the French.[83] The Condominium also received various letters from non-mission Tannese written by French traders on their behalf, protesting the actions of the missions, and non-converts greeted French naval vessels with enthusiasm.[84] As a result of simmering discontent against mission power, after visiting the island in late 1912 the British and French Residents legislated that all courts must be presided over by local government agents.[85] With the missionaries subsequently losing ground, old practices such as sexual initiations were revived.[86] While Wilkes was extremely active in ensuring there was no missionary interference until his resignation in 1914, from 1916 onwards his successor James Nicol tacitly allowed the Presbyterians to hold sway over the courts once more.[87]

Concurrently, debate simmered over what punishments the courts could enforce. Prior to 1909 the Tanna mission court-imposed fines and hard labour upon those convicted, providing a semblance of civilized governance in the eyes of missionaries and Europeans. The French were opposed to monetary fines in an Indigenous tribunal and from 1909 only hard labour was condoned. Such was the scope and influence of the courts that these sentences contributed to the colonization of the island landscape:

> The result of these wise measures can be seen today in the excellent roads which traverse the island from East to West and from North to South, and which make it possible for a mounted traveller to ride with ease all over the formerly impassable island.[88]

Though not officially sanctioned, records also show physical punishments were enforced by Wilkes in 1913, including the flogging of women who had 'offended against the proprietorial rights of their men' or in one case raped a young man.[89]

Overall, the debates over Tannese courts reveal the tensions between Tannese converts and non-converts; Presbyterian missions and local traders and recruiters; British and French officials in Vila; and administrators (such as Wilkes) and missionaries.[90] Missionaries sought to reform the island, aiming to enforce Christian morality and sexuality, and to end recruitment. The British generally saw this as a positive step towards 'native governance', while Christian chiefs found opportunities within the mission and the courts to increase their own influence and support. Non-converts resisted the encroachment on their lives and were supported by French traders and officials who argued that Islanders had the right to choose to sign up as labour recruits. Although a British agent, Wilkes branded the missionaries as authoritarian and advanced the need for Condominium oversight of the Tannese courts. At the heart of these debates lay questions of recruitment, morality, sexual norms and the right to define and police them. More broadly the debate questioned the suitability of indirect rule (through Christian chiefs) or direct rule (through appointed European officials as the French advocated), as colonial opinion diverged on whether the Islanders could engage with and adopt European legal structures or whether they were simply obeying the laws of the missionaries imposed on unsophisticated Islanders.

Fiji

Similar concerns over sexual relationships and marriage animated early debates among chiefs and officials in Fiji. At the first gathering of the Bose Vakaturaga in 1875, Native Stipendiary Magistrate (NSM) Mafi stated:

> The white man's style of simply cohabiting with a woman is the rule now at Bau, and the land has become filthy through it, and we have been much pained and annoyed. The elders of the people have cried out 'what is to be done in this matter?' We have tried to prevent it but are met by 'All are now British subjects and it is Vakapiritania and all please themselves.'[91]

He articulated the concerns of the Fijian elite over perceived threats to their authority from increasing cultural contact. Governor Gordon's establishment of the Bose Vakaturaga as the apex of the system of indirect rule served to reify chiefly, and by implication male, power over Fijian villages and villagers.[92] Through their influence on the Native Regulations, chiefly interpretations of custom were codified that did not necessarily reflect the fluidity and flexibility of social practices. The regulations limited physical and economic mobility for men and women and paid particular attention to the private and intimate lives of villagers.[93]

The control of marriage, divorce, and adultery, and especially authority over Fijian women living with newcomer men, were amongst the key concerns of Fijian chiefs during the early colonial period. Their concerns aligned with those of the colonial state, as Gordon and his successors situated the village and its communal and family life as the key to Fijian cultural and physical survival.[94] The conversations in the Bose Vakaturaga reveal much about the preoccupations of the chiefs in the late nineteenth century, including disagreements, debates and alliances between chiefs from different regions. The records of the Bose Vakaturaga can also be read for fragments of subaltern agency, especially those considered problematic or contrary to chiefly views of acceptable social norms.

Debate over the regulation of marriage began from the first meeting of the Bose Vakaturaga at Draiba, Ovalau in September 1875.[95] Much discussion centred on who had the right to sanction marriage, with Ma'afu and others concerned that the custom of *ai duguciniyalewa* or gifting property to obtain a wife gave the family and friends of potential partners too much influence.[96] They argued that love and mutual affection provided a firmer basis for a lasting relationship, and recommended the presentation of property be replaced with an application for a marriage license from the local NSM.[97] The debate articulated a desire to create stable marriages (in line with Christian values) and to ensure chiefs and magistrates (rather than parents or relatives) gave permission to marry. The lengthy subsequent discussion over the laws for divorce and adultery similarly reflected an attempt to regularize village unions while reifying chiefly power.[98]

In the discussions on homogenizing marriage customs, evidence of the variety of existing practices emerges. The recurrent concerns expressed by chiefs and NSMs in subsequent meetings suggest that the chiefly elite were struggling to control this aspect of Islander life.[99] The refrain 'what is to be done?' was echoed throughout these conversations, and highlights frustrations at the failure of villagers to conform to the expectations enshrined in the Native Regulations.[100]

The examples of troublesome behaviour cited in these meetings provide a sense of the changes occurring within Fijian society during colonization. For example, in 1875 an incomplete table listed 22 unconsummated marriages and 209 married couples living apart across the different provinces of Fiji.[101] Five years later, the Roko Tui Ba noted that cohabitation and refusal to marriage were still increasing:

> 'How can the population increase when the people refuse to marry?' In some towns it is reported that there is a large number of marriageable women, and that they positively refuse to be married to anybody … It is said that many women now prefer to have no children.[102]

Other chiefs and magistrates recounted incidents in which the regulations on marriage, divorce and adultery had been defied. In 1876, the Roko Tui Bua reported on the many couples who had separated without divorce and who had long been living with others. Further accounts from 1876 to 1879 noted married women 'absconding' from their homes and villages, to take up labour opportunities or build new relationships.[103] Nor did chiefs themselves avoid criticism, as Uluilakeba pointed out 'a great inconsistency' that some chiefs with government appointments had multiple wives, which was 'unbecoming' and set a poor example. The chiefs resolved that Roko and Buli should marry and those with multiple wives would either give up their wives or their government appointments.[104] These incidents demonstrate the difficulties in enforcing unified practices across the colony, with polygamy persisting in certain regions. Individuals subverted or disobeyed the orders of the chiefs in matters of private life, exercising choice in their relationships and movements. Fijian men and women thus capitalized on the changing circumstances and shifting authority of the 1870s to engage in new relationships or escape difficult ones.

Every year, anxieties over relationships between Fijian women and European men were revisited by the council, indicating the frequency of such relationships and the level of disquiet they generated. Of particular concern were the cases of Fijian women who ran away from their husbands and received protection from European men, some of whom threatened or fired upon the unfortunate person who attempted to return the woman to the village.[105] Ratu Golea (Roko Tui of Cakaudrove) and Ratu Maika recounted a case of an unnamed married Fijian woman of Kanacea. She left her husband and village in 1876 to live 'incontinently' with a European man in Selia Levu. The husband complained to Ratu Maika who 'sent for the woman'.[106] Though she denied the accusations of adultery, she was convicted to a year's imprisonment. Soon after, her pregnancy became obvious.

In Ratu Maika's absence and following letters from the white man offering to cover any expenses to free her from her marriage, European Stipendiary Magistrate (ESM) Hunter released the woman from custody and she returned to Seria Levu with her European partner. The *vunivola* (scribe) Mosese reported how Mr Hunter tried to give him $100 as 'the woman's "sere" (liberating her from her husband)', which was refused as Mosese was 'afraid of it, not knowing or understanding the meaning or way of it'.[107] This case highlights the development of affective relationships across the lines of race: the European man was prepared to pay fines and reparation for the woman's freedom and return. Such relationships were clearly attractive to some Fijian women, potentially offering an escape from an unhappy relationship or from village life as well as material or emotional gain. The Karacea case also underlines the clash of values and confusion over procedures such relationships generated between the Fijian chiefs, magistrates and the ESM: over the punishment of the woman, the payment of 'sere' and the question of to whom to return her. Throughout this episode, the woman's actions, emotions and even name are unrecorded, but her imprint on the events are visible if unacknowledged.

More broadly, chiefs were concerned that the discontented 'murmurings of the people' might threaten their control over village life. Doubts over their prerogative to police interracial relationships surfaced.[108] Buli Kubulau asked in 1878 'what can be done when white men take other men's wives?'[109] The debates were linked to broader questions about Indigenous authority over Fijian labourers working for Europeans as well as the women living with them, who were considered 'at the back of, or beyond, the law'.[110] The *vunivola* of Tailevu reported that women of his district were living unmarried with white men, raising questions among Fijians over the influence of traditional authority:

> The people say 'why should we be punished when the white man goes free?' This is called 'Vakapiritania' and causes much talk, and Fijians are following in their steps, saying we are all English now.[111]

Fijian villagers were clearly aware of and attentive to the shifting dynamics of power and the opportunities these created.

Though vexed by the inability to intervene in relationships between Fijian women and European men, the emerging consensus in the Bose Vakaturaga was that the punishment of white men who 'dishonoured' Fijian women must be left to the governor.[112] These discussions were central to the negotiation of the bounds of colonial and chiefly authority over Fijian and settler communities. In the spaces between, Fijians lived in ways that actively defied or unintentionally subverted the attempts to standardize customs of marriage, adultery and divorce: co-habiting together before marriage, separating with their spouse if unhappy or to pursue new employment or relationships, and, for women, 'absconding' to live with European men.

In subsequent decades, provincial court sittings in the villages reflected continued preoccupations with personal and intimate life. Ordinary Fijian men and women found themselves constrained by new regulations over adultery and mobility, though they frequently did not conform. The majority of the Provincial Courts' work was concerned with adultery and fornication, catch-all categories for sexual offences and promiscuity. Adultery involved sexual intercourse where one or both parties were married; fornication was between unmarried individuals. For example, in April 1876, a return of twenty-two cases tried at Nakasaleka by the NSM included eight counts of adultery and five of fornication. In the Lau Provincial Courts for 1895, fifty cases were heard, thirty were charges related to sexual violence, adultery (n = 16) and domestic life.[113]

These charges appear to have been treated as one and the same in the Provincial Courts, much to the frustration of some European magistrates.[114] Attempts to impose European categories of crime (and by extension moral behaviour) had limited success. Adultery and fornication were 'omnipresent moral crimes' within Fijian communities; they functioned as blanket terms for sexual behaviours on a spectrum from sexual intercourse outside marriage to rape.[115] The nature and understanding of normative and criminal behaviour was fluid and ESMs encountered problems asserting the hegemony of European legal definitions. NSMs and chiefs held significant influence in interpreting legislation and deciding who would go to court and on what charges. The cases nevertheless reveal the difficulties ensuring Fijians conformed to the chiefly and colonial vision of Islander society.

Sexual relationships also featured prominently in discussions of indentured plantation life. Reflecting on his time as chief police magistrate in Fiji, Gilchrist Alexander wrote that

> in the days of indentured Indian immigration in Fiji the bulk of the criminal work of the Courts was concerned with the coolie classes ... '*Cherchez la femme*' could literally be said in almost every serious criminal case which came from the sugar-plantations.[116]

This statement embodied the widely held view that Indian women were at the heart of myriad social problems characterizing plantation life: promiscuity, marriage breakdown, violence, murder and suicide. While the gender imbalance inherent in the indentured migration system was acknowledged, official and missionary-led reports fixated on female labourers as low-caste, licentious and predominantly of the 'prostitute class'.[117] With the perception of Indian men's temperament as sexually jealous, volatile and violent, gender and racial prejudices together explained the notoriety of 'the Indian … as the criminal of Fiji'.[118] Such racist explanations of plantation violence have been thoroughly debunked by Brij Lal and others, who highlight the systemic violence of indenture.[119]

From the perspective of missionaries such as John W. Burton, Charles F. Andrews and Hannah Dudley and observers such as overseer Walter Gill, the breakdown of marriage as the basic social unit was emblematic of the decay of Indian society in Fiji.[120] In fact, around a third of female indentured migrants arrived in Fiji with their husbands or family, while the remainder arrived single.[121] Nevertheless, the gender imbalance placed new pressures on immigrants, making it difficult for men to find a partner, creating rivalry over women and placing Indian women at the heart of sexual tensions and subject to coercion and abuse.

Despite attempts to attribute these social issues to the poor calibre and low morality of recruits, the administration's policy towards marriage registration, alongside the structure of plantation life, greatly contributed to the lack of stable marriage and gender relations. All Indian marriages had to be registered by a government official in Fiji, or in India prior to departure, to be considered legal. Religious marriages conducted on the plantation were not formally recognized. Since the five shilling cost of the official *marit* (marriage certificate) was prohibitive for many couples, the administration reported with some despair that few indentured Indian (or Islander) marriages were registered each year.[122] Many men and women formed partnerships and considered themselves married despite lacking state documentation.[123] The imbalance and lack of formalized relationships created a degree of fluidity, providing women with the opportunity to walk away from husbands or partners, while also creating competing claims to marital or sexual rights over individual women. The flexibility in marriage practice on the plantation not only offered indentured women freedom and choice but also exacerbated conditions for sexual and physical violence.

The Blue Books and court records substantiate disproportionately high levels of violence against women in the plantation, including assaults, rape and murder. Between 1890 and 1919 when women formed just over a third of the indentured labour force, sixty-eight indentured women were murdered compared to twenty-eight men. Between 1885 and 1920, 128 cases of rape were recorded, though many more cases were excluded from official statistics.[124] While official reports and some labourers themselves pinpointed sexual jealousy as the cause of violence against women and conflict between men, Shameem,

Kelly and Nicole all highlight that conflict over domestic life more generally was at the heart of many disputes.[125]

Although the immorality of indentured labourers occupied official attention, they ignored the widespread and often coercive sexual relationships between Indian women and the managers or employers of labour. Andrews and Pearson implicitly acknowledged this problem, arguing against the employment of unmarried European overseers or Indian *sirdars* as 'the temptation of such a position was too great'.[126] John Kelly writes that colonists 'never really registered the fact that there was a lot of rape going on, as well as other forms of sexual coercion for which we do not have a serious vocabulary'.[127]

This was the result of concurrent perceptions of Indians as 'labour units' and as property and therefore sexually available. Running parallel to European beliefs in Indian promiscuity was the perception that Indian society treated women as property. India was visualized as a country where women were worthless, 'a chattel design expressedly for man's sexual pleasure … [and] a breed utensil'.[128] Such views underpinned the attitudes of overseers and managers: as J. W. Davidson reported, 'it is sufficiently evident that Indian women are available to the males of every race in the Colony'.[129] These views justified some overseers and *sirdars* using women as a means of labour control by providing women to *sirdars* and favoured labourers in exchange for their loyalty.[130]

These themes are visible in overseer Walter Gill's account, published in 1970, of his relationship with Appelema, a young Muslim *ayah* (nursemaid) in a nearby European household, and in his discussion of Indian women generally. As a young man, Walter Gill worked as an overseer during the sunset of the indenture regime in Fiji. Like Fletcher in the New Hebrides, Gill was ambivalent about the colonial plantation system and his place within it. Despite his critique of indenture as a 'rotten system … fathered by Big Business on that most fecund of whores, cheap Asiatic labour' in which labourers were 'near human apes' and the women had 'the morals of an alleycat', he excused his own participation in the brutal system: 'the system and the conditions bred men to administer them'.[131]

His relationship nevertheless was a source of pleasure. Appelema visited twice weekly and, Gill wrote:

> because, for her, life was a nightmare of poverty, she eagerly accepted the few shillings I was able to let her have … Hers was a wide-eyed acceptance of the reason for her being there. I needed her body so she was content.[132]

Appelema's experience is filtered through the racist and patriarchal writings of her partner, obscuring her desires and choices in managing the partnership to her advantage. Gill echoes Fletcher in the New Hebrides, in the infantilization of non-European women and his own growing affection. Gill continued to arrange visits after he moved plantations, though the relationship was the subject of local gossip and disapproval.[133]

Many similar encounters or relationships were kept quiet: intimacies crossing racial boundaries were frowned upon by emergent 'polite' European society in Fiji, especially when these relationships were evidently more than sex. By 1909, the administration advised against such relationships as they were a cause of jealously and discontent among labourers and considered damaging to British prestige across empire, though there were no enforceable laws against miscegenation.[134] Sexual relationships (often coercive rather than consensual) between indentured women and *sirdars* or overseers were commonplace but discreet: cases came to official attention when the behaviour of the *sirdar* or overseer caused discontent and threatened the stability of the plantation economy.[135]

In spite of their disadvantaged position, Indian women like Appelema found some freedom from traditional social or kinship obligations on the plantations.[136] Their scarcity, coupled with the removal of family expectations, made possible a greater degree of choice and mobility in relationships. Speaking of multiple marriages, immigrant labourer Marda Naicker thus commented, 'I am the King of my mind.'[137] Critiques that they were mercenary suggest that Indian women took advantage of the limited opportunities to improve their social or economic position.[138] For example, the 1888 Annual Report on Immigration expressed concern that 'these women are prone to resort to means of livelihood which render them independent of the employment secured to them by indenture'.[139]

Some women certainly used prostitution to support themselves and were at times supported by their partners.[140] They found in sexual relationships, and even prostitution, opportunities to take some control of their lives from a position of vulnerability, gaining protection, gifts or money. Appelema, for example, was able to supplement her indentured salary through her relationship with Gill.[141] Within circumstances circumscribed by the inequalities of the plantation, Indian women were active in shaping aspects of their domestic and intimate lives in meaningful ways, the emotional labour of which is rendered invisible by patriarchal accounts.

Moreover, indentured women (and men) were not passive victims in situations of physical or sexual violence but actively sought retribution against physical assaults or sexual attacks. Gill recounts an incident at Rarawai where a work gang of indentured women urinated upon an abusive overseer, who subsequently departed in shame.[142] Other accounts note that women banded together and physically attacked an overseer or *sirdar* who was too heavy-handed in his treatment or too forceful in his sexual advances. At times, indentured men and family members supported indentured women. For example, *sirdar* Din Mohamed attempted to protect the women in his work gang from the overseer's advances.[143] Whereas *sirdars* and overseers used the colonial courts, coercion and violence as means of keeping order, otherwise disempowered indentured labourers employed tactics of co-operation, resistance or violence outside the courtroom.

The argument that structural elements of the system were the root of problems on the plantation gained traction among observers and missionaries and contributed to the winding down of indentured immigration between 1916 and 1920 (see Chapter 5). Inequalities and frequent violence along race, gender and class lines were nevertheless an undeniable part of the plantation experience in Fiji. Sexual and domestic relationships were a significant cause of conflict, as women negotiated opportunities for themselves in the transformation of family and kinship ties, sometimes pursued redress for abuses perpetrated by fellow labourers, *sirdars* and overseers, and as indentured men and women grappled with the challenges of reconstituted domestic life in the lines.

New Caledonia

The nineteenth-century engraved bamboo that opens this section (Figure 3) depicts a sexual relationship between a Kanak woman and a colonist, identifiable by his beard. Nicholas Thomas argues that these erotic portrayals spoke to the 'tensions and resentments around interracial sex, which were said to loom so large among Kanak grievances'.[144] For officials, settlers and Kanak, intimacy across the lines of race (and social divisions) was simultaneously a fact of colonial life and a concerning source of conflict.

As elsewhere, few statistics are available to quantify the extent of such relationships or the resulting mixed descent population (*métis)* in New Caledonia. There has been, until recently, a lack of historical attention to the subject. Divergent historiography focused either on Kanak experiences or 'pioneering' European settlers. European-Kanak relationships as well as other forms of *métissage* (between French *colons librés* and *libérés*; Kanak and indentured immigrants from the New Hebrides or later from Reunion, Japan and Indochina; or between European settlers and these other groups of newcomers) were 'a long taboo subject'.[145] This silence relates to both historical and political factors. Firstly, no distinctive *métis* community and culture emerged in New Caledonia as it did in some other French and British colonies.[146] Rather, individuals of mixed descent were generally integrated into local Kanak society or, occasionally, into French settler society. The division of the colony on racial and spatial lines through the Indigénat contributed to demarcations that left little space for individuals in-between.[147] The official emphasis from the conflict of 1878–9 to the end of the Indigénat in 1946 was on the differences between Kanak and French settlers, rather than on assimilation.

This narrative has shifted as the post-*événements* New Caledonia seeks to build the 'destin commun' outlined by the 1988 Matignon and 1998 Nouméa Accords. Historical writing in this political context has acknowledged the cultural mixing and explored *métissage* in search of a shared history between Kanak and French settlers. This parallels the greater acceptance of intermarriage in the territory itself.[148] As Isabelle Leblic notes, until recently many individuals of mixed descent preferred to claim some Tahitian ancestry rather than acknowledge their Kanak heritage.[149] This scholarship reflects broader attempts to reconcile opposing historical memories and traditions in New Caledonia, as well as enabling members of the Calédonien community to claim rights in a period of political uncertainty.[150] More entangled historical experiences and alliances were nevertheless well known and carefully navigated by nineteenth- and twentieth-century communities and officials, as Benoît Trépied's rich study of Koné demonstrates.[151]

Some years prior to 1878, a French *libéré* named Chêne kidnapped a Dogny woman from the Bouloupari area of the Grande Terre, New Caledonia, before leaving the district. Upon his return with his family in June 1878, the Dogny decided to take retribution for the abduction. On the night of 18 June, three men crossed La Foa river and murdered Chêne, his partner and some of their children.[152] The subsequent arrests of local chiefs by French *gendarmes* precipitated the 1878–9 rebellion. Reporting on the causes of the 'insurrection', head of the inquiry Arthur de Trentitian wrote,

> The Kanak women are but an incident in this unfortunate history, but it is nevertheless necessary to speak of them, as their abduction has often given rise to massacres.[153]

Commandant Henri Rivière argued that such violence represented a more fundamental conflict between the races, while ethnographer and doctor Patouillet similarly asserted that nine of ten Kanak 'quarrels' were caused by the kidnapping or rape of women.[154] The question of intimate relationships was a recurrent element in colonial assessments of conflict, though accounts such as Trentitian's situate Kanak women as passive in a war conducted by men.

The cause of conflict between *tribus* around Ouraïl and Bouloupari-Thio and the French authorities and their Kanak allies has also subsequently been the subject of historical debate.[155] The increased incursions of grazing cattle of European pastoralists and inter-tribal politics contributed to and sustained the war. Nevertheless, contemporaneous local accounts of the 'revolt' focused on intimate relationships as a key factor in Kanak disaffection. This view reflected late-nineteenth-century official attitudes that blamed violence on inherent Kanak 'savagery' as well as on the individual colonists who provoked it, rather than with the colonial process itself.[156] Reflecting on the conflict more recently, Marie-Claire Beccalossi explained that 'the *droit du seigneur* (aristocrat's sexual rights) of the colonists, who had the right to get girls from the tribe to work on their properties' and the colonists' cattle damaging land both contributed to Kanak grievances and resistance.[157]

While varied factors underpinning the events of 1878–9, it is worth examining the place of women in the conflict more broadly. Reports on the rape and murders of European women and children made an emotive contribution to European perceptions of Kanak brutality and to calls for strong French retaliation.[158] For Kanak, as Bronwen Douglas notes, the 'booty' of war for *tribus* allied to the French (and sanctioned by the Governor) included the women of opposing *tribu*. This reflected Melanesian preferences to 'absorb the defeated … or to incorporate them within their sphere of influence'.[159] Colonial accounts nevertheless situated Kanak women as passive, in contrast to men active in the business of warfare and diplomacy. However, women were both present and actively involved in the conflict, gathering crops from defeated villages and contributing to peace negotiations.[160]

Kanak women also regularly navigated relationships in changing social and political circumstances in significant but less visible ways. Marriage was central to building alliances in Kanak society. Initially partnerships with European newcomers provided knowledge and access to another society, as occurred around the Pacific.[161] With immigration to the colony being predominately male, the practice of newcomer men establishing relationships with Kanak women as domestic and sexual partners, on a spectrum from consensual or coerced, was widespread. Kanak women were described as 'very loyal … becoming good housekeepers and good mothers of families'.[162] Female Islanders indentured in New Caledonia were also in demand as domestic servants and partners.[163] As Trentitian reported in 1879:

> The majority of settlers in the bush live with indigenous women, the Gendarmes themselves completely isolated, in the milieu of the country, do not deprive themselves in anyway to do likewise ... It is necessary to say that the popinées, as they are called here, almost all prefer to live with Europeans, and this is easy to understand; in the tribu, they do most of the work.[164]

Trentitian and others embedded women's choices to live with Europeans in a Eurocentric view of the deprivation and patriarchy of Kanak society. These accounts tend to minimize the agency of the women, who were strategic in their partnership and likely found some material or emotional advantages to such relationships. The opportunities such relationships offered must have been attractive for some women and their kin, though coercion could be equally significant for women removed from community networks.[165]

Relationships in which European men were incorporated into the *tribu* occurred throughout the nineteenth century but became increasingly rare as colonial settlement grew.[166] Instead of being located in the *tribu*, Kanak-European relationships shifted to colonial settlements. The departure of young women to stations, towns or mines deprived Kanak *tribu* of marriage partners and the bases for alliance-building.[167] Such relationships offered Kanak women an alternative to endogamous marriage but raised complex issues over the (re) integration of women and *métis* children into the *tribu* with uncertainties over their land rights and customary status. Nevertheless, many (but not all) *métis* children, as well as occasionally ni-Vanuatu, were incorporated into the *tribu*, in part due to the racism of settler society.[168] Intimate relationships between Kanak women and newcomer men required negotiation of social norms and boundaries, on a largely quotidian, interpersonal basis but occasionally flared dramatically into broader conflict.

The everyday negotiations are occasionally evident in the official archives, since some individuals in mixed marriages, as well as *métis* children, sought official guarantees of their rights and status from the colonial government. Mixed-descent individuals, especially those who were culturally *métis*, were an administrative headache for officials working within a system predicated on clear-cut divisions of race and identity between *citoyens français* and *indigènes*. Individual lives and relationships did not neatly align with official categories. However, beginning as a penal colony, the development of French settlement in New Caledonia was distinct from that of the colonial townships of Franceville (later Port Vila) or Levuka, where European expansion was haphazard, organic and preceded formal colonization.[169] There were limited attempts at self-government comparable to Franceville. Individuals instead petitioned or contested official definitions of their racial status and associated rights, highlighting the instability of colonial definitions and the fluidity of individuals' identities.[170]

Colonial officials were unsure who could be tried under Indigénat regulations, or even whether *indigènes* or *métis* could marry under French law.[171] As an example, in 1907, on the eve of annexation, Messieurs Rossi and Rodin sent a petition from the New Hebrides to the New Caledonian administration to become naturalized Frenchmen. The men claimed to be sons of French and Swedish fathers and a Kanak mother. Their request stirred debate between the Procureur-Général, the Governor and the Minister of Colonies, as their education placed them 'well above the social and intellectual level of Kanak' and Rossi's sister, having married a French national, was already a French citizen.[172] On the other hand, their paternity was not recognized, meaning that their legal status should derive from their mother.[173] By the time the case received the Minister's attention, the New Hebrides Condominium had been established, further complicating the situation, since French law could not simply be applied to the case as New Caledonian officials had previously assumed. The Minster argued that, as the men had been educated for some years in New Caledonia and the British administration in the New Hebrides recognized them as French, their naturalization should be possible under New Caledonian (rather than Condominium) law.[174] This case, crossing jurisdictions as well as racial categories, highlighted the ways in which racial and national status were linked to social markers such as education as much as to descent.

In 1910, the Head of the Judicial Service and the Commandant of the Pacific region attempted to establish general principles to address the question of *métis* identity in New Caledonia. In France, the Procureur-Général noted that children of unknown parentage are 'naturally' assumed to be French, but 'the application of these principles in a colony where alongside French *citizens*, there are indigenous French *subjects*, could lead to very strange consequences'.[175] His letter listed which *métis* he believed should be categorized as French citizens. These included individuals born of marriages between Frenchmen and Indigenous women or a French woman and an *indigène sujet français*; those born of Frenchmen and an Indigenous woman if the father recognized the child or vice versa; and those born to Indigenous women previously married to a French citizen and who retained their French nationality. Finally, for those of totally unknown parentage, individuals raised in a 'milieu européenne' could be considered French, again emphasizing the importance of cultural and social background in determining colonial and racial identities.

Conclusion

The gendered nature of European imperialism and penal, free and indentured immigration meant colonization had a particular impact on women. While racist rhetoric of morality and civilization underpinned simplistic official views of Pacific societies, the depths of individual experiences of intimacy, sex and sometimes violence is only glimpsed through the colonial archive and men's writings, most often surfacing were they contravened colonial authority. New relationships were enabled by contact and colonial expansion, as well as the transformation of old practices. Multiple, adaptable intimacies characterized the early period of colonial rule, frequently defying categorization or management by colonial states, Islander elites, missionaries and colonists.

Intimate relationships between different indentured labourers, managers, Islanders and other newcomers emerged during indentured recruitment and plantation life. These relationships could be non-consensual and abusive, as emphasized by court cases in Chapter 3 and protests against recruitment discussed further in Chapter 5. However, as the relationships between Kohkonne and Fletcher and Appelema and Gill demonstrates, the picture was more complex: discriminatory racial attitudes co-existed with affectionate relationships and family life and women were strategic and active in emotional management. Given the systemic imbalance of power, such relationships existed less on a spectrum from, than a synchrony of, coercive to consensual elements.

Various groups attempted to control sexuality, morality and community life in this period of change, often as one facet in a strategy to increase their own power and influence. Both prior to and in the early decades of colonial rule, European settlers, missionaries and Islanders contested and negotiated their own social norms where they perceived state law to be absent or inadequate. This was especially visible between the cracks in colonial governance over the New Hebrides, including Franceville settlers' attempts at self-government and in the shifting politics and influence of the Tannese mission courts. In both cases, questions about marriage, sexual relationships and religious or civil sanctions were prominent, in the rhetoric deployed and in the impact on the lives of individual Islanders and settlers. In Fiji, the disapproval and concerns aired by Fijian chiefs or European officials and missionaries, as well as occasional Indian petitions, similarly demonstrates the desire and conversely the difficulty in asserting control over intimacy.

While none of the colonies under study explicitly prohibited interracial relationships, the divisive potential social and legal quandaries they raised meant that kidnapping, sex, mixed marriage and children all demanded official attention. *Métissage* characterized the colonial experience from its earliest years. In nineteenth-century New Caledonia interracial relationships were considered a source of tension or even conflict, as much as they underpinned alliances between *tribus* or between *tribus* and European or Islander newcomers. Reporting of the 1878–9 war highlights the way in which intimate relationships could be tied into political discourse, and contributed to Kanak resistance to French expansion in the Grande Terre. On a personal level, individuals in mixed marriages or of mixed descent were more inclined to negotiate the boundaries of colonizer and colonized, petitioning colonial officials in an attempt to secure their status and rights in the colony. The headaches that such cases posed for the colonial administration indicate the fiction upon which the perceived natural divisions between Kanak and European rested.

In each colony, though shaped by differing economic and political contexts, predominantly male colonial and Indigenous elites demonstrated a common concern to monitor and maintain some control over the intimate relations of Islanders, especially in their relationships with Europeans. Some colonists and missionaries were similarly interested in establishing social, moral and economic order amongst their communities. The examples in this chapter highlight local cultures of intimacy as well as of making and maintaining the law across New Caledonia, Fiji and especially the New Hebrides. While the colonial state was invested in controlling internal and intimate frontiers, so too were Islanders, missions and colonists. Throughout this period, these interests variously conflicted and converged as women navigated the opportunities, constraints and violence of the period.

Notes

1 Jesse Hopson to J. O'N. Brenan, Immigration Agent Brisbane, 23/3/1909, Folder 22A/1908, NHBS 1/I Vol. 1, WPA.

2 J. W. Bleakey Pro Chief Protector of Aboriginals to Resident Commissioner, 15/7/1909, Folder 22A/1908, NHBS 1/I Vol. 1, WPA.

3 Shineberg, 'The New Hebridean Is Everywhere', 13, and footnotes 76 and 77.

4 Tracey Banivanua Mar and Nadia Rhook, 'Counter Networks of Empires: Reading Unexpected People in Unexpected Places', *Journal of Colonialism and Colonial History* 19, no. 2 (2018).

5 Thomas, *Islanders.*

6 Stoler, *Carnal Knowledge*, 110.

7 Paula J. Bryne, *Criminal Law and Colonial Subject: New South Wales, 1810–1830* (Cambridge: Cambridge University Press, 1993), 2.

8 Nicholas Thomas, 'Colonial Conversions: Difference, Hierarchy, and History in Early Twentieth-Century Evangelical Propaganda', *Comparative Studies in Society and History* 3, no. 2 (1992), 366–89; Thomas, *Colonialism's Culture*, 112–14.

9 Douglas and Ballard, 'Race, Place and Civilisation', 255.

10 Neil Gunson, *Messengers of Grace: Evangelical Missionaries in the South Seas 1797–1860* (Melbourne: Oxford University Press, 1978); Jolly and Macintyre *Family and Gender.*

11 No. 104 Affaires Indigènes, Inspecteur Bougourd à Ministre des Colonies, 23 mai 1919, ADC Carton 826, ANOM.

12 Belich, *Making Peoples*, 223. Jocelyn Linnekin, 'New Political Orders', in Donald Denoon (ed.), *The Cambridge History of the Pacific Islanders* (Cambridge: Cambridge University Press, 2004), 203.

13 Alexander, *From the Middle Temple*, 146; Burton, *The Fiji of To-Day*, 55. See also des Voeux, *My Colonial Service*, vol. 1, 357.

14 Ernest Davillé, *La Colonisation Française aux Nouvelles-Hébrides* (Paris: Librarie Africaine et Coloniale, 1895), 70; Service de l'Administration Générale–Rapport fait par M. Bougourd, 20 novembre 1918, SG-NH, Carton 31, ANOM; British Resident Commissioner to French Resident Commissioner, 10 April 1913, Folder 106a/1912, and Minutes of the Meeting of the JNC, HMS *Pegasus*, 21 October 1909, Folder 71/1909, NHBS 1/I Vol. 1, WPA.

15 Burton, *The Fiji of To-Day* is characteristic of such narratives.

16 Thomas, *Colonialism's Culture*, 112–13; Burton, *The Fiji of To-Day*, 8, 197–210, 233; Jacomb, *The Future of the Kanaka*, 37, 48–9, 61–5.

17 Inspecteur Adam à Ministre des Colonies, 15 mars 1896, ADC Carton 821; and No. 104 Affaires Indigènes, Inspecteur Bougourd à Ministre des Colonies, 23 mai 1919, ADC Carton 826, ANOM.

18 O'Brien, *The Pacific Muse*, 13, 161; Phillipa Levine, 'What's British about Gender and Empire? The Problem of Exceptionalism', *Comparative Studies of South Asia, Africa and the Middle East* 27, no. 2 (2007), 273–82; Jane Samson, 'Rescuing Fijian Women? The British Anti-Slavery Proclamation of 1852', *Journal of Pacific History* 30, no. 1 (1995), 22–38; Knapman, *White Women in Fiji*, 20–1, 27–8.

19 Davillé, *La Colonisation*, 69. See also Capitaine H. Buchard à Ministre de la Marine, 26 août 1907, SG-NH Carton 5, ANOM. For Fiji, see *Report of the Commission on Decrease of the Native Population 1893* (Suva: Government of Fiji, 1896), 38. See also: Alan Berman, 'Kanak Women and the Colonial Process', *International Journal of Law in Context* 2 (2006), 23; Bullard, *Exile to Paradise.*

20 See: Basil Thomson, *The Fijians: A Study of the Decay of Custom* (London: Dawsons of Pall Mall, 1968 [1908]); Burton, *The Fiji of To-Day*, 236–7, 253–5; Davillé, *La Colonisation Française*, 80; Speiser, *Two Years*, 4, 12–15. On abortion in New Caledonia, see No. 46 Affaires Indigenes, Inspecteur Revel à Ministre des Colonies, 10 juin 1912, ADC Carton 822, ANOM; and Discours prononcé par M. Paul FEILLET Gouverneur de la Nouvelle-Calédonie et Dependancies, à l'Ouverture de la Session Ordinaire du Conseil Général, 3 juin 1901, DAP AFFPOL Carton 266, ANOM. For discussion of law to prevent knocking women's teeth out on Malekula, see Folder 219A/1908 (Complaint against native customs in Malekula from Rev. F. J. Paton), NHBS 1/I Vol. 1, WPA.

21 *Report of the Commission on Decrease of the Native Population 1893* (Suva: Government of Fiji, 1896); Jacomb, *The Future of the Kanaka*, 48–9 (but compare 62); Thomas, *Colonialism's Culture*, 112–15; Vicki Luker, 'A Tale of Two Mothers'; Jolly, 'Other Mothers'.

22 Thomas, *Islanders*, 211–13.

23 Shineberg, *The People Trade*, 96–100, 112–13.

24 Ibid., 84–7, 94–5; Moore, 'Australian South Sea Islanders' Narratives of Belonging'; Banivanua Mar, *Violence and Colonial Dialogue;* Deryck Scarr, 'Recruits and Recruiters: A Portrait of the Pacific Island Labour Trade', in J. W. Davidson and D. Scarr (eds), *Pacific Island Portraits* (Canberra: Australian National University Press, 1970), 225–51.

25 Margaret Rodman, Daniela Kraemer, Lissant Bolton and Jean Tarasesei (eds), *Housegirls Remember: Domestic Workers in Vanuatu* (Honolulu: University of Hawai'i Press, 2007).

26 Rodman, *Houses Far from Home*, 19.

27 Stober, 'Isles of Illusion', 353; Michael G. Young, 'Gone Native in Isles of Illusion: In Search of Asterisk in Epi', in James G. Carrier (ed.), *History and Tradition in Melanesian Anthropology* (Berkeley: University of California Press, 1992), 194.

28 'Asterisk', *Isles of Illusion*, 149, 194. Also recorded as Ouéla Kohkun in *Gone Native.*

29 Ibid.; Daniel Defert, 'Fletcher, Robert James. Iles Paradis, Iles d'Illusion, Lettres des Mers du Sud. Un Cas d'hébridisation: Robert James Fletcher', *Journal de la Société des Océanistes* 37, no. 70 (1981), 130.

30 The first French edition appeared in 1926 as *Lettres des Îles-Paradis*, translated by Marthe Coblentz (Paris: F. Roeder, 1926); it was re-issued in French and English and inspired the film *Inseln der Illusion*. Fletcher rewrote his experience as a novel, *Gone Native.* See: Jean Jamin, 'Note sur l'étrange cas de Robert James FLETCHER', *Journal de la Société des océanistes* 37, no. 70 (1981), 131–2. Stober, 'Isles of Illusion', 354; Young, 'Gone Native', 203.

31 Defert, 'Fletcher', 131; Young, 'Gone Native', 194–6.

32 'Asterisk', *Isles of Illusion*, 181.

33 Ibid., 237, 215.

34 Ibid., 195, 237.

35 Lissant Bolton, 'Women, Place and Practice in Vanuatu: A View from Ambae', *Oceania* 70, no. 1 (1999), 43.

36 'Asterisk', *Gone Native*; see also Shineberg, *The People Trade*, 94–5.

37 Shineberg, *The People Trade*, 104; Karin Speedy, *Georges Baudoux's Jean M'Barai The Trepang Fisherman* (Sydney: UTS Sydney ePress, 2015), 58–9.

38 'Asterisk', *Isles of Illusion*, 165–7.

39 Ibid., 155. See also Thomas, *Colonialism's Culture*, 143–9 on British colonial attitudes towards 'half-castes', mission-educated 'natives' and assimilation.

40 'Asterisk', *Isles of Illusion*, 208–9; O'Brien, *Pacific Muse*, 228.

41 'Asterisk', *Isles of Illusion*, 237.

42 Ibid., 104.

43 Ibid., 167, 237.

44 Ibid., 245.

45 See Minute S. P. to R. C., 29/7/1924, Folder 131/1924, NHBS 1/I Vol. 2, WPA; Letter from R. J. Fletcher, 9 September and 5 October 1919, MS 894/28 Edward Jacomb Diary 1918–19, SHL.

46 'Asterisk', *Isles of Illusion*, 215; see also 51.

47 Ibid., 172.

48 Captain Kane to Admiral Fairfax, 19 August 1889, SG-NH Carton 3, ANOM.

49 Ibid.; Katherine Stirling Kerr Cawsey, *The Making of a Rebel: Captain Donald Macleod of the New Hebrides* (Suva: Institute of Pacific Studies, University of the South Pacific, 1998), 391–2, 398.

50 For other attempts at chiefly and community governance of emerging settlements, most notably by Kamehameha I in Honolulu and David Whippy in Levuka, see: Caroline Ralston, *Grass Huts and Warehouse: Pacific Beach Communities of the Nineteenth Century* (Canberra: Australian National University Press, 1977), esp. 69–76; Legge, *Britain in Fiji*, chapter 4.

51 'Wee Small Republics: A Few Examples of Popular Government', *Hawaiian Gazette*, 1 November 1895.

52 Cawsey, *The Making of a Rebel*, 387–8.

53 Julian Bourdiol, *Condition Internationale des Nouvelles-Hébrides* (Nîmes: Imprimerie Cooperative 'La Labourieuse', 1908), 92, 133.

54 Bourdiol, *Condition Internationale*, 133–8.

55 'Wee Small Republics: A Few Examples of Popular Government', *Hawaiian Gazette*, 1 November 1895.

56 Auguste Brunet, *Le régime international des Nouvelles-Hébrides: le condominium anglo-français* (Paris: Arthur Russeau, 1908), 65.

57 Bourdiol, *Condition Internationale*, 107. Cawsey, *The Making of a Rebel*, 397–8; Davillé, *La Colonisation Française*, 101.

58 'Under Two Flags. In the New Hebrides, the Anglo-French Condominium', *Poverty Bay Herald*, 22 February 1911. See also No. 1020 à 1028 Commissaire Délégue aux Nouvelles-Hébrides, 23W C13, ANC, for official discussion over the lack of jurisdiction in the New Hebrides over marriage and divorce.

59 Ralston, *Grass Huts and Warehouses*, 69.

60 John Davies, *The History of the Tahitian Mission, 1788–1830*, edited by Colin Newbury (Cambridge: Cambridge University Press for the Hakluyt Society, 1961); Merry, *Colonizing Hawai'i*, chapter 3; Colin Newbury, 'Pacts, Alliances and Patronage: Modes of Influence and Power in the Pacific', *Journal of Pacific History* 44, no. 2 (2009), 150; Louis-Joseph Bouge, 'Première législation tahitienne. Le Code Pomaré de 1819. Historique et traduction', *Journal de la Société des océanistes* 8 (1952), 5–26.

61 Rodman, *House Far from Home*, 136.

62 British Resident Commissioner to High Commissioner, 30 December 1912, Folder 115/1912, NHBS 1/I Vol. 1, WPA.

63 Wilkes to British Resident Commissioner, 9 October 1912, Folder 115/1912, NHBS 1/I Vol. 1, WPA.

64 British Resident Commissioner to High Commissioner, 30 December 1912, Folder 115/1912, NHBS 1/I Vol. 1, WPA.

65 Scarr, *Fragments of Empire*, 243; Bonnemaison, *The Tree and the Canoe*, 199.

66 Bonnemaison, *The Tree and the Canoe*, 201.

67 Wilkes to British Resident Commissioner, 9 October 1912, Folder 115/1912, NHBS 1/I Vol. 1, WPA.

68 Folder 15/1926 (Tanna Native Courts. 1925–7), NHBS 1/I Vol. 2, WPA.

69 Bonnemaison, *The Tree and the Canoe*, 200; Wilkes to British Resident Commissioner, 9 October 1912, Folder 115/1912, NHBS 1/I Vol. 1, WPA; Jean Guiart, 'Culture Contact and the "John Frum" Movement on Tanna', *Southwestern Journal of Anthropology* 12, no. 1 (1956), 109–10. See also Ron Adams, 'Homo Anthropologicus and Man-Tanna: Jean Guiart and the Anthropological Attempt to Understand the Tannese', *Journal of Pacific History* 22, no. 1 (1987), 10–12 on how male perspectives dominate Guiart's anthropological accounts of women in Tanna.

70 Ron Brunton, *The Abandoned Narcotic: Kava and Cultural Instability in Melanesia* (Cambridge: Cambridge University Press, 1989) 117; Jean Guiart, *Un siècle et demi de contacts culturels à Tanna* (Paris: Musée de l'Homme, 1956), 134, 139.

71 Wilkes to British Resident Commissioner, 9 October 1912, Folder 115/1912, NHBS 1/I Vol. 1, WPA.

72 Bonnemaison, *The Tree and the Canoe*, 215–17; David J. Richardson, 'Kastom versus Cross: A Battle for Cultural Hegemony on Tanna', in Brij Lal (ed.),

Wansalawara: Soundings in Melanesian History (Honolulu: University of Hawai'i Pacific Islands Studies Program, Working Paper Series, 1987), 104.

73 F. H. May High Commissioner to Lewis Verson Harcourt (Secretary of State for Colonies), 30 November 1911, Folder 77/1912, NHBS 1/I Vol. 1, WPA. See: Scarr, *Fragments of Empire*, 236–7 and 243.

74 For example: *Le Néo-Hébridais,* December 1910, in Bonnemaison, *The Tree and the Canoe*, 202, and *Le Néo-Hébridais,* 1 September 1910 in Scarr, *Fragments of Empire*, 237.

75 Ordre Conjoint du 2 Janvier 1909, Folder 115/1912, NHBS 1/I Vol. 1, WPA.

76 Wilkes to British Resident Commissioner, 9 October 1912, Folder 115/1912, NHBS 1/I Vol. 1, WPA.

77 Translation of letter from Koukarei, Tanna, to Resident Commissioner Mahaffy, November 1912, Folder 115/1912, NHBS 1/I Vol. 1, WPA.

78 Wilkes to British Resident Commissioner, 9 October 1912, Folder 115/1912, NHBS 1/I Vol. 1, WPA.

79 Commander HMS *Pegasus* to BRC, 14/10/1909, Folder 71/1909, NHBS 1/I Vol. 1, WPA.

80 Inspecteur Revel à Ministre des Colonies, 3 juin 1912, SG-NH Carton 31, ANOM.

81 Bonnemaison, *The Tree and the Canoe*, 201. He is remembered locally as having been a great supporter of kastom; see: Brunton, *The Abandoned Narcotic*, 118; Scarr, *Fragments of Empire*, 244.

82 BRC to High Commissioner, 30 December 1912, Folder 115/1912, NHBS 1/I Vol. 1, WPA.

83 Translation of letter from Koukarei to Resident Commissioner Mahaffy, November 1912, Folder 115/1912, NHBS 1/I Vol. 1, WPA.

84 Bonnemaison, *The Tree and the Canoe*, 202, 205–8.

85 BRC to High Commissioner, 30 December 1912, Folder 115/1912, NHBS 1/I Vol. 1, WPA. See Folder 5/1 Part I, NHBS 15/I, WPA, for the draft Regulation No. 3 of 1912 on Tanna Native Courts.

86 Scarr, *Fragments of Empire*, 246.

87 Guiart, 'Culture Contact', 5–6.

88 BRC to High Commissioner, 30 December 1912, Folder 115/1912, NHBS 1/I Vol. 1, WPA.

89 Wilkes to BRC, 9 March, encl. to Resident Commissioner to High Commissioner, 27 March 1914, NHBS 1/I Vol. 1, WPA; Adams, 'Homo Anthropologicus', 14.

90 Marc Tabani, 'Dreams of Unity, Traditions of Division: John Frum, Kastom and Inter-Manipulation Strategies as Cultural Heritage on Tanna (Vanuatu)', *Paideuma* 55 (2009), 27–47.

91 Mafi (Native Magistrate), 29 September 1875, 'Proceedings of the Native Council', Draiba, September 1875, NAF.

92 Newbury, '*Bose Vakaturaga*'.

93 Thomas, *Colonialism's Culture*, 108–12; Thomas, 'Seeing like a State'; Nicole, *Disturbing History*, chapters 5 and 7.

94 Thomas, *Colonialism's Culture*, 108.

95 'Proceedings of the Native Council', Draiba, September 1875, NAF.

96 Ma'afu (Roko Tui Lau) was support by the Roko Tui Bua and Native Magistrates Ratu Ilaitia and Mafi. See discussion of 20 September 1875, 'Proceedings of the Native Council', Draiba, September 1875, NAF.

97 'Proceedings of the Native Council', Draiba, September 1875, NAF. See also Native Regulation No. 12 of 1877 regarding Marriage and Divorce, *Fiji Government Gazette*, no. 17, vol. 3, 26 May 1877, CO 86/1, NAK.

98 Native Regulation No. 11 of 1877 regarding Adultery and Fornication and Native Regulation No. 12 of 1877 regarding Marriage and Divorce, *Fiji Government Gazette*, no. 17, vol. 3, 26 May 1877, CO 86/1, NAK; Stanmore, *Fiji*, vol. 1, 323–4.

99 For example: 1 December 1976, 'Proceedings of the Native Council', Waikava, November–December 1876, NAF; 1 January 1878, 'Proceedings of the Native Council', Rewa, December–January 1877–8, NAF; 19, 20 and 28–29 November, 'Proceedings of the Native Council', Bua, November–December 1878, NAF; 11 and 17 December 1879, 'Proceedings of the Native Council', Na Vatanitawake, December 1879, NAF; and 27 November and 4 December 1880, 'Proceedings of the Native Council', Mualevu, 1880–1, NAF.

100 For example: Buli Kubulau, 1 January 1878, 'Proceedings of the Native Council', Rewa, December–January 1877–8, NAF.

101 'Proceedings of the Native Council', Draiba, September 1875, NAF.

102 Roko Tui Ba, 19 November 1880, 'Proceedings of the Native Council', Mualevu, 1880–1, NAF. See also Burton, *The Fiji of To-Day*, 204–5 for a missionary perspective.

103 For example: 5 and 15 December 1876, 'Proceedings of the Native Council', Waikava, November–December 1876, NAF; 29 November 1878, 'Proceedings of the Native Council', Bua, November–December 1878, NAF; and 17 December 1879, 'Proceedings of the Native Council', Na Vatanitawake, December 1879, NAF.

104 22 September 1875, 'Proceedings of the Native Council', Draiba, September 1875, NAF. See also: No. 316/83 Swayne to Geo. Garrick, 15 November 1883, S. M. Lau-Outward Letter Book 1882–3, Lau Provincial Council Records, NAF.

105 For example: 5 and 9 December 1876, 'Proceedings of the Native Council', Waikava, November–December 1876, NAF.

106 Ratu Maika, 1 December 1876, 'Proceedings of the Native Council', Waikava, November–December 1876, NAF.

107 Mosese, 1 December 1876, 'Proceedings of the Native Council', Waikava, November–December 1876, NAF; further examples in Stanmore, *Fiji*, vol. 1, 372–4.

108 Nicole, *Disturbing History*, 130–1.

109 For example: 1 January 1878, 'Proceedings of the Native Council', Bua, November–December 1878, NAF.

110 Roko Tui Ba and Yasawa, 22 September 1875, 'Proceedings of the Native Council', Draiba, September 1875, NAF. See also: P. S. Friend (Stipendiary Magistrate for Lower Rewa) to Colonial Secretary, CSO 76/1583; P. S. Friend to Colonial Secretary, CSO MP 76/1585; and G. R. Le Hunte (Stipendiary Magistrate for Loma Loma) to Colonial Secretary, CSO MP 77/330, NAF.

111 22 September 1875, 'Proceedings of the Native Council', Draiba, September 1875, NAF.

112 See, for example, Roko Tui Tailevu, 22 September 1875, 'Proceedings of the Native Council', Draiba, September 1875, NAF; though contrast ESM Le Hunte to Gordon 3/12/1875. Stanmore, *Fiji*, vol. 1, 373.

113 R. Swanston to Colonial Secretary, CSO MP 76/742, NAF. See also: G. R. Le Hunte (Stipendiary Magistrate for Loma Loma) to Colonial Secretary, CSO MP 77/330, NAF; and Stipendiary Magistrate–Lau Provincial Court Book 1893–1902, Lau Provincial Council Records, NAF.

114 A. Eastgate, Stipendiary Magistrate Tai Levu, to Colonial Secretary, 30 October 1880, CSO MP 80/1876; Henry Anson, Stipendiary Magistrate Na Wi, to Colonial Secretary, 1 September 1880, CSO MP 80/1566, NAF.

115 Minute to Native Commissioner, 19/6/1899, CSO 2778/1899, NAF.

116 Alexander, *From the Middle Temple*, 88.

117 Andrews and Pearson, *Indian Indentured Labour*, 27; C. F. Andrews, 'Report of Mr. Andrews' Speech to the Planters' Association Executive Committee', 7 December 1915, MOM 520, Mitchell Library, 9; see also Annual Reports on Indian Immigration. Conflict between 'Polynesian' immigrants was similarly attributed to 'challenges based upon the infringement of vest rights with regard to women'; Council Paper No. 25: Annual Report on Polynesian Immigration 1884, 23, *Journal of the Legislative Council*, 1886.

118 Report of Mr Andrews' Speech to the Planters' Association Executive Committee, Fiji, 7 December 1915, MOM 520, Mitchell Library, 9; Council Paper No. 51: Report on the Fiji Constabulary for the Year 1909, 18, Legislative Council Papers 1910; Brij Lal, 'Veil of Dishonour'.

119 Lal, *Chalo Jahaji*; Naidu, *The Violence of Indenture*; Kelly, *A Politics of Virtue;* Nicole, *Disturbing History*.

120 Burton, *The Fiji of To-day*; Andrews and Pearson, *Indian Indentured Labour;* Gill, *Turn Northeast*.

121 Lal, *Chalo Jahaji*, 197.

122 Council Paper No. 14: Matrimonial Causes. Scale of Fees, 131, Minutes of the Proceedings of the Legislative Council 1907; Council Paper No. 29: Annual Report

on Indian Immigration 1887, 4, Legislative Council Papers 1888; Council Paper No. 20: Annual Report on Indian Immigration 1902, 15, Legislative Council Papers 1903; Naidu, *The Violence of Indenture,* 42; Council Paper No. 23: Annual Report on Polynesian Immigration 1884, 23, *Journal of the Legislative Council,* 1886.

123 Burton, *The Fiji of To-Day*, 315–16.

124 Statistics distinguish between the gender of the murder victim from 1890. Naidu, *The Violence of Indenture*, 71, 79.

125 Ibid., 41; Shameem, 'Sugar and Spice'; Kelly, *A Politics of Virtue*; Nicole, 'Disturbing History', 346.

126 Andrews and Pearson, *Indian Indentured Labour*, 56.

127 Kelly, '"Coolie" as Labour Commodity', 261–2.

128 Gill, *Turn Northeast*, 48.

129 Council Paper No. 20: Annual Report on Indian Immigration 1902, 19, Legislative Council Papers 1903.

130 Andrews and Pearson, *Indian Indentured Labour*, 17, 27; Naidu, *The Violence of Indenture*, 41–2. See Petition from Indenured Indian Indr Singh, as to treatment of coolies in Fiji, Government of Indian to Colonial Secretary of Fiji, 10/5/1909, CSO 5050/1909, NAF for a petition from sahibs taking Indian women.

131 Gill, *Turn Northeast*, 38, 65, 71.

132 Ibid., 80.

133 Gill, *Turn Northeast*, 80; Kelly, *A Politics of Virtue*, 35–40; Knapman, *White Women in Fiji*.

134 Colonial Secretary to Secretary to the Government of India, 29 June 1909, CSO 5050/1909, NAF; Ronald Hyam, 'Concubinage and the Colonial Service: The Crewe Circular (1909)', *Journal of Imperial and Commonwealth History* 14, no. 3 (1986), 170–86; Knapman, *White Women in Fiji*.

135 For example, see: CSO 4431/1908, NAF.

136 Shameem, 'Sugar and Spice', 248; Ali, *Girmit*, 55 and 91.

137 Naidu, *The Violence of Indenture*, 41.

138 J. W. Davidson, quoted in Paper No. 20: Annual Report on Indian Immigration1902, Fiji Legislative Council Papers 1903, 19.

139 Council Paper No. 17: Annual Report on Indian Immigration, Legislative Council Papers 1889, 5.

140 For example: Council Paper No. 25: Annual Report on Indian Immigration, Legislative Council Papers 1887, 13; and Agent-General of Immigration to Colonial Secretary, 23 March 1916, CSO MP 2402/16, NAF.

141 Gill, *Turn Northeast*, 80, 34, 39.

142 Ali, *Girmit*, 72; Naidu, *The Violence of Indenture*, 66.

143 Burton, *The Fiji of To-Day*, 291–4; Nicole, 'Disturbing History', 360–1.

144 Thomas, *Islanders*, 180.

145 Frédéric Angleviel, 'Le métissage en Nouvelle-Calédonie: Réalité biologique et question culturel', in Frédéric Angleviel (ed.), *La Nouvelle-Calédonie: Terre de Métissage* (Paris: Les Indes Savantes & GRHOC, 2004), 19.

146 For example: Jacqueline Peterson and Jennifer H. S. Brown (eds), *The New People: Being and Becoming Métis in North America* (Winnipeg: University of Manitoba Press, 1985).

147 Christiane Terrier, 'Calédoniens ou métis?' in Frédéric Angleviel (ed.), *La Nouvelle-Calédonie: Terre de Métissage* (Paris: Les Indes Savantes & GRHOC, 2004), 74.

148 Angleviel, 'Le métissage', 21–2; Hamid Mokaddem, 'Nouvelle-Calédonie, un pays métissé?' *Hermes* 32–3 (2002), 537; Angleviel (ed.), *La Nouvelle-Calédonie: Terre de Métissage.*

149 Isabelle Leblic, '«Métissage» et parenté: Assimilation de non-Kanaks dans le système des moitiés matrimoniales à Ponérihouen', in Angleviel (ed.), *La Nouvelle-Calédonie*, 36.

150 Mokaddem, 'Nouvelle-Calédonie' 537; Muckle, 'Tropes of (Mis)understanding'; Terrier, 'Calédoniens ou métis?' 65; Frédéric Angleviel, 'Du pays du non-dit à une libération de la parole: L'histoire comme enjeu culturel en Nouvelle-Calédonie', *Historical Reflections* 34, no. 1 (2008), 104–21.

151 Benoît Trépied, *Une mairie dans la France coloniale: Koné, Nouvelle-Calédonie* (Paris: Karthala Editions, 2010).

152 Martyn Lyons, *The Totem and the Tricolour: A Short History of New Caledonia since 1774* (Sydney: New South Wales University Press, 1986), 56; Latham, 'Revolted Re-Examined', 50.

153 'Rapport de la commission de l'enquete sur l'insurrection canaque', President de la Commission, A. de Trentinian, 4 février 1879, SG-NC Carton 43, ANOM.

154 Henri Rivière, *Souvenirs de la Nouvelle-Calédonie: L'Insurrection Canaque* (Paris: C. Lévy, 1881), 89–90; Douglas, *Across the Great Divide*, 115. Swinburne's *Histoire authentique de l'Insurrection* echoed this view.

155 Latham, 'Revolt Re-Examined'; Douglas, *Across the Great Divide*, chapter 5.

156 Davillé, *La Colonisation Française,* 165; Merle, *Expériences Coloniales,* 91–3; Douglas, *Across the Great Divide,* 127–9, 130–1, 205–6; Muckle, 'Tropes of (Mis) understanding', 110.

157 Marie-Claire Beccalossi, President of the Federation of Melanesian Women's Associations and New Caledonian Council of Women, quoted in Alan Berman, 'Kanak Women and the Colonial Process', 34.

158 *Histoire authentique de l'insurrection des indigenes de la Nouvelle-Caledonie en 1878* (Nouméa: Imprimerie Nationale, 1909), translated by Frank C. Swinbourne, 19–21, in A3201, Mitchell Library, Sydney.

159 Douglas, 'Winning and Losing?' 230–1. See also 'Memoires d'un forçat écrit par lui-même à l'âge de 44 ans', Manuscrit du Bagnard M. Ernest Dessaud, 1888, 1J 102,

ANC, 179–213, on the capture of women and children in the conflict, including one woman who remained with the author.

160 Douglas, *Across the Great Divide*, 118–20.

161 Eddy Wadrawane, 'Métissage et culture du métissage en Nouvelle-Calédonie', in Frédéric Angleviel (ed.), *La Nouvelle-Calédonie: Terre de Métissage* (Paris: Les Indes Savantes & GRHOC, 2004), 26–9; Maurice Leenhardt, *Do Kamo: Person and Myth in the Melanesian World*, translated by Basia Miller Gulati (Chicago: University of Chicago Press, 1979 [1947]), 94–7 and Maurice Leenhardt, *Notes d'Ethnologie Néo-Calédonienne* (Paris: Institut d'Ethnologie, 1930), 69–79.

162 'Memoires d'un forçat écrit par lui-même à l'âge de 44 ans', Manuscrit du Bagnard M. Ernest Dessaud, 1888, 1J 102, ANC, 164. Latham, 'Revolt Re-Examined', 60; Berman, 'Kanak Women and the Colonial Process', 18–19.

163 Shineberg, *The People Trade*, 106–15.

164 'Rapport de la commission de l'enquete sur l'insurrection canaque', President de la Commission, A. de Trentinian, 4 février 1879, SG-NC Carton 43, ANOM.

165 Shineberg, *The People Trade*, 109.

166 See for example: Docteur C. Nicolas, 'Memoire sur les Iles Loyalty. Hygiène publique et privée, Moeurs et Coutumes, Administration. 1908', encl. to 1918 Mission, ADC Carton 828, ANOM.

167 Angleviel, 'Le métissage', 17–19; Jean-Pierre Doumenge, Éliane Métais and Alain Saussol (eds), *La Nouvelle Calédonie: occupation de l'espace et peuplement* (Bordeaux: Presses universitaires de Bordeaux, 1986), 271–2.

168 Angleviel, *Terre de Métissage*; Shineberg, *The People Trade*, 111–12.

169 Thomas, *Islanders*, 166; Ralston, *Grass Huts and Warehouses*, 47.

170 No. 276 Secretaire Général, 4 février 1907, 23W C13; and No. 540 Chef Centre Poembout, 24 mars 1910, 23W C14, ANC; Commissaire Délégue aux Nouvelles-Hébrides, 15 juin 1903, 23W C12, ANC.

171 For example: No. 837 Directeur de l'Interieur, 4 octubre 1895 and No. 838 Procureur de la République, 4 octubre 1895, 23W C11, ANC; No. 3713 Gouverneur, 22 décembre 1905, 23W C13, ANC. See also: Muckle, 'Presumption of Indigeneity'.

172 Gouverneur à Ministre des Colonies, 20 août 1907, SG-NH Carton 7, ANOM.

173 Procureur-Général à Gouverneur, 3 juillet 1907, SG-NH Carton 7, ANOM and No. 1296, 23W C13, ANC.

174 Ministre des Colonies à Gouveneur, 20 septembre 1910, SG-NH Carton 7, ANOM.

175 No. 1130 Procureur-Général et Chef du Service Judiciaire à Chef du Bataillon, 24 août 1910, 23W C14, ANC.

5

Justice debated

While the interplay of sexual consent, coercion and violence often took place beyond and below the law, occasionally cases erupted into public view. In this chapter I turn to the debates concerning the application of criminal justice that extended out of the courtroom and encompassed discussions in the local and, in some cases, international press, between settlers, Islanders, indentured labourers, missionaries and officials. Using two case studies from the New Hebrides and Fiji, I examine the way in which different groups mobilized to protest perceived faults of the colonial justice system and the official responses to these challenges to their authority. The first comes from New Hebrides where, in 1915, a missionary doctor and his nursing staff brought the British hospital on Iririki Island to a standstill in protest over the Joint Court's failure to try, convict or punish Indigenous trespassers in the nursing quarters. These incidents aroused anxiety over the threat from the uncivilized and rampantly sexual 'native' man, despite little history of sexually motivated attacks by ni-Vanuatu.[1] This example highlights the widely held perception that the law and courts of the colony and of each national administration existed to protect the interests of national citizens ahead of Indigenous subjects or other Europeans, and regardless of proper procedure and evidence. It also underscores the ongoing tension between official attempts to adhere to the principle of colour-blind justice and the popular belief that Indigenous men who transgressed the boundaries of race and morality needed to be convicted and punished to reinforce the proper racial hierarchy in the colony.[2] As the defendant stated, 'it is not I who am on trial here today, but the Law of the New Hebrides'.[3]

The second microhistory takes us from rural Fiji to Calcutta and back again, as an attempted sexual assault on a young Indian woman was publicized to spotlight the way in which the colonial administration failed to protect Indian indentured women from the violence of the plantation lines. As agitation against indenture increased throughout the 1910s, Kunti's story, and her quest for justice and protection against the sexual advances of her overseer, resonated in anti-indenture circles, gaining traction in the Indian press and adding momentum to the movement to end the system. Her actions demonstrated one avenue by which marginalized groups could draw attention to the inadequacy and inequality of colonial law in situations where the courts did not provide them with a voice. The dissemination of Kunti's narrative also suggests the wider scope of debates concerning the protection of Indian women and the public interest in colonial law and courts. Though Kunti's story was prominent in 1910s anti-indenture circles, in this chapter I seek to place her account and impact in a comparative context, examining the different networks available to indentured Indians compared with Islanders in protesting injustice.

The anxieties aroused by these two cases and the politics surrounding them were quite distinct. The New Hebrides hospital case illustrates a typical case of anxieties of 'black peril', while Kunti's experience of 'white peril' in plantation Fiji brought public attention to the more common but frequently ignored sexual exploitation of Indian women by European men.[4] Nevertheless both cases are connected in the way they illustrate how women's bodies could be mobilized or co-opted to underpin political agendas and wider imperial debates. In debating the protection of white women and the defence of the legal system in the New Hebrides and advocating the end of indenture in Fiji, women's bodies served as a slate for both colonial and patriarchal as well as anti-colonial agendas.

Throughout the late nineteenth and early twentieth centuries colonists in the Pacific were generally well informed regarding local court dealings. In all three colonies, the local press provided significant reporting on laws, court cases and convictions, which were clearly of public interest.[5] For example, the *Fiji Times* and *Fiji Argus* (later the *Suva Times*) of Fiji, *La France Australe* and *Le Moniteur de la Nouvelle-Calédonie* (later *Le Journal Officiel de la Nouvelle-Calédonie*), and a wealth of short-lived private newspapers in New Caledonia,[6] and the *Néo-Hébridais* all published regular columns or features of court news, which might include verdicts, sentences and additional details such as the judge's commentary. Norman Etherington's study of Suva magistrate records and newspaper reports for the year 1882 found a high degree of coverage in the press accounts: 90 per cent of cases were covered in the local press.[7] Newspapers in Australia and New Zealand also covered noteworthy or scandalous cases from the Pacific and reported more generally on issues such as labour recruiting and Islander violence. Colonial authorities, particularly the French in the New Hebrides, were aware and sensitive to such reporting and its possible impact on public opinion, gathering newspaper clippings now available for historians in archival folders.[8] The literate settler community had ample opportunity to keep informed, develop opinions and discuss the goings-on of the local courts.

However, in reporting cases of violence against Europeans on the plantations, John Kelly notes that the *Fiji Times* omitted key details (such the overseer's interference with Indian women) suggesting their limits and bias.[9] Edited by colonists for a colonial audience, newspaper accounts frequently made non-European experiences and perspectives less visible, even if at the time Islanders and indentured labourers caught up in the legal system were not silent as these case studies demonstrate.

Perceived sexual perils

In September 1915, Dr David Crombie, the Director of the British hospital in the New Hebrides, threatened imminent and permanent closure of the establishment, a drastic action apparently necessitated by the failure of the bumbling colonial administration to protect the female nursing staff from 'drunk and dissolute natives' roaming the premises in the dark tropical twilight.[10] His frustration was enhanced by the fact a ni-Vanuatu intruder had been captured and charged but escaped conviction the previous year: 'The idea will get abroad among these half-savage creatures, that the Law of the New Hebrides is the protector of their lawlessness.'[11] Both events incited local European anxiety, anger and debate over the application of justice. The reverberations demonstrate the incendiary power of fears of 'black peril' (the exaggerated danger that Indigenous men posed to white women) and the perceived limits of British authority in the archipelago.

The Presbyterian mission-run John G. Paton Memorial Hospital, along with the British Residency, was located on Iririki Island in Port Vila harbour. However, the location less than 200 m from the mainland did not offer protection from an increasing stream of unwanted native midnight visitors, much to the disquiet of hospital director, Dr Crombie. The issue first came to a head in March 1914. A Tanna man and member of the British Resident's boatcrew, Numbus, disembarked on Iririki in the depth of the night, and in his quest to meet one of the Indigenous nurses, found himself instead in the quarters of the European nurses. Disturbed, Nurse Matson emerged from her cottage seeking to identify the source of the noise that had woken her. She called into the lurking shadows when the ni-Vanuatu man 'suddenly sprang at her, seizing her by the arm and bent his head down to look closely in her face'.[12] Matson screamed and fled; Numbus was apprehended.

We have little evidence of Numbus's perspective on that night, with European anxieties and anger dominating the discussions and obscuring the motivations and emotions of either Numbus or the ni-Vanuatu nurses. In many ways, the incident appears a fairly minor one. Numbus did not physically harm Matson nor demonstrate clear intention to do so, perhaps only seeking to identify her when she followed him in the dark. However she was very shaken by the midnight meeting, and her fear instilled a sense of insecurity and panic around the hospital. A small wave of anxiety over 'black peril' erupted around the British Residency, despite the fact that

> [the] natives are not in the habit of attacking white women here. They are merely after their own women, which though no doubt reprehensible is natural and not dangerous to us.[13]

The inept response of colonial officials caused even greater consternation and complaint amongst the hospital staff.

The most detailed commentary on the drama is provided by Edward Jacomb, the English lawyer and vocal Native Advocate who we encountered in Chapter 2. The various incidents of nocturnal intrusion at the hospital feature in his diaries and correspondence, as do the court cases that resulted, in which he advised Dr Crombie. His reports are supported by the French official correspondence on the matter. Jacomb's perspective should be situated in the intellectual context of humanitarian and liberal empire, as well as his difficult relationship with many officials and colonists. The so-called 'natives' friend', Jacomb, was highly critical of the competency of Condominium officials and disliked for his work supporting ni-Vanuatu land and labour rights.[14]

Jacomb realized soon after his arrival in the New Hebrides in 1907 the economic possibilities for a lawyer representing ni-Vanuatu land claims, and this undoubtedly also shaped his attitudes.[15] He remained on good terms with the missionary community, which further frustrated his fellow colonists. They expected him to naturally support their perspective and rights above those of ni-Vanuatu with anything less being seen as a betrayal of his race. Within the 'judicial monstrosity' of the Joint Court, Jacomb was aware that 'in fighting for natives one has usually to be content with a portion of their rights'.[16] He further mused:

> No wonder the natives are dying out. Recruiters care for nothing but their immediate profit, the French Administration cares for nothing but the

immediate profit of its fellow countrymen, the British Administration cares for nothing at all.[17]

The inaction of the British administration was thus a frustration Jacomb and Crombie held in common, for quite different reasons.

The Natives' Prohibition Regulation of 1909 gave officials sufficient power to prevent the much-feared nocturnal intrusions but was never adequately enforced, in part given to the inadequate resources of the colonial government.[18] As a result, midnight arrivals on Iririki continued unchecked. Crombie was particularly aggrieved by the fact that the policing in Port Vila was insufficient to prevent the theft of a boat from the short shoreline along the township, enabling undesired visitors to reach Iririki unfettered. The short stretch of sea between the island and the mainland was supposed to act as a sort of moat for the British Residency, creating a sense of isolation from the growing colonial town.[19] As much an ideological as a practical defence, this barrier – an attempt to exclude the unsavoury aspects of colonial society from the heart of British power in the New Hebrides – was easily breached. In this manner, the island was an appropriate metaphor for Britain's reluctant imperialism in the New Hebrides, as well as the permeability of the artificial boundaries and hierarchies underpinning the colonial project. By contrast, the French Residency in the township of Vila arguably reflected the French empire's more welcome embrace of the New Hebrides into its colonial possessions.[20]

Numbus's presence alone on the hospital grounds was not enough to bring criminal charges against him and so there was confusion amongst the judicial officers over how to best deliver the legal punishment they felt he clearly deserved. A bureaucratic error resulted in eventual charges of breaking and entering with attempt to commit larceny being brought before the Joint Court, a count for which the prosecution had no evidence.[21] To the fury of many British officials and local European residents, Numbus was acquitted.[22] Had he instead been charged with intent to commit assault, Jacomb suggests the outcome of the court case would have been quite different.[23] In the ensuing debate, contested visions of justice and punishment emerged amongst the colonizing community.

Much to the ire of those who felt Numbus must be punished irrespective of how his crime was defined, in this case the law did appear to be colour-blind. However, Jacomb suggested that this was not always the case, making a jibe at the French judiciary at the same time: 'We have had a great deal too much down here of the French idea of accusing natives of one thing and convicting them of another.'[24] While Jacomb clearly believed Numbus's actions fell on the wrong side of the law and expressed disappointment in the incompetent functioning of the legal bureaucracy, his voice was one of the few who advocated against inappropriate conviction. His stance against the potentially 'rotten' results of inattention to proper procedure reflected his disillusionment with the management of the New Hebrides Condominium by Britain and France alike.

By contrast, Crombie led the crusade for conviction, arguing that an example needed to be made of Numbus to protect the virtue and peace of mind of both ni-Vanuatu and white women. Calling for new and stricter regulations controlling 'native' movements in the Port Vila area, he subsequently gave this account of the case:

> Every help was given by the staff of the Hospital to the prosecution, but this man was found not guilty, and walked out of the Court, a free man, without a word of blame or censure being said to him. It is said the prosecution was bungled, but whether this was so or not, the result was most unfortunate, as it left on the native mind the impression that they could trespass on private property during the night, and even enter private houses, and insult women, and that the law could not touch them.[25]

His statement demonstrates a concern for the status of Condominium and British law in the eyes of colonial subjects, highlighting the constant struggle to assert dominance in the face of unruly, untamed and often disinterested 'natives'. Indeed individuals like Crombie expressed far greater apprehension over the effectiveness of British rule in New Hebrides than the colonial state itself demonstrated in its half-hearted process of colonization.

The British administration reacted in typical fashion to the furore: with complete inaction. The British Resident Merton King neither passed new regulations nor increased police patrols, brushing off Crombie's indignant letters and growing frustration.[26] Meanwhile, according to Crombie at least, life at the hospital deteriorated for the nursing staff due to increased nocturnal visitations and an underlying sense of anxiety. To the staff, it appeared that 'continued impunity ha[d] apparently bred greater daring'.[27] Crombie spoke for the nurses, but given limited accounts from other, female staff it is unclear to what extent such feelings were held across the hospital and to what extent he played up such anxieties to bolster his calls for action. Nevertheless, the uneasy status quo continued until the night of 17 August 1915, when tensions again erupted.

Shortly after 9.00 pm, a small boat drew into the Iririki beach. Apparently somewhat intoxicated Jack and Toby (or Tobie), two Aneityum men along with a third unnamed man, made their way around the hospital premises, trying and failing to open the front door to the nurses' cottage before departing. As in the previous incident, the ni-Vanuatu men appeared to be desirous of visiting the Indigenous nurses. In his account to the *gendarme*, Toby stated that they had invited the nurses out, but the women had declined so the men re-embarked towards Vila.[28] The movements across the harbour speak to network of relationships largely unseen and not understood by colonial state and missionaries, despite the attempts to regulate ni-Vanuatu presence in the township.

On this occasion, Crombie caught sight of the men departing. At the end of his wits, the doctor took the law into his own hands, taking action in a manner that he felt the Condominium was unable or unwilling to do. He pursued their boat, still in sight within the harbour, intent on retributive justice. One of the ni-Vanuatu men jumped into the water and successfully swam to Vila. Claiming the other drunken men attempted to strike at him with a knife, Crombie forcibly took them back ashore to punish them in 'a fitting manner'.[29] He describes himself using the humane 'method of suggestion' and causing no physical injury.[30] Toby and Jack's statements suggest Crombie made the only blows, dragging them to ground and violently striking them with some sort of baton before returning and locking them to the hospital verandah.[31]

Crombie's subsequent punishment, recounted here by Jacomb, highlights the everyday violence of colonial rule:

> Crombie then did a very foolish thing, or rather series of things. What he should have done was to give them both a jolly good licking and let them go. Instead he tied them up, got all the women employees to smack their faces with their hands, then gave them chloroform, marked both their forearms with a letter H (for Hospital), and ended up by shaving their heads![32]

Toby recounted losing capacity from the chloroform as his arm was inscribed, and *gendarme* Boibelet's physical examination of the men confirmed their still-bloody injuries.[33] While Jacomb took issue with Crombie's drastic and humiliating methods, his statement suggests that physical violence alone against the ni-Vanuatu men would likely have passed without note. There was however a longer history of the use of tattooing in missionary and colonial punishment that perhaps influenced Crombie's actions.[34] In any case, using corporal discipline clearly lay within the bounds of acceptable colonial violence; it was the other more humiliating aspects of Crombie's devised punishment that overstepped the boundaries of moral and legal permissibility.

The following morning the two men were returned to the mainland to their French employer, the Comptoirs Français des Nouvelles Hébrides, with a note from Crombie that he did not intend to inform the authorities as he had punished them himself.[35] Herein lay Crombie's misfortune. His actions came to the attention of the French Resident, and the matter was quickly passed to the French police.[36] Crombie's punishments were interpreted in the context of ongoing French frustrations with Presbyterian missionaries. As early as 1910, official French reports identified abuses by Presbyterian missionaries as a hindrance to French colonization and economic development as their actions spread discontent amongst ni-Vanuatu while they hypocritically criticized French settlers. The well-resourced Presbyterians were accused of 'abusing their spiritual power' to become 'true political chiefs', noting that 'the majority of missionaries intervene directly into the repression of crimes and offences', just as Crombie had done.[37] Reminiscent of missionary attempts to create their own jurisdiction on Tanna, the case reignited French anxiety and anger towards the Presbyterians. The reporting policeman accused Crombie of being guilty of forgetting the sentiments of humanity.[38] While Crombie emphasized that he acted in self-defence and humanely, the French argued that ni-Vanuatu men had endured 'a veritable torture' and 'a night of cruel suffering'.[39] Lacking the jurisdiction to prosecute, the French Resident forwarded a complaint to his British counterpart.

Small as the colony was, news of the event had already made its way to King's ears, but it was the French complaint that spurred the British Administration into action. Crombie received summons to appear in the High Commissioner's Court, charged with the assault and false imprisonment of Toby and Jack. Piqued, Crombie sought Jacomb's counsel who advised him to plead guilty: to plead otherwise would have dire consequences for Britain's reputation in the New Hebrides, involving as it would a harsh and unwelcome critique of the Condominium for continuing to allow roaming natives to disturb British employees. He correctly surmised that the judge would take a more lenient view if Crombie avoided an overt condemnation of colonial rule. On 6 September 1915, Crombie was found guilty of both charges, and fined ten shillings.[40]

The fine was a minor punishment, but both Crombie and the French Resident Jacques Miramende were indignant. Miramende protested to his British counterpart as well as to his superior, the High Commissioner of France for the New Hebrides, who reported to the Minister of Colonies on the insignificance of the fine, especially given the profile of the offender as 'the most prominent Presbyterian missionary in the archipelago'.[41] The French administration reported that the judge had shown extreme leniency to his 'compatriote et coreligionnaire'.[42] The outcome added fuel to French official disenchantment that 'certain Englishmen, the missionaries in particular, can do anything without ever being punished'.[43]

By contrast, Crombie accepted that he had technically breached the law, though he asserted the righteousness of his actions in seeking to protect women's virtue. To his frustration, once again as in the Numbus case, when it finally awoke from its inactivity the British national court of the Anglo-French Condominium proved willing to support Indigenous rights and convict Europeans for offences against ni-Vanuatu subjects. Unfortunately for Dr Crombie and to the ongoing frustration of British settlers, Resident Merton King and the British administration proved disinclined to offend the French and more than willing to enforce the law.[44]

This was arguably because the British were aware of French interest in the incident, and because the British administration was generally less invested in the colony's economy and less beholden to settler opinion. As noted in Chapter 1, the French government's stake in the SFNH, its land claims and plantations meant the French administration was directly involved in and affected by French economic development in the New Hebrides in a way that the British were not. Such differences in economic strategy influenced and overlapped with their ideological outlook, as the French advocated against the paternalistic British and missionary interference in ni-Vanuatu society that sought to repress custom and prevent ni-Vanuatu engagement in labour and trade.[45]

These economic and political divisions were reflected in the courts. For example, the most common infraction of the Anglo-French Convention to come before the Joint Court was the sale of liquor to natives. The majority of offenders were French. However, a far greater proportion of the fines collected were from British subjects as the French administration made virtually no effort to enforce the penalties imposed on individuals convicted under their jurisdiction.[46] Indeed the head of the French police Berhault stated in 1923 that he 'had no intention of bringing French citizens before the Joint Court whatever their offences might be'.[47] His statement reflected a long-standing French policy aimed at advancing the economic interests of their nationals, and the High Commissioner argued, 'if French law is sweeter and less brutal than English law, the fault is not with those charged with applying it'.[48]

Jacomb felt that this difference stemmed from the fact that the French Resident and his officials sought to maintain favour with the settlers, as Residents unpopular with the local community were quickly replaced. The

French Resident was, according to Jacomb, at the 'beck and call' of his nationals.[49] Certainly, the French administration had eleven resident commissioners come and go during the term of British Resident Merton King from 1907 to 1924. In this way, British disinterest and differences in official appointments to the colony seemingly resulted in a stricter adherence to the letter of the law, while the French administration appeared far more sympathetic to their own citizens in dealings with ni-Vanuatu: 'Frenchmen can break it [the law] with apparent impunity. One would wish that the law could be applied impartially.'[50] Of course, Crombie's notion of impartiality was itself questionable and as noted above, the French had their own complaints about British partiality towards missionaries.

While Crombie accepted that he had technically breached the law, he asserted the righteousness of his actions:

> Here am I, a man who has never lifted a hand against a native in my thirteen years career in the New Hebrides, who has hardly even raised his voice in speaking to them, called out in the middle of the night by terrified women asking for protection, ill for a week after with the nervous and physical strain involved; while these two degraded beings brutalized by the vices of civilisation, these potential assassians [*sic*], are allowed to go free, and boast that they can terrify women, white and black, and try to force a way into their sleeping apartments, and that no one can touch them. I feel, your Honour, that is not I who am on trial here today, but the Law of the New Hebrides.[51]

To Crombie and apparently to his Australian nursing staff, it appeared the Condominium, and especially their national British administration, had condemned them to live in constant fear, without recourse to justice. The law of the colony seemed neither to offer them protection nor tolerate them applying justice as they saw fit in the absence of hegemonic imperial rule.

Protesting this intolerable state of affairs, the European nursing staff, Matson and Finlay, resigned and planned to leave 'by the next steamer':[52] 'no women with any feeling of self-respect would live on the island, where brutalized men could roam at will'.[53] There is little other archival trace of their perspective on the incident. More drastically, Crombie wrote to the British and French resident commissioners advising them of the resultant closure of the hospital.[54] Crombie felt compelled to follow this course of action and spelt out the likely consequences for the colony:

> Both the European nurses have given notice and will leave for Sydney by the next steamer. I myself can no longer take the responsibility of having native women helpers in the hospital and intend returning them at once to their villages. It

> naturally follows from this that the hospital can no longer be kept open … I shall be unable to receive any more patients, native or European … I fear that it may be a very long time before [the hospital] will be reopened, for the story which Miss Matson and Miss Finlay will have to tell to the Sydney and Australian Press on their return to the Commonwealth will hardly be likely to encourage other ladies, or doctors, to come to Vila to suffer similar indignities.[55]

Presenting himself as the lone and valiant defender of female respectability and peace of mind amid the many threats of the colonial outpost, Crombie implied that the British administration had forced his hand in the matter. His message is clear: colonial officials must now take responsibility for protecting the women against the 'plague' of the black peril. We thus see a clash of differing ideologies of humanitarianism, between the administration's emphasis on the legal protection of 'natives' and Crombie's assertion of the need for protection for medical services and practitioners (especially women) serving the settler and Indigenous population.

The threats of resignation and hospital closure appeared to be as much for theatrical effect, aimed to spur government action, as they were borne out of fear and anxiety.[56] This is not to say that the women involved did not feel genuinely insecure because of the midnight intrusions, but that the actual menace was exaggerated to achieve a certain result. Any harm done was psychological, yet it proved a powerful stimulus behind cries for the Condominium to more closely control ni-Vanuatu in Vila. The action of closing the hospital is described variously by Jacomb and by Crombie as a 'game' and a 'bomb', designed to send ripples through the British Residency.[57] Jacomb in particular felt the controversy was rather exaggerated.[58] As Amirah Inglis has explored in the case of Papua New Guinea, the notion of 'black peril' could be invoked to serve a political end.[59] Many British residents (predominantly missionaries) wanted their administration to take a more proactive stance in advancing and protecting their affairs above those of ni-Vanuatu or French residents, and such desires clearly feed into the frustrations surrounding this 'black peril' case.

After November 1915, correspondence on the issue ceased. Later that year, Dr Crombie relocated to Macarthur in New South Wales, his departure seemingly prompted by the unsatisfactory resolution of these events.[60] It is unclear for exactly how long the hospital remained closed, but by mid-1916 a new doctor, Hogarth, had arrived in the New Hebrides to replace Crombie.[61] Overall, the furore caused by these nocturnal commotions did not leave a lasting mark on the operation of the colonial administration in the New Hebrides. However, they do reveal much about the colonial unease over the control of the (male) Indigenous population and the contested nature of the colonial legal regime, which was far from hegemonic in the New Hebrides.

Iririki, as an island slightly removed from the larger populace of Port Vila, seems an odd and inconvenient place to build a hospital but must be understood in the context of the reluctant British colonization of the New Hebrides. The security of women, especially white women, in the colonial hospital was predicated on a façade of separation from the unsettling and uncivilized elements of what remained an unfamiliar and largely unconquered environment for European settlers, as well as political separation from the French. There had been no previous incidents of rape at Iririki hospital, and just one at the French hospital in Vila. Willy (a ni-Vanuatu labourer engaged by M. Milliard) was convicted of raping a patient while drunk and imprisoned in Vila for five months by the Joint Naval Commission in June 1909, but it is notable that this case did not attract the same level of attention as the perceived threats to the European women.[62] However, the ease and frequency with which unexpected male visitors appeared on the premises highlights the porous nature of the boundaries upon which the fiction of separation was built. Numbus, Toby and Jack did not seek white women on their nocturnal jaunts, all admitted to visiting or looking for the ni-Vanuatu nurses.[63] The voices of the ni-Vanuatu nurses do not feature in Jacomb's correspondence, and thus their relation to the men and their feelings about the hospital's visitors is unknown. Yet the possibility of an attack was sufficient to motivate colonial anxiety over 'black peril' expressed by Crombie, and apparently by Nurses Matson and Finlay. The very presence of the unknown ni-Vanuatu men created an atmosphere of disquiet, a reminder of how tenuous Condominium rule was in the early twentieth century.

These fears of the possible sexual or violent intentions of Indigenous men and of the ability of colonial rule to control them existed in tension with the fact that, as Margaret Rodman has explored, male ni-Vanuatu prisoners roaming unconstrained, and often with knives (as tools), around Iririki were not perceived as a threat.[64] The contradiction can be partially resolved when we examine the broader contest over the application of justice in the colony as presented in the two court cases discussed. Certain British residents and officials clearly felt the law existed to protect and promote their own safety and interests, rather than to provide justice for all. Confident of their own superiority and of their superior rights, the acquittal of Numbus and conviction of Crombie upset their hierarchically ordered view of the colonial world, and of the law's function in upholding the racial order. The perceived inadequacy of the legal and police system led Crombie to impose his own system of vigilante justice. He did so because the colonial legal regime had failed to establish its legitimacy among both the missionaries and the colonized subjects.

However, for the French employers of the ni-Vanuatu labourers, the French police and French administration, this was a story of Presbyterian overreaching in a narrative that stretched back into the pre-Condominium era. In general, the French were more concerned about the influence of Presbyterian missions in Vanuatu than that of British officials. The French characterized their counterparts as reactive rather than proactive, and perceived them as being influenced by and biased towards the pressures exerted by missionaries within the islands, and by public opinion in Australasia.[65] They were largely correct in this assessment, as missionary agitation and Australian public opinion were an important impetus for Britain's continued involvement in colonial New Hebrides.

However, for all its shortcomings, the British administration would not stand by and see its authority blatantly undermined, especially in front of the judging eyes of the French administration and residents. So Crombie was convicted despite many colonial agents unofficially expressing support for the spirit of his actions. Clearly, the anxieties surrounding these incidents of 'black peril' at the hospital on Iririki were as much about the politics and effectiveness of Condominium administration, the Anglo-French relationship and the new legal regime as about the likelihood of sexual threats to the nursing staff.

Making visible 'white peril'

Reporting on indenture in Fiji in 1916, Andrews and Pearson stated:

> We felt … that, with the state of morals among the Indian woman which clearly existed (through no fault of their own, but because of the indenture system) it was altogether wrong to employ unmarried European overseers and unmarried Indian Sardars. The temptation of such a position was too great.[66]

In this case, it was European men and Indian *sirdars* as colonial authority figures, rather than Indigenous men, who posed the social and moral threat, this time to indentured Indian women working on Fiji's sugar plantations. In earlier decades the perceived loose morals and overt sexuality of Indian women in Fiji were blamed for social breakdown and violence on the plantation lines.[67] From the early years of the twentieth century, the indenture system itself became the subject of increased scrutiny and criticism, initially from missionaries and then from the Indian public and government. Concerns surrounding sexual jealousy in the lines, and the degradation of Indian women, their religious values and family life featured prominently in these discussions. Andrews and Pearson's report was one publication that contributed to this shifting discourse, which highlighted the realities of colonial violence. This 'white peril' was ever-present but largely ignored in comparison to the surveillance of possible Indigenous or Indian violence.

The plantations of the Colonial Sugar Refining Company (CSR) around Fiji imposed their own systems of discipline on indentured labourers, including physical intimidation and the allocation of difficult and isolated work tasks as well as taking *girmityas* to court for labour infractions. Violence as well as sexual coercion of workers by overseers and *sirdars* remained commonplace in the early twentieth century, though violence *between* labourers featured far more commonly in court trials. From the 1910s, the Indian government and the Colonial Office put increased pressure on local officials to better monitor labour conditions and remove individuals who obviously abused their workers and thus attracted negative attention to both the indenture system and the Fiji administration. This was largely a public relations exercise as in most cases, the CSR merely relocated problematic labourers, *sirdars* or overseers to a different plantation.[68] However, in 1913 one woman, Kunti, and her account of attempted sexual assault on a Rewa plantation catapulted into the media and into the heart of the growing Indian nationalist and satyagraha movement against indenture. Two minute papers containing correspondence between Fiji and India including newspaper clippings and translations held in the National Archives of Fiji allow us to reconstruct this incident as it unfolded.[69]

Just as the story circulated widely around contemporary imperial networks, Kunti has a prominent place in the history of indenture and its abolition. Brij Lal, Shaista Shameem, John Kelly and Robert Nicole have employed this incident as an example of emerging India nationalism and resistance to colonial rule in Fiji. Of most pertinence to my argument are Lal's use of this example as a starting point for exploring the social anomy that existed in the coolie lines, and Nicole's placement of Kunti in the context of quotidian acts of resistance against the injustices and violence of plantation life by indentured women aware of the difficulties in accessing justice through the court system.[70] However, as John Kelly contends, Kunti's case was clearly exceptional, owing to the attention it received across various parts of the British empire and the way it embodied mounting dissatisfaction with indentured migration generally and the Fijian administration specifically.[71]

Kunti, Indian Indentured Labourer #39934, was a woman of low caste, indentured on the plantation of Messrs Barber and Messageo Neuma at Nadewa in the Rewa district. On 10 April 1913, the overseer Cobcroft allocated her the task of weeding a remote banana patch, apparently as punishment for disobedience. She was alone, out of sight or earshot of other labourers. Kunti had not been long at her work when Cobcroft reappeared, ostensibly to inspect her progress. The overseer grabbed hold of Kunti and made 'inappropriate suggestions'. Panicked, she screamed and, resisting Cobcroft's advances, tried to free herself from his grip. Escaping, Kunti ran and jumped into the nearby Wainibokasi River, preferring an honourable death to dishonourable violation by her overseer. She was rescued by a young man passing in a small dinghy and survived to relate her experience to the Nadewa plantation manager, who refused to listen to her complaint, uninterested in hearing of 'field things'.[72] In protest or in fear, Kunti absconded from work the next day, only to be again allocated a particularly onerous task. Her husband was subsequently severely beaten.

Whether Cobcroft's actions were planned or opportunistic, his advances reflected the perception of Indian women as sexually available. European overseers and Indian *sirdars* believed that they could make such assaults with impunity. As frequently occurred, the Nadewa plantation manager turned a blind eye to the labourer's grievance and the incident never came before the court. In fact, Kunti and her husband Jal had twice unsuccessfully complained about their treatment to the Inspector of Labour when he visited the plantation the previous year, earning themselves a reputation for insubordination. This time, the attempted sexual assault did not become another archival silence. Kunti subsequently recounted her experiences to anti-indenture activist and priest Totaram Sanadhya and Arya Samaj missionary Manoharanand Saraswati. Her account was transcribed in a first-person account, apparently by Saraswati, and framed as 'a stirring appeal to the to the leaders of [India] to try to put a stop to emigration to the Fiji Islands'.[73] In August, the story appeared in the *Leader* of Allahabad under the title 'The Cry of an Indian Woman in Fiji', and by May 1914, in the *Bharat Mitra*, the most popular Hindi language newspaper of the time. Like so many experiences of indentured women (and indeed other women at the time), the version of events circulated was not transcribed by Kunti herself, leaving open questions as to the extent to which others modified the account. Through the narration of Kunti's experience and its retelling across colonial networks, the female body was inscribed with political meaning.

These articles raised Kunti to mythical status in Indian anti-indenture circles as one of the nation's 'brave and honourable ladies', who symbolized the virtuous Indian woman struggling against corrupting colonial rule.[74] For this she was praised in the press:

> We cannot refrain from admiring the patience bravery and strength of mind shown by Kunti. In spite of her being of the cobbler caste, she has surpassed many well-to-do (high class) ladies by the courage shown by her jumping into the stream to save her chastity ... Even on critical occasions one ought to stand by right ... We hope that she will get justice.[75]

Totaram Sanadhya further stressed Kunti's 'courage and fortitude' in his condemnation of Fijian indenture entitled *My Twenty One Years in Fiji*.[76] As Kelly and Nicole astutely observe, as the tale was retold Indian nationalists framed Kunti in the mould of Sita, the loyal and chaste wife of Ram in the epic *Ramayana*, which served to further reinforce her status in India as a heroine.[77]

These newspaper reports confirmed Indian suspicions regarding the violent treatment of indentured women on Fijian plantations. Kunti's experience added momentum to a groundswell of opinion against indentured immigration supported by missionary and official investigation.[78] Fiji's reputation in India was much damaged as a result, while calls to end indentured immigration were given greater moral and numerical strength. In his original study, K. L. Gillion argued that it was the strength of anti-indenture sentiments in India that eventually proved the system's downfall.[79] The desire to protect the virtuous Indian woman, as embodied by Kunti who was degraded and downtrodden by the harsh realities of life in the corrupt and immoral plantation lines of Fiji, was key to the groundswell against indenture in India: 'Having listened to the story of Kunti, will not our brothers make an effort to stop this coolie-system?'[80] Such portrayals effectively mobilized public opinion, perhaps to a greater degree than any other popular movement in Indian history.[81] Kunti's narrative, and in particular the failure of the administration to protect her or prosecute her attacker, was thus a timely catalyst for change.

Alarmed by the reaction to Kunti's narrative, the Fijian administration called for a full investigation of the allegations, hoping 'to expose the [story's] falsity' and to dispel increasing discontent.[82] Reprimanded by the Indian government and the Colonial Office, and having a vested interest in discrediting Kunti, the administration made enquiries to this end. During the investigation, the author originally credited with publishing the story (Saraswati) retracted his name and refuted he had even met Kunti.[83] Statements from the *sirdar*, overseer and

Jugdeo (who supposedly rescued the drowning woman) were used to cast doubt on the credibility of the version of the incident reported in the Indian press. Nevertheless, there was not enough evidence to definitively prove the whole story was a falsehood. However, Montgomerie, the Acting Agent General of Immigration, asserted:

> I believe the whole statement to be a fabrication. It is absolutely untrue that female indentured immigrants are violated or receive hurts or cruel treatments at the hands of their overseers. If such were the case, it would be quite impossible to manage the labourers on a plantation. It is only by fair and just treatment that labourers, at any rate in this colony, can be worked.[84]

The censure from India and London clearly put colonial officials in Fiji on the defensive. Frustrated, officials tried another tactic to discredit Kunti and her supporters. Just as undermining a woman's moral standing was a common tactic by defendants in rape trials, the colonial administration sought to deflect attention from its own embarrassing shortcomings in policing the indenture system by questioning Kunti's character and virtue. Her experience reflects the double violence of colonial rule: traumatic experiences of violence were overlaid with the violence of denial of the truth and voice for those that tried to speak publicly in court or beyond.[85] Kunti had already been labelled as a troublesome individual, needing to be disciplined and so sent to work alone. Moreover, a statement from the current *sirdar*, Ramharak, implied Kunti had unsavoury motives for tarnishing the reputation of the overseer: she had been intimate with the former *sirdar*, Sundar Singh, and the assault allegations were a means to avenge his dismissal.[86] In recasting Kunti as both immodest and malicious, officials echoed earlier annual reports on immigration in which Indian women, their licentious behaviour and lack of religious values were depicted as the root of the social and criminal problems endemic in indenture lines.

This depiction marked colonial officials as out of step with contemporary popular attitudes to indenture and failed to gain influence as a counter-narrative. The episode coincided with, and reflected, changing perceptions of the cause of immoral behaviour, vice, degraded family life and high suicide and murder rates in the indenture lines. Rather than emphasizing the low moral quality of Indian recruits, reports by Chimman Lal and James McNeill in 1913 and especially C. R. Andrews and W. W. Pearson in 1916 focused their criticism on structural aspects of the indenture system. The unequal recruitment of women (at a rate of 40 to every 100 men), deceitful recruitment practices that attempted to maintain this gender ratio and poor housing conditions were singled out and blamed for social breakdown on the lines.[87] The detrimental impacts of the system affected Indian women disproportionately:

> The Hindu woman in the coolie 'lines', having no semblance, even, of a separate home of her own, which she can cherish, and divorced from all her old home ties, has abandoned religion itself. The moral ruin is most pitiful on this side. Though there are beautiful and stately rivers in Fiji, no women are seen making their morning offerings; no temples rise on their banks; there is no household shrine. The outward life, which the Hindu women in the 'lines' lead in Fiji, appears to be without love and without worship, – a sordid round of mean and joyless occupations.[88]

In this context, Kunti powerfully personified the suffering of Indian women indentured in Fiji.

At the heart of the controversy was the issue of justice. On the termination of her *girmit* and return to India in 1915, Kunti forwarded the following critique to the Calcutta Government Emigration Agent:

> The evidence of free [Indians] is of no use in such cases, while indentured labourers do not dare give evidence … In short there is no redress. Neither the Manager nor the Coolie Agent nor the Courts care to hear or redress the labourers' grievances.[89]

As the evidence in previous chapters attests, many *girmitiyas* were pressured to withdraw their charges or testimony or, aware the legal system was biased against them, did not bother making formal complaints. Moreover the lower court sittings, which dealt with the majority of indentured labourers' cases, often sat at the plantations themselves, ostensibly for the convenience of all involved, but clearly compromising impartiality. As guests of plantation managers or overseers, magistrates had to walk a tightrope between maintaining cordial relations with their host (who was often the defendant) and fairly adjudicating on cases. These circumstances further disadvantaged Indian workers, and although officials occasionally voiced concern over the validity of such court hearings, their concerns were never acknowledged in communications with the Indian government. Kunti's statement demonstrates her awareness of what Datta terms the fleeting agency of subaltern women, whose agentic acts were often less dramatic and visible that her own though no less strategic in the context of this power imbalance.[90]

In Fiji, the indenture system was a central pillar of the colony's economy, and the colonial government, sugar companies and local planters all had a stake in its continuation. The Colonial Office requirement that the Fijian administration ensure the colony be self-supporting drove the colony to be reliant on indenture for a cheap, plentiful and constant labour source and gave the CSR (as the primary employer of indentured labour) significant political influence. Both factors provided official impetus to defend indenture against its critics, while also limiting officials' ability to monitor or interfere with conditions on the plantations. The furore over Kunti's story therefore not only caused political embarrassment but also threatened to destabilize colonial Fiji's economic viability. It is in this context that the administration's approach must be understood. Kunti's experience demonstrates the powerful way that women's bodies and sexual, violent, or intimate relationships could be imbued with much larger political significance.

Conclusion

Both case studies explore the explosion of emotions surrounding incidents of perceived and actual attempted sexual assault. However, these microhistories differ greatly in other respects. In the New Hebrides, anxiety brewed amongst British residents over the potential of sexually motivated attacks by ni-Vanuatu men on the European hospital nurses, despite no such crimes having been recorded. By contrast, the rape or sexual coercion of indentured Indian women occurred with great frequency on Fijian plantations, but the actions of *sirdars* and overseers passed largely without censure. Kunti's experience was unique in receiving a high level of attention, despite the failure to bring her grievances against her overseer before the colonial courts.

Kunti and Crombie's accounts reveal the often-conflicting pressures placed on the colonial judiciary in the Pacific. British colonists in both colonies felt that the administration owed them a duty of care, and ought to place their interests and rights ahead of those of Islanders, of indentured labourers in Fiji, or French subjects in the New Hebrides (and vice versa). In the New Hebrides, such expectations proved out of sync with British Condominium officials, who had little to gain from acquiescing to public pressure by convicting Indigenous trespassing at Iririki hospital. The British administration's economic interests in the New Hebrides were lesser than those either of the French or of the British in Fiji, a significant factor in shaping their response to settler agitation. In Fiji the attitudes of plantations managers and overseers aligned with that of the colonial government, as all parties would lose face politically and potentially face economic instability from the discrediting of the indenture system. The critique of the British legal regime instead emerged out of Indian labourers' unheeded grievances, and was advanced by increasing anti-indenture sentiment in India where activists successfully utilized print media to bolster popular support for the cause.

By contrast, many Fijians and other Islanders did not have the same imperial links or networks.[91] According to Barrow, 'the Fijian has not, like the Indian, outside friends to create trouble'. He continued:

> They dare not even appeal to their rulers: poor Oliver Twist had a more hopeful change. Whenever I have urged them to represent their grievances or petition for redress, the timorous response has been – 'Malua sa cudru na Kovana' (the Governor will be angry afterwards); or 'Malua sa cudru na Talai (Native Commissioner) – or some other official … there is little hope, in a Crown Colony, of outside assistance being of much avail.[92]

Barrow ignores the many local networks (such as Roko, Buli, Fijian and European magistrates and missionaries) on which Fijians could draw when faced with grievances and to which, according to Robert Nicole, the colonial administration felt a greater obligation to respond in line with its broader policy of 'native protection'.[93] Nevertheless, the voyages and impact of Kunti's story highlight the way in which some indentured labourers and activists were tied into and able to effectively mobilize a transnational network created through indenture. While Islanders' welfare (especially regarding 'blackbirding') also drew much international attention, the promotion of these issues was generally led by missionary organizations or the Aborigines Protection Society, rather than by Islanders themselves who were most active in local and regional networks.

Despite this distinction, in both cases, a critical motivating factor behind the actions of both colonial governments was the necessity to maintain hegemony and respect in the face of challenges to their administration's tenuous legal regime. Official inaction had given Crombie the motivation to go above the law and impose his own brand of justice on the hospital trespassers, and the colonial administration needed to reassert its authority as dominant. In this situation, the conviction of Crombie was more a signal that officials would not tolerate British citizens encroaching upon or ignoring their jurisdiction than the application of a deep-seated commitment to protecting Indigenous rights. This is not to deny that certain officials had strong humanitarian motivations. Rather, divergent and conflicting understandings of humanitarianism shaped the conflict between Crombie and officials and intersected with the official priority to protect

British colonial authority. The British administration emphasized 'natives' legal protection, while Crombie prioritized physical and violent protection of the boundaries and hierarchies of the hospital as a site of care, respectability and morality.

To understand the official response to Crombie's actions, it is also crucial to contextualize the case in terms of the tense diplomatic and missionary relationships between the dual administrations. The complaint from their French counterparts regarding the illegal detention and assault of French employees essentially forced the British administration's hand in the matter of Dr Crombie's prosecution. While the dual administrations of the Anglo-French Condominium were at liberty to disregard certain transgressions by their nationals towards ni-Vanuatu, once an issue or complaint escalated to the level of diplomatic correspondence it became much harder to ignore. The humanitarian rhetoric of justice and protection for ni-Vanuatu contributed to the successful conviction of Crombie for the violence against Toby and Jack, but in the end the need to preserve their standing with their French counterparts and insubordinate settlers spurred the British judiciary into action. Thus, the administration was motivated by pragmatics of saving face in the Anglo-French relationship, as much as by an ideological commitment to equal justice.

Colonial officials in Fiji were also put on the defensive due to censure by their superiors at the Colonial Office and counterparts in India. The Fijian administration was unwilling to give credibility to Kunti's narrative, and thereby expose the abuses of indentured labourers and admit to the inability of the Fijian Immigration Department to properly inspect and supervise the system. Officials went into damage control. The official enquiry drew on archetypal and widely circulated narratives of Indian propensity to promiscuity and dishonesty to explain away Kunti's complaint as well as the social problems associated with Fiji's plantation lines. Officials and settlers believed such explanations absolved them of responsibility for allegations of abuse of Indian immigrants, though this rationalization began to fall apart under mounting censure from missionaries and the Indian government and public. Both examples highlight the administrations' difficulties in establishing and maintaining legal authority and respect in the diverse Pacific colonies.

Crombie and Kunti's actions also demonstrate the alternative strategies by which individuals and groups pursued their own forms of justice when unsatisfied with the official legal regimes. Whereas Crombie employed violent and humiliating retributive justice, when both her superiors and the judiciary ignored her pleas, Kunti first resisted by stopping work and then employed highly public channels to bring attention to her fight for justice. Though the many obstacles to justice facing indentured labourers meant few cases attracted the attention Kunti's did, her story demonstrates the various methods by which marginalized groups actively resisted or confronted colonial violence.

In both colonies specific events dramatically revealed differing and often incompatible visions of the principles and purpose of colonial law and courts. These local fault lines come into focus through controversies over interracial sexual crimes or fears of such crimes, which, given their highly emotive character, produced some of the most intense disputes over the application of the law in colonial Fiji and Vanuatu. Crombie and Kunti each exposed the limitations of the Anglo-French and British legal regimes in their respective colonies and their counter-narratives. In both cases, the female body lay at the heart of the judicial debates: as physical body in need of protection from physical and moral assaults and as slate upon which broader colonial and anti-colonial opinions could be inscribed and circulated. The female body in the colonial Pacific thus provided a powerful and emotive image across the lines of race, religion and imperial administration.

Notes

1 For a comparative perspective from Papua New Guinea, see Inglis, *The White Women's Protection Ordinance.*

2 Wiener, *An Empire on Trial*, introduction.

3 David Crombie to British Resident Commissioner, 4/9/1908, Folder 11/1907, NHBS 1/I Vol. 1, WPA.

4 Carina E. Ray, 'Decrying White Peril: Interracial Sex and the Rise of Anticolonial Nationalism in the Gold Coast', *American Historical Review* 119, no. 1 (2014), 78–110; John Pape, 'Black and White: The 'Perils of Sex' in Colonial Zimbabwe', *Journal of Southern African Studies* 16, no. 4 (1990), 699–720. For concerns over black peril in Fiji, see Knapman, *White Women*, 124–5.

5 For Australian press commentary on the Pacific, see Roger C. Thompson, *Australian Imperialism in the Pacific: The Expansionist Era 1820–1920* (Melbourne: Melbourne University Press, 1980).

6 See Dorothy Shineberg, 'The New Hebridean Is Everywhere', 14 for a summary of New Caledonia newspapers and their print runs.

7 Etherington, 'The Gendering of Indirect Rule', 43–4.

8 For example: Dossier A4 (2) Nouvelles attaques des missions presbytériennes contre la colonisation française aux Nouvelles-Hébrides. 1924–5, SG-NH

Carton 12; 'Opinions australiennes a.s. du Condominium', in Inspection des Colonies – Mission Revel 1922, ADC Carton 828; Gouverneur et Haut Commissaire J. Repiquet à Ministre des Colonies, 5 juillet 1922, DAP Carton 1AFFPOL/1915, ANOM.

9 Kelly, *A Politics of Virtue*, 40.

10 Dr Crombie to Resident Commissioner for the French Republic, 6/9/1915, MS 894/25 Edward Jacomb Diary 1915, SHL.

11 Written Statement of Dr Combie, MS 894/25 Edward Jacomb Diary 1915, SHL.

12 Letter to Mother and Father, 2/4/1914, MS 894/24 Edward Jacomb Diary 1914, SHL.

13 Letter to Mother and Father, 11/9/1915, MS 894/25 Edward Jacomb Diary 1915, SHL.

14 While more sympathetic to ni-Vanuatu than many contemporaries, Jacomb also repeated stereotypes of 'native laziness' and unreliability. Letter from Mother, 9/9/1913, and Letter to Mother and Father, 24/1/1913, MS 894/23 Edward Jacomb Diary 1913, SHL. Entry for 22/12/907, MS 894/18 Edward Jacomb Diary 1907–08; Entry for 8/10/1909, MS 894/19 Edward Jacomb Diary 1909; Letter to Charles, 12/9/14, MS 894/24 Edward Jacomb Diary 1914; and Letter to R. J. Fletcher, 25/1/1917, MS 894/27 Edward Jacomb Diary 1917, SHL.

15 Entry for 20/8/1907, 24/8/1907, and 16/6/1908, MS 894/18 Edward Jacomb Diary 1907–1908, SHL.

16 Letter to Mother, 12/3/1914, MS 894/24 Edward Jacomb Diary 1914, SHL.

17 Letter to Mother, 3/2/1914, MS 894/24 Edward Jacomb Diary 1914, SHL.

18 See Folder 77/1914 (Presence of Unemployed Natives in Vila. 1914–19), NHBS 1/I Vol. 1, WPA.

19 Rodman, *Houses Far from Home*, 52–3.

20 Miles, *Bridging Mental Boundaries*, 40.

21 Letter to Mother, 30/4/1914, MS 894/24 Edward Jacomb Diary 1914, SHL.

22 Letter to Rev. Frank H. L. Paton, 18/4/14, MS 894/24 Edward Jacomb Diary 1914, SHL.

23 Letter to Mother and Father, 2/4/1914, MS 894/24 Edward Jacomb Diary 1914, SHL.

24 Letter to Rev. Frank H. L. Paton, 18/4/14, MS 894/24 Edward Jacomb Diary 1914, SHL.

25 Written Statement of Dr Crombie, MS 894/25 Edward Jacomb Diary 1915, SHL.

26 Dr Crombie to the Commandant of Police (British), undated [1915], MS 894/25 Edward Jacomb Diary 1915, SHL.

27 Dr Crombie to H. B. M. Resident Commissioner, 6/9/1915, MS 894/25 Edward Jacomb Diary 1915, SHL.

28 Rapport du gendarme Boibelet à Resident Commissaire, Port-Vila, 19 août 1915, SG-NH Carton 8, ANOM.

29 Written Statement of Dr Crombie, MS 894/25 Edward Jacomb Diary 1915, SHL. Drunken according to Crombie, this point is not mentioned by the men themselves.
30 Crombie to Jacomb, 2 September 1915, PANZ.
31 Rapport du gendarme Boibelet à Resident Commissaire, Port-Vila, 19 août 1915, SG-NH Carton 8, ANOM.
32 Letter to Mother and Father, 11/9/1915, MS 894/25 Edward Jacomb Diary 1915, SHL.
33 Rapport du gendarme Boibelet à Resident Commissaire, Port-Vila, 19 août 1915, SG-NH Carton 8, ANOM.
34 Anna Cole, 'Governing Tattoo: Reflections on a Colonial Trial', in Nicholas Thomas, Anna Cole and Bronwen Douglas (eds), *Tattoo: Bodies, Art and Exchange in the Pacific and Europe* (London: Reaktion Books, 2005), 109–19; Clare Anderson, *Legible Bodies: Race, Criminality and Colonialism in South Asia* (Oxford: Berg, 2004), 15–56; and Jane Caplan (ed.), *Written on the Body: The Tattoo in European and American History* (London: Reaktion Books, 2000).
35 David Crombie to M. Austin, 17 August 1915, SG-NH Carton 8, ANOM; Letter to Mother and Father, 11/9/1915, MS 894/25 Edward Jacomb Diary 1915, SHL.
36 David Crombie to M. Austin, 17 August 1915 and Gouverneur p.i./Haut Commissaire Repiquet to Ministre des Colonies, 6 octobre 1915, SG-NH Carton 8, ANOM.
37 'Rapport d'Ensemble sur la situation des Nouvelles-Hébrides en 1910', Port-Vila, 20 avril 1911, Gouverneur à Ministre des Colonies, 10 février 1910, SG-NH, Carton 11bis, ANOM. On French concerns regarding the impact of Presbyterian funding (compared to the poorly resourced Catholic mission) see 'Situation politique et économique', Inspecteur Revel à Ministres des Colonies, 3 juin 1912, SH-NH Carton 31, ANOM.
38 Rapport du gendarme Boibelet à Resident Commissaire, 19 août 1915, SG-NH Carton 8, ANOM.
39 Rapport Trimestriel sur la Situation des Nouvelles-Hebrides. Juillet–Septembre 1915, SG-NH Carton 12, ANOM.
40 Written Statement of Dr Crombie, MS 894/25 Edward Jacomb Diary 1915, SHL.
41 Le Gouverneur p.i./Haut Commissaire Repiquet à Ministre des Colonies, 6 octobre 1915, SG-NH Carton 8, ANOM.
42 Rapport Trimestriel sur la Situation des Nouvelles-Hebrides. Juillet–Septembre 1915, SG-NH Carton 12, ANOM.
43 Gouverneur et Haut Commissaire à Ministre des Colonies, 23 novembre 1923, DAP Carton 1AFFPOL/1915, ANOM.
44 On King, see Scarr, *Fragments of Empire*, 229.
45 'Rapport d'Ensemble sur la situation des Nouvelles-Hébrides en 1910', 20 avril 1911, SG-NH Carton 11bis, ANOM.

46 See for example Folder 12/1911 (Sale of liquor and explosives by the French to natives. (2 parts) 1910–1912), NHBS 1/I Vol. 1, WPA; and British Judge of the Joint Court R. S. de Vere to the President of the Joint Court, Port Vila, 23 October 1923, enclosure to Gouverneur et Haut Commissaire à Ministre des Colonies, 23 novembre 1923, DAP Carton 1AFFPOL/1915, ANOM.
47 British Judge of the Joint Court R. S. de Vere to the President of the Joint Court, 23 October 1923, enclosure to Gouverneur et Haut Commissaire à Ministre des Colonies, 23 novembre 1923, DAP Carton 1AFFPOL/1915, ANOM.
48 Gouverneur et Haut Commissaire à Ministre des Colonies, 23 novembre 1923, DAP Carton 1AFFPOL/1915, ANOM. See also Scarr, *Fragments of Empire*, 219–20 on French attempts to replace British interests with French.
49 Jacomb to A. W. Jose, 24/4/1914, Edward Jacomb Diary 1914, SHL.
50 David Crombie, Mission Station Wala, to British Resident Commissioner, 4/9/1908, Folder 11/1907, NHBS 1/I Vol. 1, WPA.
51 Written Statement of Dr Combie, MS 894/25 Edward Jacomb Diary 1915, SHL.
52 Quoted in Letter to Mother and Father, 11/09/1915, MS 894/25 Edward Jacomb Diary 1915, SHL.
53 Dr D. Crombie to H. B. M. Resident Commissioner, 6/9/1915, MS 894/25 Edward Jacomb Diary 1915, SHL.
54 Letter from Dr D. Crombie to the Resident Commissioner for the French Republic, n.d. [September 1915] and Letter from Dr D. Crombie to H. B. M. Resident Commisioner, n.d. [September 1915], MS 894/25 Edward Jacomb Diary 1915, SHL.
55 Letter from Dr D. Crombie to Resident Commisioner, n.d. [September 1915], MS 894/25 Edward Jacomb Diary 1915, SHL.
56 Letter to R. J. Fletcher, 11/11/1915, MS 894/25, Edward Jacomb Diary 1915, SHL.
57 Letter to Mother and Father, 11/9/1915 and Jacomb's notes on Written Statement of Dr Crombie, MS 894/25 Edward Jacomb Diary 1915, SHL.
58 Letter to R. J. Fletcher, 11/11/15, MS 894/25 Edward Jacomb Diary 1915, SHL.
59 Inglis, *The White Women's Protection Ordinance.*
60 Letter from Dr David Crombie, n.d. [December 1915], MS 894/25 Edward Jacomb Diary 1915; Letter from Dr David Crombie, 31/3/1916, MS 894/26 Edward Jacomb Diary 1916, SHL.
61 Letters from Dr David Crombie, 31/3/1916 and 20/8/1916, MS 894/26 Edward Jacomb Diary 1916, SHL.
62 Minutes of Meeting of Joint Naval Commission held on board HMS Prometheus at Vila on 5 June 1909, Folder 71/1909, NHBS 1/I Vol. 1, WPA.
63 Letter to Mother and Father, 11/9/1915 and Written Statement of Dr Crombie, MS 894/25 Edward Jacomb Diary 1915, SHL.
64 Rodman, 'My Only Weapon'.

65 'Rapport d'Ensemble sur la situation des NH en 1910', 20 avril 1911, Gouverneur à Ministre des Colonies, 10 février 1910, SG-NH Carton 11bis, ANOM.
66 Andrews and W. W. Pearson, *Indian Indentured Labour*, 56.
67 See annual comments in the Annual Reports on Indian Immigration, published in the Legislative Council Papers, NAF, or the *Fiji Blue Books* (Suva: Government Printer, 1880–1900), NAK; Gill, *Turn Northeast*, 73–4; and Brij Lal, 'Veil of Dishonour'.
68 Naidu, *The Violence of Indenture in Fiji*; Council Paper No. 22: Annual Report on Indian Immigration 1910, Legislative Council Papers 1911, NAF, which notes eight adults transferred.
69 See CSO 13/8779 and CSO 14/6609, NAF.
70 Brij V. Lal, 'Kunti's cry'; Shameem, 'Sugar and Spice', 239, 309–11; Kelly, *A Politics of Virtue*, 45–54; Nicole, *Disturbing History*, 210–11. For a comparative case in Assam, see Ashley Wright, 'Gender, Violence, and Justice in Colonial Assam: The Webb Case, c. 1884', *Journal of Social History* 53, no. 4 (2020), 990–1007.
71 Kelly, *A Politics of Virtue*, 55.
72 'Kunti's Story', *Bharat Mitra*, 8 May 1914 with translation, CSO 14/6609, NAF.
73 'The Cry of an Indian Woman in Fiji', *Leader*, 13 August 1913 with translation, CSO 13/8779, NAF.
74 Ibid.
75 'Kunti's Story', *Bharat Mitra*, 8 May 1914 with translation, CSO 14/6609, NAF.
76 Totaram Sanadhya, *My Twenty-One Years in Fiji and the Story of the Haunted Line*, translated and edited by John Dunham Kelly and Uttra Kumari Singh (Suva: Fiji Museum, 1991).
77 Kelly, *A Politics of Virtue*, 43–4; Nicole, *Disturbing History*, 211.
78 James McNeill and Chimman Lal, *Report to the Government of India on the Conditions of Indian Immigrants in Four British Colonies and Surinam* (London: His Majesty's Stationery Office, 1915); Andrews and Pearson, *Indian Indentured Labour; Report of Mr. Andrews' Speech to the Planters' Association Executive Committee, Fiji, December 7th, 1915,* and other reports by Miss Garnham, Richard Piper and Andrews in MOM 520, Mitchell Library, Sydney.
79 Gillion, *Fiji's Indian Migrants.*
80 Sanadhya, quoted in Kelly, *A Politics of Virtue*, 49.
81 K. L. Gillion, *The Fiji Indians: Challenge to European dominance 1920–1946* (Canberra: Australian National University Press, 1977), 7–10.
82 Secretary to the Government of India to Colonial Secretary, 17 September 1913, and A. Mongomerie to Colonial Secretary, 8 January 1914, CSO 13/8779, NAF.
83 See Minutes to CSO 14/6609, NAF for discussion.
84 A. Mongomerie to Colonial Secretary, 8 January 1914, CSO 13/8779, NAF.

85 Kate Stevens, 'Violence of the Law: Prosecuting Gendered Violence in Colonial Fiji', in Lyndall Ryan and Angela Wanhalla (eds), *Aftermaths: Colonialism, Violence and Memory* (Dunedin: Otago University Press, forthcoming).

86 Inspector of Immigrants to Colonial Secretary and A. Mongomerie to Colonial Secretary, 8 January 1914, CSO 13/8779, NAF.

87 McNeill and Lal, *Report to the government of India*; Andrews and Pearson, *Indian Indentured Labour.*

88 Andrews and Pearson, *Indian Indentured Labour,* 36.

89 Quoted by Government Emigration Agent, Calcutta, to Colonial Secretary, n.d. [1915], CSO 14/6609, NAF.

90 Datta, *Fleeting Agencies*, introduction; see also Nicole on 'everyday resistance' in *Disturbing History.*

91 But see Tracey Banivanua Mar, 'Imperial Literacy and Indigenous Rights: Tracing Transoceanic Circuits of a Modern Discourse', *Aboriginal History* 37 (2013), 1–28.

92 Barrow, *Fiji for the Fijians*, 7.

93 Nicole, 'Disturbing History', 297.

6

Alternative pursuits of justice

In early September 1908 David, a Nguna man working on an Undine Bay plantation, refused to return to work and asserted that 'he did not care for the Bl–dy Government as he was a Nguna man and the Government could not touch the Nguna men'.[1] The incident had begun with a complaint from two married labourers, Torr and the other unnamed, that David and Tismalla had interfered with their wives. The molestation or adultery was a cause of friction, though the perspective of the wives were subsequent absent in the correspondence and investigation; their agency unrecognized in discussions between men. Planter Ernest Seagoe publicly reprimanded David and warned against continuing improper relations with Torr's wife Alice. Seagoe was then 'subjected to a brutal and unprovoked attack' as David 'rushed' at him with 'murderous intent'.[2] Kupen and Johnny joined the assault, until Seagoe got hold of a stick, causing the men to stop the attack. David then declared his impunity from government power.

Emphasizing the danger to himself and his partner, Seagoe requested government assistance to 'save possible bloodshed'. He asked that the 'boys' be arrested and punished, and 'shown that inasmuch as there is a law to punish planters who ill-treat their labour there is also a law to punish labourers who make murderous attacks on their employers'. As the nephew of the first (and pre-Condominium) British Resident, Captain Ernest Rason, and subsequently commandant of police in the 1930s, Seagoe was invested in colonial authority and well-connected to request official support.[3]

Investigating, Commandant of Police Edwin Harrowell found the situation 'unsatisfactory' as according to local planters, ni-Vanuatu 'state openly that the Government is weak and can do nothing to them if they transgress'.[4] Accounts from ni-Vanuatu witnesses point a more complex picture. Labourers Batella, Willie and Sigari supported Seagoe's account that David struck the first blow, though others including Louis, Torr, Basil, Boy, Tismas and Lop all pointed to Seagoe as the instigator.[5] Harrowell's report echoed frequent colonial concern over testimony: 'as is usual with native statements, the result is of a contradictory nature'.[6] He nevertheless held responsible the Indigenous men, who had deserted the plantation on 4 September. He advocated that David, Kupen and Johnny be dealt with 'firmly', suggesting more frequent naval patrols and labour inspections to prevent further trouble arising.

After 'securing' the accused at Kakula and Pele Islands, Harrowell returned to Vila with the men on 9 September. At the planter's request, David, Kupen and Johnny were charged with desertion, attempting to incite desertion and assault before the Joint Naval Commission (JNC) on 20 October 1908. The men were discharged of assault but were convicted of desertion.[7] As the three men had already been detained for six weeks awaiting trial, they were sentenced to three weeks imprisonment. The men's impending release raised further anxiety, as they had the majority of their contracts still to serve. The 'boys' wrote to British Resident Merton King, emphatic that they did not wish to return to Seagoe's plantation: 'And you know, father, that he put us in prison for naught. Please father, we want to go home when we out from the prison.'[8] Their plea places the injustice of arrest squarely upon Seagoe, while making a strategic appeal or conceptualization of a familial relationship with the British Resident as their protector and authority over European men, a view perhaps encouraged by the missionaries.

Nor did Seagoe want the men back, requesting that they instead serve out the remainder of their indenture with MacKenzie, who agreed to take them on. He explained:

> We are not quite near enough to the Government for that, in the event of the boys wishing to take command again I should have to protect myself, which would probably result in a visit to Fiji for me. If Johnson could come round here occasionally it would make a wonderful difference. The n___ could get justice against the white man and also the white man against the n___ in the petty cases which never reach the Office at Vila and which are in reality of much greater importance than the reported cases.[9]

He emphasized disadvantages of distance from the centre of colonial order and the threat of violence – European as much as Indigenous – in the absence of government oversight. He further hints at the unseen: the many incidents never recorded in judicial archives.

Kupen and Johnny subsequently transferred to MacKenzie but the planter refused to take David, who was perhaps perceived as the main troublemaker.[10] This incident illustrates the anxious violence provoked by the limits of legal authority in the New Hebrides.[11] Whether genuine sentiment or bravado, the ni-Vanuatu men reportedly felt that the government had no reach over their actions. Once imprisoned in Vila their tone changed as they sought aid from the colonial administration against their employer.[12] Planters felt at risk of racial insubordination and of violence, as chronicled in their requests for naval presence at Undine Bay and Nguna, which were 'not quite near enough' to the spaces of Condominium authority.

This chapter explores the many ways in which officials and administrations addressed cases of sexual (and other) violence without going to trial. As explored in previous chapters judicial power was limited, at times ineffectual, and often critiqued. Trials heard before the courts represented only a fraction of incidents, as Seagoe himself stated. However, the limits of the judiciary's extension into Indigenous communities and colonial plantations were not always owing to practical constraints, but rather a conscious strategy by colonial administrations and magistrates to circumvent the judicial process. While Indigenous elites and missionaries established their own codes and systems of punishment, the New Caledonia and New Hebrides administrations themselves pursued strategies to removed Islanders from the jurisdiction of courts. Racial and gendered narratives of violence provided a rationale to dispense with the courtroom in favour of punitive alternatives or 'trial without witnesses' in the New Caldeonian Conseil Privé or New Hebrides JNC.

I argue that government violence remained a basic response to non-European crime, both sexual and otherwise. Despite the introduction of colonial courts and the rhetoric of law's civilizing power, arbitrary tribunals, naval expeditions and bombardment remained key means of enforcing rule well into the twentieth century, justified on the grounds of Islander 'savagery' but also tied to imperial politics and rivalries of the period. Indeed the very existence of the courts functioned to obscure the continued use of violent tactics. While the courts had real impact for those appearing on trial or denied the opportunity to go to trial, the proliferation of other forms of justice, retaliation and punishment was testament not only to the continued vibrancy of local cultures of maintaining order, but also the state's willingness to bypass legal procedure. To rephrase Dr Crombie's words from the previous chapter, the law was the protector of colonial lawlessness.

Arbitrary tribunals and courtrooms without witnesses

Many cases that reached the ears of the colonial administrations were dealt with behind closed doors. From 1887, the Indigénat removed the separation of executive and judiciary in the governance of Kanak in New Caledonia. One result was a reduction in the number of trials involving Kanak, especially outside Nouméa. Officials representing the Service des Affaires Indigènes (SAI) were instead authorized to impose summary justice for minor offences with fines or short-term imprisonment. From 1898, gendarmes were appointed as *syndics*, but often lacked training and capacity (see Chapter 1). Though the Indigénat included an evergrowing list of infractions, many crimes, such as murder, rape, theft and other violent acts, were covered by the penal code. These could equally be pursued through the courts and serious offences were to be referred to the administration in Nouméa. Many were discussed and decided privately by the Conseil Privé (Privy Council), which meant Kanak lost the right to trial and to appeal the governor's decision. As Jean Guiart underlines, this 'had the principal consequence of placing the indigènes outside common law'.[13] Kanak lost their right to go to court.

The Conseil Privé was established in 1885 and consisted of the Governor and senior members of the colonial bureaucracy.[14] The Governor consulted the council on the governance of the colony including discussion of court sentences in serious cases, and on Indigenous affairs such as proposed punishments under the Indigénat. Requests for and adjudication of internment sentences for serious Kanak offenders (or at least those who were perceived as a threat) were deliberated with reasonable frequency. The relationship between criminal offences and political concerns was blurred, for the Conseil Privé acted as both judge and jury and its preferred sanctions, exile and internment, effectively removed 'unruly' individuals from causing further trouble. Focusing on the years from 1890 to 1905 when internment was most frequently deployed for serious, but primarily non-political, crimes, I examine how the motivations and justifications featured concerns around sexual conduct.[15]

Deportation had a prior history in New Caledonia and the wider French empire. The removal of Kanak from their community under the Indigénat mirrored the removal of criminals from the metropole to penal colonies.[16] Even before the consolidation of the Indigénat regime, numerous Kanak were deported or interned during periods of violent conflict with the colonial state. However, Adrian Muckle has demonstrated that internment was a management strategy employed to govern the quotidian as much as the political, and was a defining aspect of Kanak colonial experience. I draw on Merle and Muckle's excellent scholarship in situating the Indigénat as a range of policies that limited the judiciary's role in sexual crimes involving Kanak, while simultaneously increasing colonial authority over their intimate and personal lives.[17]

One justification for dealing with Kanak under the Indigénat rather than the court system was a concern that Kanak appearing before juries did not receive justice. This enabled greater administrative oversight of sentencing and punishment where Kanak were involved. Concerns regarding the partiality of settler juries and perceptions of cultural differences relating to violence, conflict and the treatment of women underpinned discussions of the limitations of courtroom justice, paralleling the situation in the Fiji Supreme Court. For example, despite a strong case including witnesses and a history of violence, Léon Leconte was acquitted by the jury in the Cour d'Assises in 1909 of 'coups et blessures' inflicted upon chief Tiéou of Paola, Koné after he entered the colonist's courtyard to try and visit a Kanak woman. The attack was so brutal the chief lost his right eye.[18] Tiéou described to *gendarme* Henri Chabert how he had been made to sign a letter retracting his complaint but only found out its contents afterwards. Despite the settler jury's verdict, officials believed Leconte was at fault. Noting Leconte's previous convictions, his theft of the tax money the chief was carrying, and his attempts to force Tiéou to drop the complaint, he was fined 3,000 francs in damages. The Governor explained that the family 'deserves the reputation for brutality they have … and it is regrettable that the sanction … was only monetary'.[19] He added that the outcome was justified because, though small, the fine gave Kanak assurance they could gain protection from the administration – likely small comfort if any at all.

Commenting on the case, the Paris-based Director of Political and Administrative Affairs Vasselle felt 'the violent acts committed against indigènes are not assessed by the jury with the desirable impartiality'. For such cases to be resolved in a manner 'more consistent with justice and bon droit', he recommended their referral to the *tribunal correctionel*, a proposal rejected by the local administration who argued that this court lacked the requisite jurisdiction.[20] The alternative, utilizing the provisions of the Indigénat, avoided trial altogether.

Anxieties that Kanak would be acquitted in the courts recurred frequently.[21] In the 4 July 1892 Conseil Privé sitting, Director of the Interior Gauharou proposed the internment of Boé of Ponérihouen, an ex-administrative chief accused of murdering convict Signolo the previous September. Despite speaking fluent French and visiting France, Boé apparently 'had taken nothing from civilization but the worst vices'.[22] Gauharou further reported that Kanak and colonists alike believed Boé was responsible for the murder of *libéré* Debatebe and his *popinée* (Kanak woman or partner) at Tebemba in 1884. He had allegedly committed multiple murders, including burying alive a woman of his *tribu* in 1875. The case was brought to the administration because there was deemed neither sufficient evidence nor suitable witnesses (being *indigènes* with overly consistent statements) to take Boé to trial.[23] The Conseil Privé approved the proposal that Boé be interned on the Île des Pins under the same conditions of the 1878 'insurgents'. This case demonstrates the willingness of the administration to rely on rumour and reported knowledge in governing the Indigenous population and determining the fate of non-European suspects. The outcome attempted to maintain settler calm and confidence in the Ponérihouen area, part of an ongoing project after 1878–9 to dispel anxieties over the 'fantôme' of another Kanak uprising.[24]

Whether justified to protect Kanak from injustice or to protect others from Kanak violence, the effect was to concentrate power in the hands of the Governor and executive, bypassing the judicial process. It enabled direct oversight of Indigenous affairs, a particularly centralized and authoritarian system. By 1902, the Inspector of Colonies Rheinhart noted twenty-five *indigènes* were interned under this policy.[25] Often, cases reported to and decided by Conseil Privé prevented Kanak victims, witnesses and defendants from presenting their cases in the courtroom. In contrast to the Indigenous testimony recorded in the Fijian Supreme Court in Chapter 3, Kanak voices were marginalized. Defendants had no opportunity for defence or appeal, did not appear before the Conseil Privé and could be sentenced before they had been arrested.[26]

These limits to legal recourse or appeal were critiqued by Colonial Inspectors in their tours in the colony during the early twentieth century, though to little effect. In 1902, Maurice Meray was troubled by

> the ease with which the penalties of the Decrét of 18 July 1887 are applied in Nouméa, notably in regards to the sentence of internment … The sentence of internment thus changes in character here, in fact becoming one of containment. Moreover, [the punishment] is always considered definitive as it has been delivered by the Government in Conseil Privé, whereas Article Five of the Décret states that the decisions taken must, in all cases, be submitted for your approval.[27]

Subsequent inspectors echoed Meray's assessment, emphasizing the entrenched use of Indigénat legislation in place of the courts. As Inspector Fillon reported in 1907, 'I do not believe that the caprice of a local government has, in any other colony, subject[ed] the rights of the first Indigenous inhabitants to so many variations.'[28] The repeated attention such reports drew to the misuse and abuse of administrative power through the Indigénat did not trigger reform.

The one notable exception was in the aftermath of the 1917–18 war in Koné, Hienghène and Tipindjé, which left over 250 Kanaks imprisoned in Nouméa. On the insistence of the Ministry of Colonies, seventy-eight individuals against whom there was sufficient evidence were given a criminal trial rather than automatically subjected to Indigénat regulations.[29] Overall however, the Conseil Privé continued to act as a courtroom without an audience, witnesses or defendant in adjudicating Kanak crimes.

Criminal, rather than political, cases by Kanak formed the subject of the bulk of Conseil Privé deliberations. Interned Kanak were charged with a wide range of offences, often involving rape and causing local disharmony through kidnapping and marriage against the community's will. For example, in October 1901, Difoudio, Liuo, Jean and Ami were described as 'inveterate drunks' who 'stole settler property, battered women, forced young girls and did not recognize any authority'. They were each interned for two years on the Île des Pins. The dossiers thoroughly denigrated their character, leaving little room for any decision other than internment.[30] In another case, when the Governor questioned the length of the proposed sentence, the Head of the SAI assured that the accused Demoin was the source of constant trouble and habitual misconduct.[31] Removing disruptive individuals from their communities was justified because it helped achieve 'public tranquility', including the protection of women. Public tranquillity here meant reassuring settlers of colonial control as much as the disciplining of Kanak.

Adjudication on abduction and rape offences specifically reflected officials' view that the kidnapping of women (and related conflict over marriage and the control of persons) lay at the heart of many pre-contact and internal conflicts within Kanak society.[32] Kanak too sometimes strategically utilized the administration to make complaints against individuals who disrupted social norms or as part of ongoing rivalry between groups. In May 1902, Amoux had his position as the *petit chef* of Nindia *tribu* (Haouïlou) revoked and found himself sentenced to internment on Maré for six years. The Conseil Privé was concerned, as Amoux 'had sought women from the neighbouring tribus to marry by force to the tayos [friends, Kanak men] of the mission, seriously displeasing the men of these tribus, and risking creating regrettable conflicts'.[33] The disruptive nature of Amoux's behaviour and the potential for such disputes to escalate to greater violence spurred his long sentence.

Conseil Privé cases involving rape and kidnapping also drew upon racist views of Kanak society as rooted in 'barbarism', with ill treatment of women seen as a marker of their lack of civilization (see Chapter 4). In 1900, for example, the

Head of the SAI reported to the Conseil Privé on the rape of two children, Dj and Dr of Mia, aged twelve and nine years, by Diénima and others. These attacks appeared to be in retribution for the rape of Diénima's wife by a group of men from Mia. One official situated the root of the attacks in the moral deficiency of the accused, and by implication in Kanak society more broadly, while also emphasizing the potential to reform and civilize such men through the example of appropriate punishment. He stated:

> These crimes, which are unfortunately nothing but the consequence of the barbarous customs of these indigènes, merit a severe punishment; the Kanak population must know that the administration will not allow such monstrosities.[34]

While rape was one in a long list of offences resulting in internment, it powerfully signified a lack of civilization and morality that justify individual removals and the Indigénat regime more generally.

In the rape of Dj and Dr, Procureur-Général and the Procureur de la Republique agreed that the case should not be passed to the judiciary, as they feared acquittal for the 'odious act' would 'have a deplorable effect on members of the tribu'. Believing the initial sentences – ranging from a fine of 100 francs for Bouché, Bouénore and Doya to a year's internment and a fine for Ombine and Pecounou – were not long or severe enough, the Conseil Privé increased the punishment to one year's internment at Phare or Maré and 100 francs fine for each man.[35] These were still not long sentences compared to others imposed by the Conseil Privé, arguably on lesser grounds. The incident nevertheless highlights how the administration framed the judiciary as unreliable: uncertain to punish offenders or ensure a reformatory example was impressed upon colonial subjects.

Similar discussions about the internment of Demoin in 1905 reveal how colonial perceptions of Kanak gender relations shaped the dispensation of justice. During the Head of the SAI's tour of Ponérihouen in July 1905, 'all the chiefs' and the *gendamerie* requested that Demoin be exiled, demonstrating local engagement with the administration as one way to deal with problems within the *tribu*. Leclere reported that Demoin had raped Dohi, and beaten her husband Santo and two others who had tried to intervene. The SAI proposed five years internment on Maré. Noting that rape was a crime that fell under *droit commun* (common law), the Procureur-Général questioned why the *gendarmes* did not forward the report to court. The subsequent conversation problematically suggested rape was ubiquitous in an 'uncivilized' society and beyond the bounds of colonial authority to adjudicate. Head of the SAI Leclere's defence was that 'in fact it is a simple matter between Kanaks as occurs in the tribes of the interior.

The indigènes do not attach the same importance to this act as us'. Colombeix backed him, asserting, 'I know that the indigènes have barbaric customs in this regard, and it happens that the young nubile girls sometimes are used by all the men of the tribu.'[36] Governor Rognon concluded such violence was ubiquitous in Kanak society:

> It is rather an internal matter for the tribu. If each time something of this nature occurred within a Kanak tribu, we would be obliged to put justice in action; I believe that we would thus create difficulties beyond count and that the local magistracy would not know how to cope with it.[37]

In contrast to the rape of Dj and Dr, the Conseil Privé decided here that officials did not have a role in policing and punishing sexual violence, showing the fluidity if not inconsistency in how gender and violence were understood by the administration.

By contrast, the Conseil Privé deployed its powers to control the movements of Indigenous women whose conduct was deemed immoral, particularly in Nouméa. The administration attempted to delimit the morality and sexual behaviour of Indigenous women in their interactions with Europeans, despite refusal to address gendered violence. For example, Céline Sélika, an Indigenous woman of Ponérihouen described as living dissolutely with *libérés*, was charged for attempting to hand over her infant to settlers at Thio in January 1900 and confined to an orphanage.[38] The Conseil Privé also had broader power to intervene into aspects of Indigenous women's private lives. To officially marry a European, Kanak women needed proof of their age and identity. If they lacked suitable documentation (which many Kanak did), Indigenous women had to apply to the Conseil Privé for a notarized birth certificate. While the administration initially had little power or oversight of relationships within Kanak society, the behaviour and relationships of Indigenous women with settler men or in colonial settlements was open to greater surveillance and intervention.

Tension nevertheless existed between the judiciary and the Indigénat in addressing violence and crime, as their methods were fundamentally opposed: the colonial judiciary upheld the ideal of, and right to, a fair and open trial while the Indigénat enabled conviction and sentencing through the arbitrary and obscure Conseil Privé. While concerns were raised by Colonial Inspectors and occasionally within the administration itself (particularly by the Procureur-Général, who sought to protect his jurisdiction), the systems effectively operated in parallel from the introduction of the regime in 1887. The Indigénat provided the administration with authority to intervene in Kanak lives unfettered by judicial rules of evidence and procedure. Specific instances of rape and kidnapping were problematically extrapolated as evidence of barbaric nature of all Kanak society. As the accused had no opportunity to defend themselves in closed meetings of the Conseil Privé, the colonial administration's stereotypes went largely unchallenged.

Like the Conseil Privé in New Caledonia, from 1887 the JNC functioned as a courtroom without witnesses.[39] Between 1887 and 1907, the JNC was the only form of limited jurisdiction over the New Hebrides, and from the 1890s the JNC developed an 'ad hoc system … of flogging and fines' and imprisonment.[40] The formation of the JNC into a court was initially a means to obviate undertaking violent reprisals against ni-Vanuatu, technically the JNC's only mandated action. However, even beyond the advent of Condominium rule and the opening of the Joint Court, the JNC worked within a judicial lacuna to police and prosecute ni-Vanuatu in the New Hebrides. The failure to include the ni-Vanuatu population under Joint Court or other jurisdiction thus created a broad and flexible continued role for the JNC.

Cases before the JNC concerned recruitment-related conflicts, especially the recruitment of women against the wishes of the husband or chief, violence against women, such as uxoricide and rape, and the sale of alcohol. The JNC sitting aboard the *Saóne* on 16 October 1891 heard five cases including the illegal sale of women into indenture, a case of theft, and the murder of British planter Peter Sawers and his Malekula 'boy' at Tangoa on 12 September 1891.[41] After the inauguration of the Condominium and before the Joint Court opening, the JNC heard sixty-three cases.[42] The Native Advocate was banned from the JNC proceedings, as were private lawyers. As the JNC allowed neither witnesses nor counsel for the defence, it was remarkably efficient in dispensing with cases: up to thirty convictions could be made in a single afternoon's sitting.[43] Punishments were typically short sentences of imprisonment at Port Vila or longer periods of deportation to Fiji. In some rape and sexual assault cases, the sentences imposed were short compared with those imposed in Fiji or by the New Caledonian *Counsel Privé*. For example, in September 1909 two rape cases (one involving a ten-year-old girl) and a case of incest came before the JNC, all resulted in convictions but with sentences of just three to six months.[44] In each case, one power brought the case and proposed the punishment, which the other appears to have agreed to largely without question.[45]

In short case reports, the JNC made observations and recommendations. For example, sitting aboard the *Kersaint* on 13 June 1908, the JNC suggested that Berk be deported to Fiji for five years hard labour for the murder of his wife at Port Vato, Ambrym. Noting it was the third case of uxoricide in two JNC sittings, the commission felt that 'more severe measures are necessary to check the prevalence of the crime'.[46] Drunkenness, and the resultant violence, was also a recurrent frustration through the reports. On 5 June 1909 sitting aboard the *Prometheus*, the JNC commented on a case of rape at the Vila hospital, where the accused Willy 'plead[ed] he had drink': '[The] Commission wishes to point out this is the second case of natives obtaining drink in Port Vila and subsequently being brought before them.'[47] Nevertheless, it appears resident commissioners rarely took action on JNC suggestions.

Prior to the First World War, the JNC continued to meet sporadically.[48] Suspects could be held in gaol for long periods without formal trial, and where internment was not possible, punitive strategies were employed as discussed in the following section. Despite earlier complaints by Jacomb on behalf of ni-Vanuatu clients, this situation was deemed acceptable and uncontroversial until 1913–14.[49] As acting New Caledonian Governor Ancelin noted, there had previously been a 'tacit tolerance' from both sides of the administration despite the technical illegality of JNC's arrests. They were justified by the circumstances: 'in an exceptional country, an exceptional regime'.[50]

In 1913 the French *Kersaint* toured the archipelago. Taking advantage of the absence of their British counterpart and a loose interpretation of the instructions that naval vessels could only act unilaterally in cases of urgency, the *Kersaint* made 'wholesale arrests', not only for serious crimes of rape and murder, but also for petty charges outside its mandate. This voyage revealed the divergence between law and practice.

In 1914, Edward Jacomb accused the JNC and specifically *Kersaint* of making arrests beyond its jurisdiction. His article engaged in an emerging dispute over the role and activities of the JNC and the naval vessels empowered to act under the terms of the 1887 and 1906 Conventions. Jacomb reported in *The Daily Telegraph*:

> Once arrested, the natives are liable to be detained for many months in prison, where some of them have died whilst awaiting trial, for the sittings of the Joint Commission take place only when the British and French men-of-war are in Port Vila at the same time, and on one occasion there was an interval of 10 months between the sittings.

Moreover, he noted:

> Practically no natives brought before the Joint Naval Commission have ever been acquitted, for the simple reason that no witnesses for the defence are ever heard, and the accused are not allowed to be defended by counsel. It

> goes without saying that they are quite unable to defend themselves, as even the most intelligent of them speak 'pidgin' English only. At the same time, the members of the commission do not understand 'pidgin' English … And there is no disinterested interpreter. Often the unfortunate natives are quite innocent of the charges against them; often they are arrested, kept in gaol for months, doing hard labor, tried, and sentenced for further periods, for no apparent offence.[51]

As well as drawing attention to injustice, this account echoes the difficulties of translation and mutual incomprehension in the various satirizations of the Joint Court.

Jacomb argued that *Kersaint*'s actions represented significant worsening of the already problematic actions and questionable legality of the JNC:

> Nowhere and at no time can be found a shadow of legal justification for the Joint Naval Commission forming itself into a court of justice, trying people and awarding sentences … the Joint Naval Commission has calmly stepped in and undertaken this most important judicial responsibility, without any legal power to do so, or, indeed, without any knowledge or capacity for the work.[52]

Missionaries made similar protests.[53]

Ni-Vanuatu accounts of their harsh treatment onboard the *Kersaint* added weight to these objections: they were 'kicked along' and 'capsized into the boat head first', where they were chained and fed minimal rations. In the Guitel murder case, when Jimmy Tarames would not say who told him to kill the planter, the head Maré policeman 'cut him over the head' with a lash or whip until Tarames answered as desired. Similar physical assaults were used on the other arrested men until they gave the same answers.[54] Expressing concern about the high level of convictions and lack of judicial process, Commonwealth solicitor Wallace described the JNC as 'an instrument for the oppression of the natives by the French … as a court it simply convicts at the request of the Administration'.[55] These critiques stemmed from humanitarian concerns as much as frustration that unilateral French action undermined joint governance and British prestige.

Spurred by the *Kersaint* tour, Jacomb attempted to gain entry to the JNC as a lawyer and representative for ni-Vanuatu in December 1913 but was denied. The French Commandant Roque explained that military or police officers had made their own investigations, which were quite sufficient to get to the heart of matter.[56] The French resident commissioner argued that there were 'many more disadvantages than advantages in admitting lawyers' to the JNC.[57] He justified this in the interests of the defendants, noting that lawyers were not permitted to represent *indigènes* in the French West African colonies either. French refusal and apparent British acquiescence prompted Jacomb's complaints to the resident commissioner and the press. In his 1914 book he wrote:

> Who in England would think that a British Naval Officer would consent for one moment to associate himself with such a travesty of justice, or that a British Resident Commissioner should dare execute sentences arrived at by such means?[58]

Much of the criticism emerged in the context of imperial and religious rivalries in the colony, with the *Kersaint* primarily arresting Presbyterian mission converts and teachers.[59] French officials argued that the JNC was essential to maintaining French influence in the territory given the concerted efforts by missionaries to increase British power. That missionaries made their own arrests, conducted trials and imposed punishments irked French officials and colonists, underpinning support for the French Navy's role in safeguarding French interests. Adding to French frustration was their belief that missionaries were instrumental in influencing ni-Vanuatu to contribute money for Jacomb to represent their land claims in the Joint Court, and that he was thus usurping the Native Advocate's role. Labelling him the 'Gouvernement de M. Jacomb', the French resident commissioner felt that the lawyer interfered with Condominium sovereignty and French rights in the New Hebrides.[60]

War changed the landscape of the debate, for the JNC was not able to convene regularly and the Joint Court also closed. Delays in trying ni-Vanuatu held in the Port Vila prisons became the focus of official attention, and both powers agreed that clarification of the law was needed.[61] Yet the lacuna in dealing with Islander crime and dissent remained. The administrations fully divested JNC of its jurisdictional power over ni-Vanuatu in 1916, 'without these powers being regularly assigned to another court'. Thus in 1921 French officials complained, 'There does not exist therefore, after six years, any legal means to punish the culprits of these crimes.'[62] Similarly exasperated with the lack of change, George W. Paton in 1923 declared, 'It is a disgrace to any administration that the greater part of its inhabitants should not be subject to any criminal law and should be at the mercy of an arbitrary tribunal.'[63] The political inertia of wartime meant legislative changes to the Condominium and JNC were not enacted until the early 1920s (see Chapter 1).

The lack of jurisdiction over island subjects and the inability to enforce Condominium authority meant that the JNC effectively replaced the Joint Court as the key colonial legal presence outside Port Vila. From the 1890s to the 1910s, it resembled the role of the Conseil Privé in New Caledonia, functioning as a courtroom without witnesses, allowing neither representation or defence witnesses for Islanders accused of crimes ranging from rape to murder to theft. Similarly, there were few checks on its operation despite its technically restricted role after 1906. Nevertheless, the local inter-imperial rivalries made the JNC the subject of fierce criticism when either navy seemed to overstep the boundaries of joint sovereignty. The negotiations towards the 1914 Protocol combined with reduced naval capacity during the First World War meant the JNC was technically relieved of its judicial powers. However, as so often characterized New Hebrides' colonial history, change was slow to come.

Punitive expeditions

Throughout the early decades of the Condominium the ship remained a space of law: sitting as a tribunal, naval vessels under the JNC were key to the performance and enactment of justice across the archipelago. However, these ships were also spaces of violence. Alongside investigations, arrests, imprisonment and deportation, the JNC threatened violent reprisals, undertook punitive expeditions and the burning and shelling of villages and crops if the guilty were not found or handed over by ni-Vanuatu communities. The JNC reports made little differentiation between tactics, suggesting they were deemed substitutable. It thus retained an underlying military character both in the handling of cases and in the use of other violent tactics.

State-endorsed violence through naval bombardments endured well into the twentieth century. The Condominium condoned punitive naval expeditions against Indigenous crime well after the establishment of the colonial judiciary and in the face of continued questions and criticism over the legitimacy of such actions. The ongoing use of naval visits and attacks was predicated on European perceptions of ni-Vanuatu understandings of justice. Like the courts, such expeditions did performative work for the colonial state: they were essential in pacifying settler voices for greater government intervention as much as visibly demonstrating Anglo-French authority to Islanders. As the same time, the performances and the performative ineptness of the Joint Court (Chapter 3) has helped to obscure these violent strategies.

I build here on Martin Thomas's argument that violent tactics by colonial law enforcement were a sign of colonial weakness rather than of strength.[64] Punitive practices were framed as a logical response to local exigencies: where justice was circuitous and Islanders constructed as 'savage', officials deemed extrajudicial methods necessary to manage a difficult and 'uncivilised' population. Despite criticism, racialized narratives provided a convenient rhetoric to justify authoritarian and violent actions by officers, and responded to settler fears and petitions, many of which were inflected by gendered claims about the need to protect white women and children. Gender thus played a part in the discursive strategies used to justify repressive tactics as well as to critique them, especially when Indigenous women and children fell victim to naval attacks. In these debates, liberalism sat in tension with repressive justice.

Pre-Condominium punitive expeditions were generally undertaken as retribution or punishment for the murder of Europeans in the New Hebrides, though naval vessels occasionally intervened to halt intra-Islander conflict.[65] These incidents were often connected to the labour trade, as Islanders avenged underpayment, the kidnapping of women, the death or non-return of indentured labourers, or sought the material goods offered by recruiters. In general, Joel Bonnemaison argues that 'most murders were single acts of violent retaliation whenever the rules of Melanesian society had been challenged'.[66] As the Earl of Kimberley explained in 1881, traders similarly responded to challenges with violence: 'the absence of protection in any regular manner leads the white traders to take the law into their own hands, and to avenge themselves by acts as violent as those from which they suffer'.[67]

Though annexation shifted the purely naval oversight of the JNC to the firmer land-based rule of Condominium, for most Islanders outside Port Vila or Efate little change was discernible in their encounters with imperial agents. Despite their often-limited success, naval violence against ni-Vanuatu remained a key strategy of imperial governance in the decades after the establishment of the rule of law. The perceived need for punitive expeditions indicates how, even when available, the legal system was not always the vehicle of redress for individuals, communities or the administration itself.

Though used elsewhere, the regular use of repressive naval tactics was particularly prominent in the New Hebrides, even increasing after annexation.[68] As Jacomb wrote in 1919:

> The white man is satisfied if in lieu of catching a murderer he sacks the tribal village from which he comes, and destroys a number of the villagers who probably had no connexion whatever with the crime. Again, it is in the New Hebrides, that unfortunate Group where all the evils of the South Seas seem to find their happiest hunting-ground, that we find this miserable practice in full vigour.[69]

Both Fiji and New Caledonia administrations also resorted to military intervention against Islanders, often on a larger scale, but with less frequency than occurred in the New Hebrides.

The 1876 war in Fiji, known as the 'Kai Colo'[70] war, *valu ni lotu* (church war) or Gordon's 'little war', sought the subjugation and integration of the troublesome 'hill-tribes' of Viti Levu into the broader colonial project. The so-called 'Kai Colo' peoples had not been present at the cession of Fiji, and their resistance to colonial rule owed much to the alliance of Gordon's administration and Christianity with the eastern Bauan chiefs, long-standing rivals of those from inland Viti Levu. The killing of Reverend Thomas Baker in 1867 at Nabutautau and of planters Spiers and Macintosh in 1871, Cakobau's failed reprisals for these murders and the more 'successful' 1873 expedition (in terms of numbers killed or captured and damage to local power) against other murders, as well as increasing incursions on 'Kai Colo land and autonomy by other chiefs, missionaries and settlers, created the conditions for intra-tribal and colonial confrontation in the 1870s. From April to June 1876, Gordon led a predominantly Fijian force on a military campaign to pacify the 'heathen' of the interior. He suspended Supreme Court jurisdiction so many of the Kai Colo leaders could be tried and executed, a forceful demonstration of colonial power and the risk of open dissent against it. This and other legislation reinforced the colonial view of this region as a 'disturbed district'. Kai Colo sought (and continued to seek) to maintain their land, their independence vis-à-vis the Bauan chiefs and their own religion and customs such as polygamy. The end of the Colo war did not mark the end of Kai Colo resistance, but did mark a shift away from warfare as a strategy of asserting authority for both the British administration and for the Kai Colo peoples.[71]

Kanak relationships with the New Caledonia administration were punctuated by a series of local wars from 1856 to 1879, and again in 1917, the so-called last Kanak revolt. In each case, Kanak *tribus* sought to actively prevent and defend encroachments on their society and lands though, as in Fiji, pre-colonial political conflict persisted with Kanak represented on both sides. The legacy of these conflicts was great, not only in practical terms (the loss of land, crops and resource access) but also in the construction of Kanak as a threatening other, needing to be contained and excluded from the project of settling and transforming the Grande Terre agriculturally and economically. These wars, which have been ably discussed by other scholars, indicate that recourse to military measures to instil or to resist colonial order was not unique to the New Hebrides.[72] However, the longevity of the JNC and the continuation and frequency of punitive expeditions well into the twentieth century seem peculiar to the New Hebrides, enabled by the combination of the limited official presence outside Vila, racial discourse and inter-imperial politics.

Though technically identified as 'acts of war', repressive naval measures were generally deployed against individual acts of violent crime, rather than political threats to the colonial state. The legality of such actions were the subject of debate and critique within official circles but continued nonetheless at least until 1918.[73] Alongside the troublesome island geography, racialized constructions of Indigenous society were deployed to counter critiques, and some officials argued that swift and violent retribution was the only form of justice 'natives' were capable of understanding.

The role of gunboat diplomacy in the contact era has been the subject of historical debate. Jane Samson's work on the role of the British Navy in Pacific colonization pre-1874 shows how naval officers constructed their mission as one of 'imperial benevolence'. The navy had a crucial role in drawing British authority into the region and legitimizing it 'through the crafting of a humanitarian mission to protect Islanders'.[74] Naval intervention is framed as a pre-cursor to formal imperialism, though they subsequently co-existed as both British and French navies pursued punitive justice around the islands well after colonization. Hardened racial bias triumphed over humanitarian ideals, and practical expediencies trounced ineffective and time-consuming legal procedures. The simultaneous condemnation of the violence between European traders, recruiters and planters (who were often subject to vitriolic assessments in official reports) and Islanders, and the continued condoning of imperial acts of violence in the colonial period is a tension that highlights the limits to imperial benevolence in the early twentieth century.

Focusing on New Caledonia, Isabelle Merle identifies similar language and ideals of humanitarianism at play as France, the 'nation of human rights', sought to 'protect a certain international image'.[75] The instructions of the Ministry of Colonies regarding the treatment of Kanak, and advising against repressive military expeditions, were constantly at odds with the views and actions of local colonial authorities. In particular, the entrenched characterization of Kanak as guerrillas and 'savages' rather than honourable soldiers in early conflicts enabled continued violent reprisals by the state.[76] Although British protectionism has received greater historiographical attention, both British and French colonial ministries decried excessive violence against Indigenous subjects in the Pacific and asserted their humanitarian motivations and credentials. Nevertheless, as the realities of local circumstances and the pressure of anxious settlers undermined such ideals, authoritarian repression remained a key component in managing Islanders in the New Hebrides and New Caledonia.

Throughout much of the nineteenth century, men-of-war constituted the only form of British and French imperial presence around the New Hebrides and other uncolonized islands. The 1877 British Order in Council establishing the Western Pacific High Commission, the establishment of British and French Naval Divisions in the Pacific and the 1887 Anglo-French Convention establishing the JNC all served to formalize the role of the British and French Navy as the vanguard of imperial contact with Islanders. As Scarr explains, during the 1880s 'in the absence of any jurisdiction over Islanders for offences against British subjects, [Islanders] continued to be regarded as members of responsible communities whose occasional violent acts must be interpreted as acts of war and be answered accordingly'.[77] Naval bombardments were the preferred sanction, especially when difficulties arose establishing the identity of specific offenders.[78] This is clear in the tour of the *Dives* around the New Hebrides in 1886, where Commandant Legrand reported on the attempt to avenge the murder of Joachim on Malekula. In attempting to isolate the guilty parties among the various allied and rival groups, he noted that 'the number of guilty increases each day, soon all Malicolo [Malekula] will have taken part in the murder'. In the end, he reported satisfactorily achieving his goal of 'inflicting a punishment they will remember', shelling and burning the villages on Orembao from the ship as well as sending in Indigenous auxiliaries to reconnoitre.[79] British naval commanders engaged in such tactics with some unease and reluctance though alternatives were limited as their jurisdiction was severely curtailed.

Colonists and officials advocated punitive justice for Islanders on the basis of racial theories of criminality. Petitions, reports and correspondence repeatedly asserted that swift and forceful eye-for-an-eye action was the only form of retribution that 'natives' understood. In 1897 the president of the SFNH drew attention to recent violence by ni-Vanuatu around Port Sandwich, Malekula. He argued that more numerous and lengthy patrols of warships were essential to prevent such incidents:

> These violences are unfortunately neither a new nor exceptional thing. Each year, from January to April, the European settlers are exposed to them and the list is already long of those who have been victims in recent years. They coincide too exactly with the absence of French and British warships in these passages for it to be possible to doubt that they should be attributed to it and that the indigènes believing their impunity, take advantage of this absence

> to satisfy their vengeance against Europeans and their flagrant natural instincts.[80]

The salutary effect of naval visits on the European settler and trader community were also acknowledged, as 'everybody, traders and natives, is on highest behaviour when the Man-of-war is in the neighbourhood'.[81]

In the pre-Condominium era, official reports complained equally of the role of reprobate European beachcombers and settlers in inciting intra-racial conflict, through their recruiting practices, poor treatment of indentured labourers, and interference with Indigenous women.[82] Scarr notes that 'men of known bad character killed on the scene of their operations were generally not avenged'. For example, no warship arrived to avenge Peter Cullen, a copra trader and recruiter murdered after disturbing communities from Epi to the Maskelyne Islands in the early 1880s and stealing women and children from Tomman Island, not far from his Lemua Island station off southeast Malekula.[83] Naval officers agreed: Cullen was culpable for his own demise. Naval officers similarly declined to intervene in other cases, such as the murder of recruiters from the *Petrel* in 1904 or of British settler Trumble in 1905. Commander Bigaut spoke for many when he said Europeans were 'very violent and too forceful; they pay for their recklessness with their lives'.[84]

In 1890, the Earl of Derby summed up the relationship between 'savage' Islanders and unscrupulous Europeans, linking troublesome Europeans, violent Islanders and the deleterious impact of interaction:

> Europeans of adventurous disposition or of damaged reputation visit or settle down among the islands. They then trade with the natives for copra, bêche-de-mer, tortoiseshell, &c., and not infrequently in men and women. In return, they, among other things, supply arms, powder, lead, dynamite, and spirits … the general effect of such intercourse is to make the savage more untruthful, treacherous, and bloodthirsty than he was in his original state.[85]

Such views underpinned calls for greater colonial oversight in the islands and continued to influence official reactions to violence and conflict in subsequent decades.

There were ongoing critiques of this punitive style of Indigenous governance. The reprisals, arrests and internments made by warships under the JNC banner were condemned as early as 1894 as 'retaliation and not an act of justice'.[86] New Caledonia Governor and French High Commissioner Feillet reported to Paris that 'the rights of indigènes against whites have no guarantee; the acts of the commandants of British and French vessels which are the police of the New Hebrides do not fall within any jurisdiction and are subject only to public opinion'.[87] Such critiques were advanced to debunk the JNC and assert the need for full French annexation. Indeed, as Rear Admiral Regnault de Premesnil explained, repressive tactics were related to the lack of competent jurisdiction over the territory:

> The authorities of New Caledonia and Australia rightly refuse to receive and judge indigènes arrested as guilty of a crime or an offence meriting a conviction, and the only means of repression by the cruisers consists of sometimes burning villages and killing, if they can, the indigènes who might not always be the culprits.[88]

In the settler press of Australia and New Zealand, Presbyterian missionaries similarly protested against punitive justice, critiquing French activities as inhumane while advocating for British sovereignty over the isles.[89]

As the numbers of settlers increased, the colonial administrations felt increasingly bound to protect them and their commercial interests. This was particularly true for the French, who had greater economic interests in the New Hebrides after the acquisition of Higginson's land and trading interests in 1894. As planters and traders could no longer be collectively dismissed as lazy beachcombers or escaped criminals, eruptions of ni-Vanuatu-European conflict or murders could not automatically be blamed on the newcomers' poor character or unscrupulous actions. The organization of planters and traders into large-scale commercial and advocacy groups, such as SFNH or the New Hebrides British Association, further swayed the national administrations and the Condominium in the period after 1906. Not barring the continued vocal confrontation between missionaries and other settlers (particularly regarding labour recruitment and the sale of alcohol), the reconfiguration of the European community's reputation from disreputable to decent, economically productive citizens facilitated the continuance of repressive tactics against ni-Vanuatu. As early as 1881 the Earl of Kimberley noted 'the strong feeling which prevails in the Australian colonies that some steps are urgently needed for the better protection of attacks on peaceful traders deserves consideration'.[90]

Two decades later the French High Commissioner commended settler patience in abstaining from 'armed demonstration' against ni-Vanuatu but questioned whether they could be expected to maintain this in the face of continued provocation and violence.[91] In December 1904 reports from New Caledonia to Paris complained of the inability to legally detain, try or punish the men believed guilty of the murders of M. Le Bouhellec and his second Willy Champion of the *Perle*.[92] Naval commander Adigard proposed using force as 'no injustice, no exaction, no act of brutality is alleged against the victims of recent attacks. The indigènes only want to kill the whites, and they proclaim it bluntly'.[93] A scribbled margin note proclaims this view is 'faux', indicating some internal dispute over understanding of ni-Vanuatu motivations and the appropriate response. But it was unlikely to have dissuaded Adigard or local settlers from viewing Indigenous attacks as unprovoked affronts on the rights of hardworking planters to pursue their commercial ventures undisturbed.[94] On the eve of Condominium annexation in 1905, Adigard argued:

> The settled whites became sedentary and colonists, consequently having a vested interest to behave well towards neighbours and live in peace with them, on the other hand monitored by warships that would not let them exercise abuse on the Kanaks.[95]

By contrast, ni-Vanuatu were framed as suffering from the deleterious effects of contact and had become, according to one commandant, 'not more intelligent but … more scoundrel'.[96] This racial narrative set the scene for further settler petitions and for aggressive naval intervention to continue.

Between 1904 and 1905, as Anglo-French negotiations over the archipelago proceeded in Europe, a flurry of attacks, murders and discussions of punitive activity occurred. On 3 July 1904 Sirguey, Pentecost and three Indigenous crew of the French galley *Charlaise* were murdered at Malekula, and the murderers disappeared into the interior, prompting the Governor of New Caledonia to complain about the problems of surveilling recruiters and labour employers as well as the general insecurity facing Europeans. If anything, he argued, it was surprising violence was not more common when one took account of 'the extreme savagery of the New Hebrideans, their vindictive character, of the superstitions that reign among them'.[97] The following year, *La France Australe* reported on the expedition to avenge their deaths, where a village was burnt by the *Meurthe* after the *tribu* failed to hand over the guilty parties as demanded.[98] Referring to the incident and to the *Perle* murders of the same year, the New Caledonian Governor drew attention to the accuseds' impunity owing to the curious diplomatic situation of the territory, which was exacerbated by the suspected perpetrators being mountainous *tribus* and out of reach of all but military expeditions. In consequence, he stated, 'these tribus have become extremely insolent'.[99] The focus of anxieties on inland communities or 'bush natives' reflected official views that the coastal Islander communities were more civilized, less treacherous and more accommodating of European settlement, an idea reinforced by missionary distinctions between Christian Islanders, located primarily around coastal mission stations, and the heathen Islanders of the interior.[100]

The Condominium thus inherited recurring patterns of interaction between naval vessels, settlers and Islanders as well as narratives of race and rival political imperatives that justified continued repressive tactics. As the French resident commissioner asserted in 1908, 'the presence of warships is still necessary in the archipelago. It helps maintain the indigènes' respect while ensuring, through the supervision exerted over recruiting vessels, the legality as well as the safety of their operations'.[101] Indigenous responses to naval violence sometimes reinfored colonial belief in its efficacy. After Lanebon village was shelled by the *Kersaint* in 1909 following a murder, the chief apparently 'came on board of his own free will and deposited £20 as a surety for good behaviour and stated that they were much impressed by the firing … The French Officials of the Commission having declared themselves satisfied, the case is finished'.[102]

By 1910, the JNC was instructed no longer 'to punish the tribes en masse but to search for the guilty and to seize them to remand them to justice'.[103] Though almost annual naval expeditions in following years sought to arrest the perpetrators of violent crimes, these attempts also involved the destruction of villages, crops and pigs, resulting in gunfire and conflict between Islanders, injuries and deaths on both sides.[104] The expeditions thus remained military in nature. While in principle the guilty individuals were sought, warships frequently returned without the accused and in practice expeditions followed the concept of collective responsibility and collective punishment of the tribe.[105]

Gilchrist Alexander, serving on the bench of the Joint Court from 1912, recalled the typical punitive reaction:

> Information would be received that a white planter or trader had been murdered by natives on the island of Malekula or some equally wild place. After due inquiry, a man-of-war would be dispatched to the place of the crime. A party of bluejackets would be landed. Heavily loaded with rifles, ball ammunition, and kit, they would be marched from the beach up to a native village through a bush so dense that they could not see more than a yard or two. When, pouring with perspiration and exhausted, they reached the village, they would discover only a few old men or women and children. The supposed malefactors had fled or, more probably, had been dogging the steps of the landing-force behind the thick bush. After burning down the village and killing the pigs, the bluejackets would retrace their steps and would be lucky to reach the beach without losing one or

> more of their number. Very often snipers waited, with rifles fixed to trees and trained across the path by which the landing party made its way in single file. Or, if it was not thought desirable to land, the ship would be content … to shell the village. This would be rough justice indeed, for, as like as not, the chief sufferers would be the old men, women, and children.[106]

Alexander paints a picture of colonial agents ill at ease, with limited knowledge of Islanders and the geography, and fearful of 'natives' who were more adept in their environment and aware of their opponents' movements. His account references recurring elements in official reports of such expeditions. The outer islands and the mountainous interiors of the New Hebrides, Fiji and New Caledonia remained troublesome zones for colonial administrations lacking the resources to effectively incorporate such regions into their jurisdiction.[107]

As in the pre-Condominium era, a punitive response was promoted as most suited to local conditions. Such action was deemed more effective for its speed: the cogs of European justice turned slowly, lessening the exemplary effect for 'uncivilised' Islanders. Echoing reports from the 1880s, the first French trimestrial report for 1916 argued that the warships'

> swift justice is equally the only one that is accessible to the simplistic spirit of the Kanaks. They find it natural that a wrongdoer suffers, as soon as he can be apprehended, the punishment he has incurred. If this punishment is delayed several months as a result of the difficulties of the investigation or the complications of the procedure, they would not consider the motives anymore, and on the contrary, would be inclined to consider it as an act of revenge.[108]

The report argued the injustices of trialling ni-Vanuatu under French or British law would be greater and the Islanders – 'much inferior than the natives of our African colonies' – were incapable of fulfilling the role of assessors if cases were tried by District Agents. Continued naval tours by the JNC were presented as the only viable option for justly dealing with the Indigenous population.

Similarly, in 1915, protesting attempts to reduce the role of the JNC, the officer based on Epi, Ancelin asserted that the warship was the only real French power, because it was

> a material force that they can see, appreciate and evaluate. It is because of the fear they have of it that we can obtain respect of our people and properties. It has not always been effective, it is true, but as it is, our indigènes fear [the warship]. It exists; it can come. When? No matter, they simply know that it will come, that it will take action more or less severely … They fear the warship because it has the force and the power, and they respect it because for them it also represents

> justice. Justice in the true sense of the word, sometimes lively, a bit brutal, but more in line with the moeurs and habits of the indigènes.[109]

Ancelin linked the visible strength of the navy to its impact, suggesting the importance of performative forms of justice in maintaining European authority over the Islanders. He went on to argue that continued tours of French naval ships were crucial to mitigate Presbyterian influence.[110] The operations of commandants and naval ships were tactics in a battle to maintain influence vis-à-vis their European rival as well as their Indigenous subjects.

Enabled by narratives of race, motivated by inter-imperial rivalry and necessitated by the lack of effective law, naval vessels could take unilateral action, as the *Kersaint* did in 1913, if the situation was construed as 'urgent'. These actions could be retrospective approved by the JNC: better to ask for forgiveness than permission.[111] As Keith Woodward notes, scarcely a year passed without similar violence.[112] In 1908, the 'very highly respected' and 'popular' Peter Greig and two of his teenage daughters Ada Joyce and Elizabeth Marion were murdered at Baldwin Bay, South Santo.[113] Between October and November, the perpetrators were pursued inland by three expeditions led by John Glossop, commander of HMS *Prometheus*. Two of the murderers, Arumasanga and Tavoro, were caught and tried by the JNC after being delivered by the tribe in hope of receiving pardon and avoiding further naval violence. A third, Evunrere, was killed. French Resident Noufflard considered the local *indigènes* had learned a severe lesson.[114] However, British naval officers felt that the eventual punishment of the surviving murderers (deportation to Fiji) was inadequate:

> Here we have a native, taken from his savage home, surrounded by antagonistic tribes constantly at war with each other, committing a brutal outrage in massacring a harmless white settler and his two young daughters transported to Fiji to end his days in peace and quietness, no punishment and everything found for him.[115]

The establishment of an Indigenous police force under the Condominium meant 'for the first time' officers penetrated well into the interior, 'thanks to the endeavours of miliciens indigènes'.[116] Indeed, one of the accused himself aided the expeditionary party after his companions had handed him over to the *Prometheus*, and on this information Glossop attacked those *indigènes* sheltering the other murderers.[117] In his annual report, the French resident commissioner even optimistically suggested that, along with joint national celebrations, 'shooting side by side to avenge the triple murder' helped bring the two colonizing powers together.[118] However, the expeditions were not without collateral damage, as 'unfortunately, in the course of these operations and in the fire of the pursuit, women and children were hit by volleys fired at the fugitives who had taken refuge in the bush'.[119] Glossop and Johnson reported six women and one child dead, along with pigs killed and huts destroyed.[120]

The Greig case attracted much publicity in the Australasian and British press, partly because of the gendered element in the initial murders and the subsequent expedition. The report from the *Kersaint* noted that while the girls' clothes were disordered and their skirts pulled up, there was no evidence of rape.[121] However, the murder of the 'charming and accomplished' Greig girls and the respectable settler family were pointedly repeated in published accounts of the incident to elicit sordid horror at the barbarity of the crime and sympathy for the victims.[122] Emphasis on the physical details of the girls' murder sought to accentuate the opposition between the savagery of the murderers and the civility of the European victims.[123] In fact, the murderer-accused had formerly worked for Greig, and his aggression was seemingly motivated by the non-payment of wages.[124] Such details did not make the colonial press.

The death of ni-Vanuatu women during the ensuing punitive expedition placed a question mark over the morality of the JNC's reprisals, as it seemed the administration was equally guilty of barbaric acts. The treatment of women was used as a marker of civilization and so the killing of Indigenous women by naval officers upended European claims to moral superiority. In the House of Commons on 1 March 1909, Liberal MP Sir Charles Dilke asked about the death of 'native' women in the expedition, and the response was widely reported. First Lord of the Admiralty Reginald McKenna expressed his regret but noted that 'the shooting of the women was due to the fact that owing to the clothes they wore they could not be distinguished from the men'.[125] In noting a lack of distinction between the genders amongst South Santo Islanders, he implied a more fundamental difference between 'native' and European society: the failure to visibly conform to European gender distinctions suggested a lack of civilization. Interestingly, the first-hand report from the expedition's acting commander Johnson does not draw attention to dress; instead he only suggests the bush made it difficult for the party to see at whom they were shooting.[126] Similarly, Glossop argued that the women of Santo did not, as on other islands, wear 'grass petticoats' but noted the bush was so dense anyway it was impossible to identify them.[127] In justifying their actions to superiors and concerned London politicians, the Admiralty reworked the meaning of gender: inverting concerns for the protection of women and instead using the lack of gender division to signal the un-European and uncivilized nature of these Islanders.

Somewhat surprisingly, local missionary Joseph Annand did not express recriminations over the women's deaths. Rather he stated the 'slaughter of their women, painful though it may appear to many, had a very good effect upon the bushmen generally … this has been a severe but much needed lesson to man Santo'.[128] Certainly the impact of these expeditions was long-lasting. The Greig and the 1923 Clapcott incidents 'still soured relations' with the government in 1950s Santo, 'particularly because innocent women, including a girl, had been killed during an expedition to capture Greig's murderers'.[129] In addition, though not mentioned, rape was a frequent fact of colonial warfare and may well have occurred in naval expeditions – a further, unspoken violence.[130]

In July 1914, the HMS *Torch* and the French *Kersaint* led an expedition to Putermwomo village on Malekula to arrest the murderers of six mission teachers killed the previous February.[131] On anchoring at Wala, the landing party consisted of ninety-six men, including British and French seaman, members of the British and French 'native' police, local guides and bearers. The column trekked into the interior, where they found the village abandoned. They destroyed pigs and yams, but on the second day, having exchanged occasional gunfire, which killed one Islander of Lalip village, one guide, one Indigenous policeman, and injured another five Indigenous policemen (at least two of whom died of their wounds), the expedition was abandoned.

As Senior British Naval Officer John Ward reported somewhat laconically, 'in summing up it cannot be said that the object of the expedition has been obtained; no prisoners were taken belonging to Putermwomo village, and only the pigs and stores of yams of that village were destroyed', whereas as French commandant Roque stated, the expedition 'cost dearly'. Having suffered greater causalities, the French report was overall more critical, criticizing the quality of the arms and that it would be 'criminal' if Indigenous police were not better armed in future to suit their abilities and the local conditions.[132] This incident report recalls Alexander's account of anxiety in the deep bush, as 'there were various alarms during the night … the natives could be heard calling to one another in the surrounding hills and intermittent rain throughout the night added to the general discomfort'. The failure was attributed in part to the 'Bushman's confederacy' between various villages of the island.[133] Similarly, the losses sustained were for little return. Such events reinforced the view of Malekula as a particularly turbulent island.

Two years later, the *Kersaint* returned to Malekula, this time accompanied by HMAS *Una* to seek the men responsible for the murder of British planter Bridges and his five children on 18 August 1916. Fifty-five Australian sailors of the *Una*, ten *miliciens* from New Guinea, thirty sailors from the *Kersaint* along with twenty-five French-employed *miliciens* disembarked on the night of 2 November 1916, ready to begin the day-long march in the early hours of the next morning. Arriving at nearby Boutarmar village, the New Guineans were sent to reconnoitre and returned to report to Commander Jackson that the Islanders were having a dance so it would be possible to surprise them as dawn arose.[134] On 4 November, as the attack quickly developed:

> Four Bushmen were killed outright, one woman taken prisoner, the number of wounded Bushmen is unknown, but from the screams there number must have been considerable. The village was then burnt, including the 'Sing Sing' House, which is a matter of great importance to the Bushmen.[135]

The retreating expeditionary forces found themselves under fire, and lost nine men (predominantly Islanders), around 20 per cent of the landing party. Commander Jackson reported, 'the only method of progress was by raking the cane grass with rifle fire and advancing in short rushes', killing numerous other Islanders in the process.[136] Unable to continue the land-based expedition, the warships shelled the island.[137] The expedition was heavily criticized in the regional press.[138] The joint naval party suffered significant loss of personnel and many more suffered from malaria, though the impact on Islander communities in terms of deaths, injuries and the loss of food resources was far greater. The French report argued the need for local military posts as in New Caledonia: 'permanent military occupation is the only way to pacify the country'.[139]

The Bridges expedition occurred at a moment of rising criticism of the JNC and ambiguity about the role of the naval power in Condominium New Hebrides. The expedition was deemed a failure and described in the local press as a 'fiasco'. Critical as ever, Jacomb wrote, 'a more lamentable story of muddle and mis-management it would be hard to conceive'.[140] The killing of women in these expeditions was of particular concern in 1908–9 and again in 1918.[141] The ineffectiveness of the expeditions was critiqued more generally: Felix Speiser argued that while Islanders may have previously been frightened by men-of-war, 'to-day they know that resistance is easy'.[142] Despite cries to the contrary from settlers and some naval officers, the punitive methods of naval expeditions were out of step with the new Condominium structures of rule. Officials discussed stripping the JNC of its judicial powers in 1915 in favour of establishing courts to try ni-Vanuatu and legislation was drawn up to deal with crimes 'particular to natives' in 1916–17.[143] However, the New Caledonia Governor appealed to Paris that the JNC be allowed to continue its work for the duration of the First World

War, as the Joint Court was largely unable to sit. By 1923, concerned with unrest on Santo and the murder of Clapcott, the British resident commissioner had written that the reconstitution of the JNC was desirable.[144]

The Condominium continued to rely on naval vessels to transport officials as well as prisoners, and the island locale meant colonial power could never be limited to land-based administration.[145] The joint administrations relied on maritime support to effectively govern the archipelago. The relationship between naval actions and administrative policy was often tense and contested, particularly since naval vessels had greater scope to act unilaterally than did the national administrations in Port Vila, as highlighted by the 1913 tour of the *Kersaint*. However, the JNC was also, occasionally, a site of co-operation in an Anglo-French relationship otherwise dominated by rivalry.

The continued joint Anglo-French reliance on repressive action contrasts with a historiography that emphasizes the benign protectionist role of the British and French Navy in Pacific imperial expansion in the earlier nineteenth century and the bumbling nature of the Condominium administration in the early twentieth century. At least until 1920, there was little distinction between acts of law and acts of war in how the JNC dealt with 'native' violence in the New Hebrides. Arrests, trials and punitive reprisals were employed concurrently during naval tours of the islands.

Like the courts, punitive acts were performative: attempts to reinforce the power of the JNC as an arbiter of justice through a show of power. Expeditions often had limited efficacy for the state, but no matter when the aim was to be seen to do something. However, as the Bridges expedition demonstrated, such actions could prove costly and were increasingly hard for the colonial state to defend. Despite the rhetoric of civilizing law and the various critiques of the continued power of the JNC, the lack of effective administrative authority beyond Port Vila or Efate meant that for many Islanders, encounters with colonial rule continued to be through man-of-war visits into the 1920s and beyond.[146] The naval ship was thus a key space of law, violence, and of the performance of authority, alongside the colonial court and the mission station.

Conclusion

In contrast to the performances and narrations that dominated the New Hebrides Joint Court and the Fijian Supreme Court (Chapters 2 and 3), this chapter has demonstrated the ways that Islanders were frequently excluded from colonial courts and the resulting archives. Many Islanders and indentured labourers had no opportunity to present their case as either victim or defendant.

In New Caledonia, serious crime or disruption by Kanak were often referred to the Conseil Privé instead of the courts in the late nineteenth and early twentieth century. This forum effectively guaranteed the administration had the authority to interpret the law when a trial was unlikely to reach the outcome officials desired. The Conseil Privé served as a courtroom without witnesses, defence or right of appeal where senior colonial officials adjudicated and delivered sentences. Sexual crimes, kidnappings and violence against women were but some of a variety of offences dealt with but they often acted as potent signifiers of the uncivilized and immoral nature of Kanak society, justifying continued intervention through the Indigénat.

Similarly, in the New Hebrides the limited authority of the Joint Court left space for the continued operation of the JNC in the colonial period. While technically confined to acts of war, the humanitarian inclination of naval officers contributed to the adoption of JNC trials and sentences from the 1890s. However, the sittings of the JNC did not conform to colonial legal procedure, and Islanders were disadvantaged by the refusal of the JNC to admit representation or witnesses on behalf of the defence. Moreover those arrested and charged before the JNC in 1913–14 became pawns in a wider Anglo-French conflict, as the *Kersaint* sought to diminish Presbyterian influence while Jacomb and missionaries vehemently protested against such actions. Overall the impact of the JNC was significant, as encounters with the 'arbitrary tribunal' of the JNC or other man-of-war visits remained the primary contact for ni-Vanuatu with the colonial administration across much of the New Hebrides.

As Chapter 1 noted, the capacity to extend European law into the outer islands of the New Hebrides or 'la brousse' of New Caledonia was sometimes simply lacking. However, deliberate colonial strategies for dealing with cases outside the formal judiciary and conflicts over jurisdiction equally contributed to determining whether crimes were tried in the colonial courts. Questions of gender and intimacy were often central: sexual assaults were marshalled as evidence of Kanak and ni-Vanuatu 'savagery' to justify the continuation of the Indigénat by New Caledonia officials or punitive naval violence in the New Hebrides. These different examples are emblematic of the way colonial courts were constructed as incapable of dealing with the complex realities of Islanders' lives and relationships, and thereby legitimizing alternative and often oppressive strategies of law and governance.

Islanders in New Caledonia, Fiji and the New Hebrides actively resisted (as well as adapted to) intrusion into their society and livelihoods. The outbreak of overt conflict such as 1876 in Fiji or the various Kanak 'revolts' in New Caledonia demonstrate the ongoing negotiation of authority between the colonial state and Indigenous groups as imperial administrations solidified their rule. The engagement with varied strategies of rule in the Pacific was equally true of colonial states themselves, as such military conflicts highlight. This was most prominent in the New Hebrides, as the reprisals of the JNC co-existed with court-based jurisdiction. Courts were thus one of many spaces in which Islanders, settlers, indentured migrants as well as the colonial state itself managed interpersonal relationships, sex and conflict in colonial New Caledonia, Fiji and New Hebrides.

Arbitrary tribunals and punitive expeditions reveal the contradictory effects of law and colonialism in the islands: despite speaking the language of humanitarianism, in practice the law was disregarded when detrimental to the maintenance of colonial authority. This was most evident in the New Hebrides, where the Joint Court made a show of authority and justice in Port Vila while the JNC practiced a more authoritarian and repressive form of rule across the islands. In the face of limit resources outside Port Vila, naval vessels were a key point of contact between Islanders and the colonial administration. This is not simply a story of the anxiety and precarity of colonial rule. Rather, the weakness of the court system simultaneously and deliberately created space, and provided cover, for colonial violence.

Official reports justified resorting to summary and violent forms of justice on the basis of racialized perceptions of ni-Vanuatu, especially on the 'wilder' islands of Malekula or Tanna. Gender strengthened this discourse. Islander 'savagery' was contrasted with the respectability of European settlers and families, with the presence of women and children a signifier of the increasingly civilized and settled status of these communities as in the 1908 Greig murders. Metropolitan humanitarian critiques of punitive expeditions also drew on gender, concerned that the collateral killing of women, as in 1908 and the 1916 Bridges case, contradicted imperial ideals of benevolence and protectionism. Hence questions of race, gender and law were tied up with broader questions and political debates about the nature of empire in the Pacific. Scholars of Vanuatu from the 1940s onwards suggest the longer-term social and political influence of these punitive practices. On Santo, the intersection of local beliefs, intimate lives, violence and reprisals (such as the Greig case or the 1923 Clapcott murder) is linked to the emergence of anti-colonial movements.[147] For Islanders too, gender and justice were central to broader understandings and approaches to colonial rule.

Notes

1 Seagoe to Resident Commissioner, 3 September 1908, Folder 202/1908, NHBS 1/I Vol. 1, WPA.
2 Ibid.
3 Rodman, *Houses Far from Home*, 91.
4 Captain Edwin Harrowell to Resident Commissioner, 10 September 1908, Folder 202/1908, NHBS 1/I Vol. 1, WPA.
5 'Assault case: Labour of E.A.G. Seagoe, Undine Bay, 3 September 1908', encl. to Harrowell to Resident Commissioner, 10 September 1908, Folder 202/1908, NHBS 1/I Vol. 1, WPA.
6 Harrowell to Resident Commissioner, 10 September 1908, Folder 202/1908, NHBS 1/I Vol. 1, WPA.
7 Minute by B. G., 27/11/1908, Folder 202/1908, NHBS 1/I Vol. 1, WPA.
8 John, Kapten and David 'The Prisoners' to father Mr King, 23 October 1908, Folder 202/1908, NHBS 1/I Vol. 1, WPA.
9 Seagoe to Jacomb, 29 October 1908, Folder 202/1908, NHBS 1/I Vol. 1, WPA.
10 Minutes in Folder 202/1908, NHBS 1/I Vol. 1, WPA.
11 Thomas, *Colonialism's Culture*, 8.
12 John, Kapten and David 'The Prisoners' to father Mr King, 23 October 1908, Folder 202/1908, NHBS 1/I Vol. 1, WPA.
13 Jean Guiart, introduction to Kurtovitch and Guiart, 'Sortir de l'indigénat', 117.
14 Members included the Heads of the Service Judiciaire, Service Administrative, the Director of the Interior, the Director of the Penal Administration, and the Commandant Militaire.
15 Muckle, 'Troublesome Chiefs', 147. The use of internment declined from the 1920s as it was gradually subject to greater oversight, such as 1928 Legislation restricting length of sentences and 1937 laws that re-instated the requirement that all proposed internments must be submitted Paris for approval.
16 Merle, *Expériences Coloniales,* chapter 2. See also Dousset-Leenhardt, *Terre natale*, 177–9; Saussol, *L'Héritage*, 245–9; and Dauphiné et al., *Île d'exil, terre d'asile.*
17 Muckle, 'Troublesome Chiefs', 150; see also Merle and Muckle, *L'Indigénat.*
18 Note pour la Direction du Personnel, Directeur des Affaires Politiques et Administratives, 22 octobre 1909, SG-NC Carton 231, ANOM. A charge similar to assault and battery.
19 Gouverneur à Ministre des Colonies, 21 juillet 1909, SG-NC Carton 231, ANOM.
20 Note pour la Direction du Personnel, Directeur des Affaires Politiques et Administratives, 22 octobre 1909; and Note pour la 2me Direction (4e Bureau), Directeur de Personnel, SG-NC Carton 231, ANOM.
21 No. 298, Chef Affaires Indigènes, 7 avril 1903, 23W C12, ANC.

22 Conseil Privé No. 28, 4 juillet 1892, SG-NC Carton 51, ANOM.

23 See also No. 888, Procureur Général à Chef des Affaires Indigènes, 1 juin 1892, 23W C11, ANC.

24 Muckle, 'Killing the "Fantôme Canaque"'.

25 Maurice Méray à Ministre des Colonies, 24 mai 1902, ADC Carton 821, ANOM.

26 Ibid; 'No. 22 Régime de l'Indigénat', Inspecteur Fillon à Ministre des Colonies, 15 mai 1907, and 'No. 46 Affaires Indigènes', Inspecteur Revel à Ministre des Colonies, 10 juin 1912, ADC Carton 822, ANOM.

27 Maurice Méray à Ministre des Colonies, 24 mai 1902, ADC Carton 821, ANOM.

28 Inspecteur Fillon à Ministre des Colonies, 15 mai 1907, ADC Carton 822, ANOM.

29 Muckle, *Specters of Violence*, chapter 8 analyses this trial.

30 Conseil Privé No. 47, 26 octobre 1901, SG-NC Carton 145 à 147, ANOM.

31 Conseil Privé No. 28, 6 juillet 1905, SG-NC Carton 46, ANOM.

32 No. 298, Chef Affaires Indigènes, 7 avril 1903, 23W C12, ANC.

33 Conseil Privé No. 82, 9 mai 1902, SG-NC Carton 175, ANOM.

34 Conseil Privé No. 22, 2 mai 1900, SG-NC Carton 145 à 147, ANOM.

35 Ibid.

36 Conseil Privé No. 28, 6 juillet 1905, SG-NC Carton 46, ANOM.

37 Ibid.

38 Conseil Privé No. 5, 26 janvier 1900, SG-NC Carton 145 à 147, ANOM.

39 Jacomb, *France and England*, 125–6 describes JNC trials as 'to all intents and purposes held in camera'.

40 Scarr, *Fragments of Empire*, 241.

41 Séance du 12 octobre 1891, Commission Navale Mixte, SG-NH Carton 3, ANOM. On Sawers see: Roger C. Thompson, 'Commerce, Christianity and Colonialism: The Australasian New Hebrides Company, 1883–1897', *Journal of Pacific History* 6, no. 1 (1971), 25–38; and Rodman, 'The Heart in the Archives'.

42 Scarr, *Fragments of Empire*, 241.

43 Jacomb, *France and England*, 126.

44 Minutes of JNC meeting, HMS *Prometheus*, 5 June 1909, Folder 71/1909, NHBS 1/I Vol. 1, WPA.

45 Though see exceptional debate in 1909: Edward Jacomb to British Resident, 4 September 1909 and Case 39, Minutes of JNC meeting, *Kersaint*, 4 September 1909, Folder 71/1909, NHBS 1/I Vol. 1, WPA.

46 Minutes, *Kersaint*, 13 June 1908, Folder 91/1908, NHBS 1/I Vol. 1, WPA.

47 Minutes of JNC meeting, HMS *Prometheus*, 5 June 1909, Folder 71/1909, NHBS 1/I Vol. 1, WPA.

48 See Folder 57/1911 (Joint Naval Commission Cases 1911) and Folder 62/1912 (Joint Naval Commission Cases 1912–1913), NHBS 1/I Vol. 1, WPA.

49 Edward Jacomb to British Resident Commissioner, 19 September 1912; and Edward Jacomb to British Resident Commissioner, 20 September 1912, Folder 35/1912, NHBS 1/I Vol. 1, WPA.
50 Gouverneur à Ministre des Colonies, 7 février 1916, DAP Carton 1AFFPOL/1915, ANOM.
51 *The Daily Telegraph*, 13 February 1914, encl. in SG-NH Carton 2, ANOM; Entry for 2/4/1914, MS 894/24, Edward Jacomb Diary 1914, SHL. There is evidence in some cases that witness statements were taken and interpreters employed, either at the site of their arrest or on the vessel, such as in the JNC sittings of 10 July 1911 aboard the *Prometheus* or 17 November 1911 on the *Kersaint*: see Commander E. C. Carver to British Resident Commissioner, 16 November 1911, and Minutes of JNC meeting, HMS *Prometheus*, 10 July 1911, Folder 57/1911, NHBS 1/I Vol. 1, WPA.
52 Ibid.
53 'Meeting of Protest', in 'Rapport Trimestriel Octobre–Decembre 1913', encl. to Gouverneur à Ministre des Colonies, 25 février 1914, SG-NH Carton 11bis, ANOM.
54 Jacomb, *France and England*, 123–4.
55 Wallace to Paton, 30 March 1914, quoted in Scarr, *Fragments of Empire*, 242.
56 Commandant Roque à Commissaire-Résident de France, 19 décembre 1913, 25 Feb 1914, SG-NH Carton 11bis, ANOM.
57 'Rapport Trimestriel Octobre–Decembre 1913', encl. to Gouverneur à Ministre des Colonies, 25 février 1914, SG-NH Carton 11bis, ANOM.
58 Jacomb, *France and England*, 126.
59 Scarr, *Fragments of Empire*, 240.
60 'Rapport Trimestriel Avril–Juin 1914' in Gouverneur à Ministre des Colonies, 15 octobre 1914, SG-NH Carton 11bis, ANOM.
61 Service de l'Administration Générale–Rapport fait par Inspecteur Bougourd, 1918, SG-NH Carton 31, ANOM.
62 'Rapport trimestrial Janvier–Mars 1921', SG-NH Carton 12, ANOM.
63 Quoted in Linda A. Mander, 'The New Hebrides Condominium', *Pacific Historical Review* 8, no. 2 (1944), 156.
64 Martin Thomas, *Violence and Colonial Order: Police, Workers and Protest in the European Colonial Empires, 1918–1940* (Cambridge: Cambridge University Press, 2012), 65.
65 See Chris Ballard and Bronwen Douglas (eds), Special Issue: Punitive Expeditions, *Journal of Colonialism and Colonial History* 18, no. 1 (2017) for broader genealogy of expeditions in the Pacific.
66 Bonnemaison, *The Tree and the Canoe*, 84. See also: Michael Gilding, 'The Massacre of the Mystery: A Case Study in Contact Relations', *Journal of Pacific History* 17, no. 2 (1982), 66–85; Miles, *Bridging Mental Boundaries*, 64–5; Thomas, *Islanders*, chapter 8.

67 Quoted in Scarr, *Fragments of Empire*, 169.

68 Stuart Bedford, '"A Good Moral Effect?": Local Opposition and Colonial Persistence in Malakula, New Hebrides, 1875–1918', *Journal of Colonialism and Colonial History* 18, no. 1 (2017).

69 Jacomb, *The Future of the Kanaka*, 123–4.

70 Kai Colo, through equivalent to a tribal or ethnic name, also has derogatory connotations, implying backwardness. Ronald Gatty, *Fijian–English Dictionary: With Notes on Fijian Culture and Natural History* (Suva, Fiji: Ronald Gatty, 2009), 99.

71 Baron Arthur Hamilton–Gordon Stanmore, *Letters and Notes Written during the Disturbances in the Highlands (known as the 'Devil Country') of Viti Levu, Fiji, 1876* (Edinburgh: R. and R. Clark, 1879); Thomas, *Islanders*, 251–62; Nicole, *Disturbing History*, chapter 1; Brereton, *Law, Justice and Empire*, 113–14; Martha Kaplan, *Neither Cargo nor Cult: Ritual Politics and the Colonial Imagination in Fiji* (Durham: Duke University Press, 1995); Brewster, *The Hill Tribes.*

72 Douglas, 'Conflict and Alliance'; Douglas, 'Winning and Losing?'; Douglas, *Across the Great Divide*; Muckle, *Specters*; Thomas, *Islanders*, 163–83.

73 Scarr, *Fragments of Empire*, 208, 241; 'Instructions to the British High Commission on the issue of native labour', SG-NH Carton 11, ANOM.

74 Samson, *Imperial Benevolence*, 4.

75 Merle, *Expériences Coloniales*, 96.

76 Ibid., 93–7.

77 Scarr, *Fragments of Empire*, 167. See also chapters 6 and 7.

78 Thompson, 'Natives and Settlers', 7.

79 Rapports du Legrand, Commandant la *Dives* sur sa tournée aux Nouvelles-Hébrides, 11 avril 1886, SG-NH Carton 1, ANOM.

80 President du Conseil, SFNH, à Ministre des Colonies, 21 juin 1897, SG-NH Carton 4, ANOM.

81 Bridge to Des Voeux, 27 July 1882, quoted in Thompson, 'Natives and Settlers', 7.

82 Samson, *Imperial Benevolence*, 24–41; Ralston, *Grass Huts and Warehouses*, 24–5, 39–43.

83 Scarr, *Fragments of Empire*, 170.

84 Bonnemaison, *The Tree and the Canoe*, 84–5.

85 Quoted in J. Stewart, Assistant Colonial Secretary to the Rev. D. McDonald, 13 September 1890, SG-NH Carton 3, ANOM.

86 Governor Feillet à Ministre des Colonies, 22 octobre 1894, SG-NH Carton 2, ANOM.

87 Ibid.

88 Contre-Amiral de Premesnil, Commandant de la division navale de l'Océan Pacifique to Contre-Amiral Scott, Commandant la division navale anglaise d'Australie, 5 novembre 1890, SG-NH Carton 4, ANOM.

89 For example, 'New Hebrides Scandals', *Dominion*, 23 January 1911; 'How the French Handle Their Subject Races. Harsh Methods in the New Hebrides', *Manuwatu Standard*, 5 September 1913; Thompson, *Australian Imperialism*, 44–7, 195–7.

90 Quoted in Scarr, *Fragments of Empire*, 169.

91 Gouverneur à Ministre des Colonies, 30 août 1904, SG-NH Carton 4, ANOM.

92 Gouverneur à Ministre des Colonies, 13 décembre 1904, SG-NH Carton 4, ANOM.

93 Chef de la division navale du Pacifique Adigard à Ministre de la Marine, 26 mai 1905, SG-NH Carton 4, ANOM.

94 Scarr, *Fragments of Empire*, 170–1.

95 Adigard à Ministre de la Marine, 26 mai 1905, SG-NH Carton 4, ANOM.

96 Ibid.

97 Gouverneur à Ministre des Colonies, 30 août 1904, SG-NH Carton 4, ANOM.

98 *Le France Austral*, 30 octobre 1905, SG-NH Carton 4, ANOM.

99 Gouverneur à Ministre des Colonies, 5 octobre 1904, SG-NH Carton 4, ANOM.

100 'Service des Affaires Indigenes' Rapport fait par M. Pégourier, 20 novembre 1918, DAP Carton 1AFFPOL/742, ANOM; on Tanna, Bonnemaison, *The Tree and the Canoe*, 198–9; on Fiji, Brewster, *The Hill Tribes.*

101 'Les Nouvelles-Hébrides en 1908. Rapport d'Ensemble du Commissaire-Résident de France', DAP 1AFFPOL/1916, ANOM.

102 Minutes of JNC meeting 'Kersaint' 4 September 1909, Folder 71/1909, NHBS 1/I Vol. 1, WPA.

103 Rapport d'Ensemble sur la situation des Nouvelles-Hébrides en 1910. 20 avril 1911, SG-NH Carton 11bis, ANOM.

104 Rodman, 'The Heart in the Archives', 299.

105 See for example J. Repiquet, Haut-Commissaire à Ministre des Colonies, 23 octobre 1918, SG-NH Carton 4, ANOM.

106 Alexander, *From the Middle Temple*, 219–20.

107 The Loyalty Islands were often an exception, as inhabitants were considered more amenable to Christianity and 'civilisation' those of the Grande Terre, tied into their characterization as Polynesian rather than Melanesian.

108 Rapports Trimestriel Janvier-Mars 1916, SG-NH Carton 12, ANOM.

109 Ancelin à Commissaire-Résident, 2 octobre1915, DAP Carton 1AFFPOL/1916, ANOM.

110 Commissaire délégué à Commissaire Général de la République dans l'Océan Pacifique, 5 juin 1905, SG-NH Carton 4, ANOM.

111 In other situations, an enquiry was before the JNC was instructed to pursue the offenders. Gouverneur à Ministre des Colonies, 19 janvier 1909, and related corespondence, SG-NH Carton 6, ANOM.

112 Keith Woodward, 'Historical Note', in Bresnihan and Woodward, *Tufala Gavman*, 27.

113 Greig's fourteen-year-old son Alexander was absent and thus survived. 'Treacherous Islanders. A New Hebrides Outrage', *The Argus* (Melbourne), 24 October 1908, SG-NH Carton 6, ANOM, contains details of the expedition. See also Joseph Annand to British Resident Commissioner, 8 October 1908, Folder 33/1908, NHBS 1/I Vol. 1, WPA.

114 Noufflard à Haut Commissaire, 21 novembre 1905, SG-NH Carton 6 ANOM.

115 John Glossop to High Commissioner Western Pacific, 21/11/1908, Folder 91/1908, NHBS 1/I Vol. 1, WPA. See also *Kersaint*, Vila, 21 November 1908, Folder 91/1908, NHBS 1/I Vol. 1, WPA on the 'absolute futility of sending natives guilty of outrageous massacres of white people to be detained in Fiji during His Majesty's pleasure, such a proceeding being an incentive rather than a deterrent'.

116 'Les Nouvelles-Hébrides en 1908 – Rapport d'Ensemble du Commissaire-Résident de France', DAP Carton 1AFFPOL/1916, ANOM.

117 Noufflard à Haut Commissaire, 21 novembre 1905, SG-NH Carton 6, ANOM.

118 'Les Nouvelles-Hébrides en 1908 – Rapport d'Ensemble du Commissaire-Résident de France', DAP Carton 1AFFPOL/1916, ANOM.

119 Gouverneur à Ministre des Colonies, 25 novembre 1908, SG-NH Carton 6, ANOM.

120 John Glossop to French Resident Commissioner, 6 November 1908, and 19 November 1908, SG-NH Carton 6, ANOM; Acting Commandant Johnson to British Resident Commissioner, 10 November 1908, Folder 33/1908, NHBS 1/I Vol. 1, WPA.

121 Lieutenant Valat à Capitaine Roque Commandant le *Kersaint*, 14 octobre 1908, Folder 91/1908, NHBS 1/I Vol. 1, WPA.

122 'Murders at Santo. Sad Fate of the Greig Family', *Evening Post* (NZ), 2 November 1908.

123 'Murders in the Islands', *Argus* (Melbourne), 23 November 1908; 'Recent Island Massacres. Punitive Expeditions Landed', *Sydney Mail*, 25 November 1908.

124 'The Greig Case. The Prisoners' Statements', Folder 33/1908, NHBS 1/I Vol. 1, WPA. See Rodman, 'My Only Weapon Being a Pencil', 33, who also suggests that Greig was believed to be 'blocking the route that cargo, or wealth, would follow'.

125 'Pacific Island Punitive Expedition. The Killing of Native Women', *The West Australian*, 3 March 1909. See also 'Pacific Island Punitive Expedition', *The Straits Times*, 26 March 1909; 'Regrettable Error Native Women Killed', *Dominion*, 3 March 1909.

126 Acting Commandant Johnson to British Resident Commissioner, 10 November 1908, Folder 33/1908, NHBS 1/I Vol. 1, WPA.

127 John Glossop to French Resident Commissioner, 'Prometheus', 6 November 1908, and 19 November 1908, SG-NH Carton 6, ANOM.

128 Rodman, 'My Only Weapon Being a Pencil', 32–3.

129 Miles, *Bridging Mental Boundaries*, 65.

130 Elizabeth D. Heineman (ed.), *Sexual Violence in Conflict Zones: From the Ancient World to the Era of Human Rights* (Philadelphia: University of Pennsylvania Press, 2011); Rachel Buchanan, *The Parihaka Album: Lest We Forget* (Wellington: Huia, 2009), 158–9.

131 'Rapport Trimestriel Avril–Juin 1914', encl. to Gouverneur à Ministre des Colonies, Noumea, 15 octobre 1914, SG-NH Carton 11bis, ANOM; Report on Expedition to Putermwomo village, Malekula Island, HMS 'Torch', 6 July 1914, Folder 12/1913, NHBS 1/I Vol. 1, WPA.

132 'Extrait du Rapport de Capitaine Roque, Commandant du Kersaint', encl. to Gouverneur à Ministre des Colonies, 15 octobre 1914, SG-NH Carton 11bis, ANOM.

133 'Report on Expedition to Putermwomo village, Malekula Island', Senior British Naval Officer J. R. Le H. Ward, encl. to Gouverneur à Ministre des Colonies, 15 octobre 1914, SG-NH Carton 11bis, ANOM.

134 Miramende, Commissaire Résident de France à Haut Commissaire, 7 novembre 1916, SG-NH Carton 8, ANOM.

135 J. M. Jackson Commander R. N. to M. Boju, Commandant du *Kersaint*, 7 November 1916, SG-NH Carton 8, ANOM.

136 Ibid. The families of the deceased *miliciens* were offered 1,000 francs compensation.

137 Extrait du rapport, encl. to Gouverneur à Ministre des Colonies, 10 novembre 1916, SG-NH Carton 8, ANOM.

138 For example: 'A Tragedy to be Avenged', *Evening Post*, 9 December 1916; 'Killed by Cannibals. The Island Tragedy', *New Zealand Herald*, 29 August 1916.

139 Extrait du rapport, encl. to Gouverneur à Ministre des Colonies, 10 novembre 1916, SG-NH Carton 8, ANOM; HMAS UNA–December 1915 to June 1919, Royal Navy Log Books of the World War 1 Era, accessed 1 February 2021, http://www.naval-history.net/OWShips-WW1-18-HMAS_Una.htm.

140 Jacomb, *The Future of the Kanaka*, 127.

141 L. Nially, Commissaire-Résident à Haut-Commissaire, 9 décembre 1918, SG-NH Carton 4, ANOM; 'A Punitive Expedition. Killing of Women by Mistake', *Press* (NZ), 3 March 1909.

142 Speiser, *Two Years*, 17.

143 Ministre des Affaires Etrangères à Ministre des Colonies, 18 décembre 1915; and Gouverneur à Ministre des Colonies, 4 septembre 1916, DAP Carton 1AFFPOL/1916, ANOM.

144 Charge d'Affaires, British Embassy, Paris à Ministre des Affaires Etrangères, 21 octobre 1923, SG-NH Carton 9, ANOM.

145 Rapport Trimestriel Septembre–Décembre 1919, SG-NH Carton 12; President p.i. du Tribunal Mixte à President de cette Jurisiction, 24 décembre 1917, DAP Carton 1AFFPOL/1676, ANOM.

146 For work on later expeditions, see Hugh Laracy, 'The Pentecost Murders: An Episode in Condominium Non-Rule, New Hebrides 1940', *Journal of Pacific History* 26, no. 2 (1991), 245–55.

147 Miles, *Bridging Mental Boundaries*, 65; see also Rodman, *Houses Far from Home*, chapter 7; and compare Jean Guiart, 'Culture Contact', 109–10.

Conclusion

In 1908 Inspector of Immigration Dobson reported on recent disruption at the Waidoi plantation, near Suva in Fiji. Dobson noted that the *sirdar* DM managed his labour through intimidation and violence, while the inexperience, youth and frequent absences of the overseer meant his behaviour went unchecked. The situation came to a head with DM's attempted rape of two indentured women, J and P, the latter of whom screamed for help. Some men of the plantation came to their aid, assaulted DM, and 'thinking that they had not done wrong by taking the law into their own hands, they all trooped off to Naitonitoni and reported the affair to Mr Spence the resident magistrate there'.[1] The *sirdar* was hospitalized in Suva as a result of the attack.

No charges were taken against either the men who assaulted him or the *sirdar* despite complaints from other officials that proper procedure had not been followed and the police had not been involved. In part, there was a lack of evidence to support the case. More importantly, the plantation manager Mr Powell did not want charges laid. He explained that

> if they are proceeded with he will have much difficulty in maintaining discipline on the Estate. He point[ed] out that the Sirdar was very badly beaten by the labourers for his misdeeds and as he understood that no further action was to be taken against the Sirdar he did not prosecute those concerned in the assault for taking the law into their own hands.[2]

This incident embodies the intersecting and overlapping nature of the colonial judiciary and other forms of justice discussed throughout the book. Though not always recorded in the colonial archive, individuals and groups pursued a wide variety of strategies for redress when their sense of justice was violated. The Waidoi case underlines that direct, even violent, retribution was not necessarily considered at odds with that of the judicial system by labourers, colonists or officials.

Alongside the courtroom, naval vessels, mission stations and plantations thus remained sites of law into the twentieth century. Colonial lawmaking was adaptable and diverse, accommodating such alternatives as long as they did not directly threaten the prestige and authority of the administration. The purpose and practice of criminal justice was nevertheless frequently contested both inside and outside the colonial administrations of New Caledonia, Fiji and the New Hebrides. The fragmented nature of colonial criminal justice is reflected in the structure of the book itself, as comparisons do not easily fit into a linear narrative. Consequently this conclusion reflects more broadly on the convergences and divergences between the colonies studied, and what they suggest for our understanding of colonial rule, of judicial institutions and of the place of race and gender within them.

This history speaks to the colonial experience in other parts of the world, notably Africa and the Caribbean, where empire was similarly characterized by overlapping imperial powers, and in latter similarly across island space. I show that focusing on the pragmatics of empire – an approach centred on institutions and their functioning – is a valuable method for exploring the diversity within and differences between individual colonies as well as the commonalities between empires. Rather than comparing the differences between British and French imperialism, it is worth examining the accuracy and relevance of such comparisons by exploring the enactment of colonial rule at the local level.

The difference between French and British imperial policy for governing Indigenous subjects from the late nineteenth century is generally characterized as direct versus indirect rule. Indeed, Gordon's policy in Fiji was archetypal of British indirect rule, though it was underpinned by the administration-sponsored scheme of Indian indentured labour immigration and *girmityas* found themselves subject to direct and coercive plantation surveillance and management, akin to slavery in nature. In New Caledonia, the repressive Indigénat regime paralleled aspects of Fijian 'native policy' in co-opting and reifying appointed male chiefs as Indigenous and administrative leaders to coerce labour and maintain Kanak society at a remove from the penal and settler community. Thus, as Lauren Benton argues in West Africa, 'the French and British patterns of establishing state hegemony, though somewhat different in timing and certainly different in the rhetoric employed, were structurally similar'.[3] Whether based on the rhetoric of the Kanak threat in New Caledonia or the paternalistic approach in Fiji, both colonies legally and geographically separated colonial subjects on the basis of race and hierarchies of gender.

In Fiji this was achieved largely through the colonial judiciary itself. The court and the magistrate were key to enforcing colonial rule, though the justice that prevailed was that of the male chiefly elite in the village courts, of plantation managers in the plantation courts and of white, masculine, racialized and scientifically rationalized practice in the Supreme Court. By contrast, colonial courts in New Caledonia were supplemented and frequently supplanted by the summary jurisdiction over Kanak granted by the Indigénat to the Service des Affaires Indigènes or the Conseil Privé. Kanak accused of serious crime, including murder and rape, were thus often interned without trial, a practice justified on the grounds of the Islanders' perceived lack of civilization.

There were clear similarities between New Caledonia and the New Hebrides, as the Joint Naval Commission (JNC) also exercised summary justice, often violently, into the twentieth century. Representations of Kanak and ni-Vanuatu as 'savage', a view validated in both colonies by the perceived poor treatment of women in island society, justified the official stance in both colonies that swift and summary justice was best. Despite criticism, this rhetoric was important in sustaining the role of the JNC under the New Hebrides Condominium and the Indigénat regime in New Caledonia. The authoritarian and divided forms of colonial justice in the New Hebrides were a result of local inter-imperial politics more than deliberate policy, contrasting with the sustained adherence to Britain's 'native policy' in Fiji and France's Indigénat regime in New Caledonia.

In all three colonies, the administrations faced similar challenges regarding dispersal of personnel and resources over island space, defining jurisdiction over different communities and understanding local social practices in order to distinguish between the licit and the criminal in cases involving intimate violence. Cases of sexual crime most clearly revealed the limitations of judicial resources and knowledge: they proved particularly thorny for magistrates as they required intimate understanding of local custom and social relationships. Yet despite the constraints, the courts made a substantial contribution to colonial rule in New Caledonia, Fiji and the New Hebrides. In its opening decades, the New Hebrides Joint Court provided a theatre demonstrating Anglo-French authority and prestige. The incongruity of the multinational judiciary in the small and otherwise under-resourced colony, and of the performances of co-operation in an atmosphere of rivalry, led to satirical critiques such as Jacomb's *The Joy Court* and Cowell's 'Pandemonia'. But the restricted function of the Joint Court and its comic representations were politically useful: they supported calls from both British and French to replace the Condominium with either unilateral colonization or partition of the islands. Moreover, the theatre of the courtroom distracted attention from continued violent practices of rule over ni-Vanuatu through the JNC.

The courtrooms of New Caledonia and Fiji had greater effective power to try and sentence Europeans, Islanders and other immigrants for serious crime, including rape and sexual assault. When appearing before the courts, Kanak, Fijians and especially Indian indentured labourers faced high levels of conviction and often harsh sentences. In the Fiji Supreme Court, where the most complete trial evidence exists, the weight given to medical evidence reflected the formulation of colonial law as a modern, scientific, male and European construct. In the face of the seeming impenetrability of intimate aspects of 'native' life, and ever-present concerns over the trustworthiness of non-Europeans, the rise of medical examinations in rape and sexual assault cases seemingly promised a more reliable form of evidence.

Individuals nevertheless contested criminal justice, its practice and meanings from within the court system as well as outside it. In rape and sexual assault cases before the Fiji Supreme Court, women were sometimes able, often with the support of family, to use the court to redress violence. Even when constrained or unsuccessful, these women chose voice, one option among varied alternatives in addressing the trauma inflicted by such violence. But as defendants, men sometimes articulated different understandings of guilt and of acceptable behaviour that challenged European legal definitions of rape and sexual assault. However, the court was just one means of achieving justice for Fijians and Indians, or for Kanak and ni-Vanuatu, and many individuals were either dissuaded from using the courts or strategically choose an alternative.

Indeed, the limits to effective jurisdiction in each colony allowed space for the pursuit of justice by other means. Aside from individual acts of violence or resistance, local and non-official forms of justice (such as the Tanna mission courts, the Franceville municipality, violence and resistance on Fiji's sugar plantations and the Kanak-French wars in New Caledonia) often focused on patrolling the boundaries of intimacy and morality or creating respectability in an era of increasing cultural contact and social change. Read against the grain, concerns over the control of relationships reveal both intimate lives beyond the scope of colonial or other authorities and vibrant local cultures of lawmaking. In some cases, colonial administrations accepted these divergent systems of justice but intervened where they threatened colonial sovereignty or prestige.

In the context of flexible judicial practice, it is unsurprising that categories of gender and race intersected with law in multiple ways: ever-present yet shifting and unstable in their meaning and relevance in different cases, times and places. Perceptions of these categories shaped who had a right to trial in certain courts, who could adjudicate as judge, jury or assessor, and whose evidence would be trusted. For example, the Fiji Supreme Court placed the emphasis on women's bodies, instead of their voices. Women's bodies were also central to highly publicized and political debates in which sexual crimes spoke to broader concerns over race and the nature and purpose of imperial rule in the Pacific. The sexual threat posed by 'native' men was used by Dr Crombie to protest the inefficiency of Condominium rule in the New Hebrides, while anti-indenture activists in Fiji turned the narrative of 'black peril' on its head to decry the abuses of European men and of the indenture system. The murder of European women and children by Kanak or ni-Vanuatu in inter-racial conflict and the perceived need to protect women or avenge their death heightened settler anxiety and calls for military protection or punitive expeditions in New Caledonia and the New Hebrides. By contrast, the death of Indigenous women in Anglo-French naval expeditions in 1908 and 1916 raised humanitarian concerns over the nature of colonial rule in the New Hebrides. These varied cases indicate the way in which individual lives and intimate relationships influenced the broader functioning of criminal justice as well as imperial politics, often highlighting the fault lines between racial and gender hierarchies and between claims to liberal equality and illiberal practices in colonial contexts.

All books leave some questions unanswered as well as posing new ones. In addition, a comparative project sacrifices some depth in order to make connections and think across differing places. Future research in additional archives has potential to add weight to, or complicate, the arguments made here. In particular, the British, French and Australian naval archives would complement the Condominium records to more fully understand the continued role of naval power in the early twentieth century. Local and missionary archives, especially for New Caledonia, might illuminate the gaps in the territorial and colonial archives accessed, such as on the functioning of the Service des Affaires Indigènes. The book has emphasized the value of examining criminal justice and colonial rule through judicial institutions, their function and limits. Histories of parallel and intersecting institutions, such as police and prisons, would situate the courts as one technology of rule among others and further illuminate the diverse and contested practices that constituted the colonial experience in the Pacific. A systematic review of trial reporting in newspapers could enable a more qualitative comparison of charges, verdicts and sentences across the three colonies, aided by forthcoming digitalization of these sources. Research in Indigenous-language sources as well as oral histories would add invaluable depth by expanding on Indigenous engagements with, and perspectives on, the colonial criminal justice system and its legacies. This work is beyond my own cultural expertise and positionality but is a direction I hope other historians will pursue.

Finally, the practice of criminal justice and specifically the issue of sexual crime in New Caledonia, Fiji and the New Hebrides, as well as the Pacific generally, deserve a longer history. Sexual violence remains a recurrent problem across Pacific Island societies, as elsewhere globally. In confronting this social issue, post-colonial Pacific nation-states – and Territoire d'Outre Mer in the case of New Caledonia – face continued dilemmas over legal pluralism and the relationship between custom and law.[4] These challenges were not unfamiliar to colonial magistrates, who influenced the legal structures and practices inherited by post-colonial governments. As we have seen, colonial laws against rape and sexual assault in New Caledonia, Fiji and the New Hebrides were often ineffective in prosecuting sexual violence. Moreover, the judiciary frequently compounded the hierarchies that contributed to the subordination of women's experiences and legal rights. The complexities of legal solutions to contemporary gender-based violence thus have long roots that extend back into the earliest years of colonial rule. What remains to be investigated are the continuities and discontinuities between these years and the present, particularly in the context of the legal and institutional changes arising from processes of decolonization in the 1970s and 1980s.

Notes

1 C. D. Dobson, Inspector of Immigration to Agent General Immigration, 26/9/1908, CSO 4431/1908, NAF.

2 J. M. CO to Colonial Secretary, 7/11/1908, CSO 4431/1908, NAF.

3 Benton, *Law and Colonial Cultures,* 154.

4 Miranda Forsyth, *A Bird That Flies with Two Wings: Kastom and State Justice Systems in Vanuatu* (Canberra: ANU E-Press, 2009).

Glossary

Adi	Fijian female title
Arrêté	Decree, order (French)
Bagnards	Convicts transported from metropolitan France and other colonies to New Caledonia. In certain circumstances, they were also called forçats, recidivistes or concessionaires.
Bagne	Penal colony (French)
Bislama	One of the national languages of Vanuatu, a pidgin language that emerged between traders and ni-Vanuatu in nineteenth century Vanuatu and derived from beche-de-mer, a popular trading item of the period
Bose Vakaturaga	Council of Chiefs, Fiji
Buli	Local or minor chief/chiefs, Fiji
Brousse	The bush, the area outside Nouméa and colonial towns in New Caledonia
Canaque	Colonial term for Kanak (Indigenous Melanesian) in New Caledonia, or Islander in Vanuatu/the New Hebrides, derived from Hawaiian *kanaka* (person)
Colons	French settlers
Commissaire-Délégué de France	French Resident Commissioner, the New Hebrides
Conseil Privé	Privy Council, New Caledonia
Décret	Decree (French)
Gendarme	French police officer, representative of the gendarmerie
Gendarmerie	French military force charged with maintaining public order
Girmit	Indenture contract for Indian immigrants to Fiji
Girmitayas	Indian indentured labourers in Fiji

Grand chef	Administratively appointed high chief, New Caledonia
Indigénat	Regime of laws applied to Kanak in New Caledonia from 1887 to 1946
Indigène	Indigenous person, commonly used in colonial period, French
Indigène sujet non français	Indigenous person who was a French subject, but not a citizen
Indigène sujet français	Indigenous person who acquired French citizenship, generally by virtue of their assimilation into French colonial society through education, language fluency and social networks
iTaukei	Indigenous Fijians, the original inhabitants of the land
Kanak	Collective term for the Indigenous people of New Caledonia
Kastom	Custom, Vanuatu
Libérés	Freed convicts
Mataqali	Fijian communities or clans, tied to land ownership
Meke	Fijian dance or song
Métis	Person of mixed race, sometimes used specifically to refer to children of French fathers and Indigenous women.
Métissage	Broad French term for biological and/or cultural hybridity and interracial unions
Milicien	French ni-Vanuatu or Indigenous police constable
Miliciens	Indigenous constables in the French Police Force
ni-Vanuatu	Collective term for Indigenous people of Vanuatu
Nolle prosequi	Legal term used in English law where the prosecutor terminates the case before the trial or before a verdict is reached
Ovisa	Fijian police officer
Pétit chef	Administratively appointed petty chief, New Caledonia
Popinée	Colonial term for a Melanesian woman, often the partner of a European man, New Caledonia or the New Hebrides

Ratu	Fijian male title, equivalent of Adi
Roko Tui	Government-appointed district or provincial chief/chiefs, Fiji
Sirdar	Indian manager on Fijian plantations, responsible to a European overseer
Syndics	Officers or officials, notably of the Service des Affaires Indigènes, New Caledonia
Tribu	French term for tribe, New Caledonia and the New Hebrides
Tufala gavman	Bislama term for the New Hebrides Condominium
Turaga ni koro	Administratively appointed village head, Fiji
Turaga ni lewa	Fijian magistrate or judge
Vunivalu	Paramount chief, honorific title for Cakobau in Fiji
Vunivola	Scribe, Fiji

Bibliography

Archival sources

Archives de la Nouvelle-Calédonie, Nouméa (ANC)

Collection de documents relatif à la main d'oeuvre néo-hébridaise en Nouvelle-Calédonie 1876–1905, 1J23.

Correspondances (Procureur Général): 23W C11 - 1891–7, 23W C12 - 1887–1925, 23W C13 - 1905–7, 23W C14 - 1908–11.

'Memoires d'un forçat écrit par lui-même à l'âge de 44 ans', Manuscrit du Bagnard M. Ernest Dessaud, 1888, 1J 102.

Minutes des jugements de Tribunal correctionnel de Nouméa: 23W B2 - 1878–9, 23W B3 - 1883, 23W B8 - 1890.

Minutes des arrêts de la Cours d'Assise, Nouméa: 23W H2 - 1881–5, 23W H4 - 1890–3, 23W H6 - 1898–1900.

Archives Nationales d'Outre Mer, Aix-en-Provence (ANOM)

Archives de la Direction du Contrôle (ADC): Cartons 821, 822, 826 and 828.

DAP: Affaires Politiques Nouvelles-Hébrides Cartons 1AFFPOL/1915, 1AFFPOL/1916, and 1AFFPOL/1676.

Direction des Affaires Politiques, Ministre des Colonies (DAP): Affaires Politiques Nouvelle-Calédonie Cartons 1AFFPOL/266, 1AFFPOL/271, 1AFFPOL/741 and 1AFFPOL 742.

Séries Géographiques – Nouvelle Calédonie (SG-NC): Cartons 43, 46, 51, 145 à 147, 160, 175, 231 and 234.

Séries Géographiques – Nouvelles Hébrides (SG-NH): Cartons 1, 2, 3, 5, 8, 9, 11bis, 12 and 31.

Mitchell Library, Sydney

MOM 520: C. F. Andrews, 'Report of Mr. Andrews' Speech to the Planters' Association Executive Committee', Fiji, 7 December 1915.

A 320: *Histoire authentique de l'insurrection des indigenes de la Nouvelle-Caledonie en 1878*, translated by Frank C. Swinbourne (Nouméa: Imprimerie Nationale, 1909).

343.988/L: George Henry Lee, In the Supreme Court, Fiji: Regina v. Lee; affidavit of G. H. Lee and his remarks thereon.

PMB 1145: Judgements of the Joint Court of the New Hebrides, 1911–77, Vol. 4.

National Archives of Fiji, Suva (NAF)

Case Files – Criminal Sittings, Fiji Supreme Court (FSC), 1875–1920.

Colonial Secretary's Office Minute Papers (CSO MP), 1875–1915.

Fiji Colonial Reports, 1880–1920.

Lau Provincial Office – Official Correspondence, 1876–83.

Lau Provincial Council Records – Stipendiary Magistrate Lau – Provincial Court Books, 1893–1902.

Legislative Council Papers, 1885–1913.

Proceedings of the Native Council or Council of Chiefs, 1875–1920.

The National Archives, Kew (NAK)

CO 84/1 Fiji Certified Copies of Acts, 1875–80.

CO 84/2 Certified Copies of Acts of the Fiji Islands, 1881–7.

CO 86/1 Colonial Office, Fiji, Government gazettes, 1874–8.

Senate House Library, London (SHL)

MS894 Edward Jacomb diaries and papers, 1907–55.

Presbyterian Church of Aotearoa New Zealand Archives, Dunedin (PANZ)

Inwards Correspondence – New Hebrides Mission (Rev. W. Hewitson and Rev. A. Don), 1914–23, Mission Convenor's & Mission Secretary's Papers, Foreign Missions Committee.

Western Pacific Archives, University of Auckland Library Special Collections, Auckland (WPA)

Western Pacific archives. MSS & Archives 2003/1:

NHBS 1/I Vol. 1: General Correspondence files, MP Series 1907–42 (1907–14).

NHBS 1/I Vol. 2: General Correspondence files, MP Series 1907–42 (1915–29).

NHBS 15/I: General correspondence files c.1946 – c.1966 (1916–69).

University of Adelaide Manuscript and Archival Collections, Adelaide

MSS 0077 Thomson Reid Cowell – Papers relating to the Pacific Islands, 1961–91.

Published primary sources

Legislation, official reports and publications

'Accord sur la Nouvelle-Calédonie signé à Nouméa le 5 mai 1998', *Journaux Officiels de la République Française* 121 (27 mai 1998), 8039–8044.

'Convention between Great Britain and France, Respecting Abrogation of the Declaration of the 19th June 1847, Relative to the Islands to the Leeward of Tahiti and for the Protection of Life and Property in the New Hebrides [1887] PITSE 1 (16 November 1887)', Pacific Islands Treaty Series, Pacific Islands Legal Information Institute, accessed 19 January 2022, http://www.paclii.org/pits/en/treaty_database/1887/1.html.

'Convention between the United Kingdom and France Concerning the New Hebrides. Signed at London, October 20, 1906. (Ratifications exchanged at London, January 9, 1907.)', *American Journal of International Law* 1, no. 2, Supplement: Official Documents (1907), 179–200.

'Declaration between Great Britain and France, for the Constitution of a Joint Naval Commission for the Protection of Life and Property in the New Hebrides [1888] PITSE 1 (26 January 1888)', Pacific Islands Treaty Series, Pacific Islands Legal Information Institute, accessed 19 January 2022, http://www.paclii.org/pits/en/treaty_database/1888/1.html.

'Exchange of Notes Arrangement between Great Britain and France, Respecting the Independence of the New Hebrides Group [1878] PITSE 1 (18 January 1878)', Pacific Islands Treaty Series, Pacific Islands Legal Information Institute, accessed 19 January 2022, http://www.paclii.org/pits/en/treaty_database/1878/1.html.

Government of Fiji, *Journal of the Legislative Council*, 1886–1909.

[Fiji Government]. *Regulations of the Native Regulation Board: 1877–1882*. London: Harrison and Sons, 1883.

[Fiji Government]. *Report of the Commission on Decrease of the Native Population 1893*. Suva: E.J. March, Govt. Printer, 1896.

[Fiji Government]. *The Ordinances of the Colony of Fiji: A New Edition*. Suva: Edward John March, Government Printer, 1906.

[Fiji Government]. *Handbook to Fiji*. Suva: Government Printing Office, 1906.

Fiji Native Regulation Board. *Records of the Native Regulation Board 1887–1895*. Suva: Edward John March, Govt. Printer, 1898.

[New Caledonia Government]. *Bulletin Officiel de la Nouvelle-Calédonie*, 1887.

[New Hebrides Condominium]. Joint Regulation No. 2 of 1928 – Institution of Native Courts. Pacific Islands Legal Information Institute, accessed 19 January 2022, http://www.paclii.org/vu/legis/joint_reg/ioncr1928445/.

[New Hebrides Joint Court]. Ministère Public et Mtre Jacomb c MM. Stuart et Wright [1913] VUTM 39; [1913] No 183 (30 May 1913), Décisions du Tribunal Mixte des Nouvelles-Hébrides. Pacific Islands Legal Information Institute, accessed 19 January 2022, http://www.paclii.org/vu/cases/VUTM/1913/39.html.

'Protocol between Great Britain and France Respecting the New Hebrides [1906] PITSE 2 (27 February 1906)', Pacific Islands Treaty Series, Pacific Islands Legal Information Institute, accessed 19 January 2022, http://www.paclii.org/pits/en/treaty_database/1906/2.html.

[Royal Navy] HMAS UNA–December 1915 to June 1919, Royal Navy Log Books of the World War 1 Era, accessed 1 February 2021, http://www.naval-history.net/OWShips-WW1-18-HMAS_Una.htm.

Vanuatu Unreported Judgements Joint Court of the New Hebrides, Vol. 2 (1913–15). Pacific Islands Legal Information Institute, accessed 19 January 2022, http://www.paclii.org/vu/indices/cases/VanUnR_Cases2.html.

Newspapers and periodicals

The Anti-Slavery Reporter and Aborigines' Friend, July 1914.

Argus (Melbourne), 23 November 1908.

Dominion (New Zealand), 3 March 1909, 23 January 1911.

L'Echo de Tananarive, 7 Août 1929.

Evening Post (New Zealand), 2 November 1908, 9 December 1916.

Fiji Times.

Hawaiian Gazette, 1 November 1895.

Northern Advocate, 17 November 1923.

Manawatu Standard, 5 September 1913.

Le Néo-Hébridais, 1913–16.

Poverty Bay Herald, 22 February 1911.

The Straits Times, 26 March 1909.

Sydney Mail, 25 November 1908.

Sydney Morning Herald, 28 December 1911, 6 July 1929.

La Tamatave, 5 Août 1929.

The Times, 30 November 1910.

The West Australian, 3 March 1909.

Other published sources

Alexander, Gilchirst. *From the Middle Temple to the South Seas*. London: John Murray, 1927.

Andrews, C. F., and W. W. Pearson. *Indian Indentured Labour in Fiji: An Independent Enquiry*. Calcutta: Star Printing Works, 1916.

'Asterisk' (Robert James Fletcher). *Isles of Illusion: Letters from the South Seas*. Edited by Bohun Lynch. London: Constable, 1928 [1923].

'Asterisk' (Robert James Fletcher). *Lettres des Îles-Paradis*. Translated by Marthe Coblentz. Paris: F. Roeder, 1926.

'Asterisk' (Robert James Fletcher). *Gone Native: A Tale of the South Seas*. London: Constable, 1924.

Barrow, G. L. *Fiji for the Fijians: A Protest and a Plea*. Korolavu, [1921].

Bosch Barrett, Manuel. *Tres Años en las Nuevas Hébridas 1936–1939*. Barcelona: Alqueria, 2009 [1943].

Bourdiol, Julian. *Condition Internationale des Nouvelles-Hébrides*. Nîmes: Imprimerie Cooperative 'La Labourieuse', 1908.

Brewster, A. B. *The Hill Tribes of Fiji*. London: Seeley, Service, & Co 1922.

Brunet, Auguste. *Le régime international des Nouvelles-Hébrides: le condominium anglo-français*. Paris: Arthur Russeau, 1908.

Burton, J. W. *The Fiji of To-day*. London: C. H. Kelly, 1910.

'Colonial Medical Service', *Lancet* 202, no. 5217 (25 August 1923), 423–7.

'Colonial Medical Service', *Lancet* 198, no. 5113 (27 August 1921), 470–3.

Davillé, Ernest, *La Colonisation Française aux Nouvelles-Hébrides*. Paris: Librarie Africaine et Coloniale, 1895.

Des Voeux, William. *My Colonial Service in British Guiana, St. Lucia, Trinidad, Fiji, Australia, New-Foundland, and Hong Kong with Interludes*, vol. 1. London: John Murray, 1903.

Fison, Lortimer. 'Land Tenure in Fiji', *Journal of the Anthropological Institute of Great Britain and Ireland* 10 (1881), 332–52.

Gill, Walter. *Turn Northeast at the Tombstone*. Adelaide: Rigby, 1970.

Jacomb, Edward. *France and England in the New Hebrides*. Melbourne: G Robertson and Company, 1914.

Jacomb, Edward. *The Future of the Kanaka*. London: P. S. King and Son, 1919.

Jacomb, Edward. *The Joy Court: Comédie Rosse*. London: Braybrook and Dobson, 1929.

Leenhardt, Maurice. *Notes d'Ethnologie Néo-Calédonienne*. Paris: Institut d'Ethnologie, 1930.

Leenhardt, Maurice. *Do Kamo: Person and Myth in the Melanesian World*. Translated by Basia Miller Gulati. Chicago: University of Chicago Press, 1979 [1947].

McNeill, James, and Chimman Lal. *Report to the Government of India on the Conditions of Indian Immigrants in Four British Colonies and Surinam*. London: His Majesty's Stationery Office, 1915.

Rivière, Henri. *Souvenirs de la Nouvelle-Calédonie: L'Insurrection Canaque*. Paris: C. Lévy, 1881.

Sanadhya, Totaram. *My Twenty-One Years in Fiji and the Story of the Haunted Line*. Translated and edited by John Dunham Kelly and Uttra Kumari Singh. Suva: Fiji Museum, 1991.

Speiser, Feliz. *Two Years with the Natives in the Western Pacific*. London: Mills and Boon, 1913.

Stanmore, Arthur Hamilton Gordon. *Fiji: Records of Private and Public Life 1875–1880*, four volumes. Edinburgh: Printed by R. and R. Clark, 1897–1912.

Stanmore, Arthur Hamilton Gordon. *Letters and Notes Written during the Disturbances in the Highlands (Known as the 'Devil Country') of Viti Levu, Fiji, 1876*. Edinburgh: R. and R. Clark, 1879.

Thomson, Basil. *The Fijians: A Study of the Decay of Custom*. London: Dawsons of Pall Mall, 1968 [1908].

Secondary sources

Abrahams, Sidney. 'The Colonial Legal Service and the Administration of Justice in Colonial Dependencies', *Journal of Comparative Legislation and International Law* 30, nos. 3/4 (1948), 1–11.

Adams, Ron. 'Homo Anthropologicus and Man-Tanna: Jean Guiart and the Anthropological Attempt to Understand the Tannese', *Journal of Pacific History* 22, no. 1 (1987), 3–14.

Agmon, Danna. 'Historical Gaps and Non-Existent Sources: The Case of the Chaudrie Court in French India', *Comparative Studies in Society and History* 63, no. 4 (2021), 979–1006.

Aldrich, Robert. *The French Presence in the South Pacific, 1842–1940*. Basingstoke: Macmillan, 1990.

Aldrich, Robert, and John Connell. *France's Overseas Frontier: Départements et territoires d'outre mer*. Cambridge: Cambridge University Press, 2006.

Ali, Ahmed. *Girmit: The Indenture Experience in Fiji*. Suva: Fiji Museum, 2004 [1979].

Anderson, Clare. *Legible Bodies: Race, Criminality and Colonialism in South Asia*. Oxford: Berg, 2004.

Anderson, Clare. *Subaltern Lives: Biographies of Colonialism in the Indian Ocean World, 1790–1920*. Cambridge: Cambridge University Press, 2012.

Angleviel, Frédéric. *Historiographie de la Nouvelle-Calédonie: ou l'émergence tardive de deux écoles historiques antipodéennes*. Paris: Publibook, 2003.

Angleviel, Frédéric (ed.). *La Nouvelle-Calédonie: Terre de Métissage*. Paris: Les Indes Savantes & GRHOC, 2004.

Angleviel, Frédéric. 'Le métissage en Nouvelle-Calédonie: Réalité biologique et question culturel', in *La Nouvelle-Calédonie: Terre de Métissage*, edited by Frédéric Angleviel. Paris: Les Indes Savantes & GRHOC, 2004, 13–23.

Angleviel, Frédéric. 'Du pays du non-dit à une libération de la parole: L'histoire comme enjeu culturel en Nouvelle-Calédonie', *Historical Reflections* 34, no. 1 (2008), 104–21.

Angleviel, Frédéric, and Max Shekleton. '"Olfala Pija blong Niuhebridis blong Bifo": Old Pictures of the Early New Hebrides (Vanuatu)', *Pacific Studies* 20, no. 4 (1997), 161–85.

Anova-Ataba, Apollinaire. 'Deux exemples de réflexions mélanésiennes. 1: L'insurrection des Néo-Calédonieenes en 1878 et la personnalité du grand chef Atai. 2: Pour une économie humaine', *Journal de la Société des Océanistes* 25 (1969), 201–37.

Armitage, David, and Alison Bashford (eds). *Pacific Histories: Land, Ocean, People*. Basingstoke: Palgrave Macmillan, 2014.

Arvin, Maile. *Possessing Polynesians: The Science of Settler Colonial Whiteness in Hawai'i and Oceania*. Durham: Duke University Press, 2019.

Attwood, Bain. *Empire and the Making of Native Title: Sovereignty, Property and Indigenous People*. Cambridge: Cambridge University Press, 2020.

Bain, 'Atu. 'A Protective Labour Policy? An Alternative Interpretation of Early Colonial Labour Policy in Fiji', *Journal of Pacific History* 23, no. 2 (1988), 119–36.

Ballantyne, Tony, and Antoinette Burton (eds). *Bodies in Contact: Rethinking Colonial Encounters in World History*. Durham: Duke University Press, 2005.

Ballantyne, Tony, and Antoinette Burton (eds). *Moving Subjects: Gender, Mobility and Intimacy in an Age of Global Empire*. Urbana: University of Illinois Press, 2009.

Ballard, Chris, and Bronwen Douglas (eds). 'Special Issue: Punitive Expeditions', *Journal of Colonialism and Colonial History* 18, no. 1 (2017).

Banivanua Mar, Tracey. *Violence and Colonial Dialogue: The Australia-Pacific Labor Trade*. Honolulu: University of Hawai'i Press, 2007.

Banivanua Mar, Tracey. 'Frontier Space and the Reification of the Rule of Law: Colonial Negotiations in the Western Pacific, 1870–74', *Australian Feminist Law Journal* 30, no. 1 (2009), 23–39.

Banivanua Mar, Tracey. 'Imperial Literacy and Indigenous Rights: Tracing Transoceanic Circuits of a Modern Discourse', *Aboriginal History* 37 (2013), 1–28.

Banivanua Mar, Tracey. *Decolonisation and the Pacific: Indigenous Globalisation and the Ends of Empire*. Cambridge: Cambridge University Press, 2016.

Banivanua Mar, Tracey, and Nadia Rhook. 'Counter Networks of Empires: Reading Unexpected People in Unexpected Places', *Journal of Colonialism and Colonial History* 19, no. 2 (2018).

Banner, Stuart. *Possessing the Pacific: Land, Settlers and Indigenous Peoples from Australia to Alaska*. Cambridge, MA: Harvard University Press, 2007.

Bayly, Christopher. *Recovering Liberties: Indian Thought in the Age of Liberalism and Empire*. Cambridge: Cambridge University Press, 2012.

Bedford, Stuart. '"A Good Moral Effect?": Local Opposition and Colonial Persistence in Malakula, New Hebrides, 1875–1918', *Journal of Colonialism and Colonial History* 18, no. 1 (2017).

Belich, James. *Making Peoples: A History of the New Zealanders from Polynesian Settlement to the End of the Nineteenth Century*. London: Allen Lane, 1996.

Bensa, Alban (ed.). *Comprendre l'identité kanak*. Paris: Centre Thomas Moore, 1990.

Bensa, Alban, and Christine Salomon. *Nouvelle-Calédonie: les Kanaks face à l'appareil judiciaire*. Paris: Publications du GIP mission de recherche Droit et Justice, 2003.

Benton, Lauren. *Law and Colonial Cultures: Legal Regimes in World History, 1400–1900*. Cambridge: Cambridge University Press, 2002.

Benton, Lauren, and Lisa Ford. 'Magistrates in Empire: Convicts, Slaves, and the Remaking of the Plural Legal Order in the British Empire', in *Legal Pluralism and Empires 1500–1850*, edited by Lauren Benton and Richard J. Ross. New York: New York University Press, 2013, 173–98.

Benton, Lauren, and Lisa Ford. *Rage for Order: The British Empire and the Origins of International Law, 1800–1850*. Cambridge, MA: Harvard University Press, 2016.

Benton, Lauren, and Richard J. Ross (eds). *Legal Pluralism and Empires 1500–1850*. New York: New York University Press, 2013.

Berman, Alan. 'Kanak Women and the Colonial Process', *International Journal of Law in Context* 2 (2006), 11–36.

Biersack, Aletta, Margaret Jolly and Martha Macintyre (eds). *Gender Violence & Human Rights: Seeking Justice in Fiji, Papua New Guinea and Vanuatu*. Canberra: ANU Press, 2016.

Bingham, Adrian et al. 'Historical Child Sexual Abuse in England and Wales: The Role of Historians', *History of Education* 45, no. 4 (2016), 411–29.

Bobin, Frédéric. 'Caldoches, Metropolitans and the Mother Country', *Journal of Pacific History* 26, no. 2 (1991), 303–12.

Boetsch, Gilles, Nicolas Bancel and Pascal Blanchard (eds). *Sexualités, identités & corps colonisés. XVe siècle-XXIe siècle*. Paris: CNRS Editions, 2019.

Boittin, Jennifer Anne, Christina Firpo, and Emily Musil Church, 'Hierarchies of Race and Gender in the French Colonial Empire, 1914–1946', *Historical Reflections/ Réflexions Historiques* 37, no. 1 (2011), 60–90.

Bolton, Lissant. 'Women, Place and Practice in Vanuatu: A View from Ambae', *Oceania* 70, no. 1 (1999), 43–55.

Bonnemaison, Joel. *The Tree and the Canoe: History and Ethnogeography of Tanna*. Honolulu: University of Hawai'i Press, 1994.

Borofsky, Robert (ed.). *Remembrance of Pacific Pasts: An Invitation to Remake History*. Honolulu: University of Hawai'i Press, 2000.

Bouge, Louis-Joseph. 'Première législation tahitienne. Le Code Pomaré de 1819. Historique et traduction', *Journal de la Société des océanistes* 8 (1952), 5–26.

Bourke, Joanna. *Rape: A History from 1860 to the Present.* London: Virago, 2007.

Brennan, Russell, and Jonathan Richards. '"The Scum of French Criminals and Convicts": Australia and New Caledonia escapees', *History Compass* 12, no. 7 (2014), 559–66.

Brereton, Bridget. *Law, Justice and Empire: The Colonial Career of John Gorrie, 1829–1892.* Barbados: University of the West Indies Press, 1997.

Bresnihan, Brian J., and Keith Woodward (eds). *Tufala Gavman: Reminiscences from the Anglo-French Condominium of the New Hebrides.* Suva: Institute of Pacific Studies USP, 2002.

Brewster, David. *The Turtle and the Caduceus: How Pacific Politics and Modern Medicine Shaped the Medical School in Fiji, 1885–2010.* Bloomington: Xlibris, 2010.

Brou, Bernard. *Histoire de la Nouvelle-Calédonie: les temps moderne, 1744–1925.* Nouméa: Société d'études historiques de la Nouvelle-Calédonie, 1973.

Brown, Laurence. 'Inter-Colonial Migration and the Refashioning of Indentured Labour: Arthur Gordon in Trinidad, Mauritius and Fiji', in *Colonial Lives across the British Empire: Imperial Careering in the Long Nineteenth Century*, edited by David Lambert and Alan Lester. Cambridge: Cambridge University Press, 2006, 204–27.

Brunton, Ron. *The Abandoned Narcotic: Kava and Cultural Instability in Melanesia.* Cambridge: Cambridge University Press, 1989.

Bryne, Paula J. *Criminal Law and Colonial Subject: New South Wales, 1810–1830.* Cambridge: Cambridge University Press, 1993.

Buchanan, Rachel. *The Parihaka Album: Lest We Forget.* Wellington: Huia, 2009.

Bullard, Alice. *Exile to Paradise: Savagery and Civilization in Paris and the South Pacific, 1790–1900.* Stanford: Stanford University Press, 2000.

Burton, Antoinette. *Burdens of History: British Feminists, Indian Women, and Imperial Culture, 1865–1915.* Chapel Hill: University of North Carolina Press, 1994.

Caplan, Jane (ed.). *Written on the Body: The Tattoo in European and American History.* London: Reaktion Books, 2000.

Carrier, James G. (ed.). *History and Tradition in Melanesian Anthropology.* Berkeley: University of California Press, 1992.

Cawsey, Katherine Stirling Kerr. *The Making of a Rebel: Captain Donald Macleod of the New Hebrides.* Suva: Institute of Pacific Studies, University of the South Pacific, 1998.

Chapman, J. K. *The Career of A. H. Gordon.* Toronto: University of Toronto Press, 1964.

Chatterjee, Nandini, and Lakshmi Subramanian. 'Law and the Spaces of Empire: Introduction to the Special Issue', *Journal of Colonialism and Colonial History* 15, no. 1 (2014).

Clancy-Smith, Julia, and Frances Gouda (eds). *Domesticating the Empire: Race, Gender, and Family Life in French and Dutch Colonialism.* Charlottesville: University Press of Virginia, 1998.

Clark, Anna. *Women's Silence, Men's Violence: Sexual Assault in England, 1770–1845.* London: Pandora Press, 1987.

Clark, Michael, and Catherine Crawford. *Legal Medicine in History*. Cambridge: Cambridge University Press, 1994.

Cole, Anna. 'Governing Tattoo: Reflections on a Colonial Trial', in *Tattoo: Bodies, Art and Exchange in the Pacific and Europe*, edited by Nicholas Thomas, Anna Cole and Bronwen Douglas. London: Reaktion Books, 2005 [e-book], 109–19.

Comaroff, John L. 'Colonialism, Culture and the Law: A Forward', *Law and Social Inquiry* 26, no. 2 (2001), 305–14.

Connell, John. *New Caledonia or Kanaky? The Political History of a French Colony*. Canberra: National Centre for Development Studies, Australian National University, 1987.

Cooper, Frederick. *Colonialism in Question: Theory, Knowledge, History*. Berkeley: University of California Press, 2005.

Corris, Peter. *Passage, Port and Plantation: A History of Solomons Islands Labour Migration 1870–1914*. Melbourne: Melbourne University Press, 1973.

Counts, Dorothy A. 'Domestic Violence in Oceania: Conclusion', *Pacific Studies* 13, no. 3 (1990), 225–54.

Crowther, M. Anne, and Brenda White. *On Soul and Conscience: The Medical Expert and Crime*. Aberdeen: University of Aberdeen Press, 1988.

Datta, Arunima. *Fleeting Agencies: A Social History of Indian Coolie Women in British Malaya*. Cambridge: Cambridge University Press, 2021.

Dauphiné, Joël. *Les spoliations foncières en Nouvelle-Calédonie (1853–1913)*. Paris: L'Harmattan, 1989.

Dauphiné, Joel, Louis-José Barbançon, Sylvette Boubin-Boyer, Claude Cornet, Nicole Célestin, Thierry Cacot, Gisèle Chauvet, Luc Legeard, Claudy Chêne, Anne-Lise Pasturel, André Dubois, Philippe Palombo and Jean-Marc Regnault. *Île d'exil, terre d'asile: les déportations politiques et les expulsions en temps de guerre en Nouvelle-Calédonie*. Nouméa: Musée de la ville de Nouméa, 2005.

Davidson, J. W. 'British Policy in the South Pacific', *Pacific Affairs* 21, no. 4 (1948), 408–10.

Davies, John. *The History of the Tahitian Mission, 1788–1830*, edited by Colin Newbury. Cambridge: Cambridge University Press for the Hakluyt Society, 1961.

D'Cruze, Shani. 'Sexual Violence in History: A Contemporary Heritage?' in *Handbook on Sexual Violence*, edited by Jennifer Brown and Sandra Walklate. London: Routledge, 2011, 23–51.

Defert, Daniel. 'Fletcher, Robert James. Iles Paradis, Iles d'Illusion, Lettres des Mers du Sud. Un Cas d'hébridisation: Robert James Fletcher', *Journal de la Société des Océanistes* 37, no. 70 (1981), 129–31.

Denoon, Donald. 'An Untimely Divorce: Western Medicine and Anthropology in Melanesia', *History and Anthropology* 11, nos. 2–3 (1999), 329–50.

Denoon, Donald (ed.). *The Cambridge History of the Pacific Islanders*. Cambridge: Cambridge University Press, 2004.

Deschamps, Hubert. 'Et Maintenant, Lord Lugard?' *Africa: Journal of the International African Institute* 33, no. 4 (1963), 293–306.

Deutsch, Jan-Georg. 'Celebrating Power in Everyday Life: The Administration of Law and the Public Sphere in Colonial Tanzania, 1890–1914', *Journal of African Cultural Studies* 15, no. 1 (2002), 93–103.

Dimier, Veronique. 'On Good Colonial Government: Lessons from the League of Nations', *Global Society* 18, no. 3 (2004), 279–99.

Dorsett, Shaunnagh. *Juridical Encounters: Maori and the Colonial Courts, 1840–1852*. Auckland: Auckland University Press, 2018.

Dorsett, Shaunnagh, and John McLaren (eds). *Legal Histories of the British Empire: Laws, Engagements and Legacies*. Abingdon: Routledge, 2014.

Douglas, Bronwen. 'Conflict and Alliance in a Colonial Context', *Journal of Pacific History* 15, no. 1 (1980), 21–51.

Douglas, Bronwen. 'Winning and Losing? Reflections on the War of 1878–79 in New Caledonia', *Journal of Pacific History* 26, no. 2 (1991), 213–33.

Douglas, Bronwen. 'Doing Ethnographic History: The Case of Fighting in New Caledonia', in *History and Tradition in Melanesian Anthropology*, edited by James G. Carrier. Berkeley: University of California Press, 1992, 86–116.

Douglas, Bronwen. *Across the Great Divide: Journeys in History and Anthropology*. Amsterdam: Harwood Academic Publishers, 1998.

Douglas, Bronwen. '"Prologue" in Women's Groups and Everyday Modernity in Melanesia, Special Issue', *Oceania* 74, nos. 1–2 (2003), 1–5.

Douglas, Bronwen. 'Slippery Word, Ambiguous Praxis: "Race" and Late 18th-Century Voyagers in Oceania', *Journal of Pacific History* 41, no. 1 (2006), 1–29.

Douglas, Bronwen. *Science, Voyages and Encounters in Oceania 1511–1850*. Basingstoke: Palgrave Macmillan, 2014.

Douglas, Bronwen, and Chris Ballard (eds). *Foreign Bodies: Oceania and the Science of Race 1770–1940*. Canberra: ANU E-Press, 2008.

Douglas, Bronwen, and Chris Ballard. 'Race, Place and Civilisation: Colonial Encounters and Governance in Greater Oceania', *Journal of Pacific History* 47, no. 3 (2012), 245–62.

Doumenge, Jean-Pierre, Éliane Métais and Alain Saussol (eds). *La Nouvelle Calédonie: occupation de l'espace et peuplement*. Bordeaux: Presses universitaires de Bordeaux, 1986.

Dousset-Leenhardt, Roselène. *Terre natale: Terre d'exil*. Paris: Maisonneuve et Larose, 1976.

Dousset-Leenhardt, Roselène. *Colonialisme et contradictions: étude sur les causes socio-historiques de l'insurrection de 1878*. Paris: L'Harmattan, 1978 [1970].

Drewry, Gavin, and Charles Blake (eds). *Law and the Spirit of Enquiry: Essays in Honour of Sir Louis Blom-Cooper, QC*. London: Kluwer Law International, 1999.

Duff, Peter. 'The Evolution of Trial by Judge and Assessors in Fiji', *The Journal of Pacific Studies* 21 (1997), 189–213.

Edwards, Louise, Nigel Penn and Jay Winter (eds). *The Cambridge World History of Violence*, vol. 4, 1800 to present. Cambridge: Cambridge University Press, 2020.

Erber, Nancy, and George Robb (eds). *Disorder in the Court: Trials and Sexual Conflict at the Turn of the Century*. London: Macmillan Press, 1999.

Estrich, Susan. 'Rape', *Yale Law Journal* 95, no. 6 (1986), 1087–84.

Etherington, Norman. 'Natal's Black Rape Scare of the 1870s', *Journal of Southern African Studies* 15, no. 1 (1988), 36–53.

Etherington, Norman. 'The Gendering of Indirect Rule: Criminal Law and Colonial Fiji, 1875–1900', *Journal of Pacific History* 31, no. 1 (1996), 42–57.

Etherington, Norman. 'Afterword: The Missionary Experience in British and French Empires', in *In God's Empire: French Missionaries and the Modern World*, edited by Owen White and James Patrick Daughton. Oxford: Oxford University Press, 2012, 280–301.

Etherington, Norman. 'Law', in *Pacific Histories: Land, Ocean, People*, edited by David Armitage and Alison Bashford. Basingstoke: Palgrave Macmillan, 2014, 216–36.

Ford, Lisa. *Settler Sovereignty: Jurisdiction and Indigenous Peoples in America and Australia, 1788–1836*. Cambridge, MA: Harvard University Press, 2010.

Forster, R. A. S. 'Vanuatu: The End of an Episode of Schizophrenic Colonialism', *The Round Table: The Commonwealth Journal of International Affairs* 70, no. 280 (1980), 367–73.

Forsyth, Miranda. *A Bird That Flies with Two Wings: Kastom and State Justice Systems in Vanuatu*. Canberra: ANU E-Press, 2009.

Forsyth, Miranda. 'A Bird That Flies with Two Wings: The *Kastom* and State Justice Systems in Vanuatu'. PhD Thesis, Australia National University, 2007.

Foucrier, Annick (ed.). *The French and the Pacific World, 17th–19th Centuries: Explorations, Migrations and Cultural Exchanges*. Aldershot: Ashgate, 2005.

Fozdar, Farida, and Kirsten McGavin (eds). *Mixed Race Identities in Australia, New Zealand and the Pacific Islands*. New York: Routledge, 2017.

Fradera, Josep M. *The Imperial Nation: Citizens and Subjects in the British, French, Spanish, and American Empires*. Translated by Ruth MacKay. Princeton, NJ: Princeton University Press, 2018.

France, Peter. *The Charter of the Land: Custom and Colonisation in Fiji*. Melbourne: Oxford University Press, 1969.

Fuentes, Marisa J. *Dispossessed Lives: Enslaved Women, Violence, and the Archive*. Philadelphia: University of Pennsylvania Press, 2016.

Gatty, Ronald. *Fijian–English Dictionary: With notes on Fijian Culture and Natural History*. Suva, Fiji: Ronald Gatty, 2009.

Genever, Geoffrey. '"Worse than Murder"? Colonial Queensland's Response to the Rape of European Women by Aboriginal Men', *Queensland Review* 19, no. 2 (2012), 234–46.

Ghosh, Durba. 'Household Crimes and Domestic Order: Keeping the Peace in Colonial Calcutta, c.1770–c.1840', *Modern Asian Studies* 38 (2004), 599–623.

Ghosh, Durba. *Sex and the Family in Colonial India: The Making of Empire*. Cambridge: Cambridge University Press, 2006.

Gilding, Michael. 'The Massacre of the Mystery: A Case Study in Contact Relations', *Journal of Pacific History* 17, no. 2 (1982), 66–85.

Gillion, K. L. *Fiji's Indian Migrants: A History to the End of Indenture in 1920*. Melbourne: Oxford University Press, 1962.

Gillion, K. L. *The Fiji Indians: Challenge to European Dominance 1920–1946*. Canberra: Australian National University Press, 1977.

Glasser, Cyril. 'In Foreign Parts: Reflections on British Lawyers Abroad', in *Law and the Spirit of Enquiry: Essays in Honour of Sir Louis Blom-Cooper, QC*, edited by Gavin Drewry and Charles Blake. London: Kluwer Law International, 1999, 179–92.

Godfrey, Barry, and Graeme Dunstall (eds), *Crime and Empire 1840–1940*. Uffculme: Willan Publishing, 2005.

Gregory Robert J., and Janet E. Gregory. 'John Frum: An Indigenous Strategy of Reaction to Mission Rule and the Colonial Order', *Pacific Studies* 7, no. 2 (1984), 68–90.

Grimshaw, Patricia. *Paths of Duty: American Missionary Wives in Nineteenth Century Hawai'i*. Honolulu: University of Hawai'i Press, 1989.

Guiart, Jean. 'Culture Contact and the "John Frum" Movement on Tanna', *Southwestern Journal of Anthropology* 12, no. 1 (1956), 105–16.

Guiart, Jean. *Un siècle et demi de contacts culturels à Tanna*. Paris: Musée de l'Homme, 1956.

Guiart, Jean. 'Le cadre social traditionnel et la rebellion de 1878 dans le pays de la Foa', *Journal de la Société des Océanistes* 24 (1968), 97–119.

Guiart, Jean. 'Les évènements de 1917 en Nouvelle-Calédonie', *Journal de la Société des Océanistes* 29 (1970), 265–82.

Gunson, Neil. *Messengers of Grace: Evangelical Missionaries in the South Seas 1797–1860*. Melbourne: Oxford University Press, 1978.

Guthrie, Margaret W. *Misi Utu: Dr. D. W. Hoodless and the Development of Medical Education in the South Pacific*. Suva: Institute of Pacific Studies, 1979.

Heartfield, James. '"You Are Not a White Woman!" Apolosi Nawai, the Fiji Produce Agency and the Trial of Stella Spencer in Fiji, 1915', *Journal of Pacific History* 38, no. 1 (2003), 69–83.

Heineman, Elizabeth D. (ed.). *Sexual Violence in Conflict Zones: From the Ancient World to the Era of Human Rights*. Philadelphia: University of Pennsylvania Press, 2011.

Herzog, Dagmar, and Chelsea Schields (eds). *The Routledge Companion to Sexuality and Colonialism*. Abingdon: Routledge, 2021.

Hobsbawn, Eric, and Terence Ranger (eds). *The Invention of Tradition*. Cambridge: Cambridge University Press, 1992 [1983].

Hofman, Elwin. 'Spatial Interrogations: Space and Power in French Criminal Justice, 1750–1850', *law&history* 7, no. 2 (2020), 155–81.

Howe, Kerry R. 'Pacific Islands History in the 1980s: New Directions or Monograph Myopia?' *Pacific Studies* 3, no. 1 (1979), 81–90.

Hussain, Nasser. *The Jurisprudence of Emergency: Colonialism and the Rule of Law*. Ann Arbor: University of Michigan Press, 2003.

Hyam, Ronald. 'Concubinage and the Colonial Service: The Crewe Circular (1909)', *Journal of Imperial and Commonwealth History* 14, no. 3 (1986), 170–86.

Hyam, Ronald. *Empire and Sexuality: The British Experience*. Manchester: Manchester University Press, 1990.

Inglis, Amirah. *'Not a White Woman Safe': Sexual Anxiety and Politics in Papua, 1920–1934*. Canberra: Australian University Press, 1974.

Inglis, Amirah. *The White Women's Protection Ordinance: Sexual Anxiety and Politics in Papua*. Brighton: Sussex University Press, 1975.

Israel, Kali. 'French Vices and British Liberties: Gender, Class and Narrative Competition in a Late Victorian Sex Scandal', *Social History* 22, no. 1 (1997), 1–26.

Jackson, Louise A. *Child Sexual Abuse in Victorian England*. London: Routledge, 1999.

Jamin, Jean. 'Note sur l'étrange cas de Robert James FLETCHER', *Journal de la Société des océanistes* 37, no. 70 (1981), 131–2.

Jasanoff, Maya. 'How Can We Write the History of Empire?' in *What Is History, Now?* edited by Suzannah Lipscomb and Helen Carr. London: Weidenfeld & Nicolson, 2021, 84–100.

Jolly, Margaret. 'The Forgotten Women: A History of Migrant Labour and Gender Relations in Vanuatu', *Oceania* 58, no. 2 (1987), 119–39.

Jolly, Margaret. '"To Save the Girls for Brighter and Better Lives": Presbyterian Missions and Women in the South of Vanuatu: 1848–1870', *Journal of Pacific History* 26, no. 1 (1991), 27–48.

Jolly, Margaret. '"Women Ikat Raet Long Human Raet o No?" Women's Rights, Human Rights and Domestic Violence in Vanuatu', *Feminist Review* 52 (1996), 169–90.

Jolly, Margaret. 'Custom and the Way of the Land: Past and Present in Vanuatu and Fiji', in *Remembrance of Pacific Pasts: An Invitation to Remake History*, edited by Robert Borofsky. Honolulu: University of Hawai'i Press, 2000, 340–57.

Jolly, Margaret. 'Other Mothers: Maternal "Insouciance" and the Depopulation Debate in Fiji and Vanuatu, 1890 to 1930', in *Maternities and Modernities: Colonial and Postcolonial Experiences in Asia and the Pacific*, edited by Kalpana Ram and Margaret Jolly. Cambridge: Cambridge University Press, 1998, 177–212.

Jolly, Margaret, and Martha Macintyre (eds). *Family and Gender in the Pacific: Domestic Contradictions and the Colonial Impact*. Cambridge: Cambridge University Press, 1989.

Jolly, Margaret, Serge Tcherkézoff and Darrell Tyron (eds). *Oceanic Encounters: Exchange, Desire, Violence*. Canberra: ANU Press, 2009.

Joyce, R. B. 'Sir William MacGregor – a colonial Governor', *Historical Studies: Australia and New Zealand* 11, no. 41 (1963), 18–31.

Kaplan, Martha. *Neither Cargo nor Cult: Ritual Politics and the Colonial Imagination in Fiji*. Durham: Duke University Press, 1995.

Kaplan, Martha. 'Promised Lands: From Colonial Law-giving to Postcolonial Takeovers in Fiji', in *Law and Empire in the Pacific: Fiji and Hawaii*, edited by Sally Engle Merry and Don Brenneis. Santa Fe: School of American Research, 2004, 153–86.

Kelly, John. '"Coolie" as Labour Commodity: Race, Sex, and European Dignity in Colonial Fiji', *Journal of Peasant Studies* 19, nos. 3–4 (1992), 246–67.

Kelly, John. *A Politics of Virtue: Hinduism, Sexuality and Countercolonial Discourse in Fiji*. Chicago: University of Chicago Press, 1995.

Kelly, John. 'Gaze and Grasp: Plantations, Desires, Indentured Indians, and Colonial Law in Fiji', in *Sites of Desire, Economies of Pleasure: Sexualities in Asia and the Pacific*, edited by Lenore Manderson and Margaret Jolly. Chicago: University of Chicago Press, 1997, 73–98.

Kelly, John. 'Gordon Was No Amateur: Imperial Legal Strategies in the Colonisation of Fiji', in *Law and Empire in the Pacific: Fiji and Hawaii*, edited by Sally Engle Merry and Don Brenneis. Santa Fe: School of American Research Press, 2003, 61–100.

Knapman, Claudia. *White Women in Fiji, 1835–1930: The Ruin of Empire?* London: Allen & Unwin, 1986.

Kolsky, Elizabeth. '"The Body Evidencing the Crime": Rape on Trial in Colonial India, 1860–1947', *Gender & History* 22, no. 1 (2010), 109–30.

Kolsky, Elizabeth. 'The Rule of Colonial Indifference: Rape on Trial in Early Colonial India, 1805–1857', *Journal of Asian Studies* 69, no. 4 (2010), 1093–117.

Kolsky, Elizabeth. *Colonial Justice in British India: White Violence and the Rule of Law*. Cambridge: Cambridge University Press, 2010.

Kurtovitch, Ismet, and Jean Guiart. 'Sortir de l'indigénat: cinquantième anniversaire de l'abolition de l'indigénat en Nouvelle-Calédonie', *Journal de la Société des Océanistes* 105, no. 2 (1997), 117–39.

Laidlaw, Zoe. *Colonial Connections, 1815–45: Patronage, the Information Revolution and Colonial Government*. Manchester: Manchester University Press, 2006.

Lal, Brij. *Girmitiyas: The Origins of the Fiji Indians*. Canberra: Journal of Pacific History, 1983.

Lal, Brij. 'Kunti's Cry: Indentured Women on Fiji's Plantations', *Indian Economic and Social History Review* 22, no. 1 (1985), 55–71.

Lal, Brij. 'Veil of Dishonour: Sexual Jealousy and Suicide on Fiji Plantations', *Journal of Pacific History* 20, no. 3 (1985), 135–55.

Lal, Brij. *Broken Waves: A History of the Fiji Islands in the Twentieth Century*. Honolulu: University of Hawai'i Press, 1992.

Lal, Brij. *Chalo Jahaji: On a Journey through Indenture in Fiji*. Canberra and Suva: Australian National University and Fiji Museum, 2000.

Lal, Brij (ed.). *Wansalawara: Soundings in Melanesian History*. Honolulu: University of Hawaii Pacific Islands Studies Program, Working Paper Series, 1987.

Lambert, David, and Alan Lester (eds). *Colonial Lives across the British Empire: Imperial Careering in the Long Nineteenth Century*. Cambridge: Cambridge University Press, 2006.

Laracy, Hugh. 'The Pentecost Murders: An Episode in Condominium Non-Rule, New Hebrides 1940', *Journal of Pacific History* 26, no. 2 (1991), 245–55.

Latham, Linda. 'Revolt Re-Examined: The 1878 Insurrection in New Caledonia', *Journal of Pacific History* 10, no. 3 (1975), 48–63.

Laurent, Sylvie, and Thierry Leclère (eds). *De quelle couleur sont les Blancs? Des «petits Blancs» des colonies au «racisme anti-Blancs»* Paris: La Découverte, 2013.

Lazarus-Black, Mindie, and Susan F. Hirsch (eds). *Contested States: Law, Hegemony and Resistance*. New York: Routledge, 1994.

Leblic, Isabelle. '«Métissage» et parenté: Assimilation de non-Kanaks dans le système des moitiés matrimoniales à Ponérihouen', in *La Nouvelle-Calédonie: Terre de Métissage*, edited by Frédéric Angleviel. Paris: Les Indes Savantes & GRHOC, 2004, 35–56.

Leckie, Jacqui. *Colonizing Madness: Asylum and Community in Fiji*. Honolulu: University of Hawai'i Press, 2019.

Legge, J. D. *Britain in Fiji, 1858–1880*. London: Macmillan, 1958.

Levine, Philippa. *Prostitution, Race and Politics: Policing Venereal Disease in the British Empire*. New York: Routledge, 2003.

Levine, Philippa. 'What's British about Gender and Empire? The Problem of Exceptionalism', *Comparative Studies of South Asia, Africa and the Middle East* 27, no. 2 (2007), 273–82.

Levine, Philippa (ed.). *Gender and Empire*. Oxford: Oxford University Press, 2007.

Lightner, Sara, and Anna Naupa. *Histri blong Yumi long Vanuatu*, vol. 3, French edition. Port Vila: Vanuatu Cultural Centre, 2011.

Linnekin, Jocelyn. 'New Political Orders', in *The Cambridge History of the Pacific Islanders*, edited by Donald Denoon. Cambridge: Cambridge University Press, 2004, 185–217.

Lipscomb, Suzannah, and Helen Carr (eds). *What Is History, Now?* London: Weidenfeld & Nicolson, 2021.

Lowe, Lisa. *The Intimacy of Four Continents*. Durham: Duke University Press, 2015.

Luker, Vicki. 'A Tale of Two Mothers: Colonial Constructions of Indian and Fijian Maternity', *Fijian Studies: A Journal of Contemporary Fiji* 3, no. 2 (2005), 357–74.

Lyons, Martyn. *The Totem and the Tricolour: A Short History of New Caledonia since 1774*. Sydney: New South Wales University Press, 1986.

MacClancy, Jeremy. *To Kill a Bird with Two Stones: A Short History of Vanuatu*. Port Vila: Vanuatu Cultural Centre, 1980.

MacNaught, Timothy. *The Fijian Colonial Experience: A Study of the Neotraditional Order under British Colonial Rule Prior to World War II*. Canberra: ANU Press, 1982.

Mander, Linda A. 'The New Hebrides Condominium', *Pacific Historical Review* 13, no. 2 (1944), 151–67.

Manderson, Lenore, and Margaret Jolly (eds). *Sites of Desire, Economies of Pleasure: Sexualities in Asia and the Pacific*. Chicago: University of Chicago Press, 1997.

Manktelow, Emily J. *Gender, Power and Sexual Abuse in the Pacific: Rev. Simpson's 'Improper Liberties'*. London: Bloomsbury, 2018.

Mantena, Karuna. *Alibis of Empire: Henry Maine and the Ends of Liberal Imperialism*. Princeton, NJ: Princeton University Press, 2010.

Martínez, Julia, Claire Lowrie, Frances Steel and Victoria Haskins. *Colonialism and Male Domestic Service across the Asia Pacific*. London: Bloomsbury, 2018.

Matsuda, Matt K. *Empire of Love: Histories of France in the Pacific*. New York: Oxford University Press, 2005.

Matsuda, Matt K. *Pacific Worlds: A History of Seas, Peoples, and Cultures*. Cambridge: Cambridge University Press, 2012.

Maude, H. E. *Slavers in Paradise: The Peruvian Labour Trade in Polynesia*. Canberra: Australian National University Press, 1981.

Mawani, Renisa. *Colonial Proximities: Crossracial Encounters and Juridical Truths in British Columbia, 1871–1921*. Vancouver: UBC Press, 2009.

Mawani, Renisa. 'Law's Archive', *Annual Review of Law and Social Science* 8 (2012), 337–65.

Mawani, Renisa. 'Law and Colonialism: Legacies and Lineages', *Law and Society Handbook*, edited by Austin Sarat and Patricia Ewick. Malden: John Wiley and Sons, 2015, 417–32.

McDonnell, Siobhan. 'Exploring the Cultural Power of Land Law in Vanuatu: Law as a Performance That Creates Meaning and Identities', *Intersections: Gender and Sexuality in Asia and the Pacific* 33 (2013).

McLaren, John. *Dewigged, Bothered and Bewildered: British Colonial Judges on Trial, 1800–1900*. Toronto: University of Toronto Press, 2011.

McLaren, John. 'Chasing the Chimera: The Rule of Law in the British Empire and the Comparative Turn in Legal History', *Law in Context* 33, no. 1 (2015), 21–36.

McLintock, Anne. *Imperial Leather: Race, Gender, and Sexuality in the Colonial Context*. New York: Routledge, 1995.

Merle, Isabelle. *Expériences Coloniales: La Nouvelle-Calédonie 1853–1920*. Paris: Belin, 1995.

Merle, Isabelle. 'La construction d'un droit foncier colonial: De la propriété collective à la constitution des réserves en Nouvelle-Calédonie', *Enquête: Anthropologie, Histoire, Sociologie* 7 (1999), 97–126.

Merle, Isabelle. 'De la «législation» de la violence en context colonial: Le régime de la Indigènat en question', *Politix* 17, no. 66 (2004), 137–62.

Merle, Isabelle. 'From Algeria and Indochina to Oceania: The Indigénat's Pathways in the Pacific, 1840–1900', Pacific History Association Conference, Wellington, 6–8 December 2012.

Merle, Isabelle, and Adrian Muckle. *L'indigénat. Genèses dans l'empire français. Pratiques en Nouvelle-Calédonie*. Paris: CNRS Éditions, 2019.

Merry, Sally Engle. 'Legal Pluralism', *Law and Society Review* 22, no. 5 (1988), 869–96.

Merry, Sally Engle. 'Law and Colonialism', Law & Society Review 25, no. 4 (1991), 889–922.

Merry, Sally Engle. 'Courts as Performances: Domestic Violence Hearings in a Hawai'i Family Court', in *Contested States: Law, Hegemony and Resistance*, edited by Mindie Lazarus-Black and Susan F. Hirsch. New York: Routledge, 1994, 35–58.

Merry, Sally Engle. 'Narrating Domestic Violence: Producing the "Truth" of Violence in 19th- and 20th-Century Hawaiian Courts', *Law and Social Inquiry* 19 (1994), 967–93.

Merry, Sally Engle. *Colonizing Hawai'i: The Cultural Power of Law*. Princeton, NJ: Princeton University Press, 2000.

Merry, Sally Engle. 'Comparative Criminalization: Cultural Meanings of Adultery and Gender Violence in Hawai'i in 1850 and 1990', *Pacific Studies* 25, no. 1 (2002), 203–20.

Merry, Sally Engle, and Donald Brenneis (eds). *Law and Empire in the Pacific: Hawai'i and Fiji*. Santa Fe: School of American Research Press, 2004.

Miles, William F. S. *Bridging Mental Boundaries in a Postcolonial Microcosm: Identity and Development in Vanuatu*. Honolulu: University of Hawai'i Press, 1998.

Mishra, Margaret. '"Your Woman Is a Very Bad Woman": Revisiting Female Deviance in Colonial Fiji', *Journal of International Women's Studies* 17, no. 4 (2016), 67–78.

Mokaddem, Hamid. 'Nouvelle-Calédonie, un pays métissé?' *Hermes* 32–3 (2002), 535–41.

Moore, Clive. 'Revising the Revisionists: The Historiography of Immigrant Melanesians in Australia', *Pacific Studies* 15, no. 2 (1992), 61–86.

Moore, Clive. 'Australian South Sea Islanders' Narratives of Belonging', in *Narrative and Identity Construction in the Pacific Islands*, edited by Farzana Gounder. Amsterdam: John Benjamins, 2015, 155–76.

Morens, David M. 'Measles in Fiji, 1875: Thoughts on the History of Emerging Infectious Diseases', *Pacific Health Dialog* 5, no. 1 (1998), 119–28.

Muckle, Adrian. 'Killing the "Fantôme Canaque": Evoking and Invoking the Possibility of Revolt in New Caledonia (1853–1915)', *Journal of Pacific History* 37, no. 1 (2002), 25–44.

Muckle, Adrian. 'Tropes of (Mis)understanding: Imagining Shared Destinies in New Caledonia, 1853–1998', *Journal de la Société des Océanistes* 124, no. 1 (2007), 105–18.

Muckle, Adrian. 'Troublesome Chiefs and Disorderly Subjects: The Internment of Kanak under the Indigénat – New Caledonia, 1887–1946', *Journal of French Colonial History* 11 (2010), 131–60.

Muckle, Adrian. '"Natives", "Immigrants" and "Libérés": The Colonial Regulation of Mobility in New Caledonia', *Law Text Culture* 15, no. 1 (2011), 135–61.

Muckle, Adrian. *Specters of Violence in a Colonial Context: New Caledonia, 1917*. Honolulu: University of Hawai'i Press, 2012.

Muckle, Adrian. 'The Presumption of Indigeneity: Colonial Administration, the "Community of Race" and the Category of Indigène in New Caledonia, 1887–1946', *Journal of Pacific History* 47, no. 3 (2012), 309–28.

Muckle, Adrian. 'Civilising Mission? Calling Colonialism to Account? France's Colonial Inspectorate in Oceania', Pacific History Association Conference, Wellington, 6–8 December 2012.

Muckle, Adrian, and Benoît Trépied. 'Note on French Gendarmerie Archives Relating to New Caledonia', *Pambu News* 26 (July 2009).

Muckle, Adrian, and Benoît Trépied. 'The Transformations of the "Métis Question" in New Caledonia (1853–2009)', in *Mixed Race Identities in Australia, New Zealand and the Pacific Islands*, edited by Farida Fozdar and Kirsten McGavin. New York: Routledge, 2017, 116–32.

Munro, Doug. 'Patterns of Resistance and Accommodation', in *Plantation Workers: Resistance and Accommodation*, edited by Brij V. Lal, Doug Munro and Edward D. Beechert. Honolulu: University of Hawai'i Press, 1993, 1–43.

Munro, Doug. 'The Labor Trade in Melanesians to Queensland: An Historiographic Essay', *Journal of Social History* 28, no. 3 (1995), 609–27.

Naepels, Michel. *War and Other Means: Violence and Power in Houaïlou (New Caledonia)*. Acton: ANU Press, 2017.

Naidu, Vijay. *The Violence of Indenture in Fiji*. Lautoka: Fiji Insitute of Applied Studies, 2004 [1980].

Newbury, Colin. 'Bose Vakauraga: Fiji's Great Council of Chiefs, 1875–2000', *Pacific Studies* 29, nos. 1/2 (2006), 82–127.

Newbury, Colin. 'Pacts, Alliances and Patronage: Modes of Influence and Power in the Pacific', *Journal of Pacific History* 44, no. 2 (2009), 141–62.

Newbury, Colin. *Patronage and Politics in the Victorian Empire: The Personal Governance of Sir Arthur Hamilton Gordon*. Amherst, NY: Cambria Books, 2010.

Nicole, Robert. *Disturbing History: Resistance in Early Colonial Fiji*. Honolulu: University of Hawai'i Press, 2010.

Nicole, Robert. 'Disturbing History: Aspects of Resistance in Early Colonial Fiji, 1875–1914'. PhD Thesis, University of Canterbury, 2006.

O'Brien, Patty. *The Pacific Muse: Exotic Femininity and the Colonial Pacific*. Seattle: University of Washington Press, 2006.

O'Connell, D. P. 'The Condominium of the New Hebrides', *British Year Book of International Law* 49 (1968–9), 71–146.

Oliver, D. L. *The Pacific Islands*. Cambridge, MA: Harvard University Press, 1951.

Pape, John. 'Black and White: The "Perils of Sex" in Colonial Zimbabwe', *Journal of Southern African Studies* 16, no. 4 (1990), 699–720.

Peabody, Sue, and Tyler Stovall (eds). *The Color of Liberty: Histories of Race in France.* Durham: Duke University Press, 2003.

Peterson, Jacqueline, and Jennifer H. S. Brown (eds). *The New People: Being and Becoming Métis in North America.* Winnipeg: University of Manitoba Press, 1985.

Pillon, Patrick, and François Sodter. 'The Impact of Colonial Administrative Policies on Indigenous Social Customs in Tahiti and New Caledonia', *Journal of Pacific History* 26, no. 2 (1991), 151–68.

Pitts, Jennifer. *A Turn to Empire: The Rise of Imperial Liberalism in Britain and France.* Princeton, NJ: Princeton University Press, 2005.

Potter, Simon J., and Jonathan Saha. 'Global History, Imperial History and Connected Histories of Empire', *Journal of Colonialism and Colonial History* 16, no. 1 (2015).

Purser, Margaret. 'The View from the Verandah: Levuka Bungalows and the Transformation of Settler Identities in Later Colonialism', *International Journal of Historical Archaeology* 7, no. 4 (2003), 293–314.

Ralston, Caroline. *Grass Huts and Warehouses: Pacific Beach Communities of the Nineteenth Century.* Canberra: Australian National University Press, 1977.

Ram, Kalpana, and Margaret Jolly (eds). *Maternities and Modernities: Colonial and Postcolonial Experiences in Asia and the Pacific.* Cambridge: Cambridge University Press, 1998.

Rawlings, Greg. 'Statelessness, Human Rights and Decolonisation', *Journal of Pacific History* 47, no. 1 (2012), 45–68.

Ray, Carina E. 'Decrying White Peril: Interracial Sex and the Rise of Anticolonial Nationalism in the Gold Coast', *American Historical Review* 119, no. 1 (2014), 78–110.

Richardson, David J. 'Kastom versus Cross: A Battle for Cultural Hegemony on Tanna', in *Wansalawara: Soundings in Melanesian History*, edited by Brij Lal. Honolulu: University of Hawaii Pacific Islands Studies Program, Working Paper Series, 1987, 88–118.

Robert, Yann. *Dramatic Justice: Trial by Theater in the Age of the French Revolution.* Philadelphia: University of Pennsylvania Press, 2019.

Robertson, Stephen. 'Signs, Marks and Private Parts: Doctors, Legal Discourses, and Evidence of Rape in the United States, 1823–1930', *Journal of the History of Sexuality* 8, no. 3 (1998), 345–88.

Rodman, Margaret. '"My Only Weapon Being a Pencil": Inscribing the Prison in the New Hebrides', *Journal of Pacific History*, 33, no. 1 (1998), 29–49.

Rodman, Margaret. 'Portentous Splendour: Building the Anglo-French Condominium', *History and Anthropology* 11, no. 4 (1999), 479–514.

Rodman, Margaret. *Houses Far from Home: British Colonial Space in the New Hebrides.* Honolulu: University of Hawai'i Press, 2001.

Rodman, Margaret. 'The Heart in the Archives: Colonial Contestation of Desire and Fear in the New Hebrides, 1933', *Journal of Pacific History* 38, no. 3 (2003), 291–312.

Rodman, Margaret, Daniela Kraemer, Lissant Bolton and Jean Tarasesei (eds). *Housegirls Remember: Domestic Workers in Vanuatu*. Honolulu: Hawai'i University Press, 2007.

Roux, J.-C. 'Les Indiens de la Nouvelle-Calédonie (Une ethnie disparue par assimilation)', *Bulletin de la Société de l'études historiques de la Nouvelle-Calédonie* 58 (1984), 3–11.

Ruberg, Willemijn. 'Trauma, Body, and Mind: Forensic Medicine in Nineteenth-Century Dutch Rape Cases', *Journal of the History of Sexuality* 22, no. 1 (2013), 85–104.

Saada, Emmanuelle. 'Citoyens et sujets de l'Empire français. Le usages de droit en situation coloniale', *Genèses* 53 (2003/4), 4–24.

Saada, Emmanuelle. *Empire's Children: Race, Filiation, and Citizenship in the French Colonies*. Translated by Arthur Goldhammer. Chicago: University of Chicago Press, 2012.

Saha, Jonathan. 'The Male State: Colonialism, Corruption and Rape Investigations in the Irrawaddy Delta c.1900', *Indian Economic and Social History Review* 48, no. 3 (2010), 343–76.

Saha, Jonathan. 'A Mockery of Justice? Colonial Law, the Everyday State and Village Politics in the Burma Delta, c.1890–1910', *Past & Present* 217 (2012), 187–212.

Saha, Jonathan. *Law, Disorder and the Colonial State: Corruption in Burma c.1900*. Basingstoke: Palgrave Macmillan, 2013.

Saha, Jonathan. 'Whiteness, Masculinity and the Ambivalent Embodiment of "British Justice" in Colonial Burma', *Cultural and Social History* 14, no. 4 (2017), 527–42.

Salesa, Damon. *Racial Crossings: Race, Intermarriage, and the Victorian British Empire*. Oxford: Oxford University Press, 2011.

Salomon, Christine, and Christine Hamelin. 'Les femmes kanakes sont fatiguées de la violence des hommes', *Journal de la Société des Océanistes* 125, no. 2 (2007), 101–12.

Samson, Jane. 'Rescuing Fijian Women? The British Anti-Slavery Proclamation of 1852', *Journal of Pacific History* 30, no. 1 (1995), 22–38.

Samson, Jane. *Imperial Benevolence: Making British Authority in the Pacific Islands*. Honolulu: University of Hawai'i Press, 1998.

Saunders, Kay (ed.). *Indentured Labour in the British Empire 1834–1920*. London: Croom Helm, 1984.

Saussol, Alain. *L'héritage. Essai sur le problème foncier mélanésien en Nouvelle-Calédonie*. Paris: Société des Océanistes, Musée de l'Homme, 1979.

Saussol, Alain. 'Nouvelle-Calédonie: le choc d'une colonisation singulière', in *Comprendre l'identité kanak*, edited by Alban Bensa et al. Paris: Centre Thomas Moore, 1990.

Scarr, Deryck. *Fragments of Empire: A History of the Western Pacific High Commission 1877–1914*. Canberra: Australian National University Press, 1967.

Scarr, Deryck. 'A Roko Tui for Lomaiviti: The Question of Legitimacy in the Fijian Administration 1874–1900', *Journal of Pacific History* 5 (1970), 3–31.

Scarr, Deryck. 'Recruits and Recruiters: A Portrait of the Pacific Island Labour Trade', in *Pacific Island Portraits*, edited by J. W. Davidson and D. Scarr. Canberra: Australian National University Press, 1970, 225–51.

Scarr, Deryck. *The Majesty of Colour: A Life of Sir John Bates Thurston*, four volumes. Canberra: Australian National University Press, 1973–80.

Scully, Pamela. 'Rape, Race and Colonial Culture: The Sexual Politics of Identity in the Nineteenth-Century Cape Colony, South Africa', *American Historical Review* 100, no. 2 (1995), 335–59.

Shameem, Shaista. 'Sugar and Spice: Wealth Accumulation and the Labour of Indian Women in Fiji, 1879–1930'. PhD Thesis, University of Waikato, 1990.

Shineberg, Dorothy. 'Un nouveau regard sur la démographie historique de la Nouvelle-Calédonie', *Journal de la Société des océanistes*, 76 (1983), 33–43.

Shineberg, Dorothy. '"The New Hebridean Is Everywhere": The Oceanian Labor Trade to New Caledonia, 1865–1930', *Pacific Studies* 18, no. 2 (1995), 1–21.

Shineberg, Dorothy. *The People Trade: Island Labourers and New Caledonia, 1865–1930.* Honolulu: University of Hawai'i Press, 1999.

Shlomowitz, Ralph. 'The Fiji Labor Trade in Comparative Perspective, 1864–1914', *Pacific Studies* 9, no. 3 (1986), 108–52.

Somner, Sara H. 'Idealism and Pragmatism in Colonial Fiji', *Hawaiian Journal of History* 18 (1984), 140–55.

Soriano, Éric. *La fin des Indigènes en Nouvelle-Calédonia: le colonial à l'épeuve du politique (1946–1976)*. Paris: Karthala, 2013.

Speedy, Karin. 'Who Were the Reunion "Coolies" of 19th-Century New Caledonia?' *Journal of Pacific History* 44, no. 2 (2009), 123–40.

Speedy, Karin. *Georges Baudoux's Jean M'Barai the Trepang Fisherman*. Sydney: UTS Sydney ePress, 2015.

Spencer, Michael, Alan Ward and John Connell (eds). *New Caledonia: Essays in Nationalism and Dependancy*. Brisbane: University of Queensland Press, 1988.

Steel, Frances. *Oceania under Steam: Sea Transport and the Cultures of Colonialism, c.1870–1914*. Manchester: University of Manchester Press, 2011.

Stepan, Nancy. *The Idea of Race in Science: Great Britain 1800–1960*. London: Macmillan, 1982.

Stevens, Kate. 'Visualizing Violence and Performing Law: Postcards of the Kersaint in the New Hebrides', *New Zealand Journal of History* 52, no. 1 (2018), 69–89.

Stevens, Kate. 'Violence of the Law: Prosecuting Gendered Violence in Colonial Fiji', in *Aftermaths: Colonialism, Violence and Memory*, edited by Lyndall Ryan and Angela Wanhalla. Dunedin: Otago University Press, forthcoming.

Stober, William. 'Isles of Illusion: Letters from Asterisk to Mowbray', *Journal of Pacific History* 39, no. 3 (2004), 353–73.

Stoler, Ann Laura. 'Rethinking Colonial Categories: European Communities and the Boundaries of Rule', *Comparative Studies in Society and History* 13, no. 1 (1989), 134–61.

Stoler, Ann Laura. *Carnal Knowledge and Imperial Power: Race and the Intimate in Colonial Rule*. Berkeley: University of California Press, 2003.

Stoler, Ann Laura. *Carnal Knowledge and Imperial Power: Race and the Intimate in Colonial Rule, with a New Preface*. Berkeley: University of California Press, 2010.

Stoler, Ann Laura. *Along the Archival Grain: Epistemic Anxieties and Colonial Common Sense*. Princeton, NJ: Princeton University Press, 2010.

Strange, Carolyn. 'Masculinities, Intimate Femicide and the Death Penalty in Australia, 1890–1920', *British Journal of Criminology* 43 (2003), 310–39.

Stuart, Andrew. *Of Cargoes, Colonies and Kings: Diplomatic and Administrative Service from Africa to the Pacific*. Oxford: Radcliffe Press, 2001.

Stuart, Annie. 'Contradictions and Complexities in an Indigenous Medical Service: The Case of Mesulame Taveta', *Journal of Pacific History* 41, no. 2 (2006), 125–43.

Surkis, Judith. *Sex, Law, and Sovereignty in French Algeria, 1830–1930*. Ithaca, NY: Cornell University Press, 2019.

Swanepoel, Paul. 'Transient Justice: Colonial Judges on Circuit in Interwar Tanganyika', *Stichproben: Wiener Zeitschrift für kritische Afrikastudien* 13, no. 24 (2013), 65–91.

Tabani, Marc. 'Dreams of Unity, Traditions of Division: John Frum, Kastom and Inter-Manipulation Strategies as Cultural Heritage on Tanna (Vanuatu)', *Paideuma* 55 (2009), 27–47.

Taylor, Katherine Fischer. *In the Theater of Criminal Justice: The Palais de Justice in Second Empire Paris*. Princeton, NJ: Princeton University Press, 1993.

Taylor, John P. 'The Social Life of Rights: "Gender Antagonism", Modernity and Raet in Vanuatu', *Australian Journal of Anthropology* 19, no. 2 (2008), 165–78.

Terrier, Christiane. 'Calédoniens ou métis?' in *La Nouvelle-Calédonie: Terre de Métissage*, edited by Frédéric Angleviel. Paris: Les Indes Savantes & GRHOC, 2004, 65–81.

Terrier, Christiane. 'Le «Grand Cantonnement» des indigènes (1897–1903)', in *La Nouvelle-Calédonie: Les Kanaks et l'histoire*, edited by Eddy Wadrawane and Frédéric Angleviel. Paris: Les Indes Savantes, 2008, 255–81.

Tinker, Hugh. 'Odd Man Out: The Loneliness of the Indian Colonial Politician – the Career of Manilal Doctor', *Journal of Imperial and Commonwealth History* 2, no. 2 (1974), 226–43.

Thomas, Martin. *Violence and Colonial Order: Police, Workers and Protest in the European Colonial Empires, 1918–1940*. Cambridge: Cambridge University Press, 2012.

Thomas, Nicholas. 'Sanitation and Seeing: The Creation of State Power in Early Colonial Fiji', *Comparative Studies in Society and History* 32, no. 1 (1990), 149–70.

Thomas, Nicholas. 'The Inversion of Tradition', *American Ethnologist* 19, no. 2 (1992), 213–32.

Thomas, Nicholas. 'Colonial Conversions: Difference, Hierarchy, and History in Early Twentieth-Century Evangelical Propaganda', *Comparative Studies in Society and History* 3, no. 2 (1992), 366–89.

Thomas, Nicholas. *Colonialism's Culture: Anthropology, Travel and Government*. Princeton, NJ: Princeton University Press, 1994.

Thomas, Nicholas. *In Oceania: Visions, Artifacts, Histories*. Durham: Duke University Press, 1997.

Thomas, Nicholas. *Islanders: The Pacific in the Age of Empire*. New Haven: Yale University Press, 2010.

Thomas, Nicholas, Anna Cole and Bronwen Douglas (eds). *Tattoo: Bodies, Art and Exchange in the Pacific and Europe*. London: Reaktion Books, 2005.

Thompson, Roger C. 'Commerce, Christianity and Colonialism: The Australasian New Hebrides Company, 1883–1897', *Journal of Pacific History* 6, no. 1 (1971), 25–38.

Thompson, Roger C. *Australian Imperialism in the Pacific: The Expansionist Era 1820–1920*. Melbourne: Melbourne University Press, 1980.

Thompson, Roger C. 'Natives and Settlers on the New Hebrides Frontier, 1870–1900', *Pacific Studies* 5, no. 1 (1981), 1–18.

Thornbury, Elizabeth. *Colonizing Consent: Rape and Governance in South Africa's Eastern Cape*. Cambridge: Cambridge University Press, 2018.

Tjibaou Cultural Centre. 'La Campagne du Kersaint dans le Pacifique'. Accessed 17 January 2022, http://www.adck.nc/mediatheque/tresors-de-la-mediatheque/192-la-campagne-du-kersaint-dans-le-pacifique.

Todd, David. 'A French Imperial Meridian 1814–1870', *Past and Present* 210 (2011), 155–85.

Toth, Stephen A. 'Colonisation or Incarceration? The Changing Role of the French Penal Colony in *Fin-de-siècle* New Caledonia', in *The French and the Pacific World, 17th–19th Centuries: Explorations, Migrations and Cultural Exchanges*, edited by Annick Foucrier. Aldershot: Ashgate, 2005, 117–32.

Toth, Stephen A. *Beyond Papillon: The French Overseas Penal Colonies, 1854–1952*. Lincoln: University of Nebraska Press, 2006.

Trépied, Benoît. *Une mairie dans la France coloniale: Koné, Nouvelle-Calédonie*. Paris: Karthala Editions, 2010.

United Nations Entity for Gender Equality and the Empowerment of Women Pacific Sub-Regional Office. *Ending Violence against Women and Girls: Evidence, Data, and Knowledge in Pacific Island Countries – Literature Review and Annotated Bibliography*, 2nd ed. Suva: UN Women Pacific Sub-Regional Office, 2011.

Van Trease, Howard. *The Politics of Land in Vanuatu: From Colony to Independence*. Suva: Fiji Times, 1991 [1987].

Van Trease, Howard. 'The Colonial Origins of Melanesian Politics', in *Melanesian Politics: Stael Blong Vanuatu*, edited by Howard Van Trease. Christchurch, New Zealand: Macmillan Brown Center for Pacific Studies, University of Canterbury, and Suva, Fiji: IPS, USP, 1995, 3–58.

Veracini, Lorenzo. 'The "Shadows of the Colonial Period" to "Times of Sharing": History Writing in and about New Caledonia/Kanaky, 1969–1998', *Journal of Pacific History* 38, no. 3 (2003), 331–52.

Vigarello, Georges. *A History of Rape: Sexual Violence in France from the 16th to 20th Century*. Cambridge: Polity Press, 2000.

Wadrawane, Eddy. 'Métissage et culture du métissage en Nouvelle-Calédonie', in *La Nouvelle-Calédonie: Terre de Métissage*, edited by Frédéric Angleviel. Paris: Les Indes Savantes & GRHOC, 2004, 25–34.

Wadrawane, Eddy, and Frédéric Angleviel (eds). *La Nouvelle-Calédonie: Les Kanaks et l'histoire*. Paris: Les Indes Savantes, 2008.

Wallace, Lee. *Sexual Encounters: Pacific Texts, Modern Sexualities*. New York: Cornell University Press, 2003.

Wanhalla, Angela. 'Interracial Sexual Violence in 1860s New Zealand', *New Zealand Journal of History* 45, no. 1 (2011), 71–84.

Wanhalla, Angela. 'Intimate Connections: Governing Cross-Cultural Intimacy on New Zealand's Colonial Frontier', *law&history* 4, no. 2 (2017), 45–71.

Ward, Alan. *Land and Politics in New Caledonia*. Canberra: Australian National University Press, 1982.

Ward, R. Gerard. 'Land, Law and Custom: Diverging Realities in Fiji', in *Land, Custom and Practice in the South Pacific*, edited by R. Gerard Ward and Elizabeth Kingdon. Cambridge: Cambridge University Press, 1995, 198–249.

Ward, R. Gerard, and Elizabeth Kingdon (eds). *Land, Custom and Practice in the South Pacific*. Cambridge: Cambridge University Press, 1995.

White, Owen. *Children of the French Empire: Miscegenation and Colonial Society in French West Africa*. New York: Oxford University Press, 1999.

Widmer, Alexandra. 'Native Medical Practitioners, Temporality, and Nascent Biomedical Citizenship in the New Hebrides', *PoLAR: Political and Legal Anthropology Review* 33, no. 1 (2010), 57–80.

Wiener, Martin J. *An Empire on Trial: Race, Murder, and Justice under British Rule, 1870–1935*. Cambridge: Cambridge University Press, 2009.

Woodward, Keith. 'Historical Note', in *Tufala Gavman: Reminiscences from the Anglo-French Condominium of the New Hebrides*, edited by Brian J. Bresnihan and Keith Woodward. Suva: Institute of Pacific Studies, USP, 2002, 16–72.

Wright, Ashley. 'Gender, Violence, and Justice in Colonial Assam: The Webb Case, c. 1884', *Journal of Social History* 53, no. 4 (2020), 990–1007.

Young, Michael G. 'Gone Native in Isles of Illusion: In Search of Asterisk in Epi', in *History and Tradition in Melanesian Anthropology*, edited by James G. Carrier. Berkeley: University of California Press, 1992, 193–223.

Index

Page locations in *italics* refer to illustrations.

CPSIA information can be obtained
at www.ICGtesting.com
Printed in the USA
LVHW021540120523
746846LV00003B/87